Issued by the Ministry of Information in co-operation with the War Office and the Ministry of Home Security.

If the INVADER comes

WHAT TO DO — AND HOW TO DO IT

THE Germans threaten to invade Great Britain. If they do so they will be driven out by our Navy, our Army and our Air Force. Yet the ordinary men and women of the civilian population will also have their part to play. Hitler's invasions of Poland, Holland and Belgium were greatly helped by the fact that the civilian population was taken by surprise. They did not know what to do when the moment came. *You must not be taken by surprise.* This leaflet tells you what general line you should take. More detailed instructions will be given you when the danger comes nearer. Meanwhile, read these instructions carefully and be prepared to carry them out.

I

When Holland and Belgium were invaded, the civilian population fled from their homes. They crowded on the roads, in cars, in carts, on bicycles and on foot, and so helped the enemy by preventing their own armies from advancing against the invaders. You must not allow that to happen here. Your first rule, therefore, is :—

(1) IF THE GERMANS COME, BY PARACHUTE, AEROPLANE OR SHIP, YOU MUST REMAIN WHERE YOU ARE. THE ORDER IS " STAY PUT ".

If the Commander in Chief decides that the place where you live must be evacuated, he will tell you when and how to leave. Until you receive such orders you must remain where you are. If you run away, you will be exposed to far greater danger because you will be machine-gunned from the air as were civilians in Holland and Belgium, and you will also block the roads by which our own armies will advance to turn the Germans out.

II

There is another method which the Germans adopt in their invasion. They make use of the civilian population in order to create confusion and panic. They spread false rumours and issue false instructions. In order to prevent this, you should obey the second rule, which is as follows :—

(2) DO NOT BELIEVE RUMOURS AND DO NOT SPREAD THEM. WHEN YOU RECEIVE AN ORDER, MAKE QUITE SURE THAT IT IS A TRUE ORDER AND NOT A FAKED ORDER. MOST OF YOU KNOW YOUR POLICEMEN AND YOUR A.R.P. WARDENS BY SIGHT, YOU CAN TRUST THEM. IF YOU KEEP YOUR HEADS, YOU CAN ALSO TELL WHETHER A MILITARY OFFICER IS REALLY BRITISH OR ONLY PRETENDING TO BE SO. IF IN DOUBT ASK THE POLICEMAN OR THE A.R.P. WARDEN. USE YOUR COMMON SENSE.

III

The Army, the Air Force and the Local Defence Volunteers cannot be everywhere at once. The ordinary man and woman must be on the watch. If you see anything suspicious, do not rush round telling your neighbours all about it. Go at once to the nearest policeman, police-station, or military officer and tell them exactly what you saw. Train yourself to notice the exact time and place where you saw anything suspicious, and try to give exact information. Try to check your facts. The sort of report which a military or police officer wants from you is something like this :—

> "At 5.30 p.m. to-night I saw twenty cyclists come into Little Squashborough from the direction of Great Mudtown. They carried some sort of automatic rifle or gun. I did not see anything like artillery. They were in grey uniforms."

Be calm, quick and exact. The third rule, therefore, is as follows :—

(3) KEEP WATCH. IF YOU SEE ANYTHING SUSPICIOUS, NOTE IT CAREFULLY AND GO AT ONCE TO THE NEAREST POLICE OFFICER OR STATION, OR TO THE NEAREST MILITARY OFFICER. DO NOT RUSH ABOUT SPREADING VAGUE RUMOURS. GO QUICKLY TO THE NEAREST AUTHORITY AND GIVE HIM THE FACTS.

IV

Remember that if parachutists come down near your home, they will not be feeling at all brave. They will not know where they are, they will have no food, they will not know where their companions are. They will want you to give them food, means of transport and maps. They will want you to tell them where they have landed, where their comrades are, and where our own soldiers are. The fourth rule, therefore, is as follows :—

(4) DO NOT GIVE ANY GERMAN ANYTHING. DO NOT TELL HIM ANYTHING. HIDE YOUR FOOD AND YOUR BICYCLES. HIDE YOUR MAPS. SEE THAT THE ENEMY GETS NO PETROL. IF YOU HAVE A CAR OR MOTOR BICYCLE, PUT IT OUT OF ACTION WHEN NOT IN USE. IT IS NOT ENOUGH TO REMOVE THE IGNITION KEY; YOU MUST MAKE IT USELESS TO ANYONE EXCEPT YOURSELF.

IF YOU ARE A GARAGE PROPRIETOR, YOU MUST WORK OUT A PLAN TO PROTECT YOUR STOCK OF PETROL AND YOUR CUSTOMERS' CARS. REMEMBER THAT TRANSPORT AND PETROL WILL BE THE INVADER'S MAIN DIFFICULTIES. MAKE SURE THAT NO INVADER WILL BE ABLE TO GET HOLD OF YOUR CARS, PETROL, MAPS OR BICYCLES.

V

You may be asked by Army and Air Force officers to help in many ways. For instance, the time may come when you will receive orders to block roads or streets in order to prevent the enemy from advancing. Never block a road unless you are told which one you must block. Then you can help by felling trees, wiring them together or blocking the roads with cars. Here, therefore, is the fifth rule :—

(5) BE READY TO HELP THE MILITARY IN ANY WAY. BUT DO NOT BLOCK ROADS UNTIL ORDERED TO DO SO BY THE MILITARY OR L.D.V. AUTHORITIES.

VI

If you are in charge of a factory, store or other works, organise its defence at once. If you are a worker, make sure that you understand the system of defence that has been organised and know what part you have to play in it. Remember always that parachutists and fifth column men are powerless against any organised resistance. They can only succeed if they can create disorganisation. Make certain that no suspicious strangers enter your premises.

You must know in advance who is to take command, who is to be second in command, and how orders are to be transmitted. This chain of command must be built up and you will probably find that ex-officers or N.C.O.'s, who have been in emergencies before, are the best people to undertake such command. The sixth rule is therefore as follows:—

(6) IN FACTORIES AND SHOPS, ALL MANAGERS AND WORKMEN SHOULD ORGANISE SOME SYSTEM NOW BY WHICH A SUDDEN ATTACK CAN BE RESISTED.

VII

The six rules which you have now read give you a general idea of what to do in the event of invasion. More detailed instructions may, when the time comes, be given you by the Military and Police Authorities and by the Local Defence Volunteers; they will NOT be given over the wireless as that might convey information to the enemy. These instructions must be obeyed at once.

Remember always that the best defence of Great Britain is the courage of her men and women. Here is your seventh rule :—

(7) THINK BEFORE YOU ACT. BUT THINK ALWAYS OF YOUR COUNTRY BEFORE YOU THINK OF YOURSELF.

INVASION
The Alternate History of the German Invasion of England, July 1940

by Kenneth Macksey

WRENS PARK

Invasion
This edition first published 2001 by Wren's Park Publishing, an imprint of W.J. Williams & Son Ltd.

British Library Cataloguing in Publication Data
A catalogue record for this book is available from the British Library

ISBN 0-905778-79-0

Printed and bound in Great Britain

CONTENTS

LIST OF MAPS

PREFACE

Books dealing with Operation 'Sealion' – the projected German invasion of Britain in 1940 – tend to fall into two categories. There are those like Peter Fleming's *Operation Sea Lion* (orginally published as *Invasion 1940*) and Walter Ansel's *Hitler confronts England* which speculate with events as they unfolded, and explain why the invasion did not take place, as planned, in September. And there are those like Norman Longmate's *If Britain had Fallen* which give rather cursory and unconvincing reasons for the success of the invasion in September, but chiefly postulate what might have transpired if success had been achieved by the Germans.

When writing the biography of Field Marshal Albert Kesselring, I became satisfied that, if he had had his way and the invasion had taken place soon after Dunkirk – in mid July – a most interesting situation would have arisen. Certainly the British Intelligence people thought that this was the most dangerous period, and there was an almost audible expression of relief in Government circles when July and then August passed without the threat materializing. In coming to the conclusion that a study would be worthwhile of what might have happened if Adolf Hitler had come to a decision sufficiently early to allow the invasion to occur in July, I thought it would be more realistic to write the story in the form of a campaign history, drawing upon as many real sources as possible and using the minimum of fiction.

I was greatly helped by the following institutions and people who provided source material and opinion: Public Record Office; Dover Public Reference Library; Folkestone Public Reference Library; Kent County Council Archives Office; Maidstone Museum; Kent Defence Research Group; Whitehall Library of the Ministry of Defence; The Hydrographic Department, Ministry of Defence; Imperial War Museum; Bundesarchiv, West Germany; Duke University; National Archives and Records Service, USA; Rear-Admiral T. W. Best; Major-General H. M. Liardet; Brigadier

A. J. Trythall; Lieutenant-Commander H. M. May; Sir Oswald Mosley; Ronald Lewin Esq.; David Brown Esq.; R. S. Humphreys Esq.; Dr. D. Robinson, Ian Hogg Esq.; Herr Günter Schomaekers. The following very kindly read drafts and offered invaluable criticism: Rear-Admiral T. W. Best, Lieutenant-Commander H. M. May and Lieutenant-Colonel W. F. Woodhouse, while Mrs M. Dunn typed the manuscript. All the above have my warmest gratitude for the help they gave and also for their encouragement.

Kenneth Macksey, 1980

I

A LION IS BORN

It is unlikely that anyone had a better panoramic view of the first stage of the German invasion of England than Feldwebel Rudolf Pabst. As a crew member of a Dornier 17P reconnaissance aircraft, he had taken off before first light on the day of the invasion to photograph British route centres and airfields in the sector east and south of London. The Dornier had crossed the coast near Ramsgate in daylight at a height of 12,000 feet, hoping to make use of scattered cloud cover if British fighters made an interception – as bitter experience over the past few weeks led its crew to expect. The Hurricanes and Spitfires had made life perilous for the reconnaissance machines and losses had been serious. True there had been a considerable improvement in the situation since the major air offensive had begun a fortnight ago, but there was always the danger of an early morning enemy flight making an unwelcome appearance. Over Canterbury the cameras were started whenever gaps appeared in the clouds below, and Pabst felt increasingly confident that the greater part of the mission would be fulfilled without difficulty. They took pictures of Maidstone and set a course which would take them over West Malling and the airfields of Kenley and Biggin Hill. The three members of the crew noticed that the scene below looked different from a couple of days ago, chiefly because there seemed to be rather a lot of smoke hanging about at the lower altitudes. Over Biggin Hill the rear gunner called urgently that hostile aircraft were closing from above – three Spitfires probably and, yes, they seemed to be shaping to attack.

Immediately, the pilot dived for the clouds, with the Hurricanes (as they proved to be) hurtling down to cut him off. Just out of machine-gun range they reached safety, weaving aside and swinging south to put off the fighters, finally emerging at about 4,000 feet above East Grinstead. Wrote Pabst:

'Our pilot decided to do what he had done before, that is fly home at tree-top level, crossing the coast somewhere to the west of

Folkestone. I sat in the nose and therefore had my usual uninterrupted view of the ground as it flashed by. We careered over farms, woods and villages, skirting the larger towns as we endeavoured to avoid British anti-aircraft fire and airfields. I noticed that even the smaller country lanes had much traffic – columns of cars, lorries and carts with people either gazing up or jumping into the ditches. These, for the most part, seemed to be civilians with hardly a sign of military vehicles, so I suppose they were refugees such as we had seen in France and Belgium before. Nearing the coast the signs of war became more evident. A number of places had fires burning and we were shot at on a couple of occasions. Also the rear gunner shouted more frequent warnings about enemy aircraft, although I think a number of those were our own. But it certainly came as a surprise when we overtook a *Kette* of Ju52 transports lumbering out to sea near Hythe and it was only then, in fact, that I realized we had flown into the heart of the invasion. For to our left there pillared the dust and smoke of battle, cloaking the foreshore and the cliffs, and ahead were ships and boats, convoys of them stretching back across the Channel towards France.

At once the grandeur of this historic moment was impressed upon us. By rights our pilot should have made straight for home to deliver the results of our mission, but impetuously he swung left and followed the coastline, giving us a thrilling view of the armada at about the moment, I assume, when the first troops were going ashore to join the airborne boys. As we raced above the waves some of our men looked up, but elsewhere the others were too heavily engaged. Most boats were moving, but some were obviously in trouble, heeling over or in flames. Close to Dover we noticed gunfire above the cliffs, and farther out to sea, as we turned towards Dunkirk, we could see larger warships firing and beyond them, on the cliffs near Calais, the flash of heavy artillery in action. Just off Dover it looked as if there were a naval battle in progress. A heavy smoke screen had been laid and here the ships and boats looked as if they were in disarray, all formation abandoned. At this moment we felt both safer and yet more in peril – safer because there were a lot of our own fighters and bombers about, more at risk because a lot of trigger-happy men on the warships began firing at us and gave us a hot time most of the way across.'

Looking back on what he had seen, Pabst summed up his feelings about 'this memorable and historic occasion', as he called it. 'Excited as I was, I failed to pay sufficient attention to the suffering of those in battle below and only gradually was it brought home to me, as to other Germans, what our men had gone through. The news that a cousin of mine had been killed in the paratroop assault and that my brother, Werner, had been severely wounded in that appalling massacre at the foot of the cliffs, had a deeply personal effect. Those were the fortunes of war, but it somehow seemed especially sad that Werner should suffer so much in action out of his element, on the sea, which he had never seen before this summer. Yet, despite all that has since transpired, I cannot dismiss from my mind the splendours of our achievements on that day of destiny.'

The germ of an idea

The momentous decision which brought about the invasion of Britain was taken by Adolf Hitler, the Reichs Chancellor and Supreme Head of the Armed Forces (the Wehrmacht), on 21 May 1940. It was a day rich in euphoria when new horizons opened up in his vision of a German hegemony over the rest of Europe. German arms had just won one of the most complete victories of all time. Only days before the Wehrmacht had rolled forward in its invasion of the West. Within four days Holland had been forced to surrender and now his triumphant army overlooked the English Channel, a signal from the leading tanks of General der Panzertruppe Heinz Guderian's XIX Corps having announced the previous evening that they had arrived at Abbeville after a 300-mile dash across France from the Ardennes. It was then a question of deciding which way Guderian should go – southwards, into the heart of France, or northwards in the direction of Dunkirk in an endeavour to encircle the out-flanked French and British forces which were only just awakening to the fact that they were in imminent danger of being cut off, not only from the rest of France, but also from an escape route via the sea to England.

The orders went out to turn north to complete the envelopment. The invasion of France, stripped already of her best troops, could follow at leisure. The mainland of Europe lay at Germany's feet and Britain must surely sue for peace as soon as the defeat of France had been completed. And with that thought in mind, the attention of the German High Command turned to fresh military realities in the event of political dreams coming to nought – the question of how to tackle Britain if she refused to behave sensibly.

The rout inflicted upon the Dutch, Belgian, French and British forces had been caused by *Blitzkrieg*, the battle technique which had brought about the 30-day conquest of Poland in September

1939, and which was bringing to a successful conclusion the invasion of Norway, begun on 9 April 1940. By deftly combining the operations of groups of fast-moving tanks, artillery, mechanized infantry and bombing aircraft, the Germans had produced a war machine far superior in quality to any other in the world. Psychological warfare using skillfully directed propaganda had eased the way for the invaders and so undermined the enemy's sense of purpose and unity as to persuade him to recognize the futility of opposition. Poland had been ruined because her mobilization had been wrecked by the abrupt advance of mechanized forces; the process has been accelerated by dissent worked up among the indigenous German minority groups, and by attacks from the air on bases and communication centres. Norway had fallen to a surprise attack without declaration of war, and was stunned by the appearance in her midst of a handful of German troops who had emerged from hiding in ships in her harbours, or who had been landed from the air. In both countries German radio and newspaper campaigns had confused the people and stirred up dissidents – the so-called Fifth Columnists who actively assisted the invaders. And although total surprise was lacking prior to the invasion of Holland, Luxembourg and Belgium, the Germans still executed a lightning conquest by the adroit direction of their approach. Skill at arms, mobility and the concentrated application of fire-power had cowed their opponents; had rapidly cracked modern fortifications; had out-manoeuvred and systematically wiped out the best enemy mechanized forces by advances of more than 50 miles a day; had almost driven opposing air forces from the skies; and had convinced survivors of the pointlessness of further resistance. False reports, transmitted over the public radio networks, which announced the fall of towns prior to the event, had spread a sense of despondency, had simply and economically exploited the work of the soldiers and set the tone of *Blitzkrieg*, 1940 style.

It was a contented Hitler who received the congratulations of his senior colleagues of the Oberkommando der Wehrmacht (OKW) on the glorious morning of 21 May. The Commander-in-Chief of the Army, Generaloberst Walther von Brauchitsch, and Generalfeldmarschall Hermann Goering, C-in-C of the Luftwaffe, spoke only of complete success. But Admiral Erich Raeder, the C-in-C of the Kriegsmarine, had less to say; his units did not hold the stage because they were engaged in the closing phases of the Norwegian campaign and had played only a minor part in the conquest of the Netherlands. Yet the sudden inversion of the balance of armed power in the West had prompted Raeder to think deeply about its implications. With disturbing conclusions in mind, he waited until after the conference before asking for a private word with Hitler in order to breach again a subject which had been rejected in the past – the prospects of invading England, a project which had baffled all would-be conquerors since Duke William of Normandy had succeeded in 1066.[1]

The subject had last been raised by Raeder in November 1939 when plans to invade France through the Netherlands were under consideration. Kapitän Hans Reinicke of the Kriegsmarine had sketched out the complex problems involved in launching an invasion from German ports, and in his summing up had lacked enthusiasm. Goering had brushed aside the proposal, while the Army gave it serious study and formulated the nature of their requirements without being too hopeful.[2] So the idea had lain fallow and, indeed, when Raeder spoke again about the matter with Hitler on 21 May it was not with the intention of instigating action, but of trying to find out if there had been a change of mind: he did not imagine that anything positive would come of his enquiry. It was to Raeder's chagrin, therefore, when, in the spirit of victory, the revolutionary soul of Hitler was stirred. His eyes lit up at the vision of England's shores coming within sight of his advancing spearheads. In his imagination the doors of opportunity swung wider open to the invincible Wehrmacht. He maintained strongly his dedication to the elimination of Communism as represented by Soviet Russia in the east, and he shared the fears of his advisers concerning the dangers of a war on two fronts. If he could now strike England out of the reckoning, as well as the other West European powers, everything would fall into place. Russia could then be tackled in isolation in 1941.

At once the meeting was reconvened to enable the Führer to congratulate the nonplussed Raeder on his initiative. He commanded that the project to invade England be re-examined as a matter of urgency. From Generaloberst Wilhelm Keitel (Chief of OKW) he demanded reports within three days to enable a positive decision to be reached, and, such was the mood of astonishment which prevailed, nobody demurred. Raeder, filled with professional doubts, determined at once to quash the matter at the right time, but von Brauchitsch and Goering, whose victory syndrome at that moment saw everything as possible, were willing to comply, while Keitel, who was known as a mere recording of Hitler's voice, gave tentative assent. As for Generalmajor Alfred Jodl, the Chief of OKW Operations Office, and his deputy, Walter Warlimont, the future for them looked busier than ever; they guessed they would be responsible for the burden of welding the three separate Services into a single team for combined operations.

When the leaders met again on the morning of the 24th, a fresh development coloured their opinions, one that had appeared even as Guderian's tanks began to advance towards Dunkirk on the afternoon of the 21st. That day a strong counter-attack by British tanks at Arras had overrun part of the 7th Panzer Division and a chain reaction of doubts had shot through the German hierarchy. Generaloberst Gerd von Rundstedt's Army Group A, of which Guderian's corps was a part, had for long been exposed to counter-attack along its lengthening flanks. Its cautious commander felt that the time to pause had come. In any case he wished to conserve the tanks (which were already low in strength) for use in the second phase of the campaign – the drive southward to occupy the rest of France. Throughout the 22nd and 23rd, von Rundstedt had fretted until, with von Brauchitsch's approval (and, subsequently, early on the 24th, Hitler's too) he had called a halt – even though Guderian's tanks were at the threshold of Dunkirk and there were scarcely any Allied forces in position to bar his way. At this moment, too, it had been Goering who had intervened, claiming the right for his Nazi-orientated Luftwaffe to cover itself with glory by bombing the surviving enemy into submission while the Army held the ring. 'In any case,' remarked Hitler to a jubilant Goering, shortly before the invasion feasibility conference, 'The Army will need all its composure if it is to complete the conquest of France and then deal with England' – a clear indication of the attitude he was about to adopt.

Raeder opened the discussion by emphasizing the dangers involved. The British Fleet, barely diminished by losses and damage incurred in the Norway campaign, remained immensely powerful, whereas the German Fleet had suffered serious losses among its cruisers and destroyers, and both its battlecruisers, *Scharnhorst* and *Gneisenau*, had been slightly damaged. While admitting that the situation had arisen where the entire Channel coast might soon be in German hands and that it might be feasible to put a force ashore in Britain (and even temporarily maintain it there), there was, he declared, no guarantee of sustaining such an operation. Enemy minefields could be swept, but the 30 U-boats at his disposal were quite insufficient and, in any case, were having trouble with their torpedoes. On naval grounds he could not recommend the attempt.

Speaking for the Army, von Brauchitsch regarded an invasion rather in the nature of an up-scaled river crossing operation. Once ashore, he promised, the soldiers would rapidly overcome a weakened opponent – an opinion they had originally given to Reinicke. It was up to the Kriegsmarine to get them there and – with hearty endorsement from Raeder – for the Luftwaffe to drive the Royal Air Force from the skies, besides contributing substantially to the delivery of supplies in case the Kriegsmarine was prevented from doing so. To Goering this was more of an invitation than a challenge. The Luftwaffe had won outright air superiority everywhere and had found no great problem in dealing with the RAF. Its paratroop formations, dropped ahead of the Army, had been largely instrumental in conquering Holland, and were on the eve of attempting the destruction of an army at Dunkirk to achieve what would be, he confidently predicted, the first ever conquest of land forces by air forces.

Goering had spent the 23rd in consultation with his Chief of Air Staff, Generalmajor Hans Jeschonnek, and with the man he most trusted among his Air Fleet commanders, General der Flieger Albert Kesselring, a previous Chief of Air Staff who had commanded Luftflotte 1 in Poland and whose Luftflotte 2 had just completed the subjugation of Holland and was about to tackle Dunkirk. Kesselring, like many of the senior German airmen, was a soldier by training; he was a fine artillerist and was among the five most brilliant members of the German General Staff. To him could be credited a major share in the building of the Luftwaffe. Better than many among his contemporaries, he understood the narrow margins by which the German economy and armed forces supported the war. It was his belief that Germany's existing technical superiority, which presently enabled her to dominate the battlefield, could not last for long. Prior to every campaign he had pleaded for a strict conservation of resources. But, now that Germany was committed to a major struggle, he threw caution to the winds in the desire to reach a conclusive solution. Even at the risk of heavy losses, he deemed it essential to strike hard and without restraint, to eliminate every source of opposition in the West once and for all, before Britain's potential could be developed. Goering agreed, accepting the prospect of the Luftwaffe suffering terrible punishment in a struggle with the RAF and the Royal Navy, but guessing that those losses could be replaced at leisure once Britain had been brought to her knees.[3]

The basis of a plan

The outline scheme Goering now submitted to Hitler was the

product of Kesselring's and Jeschonnek's thinking. They effectively demolished Raeder's objections while satisfying von Brauchitsch's demands for complete air superiority. 'The invasion of England,' stated Goering, 'must be viewed as being primarily a Luftwaffe responsibility.' Air power would be substituted for sea power,[4] in that aircraft would not only be used to defeat the enemy air force, but would also carry out the preliminary bombardment besides transporting the first assault echelon to its objectives. Thereafter it would play an important part in satisfying logistic requirements. The Army, he conceded, would assume its traditional rôle after an air-head was formed in England; the Kriegsmarine, protected and supplemented by the Luftwaffe, must thereafter do all it could to keep open the sea lanes. By the middle of July, Goering reckoned, he could have available 750 of the three-engined Ju 52 transport aircraft, in addition to several of the much larger four-engined Ju 90 and Focke-Wulf Kondor, as well as about 150 gliders. These could lift, over short ranges, at least 15,500 men or, alternatively, 3,000 tons of stores and equipment. In other words, the Luftwaffe alone looked capable of delivering at least a complete division in the assault and of maintaining it, together with additional forces brought in by sea, over the days to come, allowing for the fact that most aircraft would be expected to fly an average of two sorties per day. This they had already done in Norway, using 500 aircraft, as well as in Holland. Goering demanded the satisfaction of three conditions in order to guarantee this performance. First of all, the invasion must be started with the least possible delay to enable the leading elements to arrive in England almost on the tail of any escaping enemy troops. It was essential that every advantage be taken of confusion in the enemy's ranks and to give him the least possible chance for reorganization and rearmament. For preference it was desirable to attack not later than the middle of July, and better still at the beginning of the month. Secondly, it was essential that the Luftwaffe be given every opportunity to restore its strength immediately, and to concentrate on the forward deployment of ground installations in the conquered territories. Therefore the Army would have to make do with less air support in the concluding stages of the subjugation of France than it had enjoyed during the initial assault on 10 May. Finally, he insisted that the assault be launched only when four days good weather could be guaranteed, so that air superiority over the RAF might be secured without hindrance.

Faced by such overwhelming support from Goering, neither von Brauchitsch nor Raeder were able to resist. In any case, they could see that Hitler was enthusiastic. Moreover, von Brauchitsch was about the last person in the Army who would oppose strongly his Führer; on an earlier occasion, Hitler had cowed him by the violence of his invective. The Army C-in-C had already been reduced to the sort of compliance Hitler preferred. As for Raeder, the most prescient among the Cs-in-C, he was weak in debate and preferred to argue a case in writing. At this moment he realized that if a halt were not immediately called, the invasion scheme might go ahead, out of control. By extracting an admission of fear from his colleagues and questioning them closely, he sought to convince Hitler of the dangers. Had they enough data from which an outline plan could be quickly formed, he asked? What would be the size of the forces they would wish to commit? Where would they land and on what breadth of front? When and at what rate would they require follow-up forces to arrive? Warming to the subject when they answered him evasively, he sought to undermine their confidence by asking if they knew about winds, tidal streams, the sloping nature of beaches and the problems which might be posed if an intact enemy port were not swiftly seized. He was getting nicely into his stride when Hitler stopped him short.

'The difficulties,' commanded the Führer, with a firm conviction which had burgeoned with military success, 'can and will be solved.' The attempt would be made he said, and he set 15 July as the target date for its commencement, sooner still if possible, adding his belief that it might even come earlier as a peaceful occupation if the British sued for peace – as he cheerfully expected.

Seeing that he was unsupported, Raeder bowed to his Supreme Commander's order. Who then, he asked, would be responsible for the central direction of plans and operations? Concerning this Hitler was positive too. It would be executed as in the first combined operation – 'Weserübung' – the invasion of Norway. That had been planned by a combined staff under himself through OKW – although, in truth, he had played no part at all in the actual planning of that campaign. This time, he implied, it would be different, and particularly since the Navy seemed so lukewarm to this scheme after being highly enthusiastic about its predecessor. 'In any case,' pronounced Hitler, 'this will be predominantly a Luftwaffe party in its crucial, early stages,' and he relied upon his old and trusted comrade Hermann Goering to give unstinted support – an invitation which the bulky airman eagerly accepted as a prospect of acquiring greater glory.

The joint planning staff, which was hurriedly assembled by Jodl, was already partially experienced in the task, since many of its officers had been connected with Raeder's 1939 survey, and the sailors among them had learnt much from Norway. They met in Berlin on the 26th to present the respective requirements of their Cs-in-C. At once it was apparent that common ground hardly existed except in solid agreement that air superiority over the invasion area and its approaches was a mandatory prerequisite. The stumbling-blocks to a joint plan were those of scale. The Army's representative, Oberst Heinrich von Stülpnagel, insisted that the landings be on the widest possible front between Deal and Lyme Bay. He spoke of the need to employ 13 divisions from the outset, each divided into two echelons – the first to gain a foothold, the second to exploit success. In the first echelon would be 90,000 men, 650 tanks, 4,500 horses, more than 100 mountain guns and a large number of anti-tank guns, besides such weapons as mortars and machine-guns. These the Navy must carry. The Luftwaffe, too, would need help from the Navy, for although it would transport and supply its own two airborne infantry formations, it saw the need, too, for the early arrival of 52 anti-aircraft batteries within the first echelon, comprising more than 300 88mm dual-purpose guns. The second echelon would be even larger – 160,000 men strong. Reinicke, on behalf of the Navy, reckoned it would need 45 transport ships, 640 barges, 215 tugs and 550 motorboats to lift the first echelon (less 200 of the 88mm) and something like four times that capacity to bring across the remainder while continuing to maintain those which had already got ashore.[5] Moreover, he pointed out that to assemble such a fleet as this would not be possible until mid August at the earliest. And, he added, the naval forces, already depleted by losses in Norway, could not for long protect the sea lanes, even if a mine corridor were laid in time.

When it came to the turn of the Luftwaffe representative – Generalmajor Hoffman von Waldau who, by Goering's deliberate intention, out-ranked the other members of the planning group, he did not disappoint them in inspiration. In his opinion, the Army had over-estimated the size of the force needed. If the British were so heavily defeated in France, as they were all led to believe by Intelligence reports, relatively small forces would be needed to overcome what little resistance might be encountered in England. That being so, the invasion frontage could be substantially narrowed, the naval effort cut by at least 75 per cent, the escort requirement simplified and the date for the attack could be advanced so as to meet the Führer's deadline. He was enthusiastically supported by Jodl, and the upshot of it was that von Waldau's concept, for what Jodl and Hitler now called 'Operation Lion', was adopted as the basis for a joint plan. In these conditions the Army would not be heavily stretched; therefore it could still concentrate the bulk of its forces on the final subjugation of Norway and France. The Kriegsmarine, it was agreed, would not be equal to the task; it could raise enough transport craft, but had little hope of holding at bay the Royal Navy once the landing areas had been clearly delineated. All the participants therefore depended upon the Luftwaffe to make good naval deficiencies by playing a central rôle in helping to neutralize the Royal Navy. This the Luftwaffe commanders promised to do. Indeed, its dive-bombers already were swarming above the channel ports, bombing the light naval forces which were striving to rescue the defeated Allied armies from the shores of Belgium and France. Successes in these attacks were contributing to the forthcoming Battle for Britain before the Battle for France entered its final stages.

Britain in peril

In Britain on 26 May there were few in high authority who would have taken other than a thoroughly gloomy view had they been privy to the German deliberations. From the moment when Winston Churchill became Prime Minister on 10 May and the German spearheads approached the Channel coast, his fears began to focus on the danger of imminent invasion. Having studied the lessons of Norway and Holland, the Chiefs of Staff (Admiral Sir Dudley Pound, General Sir Edmund Ironside and Air Marshal Sir Cyril Newall) had concluded that a force of 5,000 paratroops, dropping on seven selected airfields in south-east England, might bring paralysis and pave the way for reinforcements by troop carriers. At the same time, 20,000 troops with armoured vehicles, landed from the sea, might well get through – the Navy always having warned that, in certain kinds of weather, a landing could be made without interference in the first instance.[6] Within the past few weeks an organization known as Ultra, which employed a primitive computer, had come into operation and had been able to break a limited number of encyphered messages passing through the higher German communication networks. The orders to Guderian to advance on Dunkirk had been monitored and read,[7] and already the Chiefs of Staff had advised the Government that the Allied armies there would be lost within 48 hours if Guderian reached his objective and thus isolated all the northern Channel ports.[8] With so few troops left to defend France, the imminent collapse of that nation must be expected. Soon the over-stretched and, in the case of the British Army, largely disarmed fighting Services would be faced with widely expanded commitments. At any moment Italy was expected to join her Axis partner in hostilities against Britain and France, and this would make defence of the Mediterranean Sea a major commitment. If France were defeated and her Fleet neutralized, the Royal Navy would have to establish a new Fleet to defend the western Mediterranean in addition to the large force she already maintained at the eastern end. Almost every warship would have to be withdrawn from the Far East, where the United States Navy would be left alone to confront the already bellicose Japanese. Furthermore, the difficulties of defending the vital sea lanes, upon which the British Isles depended for survival, would be multiplied manifold once the Germans could base naval and air forces along the western coast of France. And, finally, it could not be expected that the Navy would manage to evacuate the Army from Norway and Dunkirk without suffering substantial losses among its most valuable vessels.

As for the Army in Britain, there remained only 15 infantry divisions and a single, incomplete 2nd Armoured Division. All, in manpower, were at half establishment, extremely limited in mobility and with only about a sixth of the field and anti-tank artillery to which they were entitled – first priority in everything having been given to the British Expeditionary Force in France which, at that moment, was on the verge of losing nearly everything it possessed. The 963 tanks remaining in Britain represented impotence; only 213 were of real combat value, the remaining 618 light tanks and 132 medium machines being either of limited fighting capability or useless. A call for Local Defence Volunteers (LDV) by the War Minister, Mr Anthony Eden, on 14 May,[9] was resulting in the enthusiastic enrolment of 250,000 volunteers who had yet to be organized, dressed in uniform, given training and, above all, provided with arms. As a supplement to the Home Defence divisions they might just be capable of raising the alarm if paratroops landed.

As the Chiefs of Staff admitted, everything depended upon the RAF keeping the Luftwaffe at bay. But, since April, the RAF had suffered heavy casualties. Losses of aircraft had substantially exceeded production, particularly in fighters, upon which the burden of the defence of the forces at Dunkirk as well as the United Kingdom depended. In three weeks of fighting in May, 430 fighters had been destroyed against a production of about 300 – the latter figure far higher than originally estimated because the aircraft factories had adopted a 24-hour day, seven day week in response to the sudden emergency. Savings which would be made by withdrawing to Britain the RAF units then in France were bound, too, to be offset when fighters from the UK Defence Forces were committed to provide air cover over Dunkirk during the attempted evacuation of the trapped Army.

The American factor

Britain could expect very little immediate outside help. Hope was about all that the British Government could pin upon the future. Churchill insisted that everything possible be done to save the Army at Dunkirk. At the same time, he tried, might and main, to stiffen French resolve, to keep them in the fight while he turned to President Franklin D. Roosevelt of the USA for whatever aid could be obtained. On 15 May, Churchill had asked Roosevelt by telegram to maintain a policy of non-belligerency, 'Which would mean that you would help us with everything short of actually engaging armed forces.' He asked, too, for fifty old destroyers, several hundred modern aircraft, anti-aircraft guns, raw materials, the indirect intervention of the US Fleet through the prolonged visit of a US squadron to the Irish ports as a deterrent to a German descent on that country, and a similar presence at Singapore to deter the Japanese. To this, Roosevelt could only respond immediately with aircraft and arms. Warships could not be sent without Congress approval; in an election year and with the existence of isolationist lobbies, the time to ask was not opportune. But the US Fleet would remain concentrated at Pearl Harbor and in an operational posture. As the days passed in deepening crisis, Churchill's long established personal relationship with Roosevelt became a matter of vital importance, but for the time being the help that could be expected from the USA was of only marginal assistance.[10] The advice Roosevelt was getting from his sources of information in Europe – and particularly the pessimistic reports being sent by his Ambassador in London, Joseph Kennedy – implied that the chances of British survival were no better than fifty-fifty.

It was apparent that, for the next seven months at least, Britain would have to look to her own salvation and, as the Chiefs of Staff put it, become 'organised as a fortress on totalitarian lines'. On 22 May, under the United Kingdom Emergency Powers (Defence) Act, which was rushed through Parliament within hours, the Government assumed sweeping powers over persons and property. Next day it interned those who were regarded as being pro-German or thought to be in contact with the enemy.[11] Fear of a Fifth

Column such as was supposed to have contributed to the collapse of Britain's allies, was already rife. Spy mania swept the nation and the Government reacted against subversive elements – real and imagined – as the people reported anything unusual as if it were sinister. As the battle for Dunkirk got into its stride and the fear of invasion increased, the nation took up what few arms it possessed and, in the initial stages of preparing their defences, accidentally shot far more of their own side than of the enemy who had yet to put in an appearance.

II

A GATHERING OF FORCES

Set-backs at Dunkirk

While it is true to say that the British Chiefs of Staff never had far from their minds the connection between the rescue of the British Army from Dunkirk and defence against the expected invasion, it is probably equally right to remember that similar considerations also influenced the Germans. Every man and weapon which could be saved from Dunkirk for the defence of Britain would make the German invasion task harder. Every ship and every aircraft destroyed in the attempt to bring the troops home damaged the nation's shield. Kesselring would have been content to prolong the battle for Dunkirk if the balance of losses came down in his favour. Unfortunately for him, however, the Luftwaffe was ill-prepared to apply a stranglehold. In four weeks of heavy combat, as much from unserviceability as from battle casualties, its operational strength had fallen. Some bomber units were 50 per cent below establishment, although the fighter units had maintained a rate of 75 per cent or more, and the single-engined Messerschmitt Me 109 had proved superior to anything it had met so far. Deployment was at fault, too; a great many formations were still operating from bases in Germany because to bring them forward all at once, was beyond the capability even of the excellent field organization then in existence. So the attacks on Dunkirk, which began in earnest on 28 May, never attained the Luftwaffe's maximum effort. Moreover, it was hampered on occasion by poor weather and, to an alarming extent, by the intervention of British Spitfire fighters, based on airfields in England.[1] Suddenly, the Messerschmitt pilots found themselves opposed by an aircraft fought by men who were their equal; the German fighters frequently failed to rendezvous with the bombers they were supposed to escort, and the bombers received heavy punishment.

The story of the evacuation of the British and French armies from Dunkirk has been recounted in detail in the British Official

1. The Battle Lines of Western Europe, 31 May 1940
Allied withdrawals
Allied front lines and bridgeheads
German occupied territories
0 100 200 300 400 500
Miles
Narvik
SWEDEN
FIN-
LAND
Trondheim
NORWAY
Bergen
Oslo
Stockholm
Gothenburg
Copenhagen
DENMARK
Glasgow
Newcastle
EIRE
Manchester
Hull
NETHERLANDS
Hamburg
Birmingham
Berlin
POLAND
Cardiff
London
Rotterdam
Plymouth
Dunkirk
BELGIUM
Prague
Cherbourg
GERMANY
CZECHOSLOVAKIA
Brest
Paris
Strasbourg
Munich
Vienna
Basel
AUSTRIA
FRANCE
SWITZERLAND
Milan
ITALY
Bordeaux
Marseilles
SPAIN
Rome
©Arms and Armour Press, 1980

History *France and Flanders* by L. F. Ellis. In summary, the Luftwaffe failed to prevent the evacuation by sea, and when, too late, the Army was ordered to seize the port it was unable to do so before 330,000 men had been snatched to safety from under their noses. Nevertheless, on 4 June, when all resistance had come to an end and the last British ship had disappeared over the horizon, the Germans could take possession of vast quantities of abandoned arms, ammunition and equipment. The British Army, alone, left behind 2,472 guns, about 400 tanks, 63,879 vehicles and all its stores – which represented a major portion of the best matériel it had possessed. Simultaneously, the RAF had lost 100 more aircraft (mostly fighters) and 85 fighter pilots, and the Royal Navy 243 ships, six of which were destroyers (invaluable for anti-invasion operations in narrow waters) together with many more ships damaged, including 19 destroyers. Therefore, although Goering and Kesselring had failed to prevent the evacuation from Dunkirk, and at a stiff price, they had succeeded in wearing down the defenders of the British Isles. Furthermore, ample opportunities to inflict additional losses, when the enemy fought on in Norway and in France, were yet to be presented. Before Dunkirk had fallen, the Wehrmacht in the West had reorganized into three groups – two designated for the conquest of France and the third for Operation 'Lion'. Only eight infantry divisions and one panzer division were, at this stage, put under the command of General der Infanterie Ernst Busch's 16th Army. The Luftwaffe, however, tended to retain a larger proportion of its resources for 'Lion' than did the Army. To Kesselring's Luftflotte 2 was allocated a strong force of bombers and fighters plus the paratroop and air landing divisions and the bulk of the transport aircraft allocated to their service. General der Flieger Hugo Sperrle received what was left over for his Luftflotte 3, except when circumstances demanded a maximum effort in support of some special operation. On 5 June, as Luftflotte 2 made its preliminary flights in preparation for 'Lion', the Germans, with supreme confidence, moved to overwhelm France with forces deficient of maximum air support. German losses had been relatively light, and the pause at Dunkirk had enabled the Army to rest its mobile troops (the ten panzer divisions and seven motorized infantry divisions) and restore their equipment to a higher state of maintenance. An inspection of the battlefields of May had satisfied the Intelligence Branch that 85 per cent of the best French mechanized divisions, 24 of their infantry divisions and the bulk of their air force had been eliminated. The latest information gained through radio intercept had pinpointed nearly all the surviving Allied formations, and painted a picture of a seriously weakened enemy in a state of disarray. British reinforcements were known to have arrived to the south of the River Somme, even while the lines of circumvallation were closing upon Dunkirk, but these consisted of a single under-strength armoured division (the 1st) and the 51st and 52nd Infantry Divisions, plus parts of the 1st Canadian Infantry Division. Their presence was to be welcomed, it was concluded! If these good formations could be mopped-up in France they would not be encountered in England.

The slightest mention of the prowess of British forces fascinated the planners of 'Lion'. They were impressed by British tenacity, and insisted to Jodl at OKW that during the forthcoming assault on France, priority be given to the destruction of the British forces and the early capture of that sector of the French seaboard which would become the mounting base for the invasion. Von Stülpnagel was both intrigued and pleased by reports of a battle which had taken place near Abbeville from 27 to 30 May, when tanks of the French 4th Armoured Division and the British 1st Armoured Division had attacked a German bridgehead which had been established south of the Somme. At first, the Allied tanks, some of them very heavily armoured, had forced the German outposts to retire, and panic had infected the infantry. But, as had been noticed so often earlier in the campaign, the enemy did not press home his attack or properly co-ordinate his infantry, tanks and artillery. The German anti-tank gunners had stood their ground and repelled the attack, although not without loss to themselves. But, after the enemy had withdrawn, they dispersed their tanks, thus exposing the remaining enemy defenders to the sort of concentrated attack on a narrow frontage which the Germans practised. Von Stülpnagel decided to insist on including the maximum number of tanks and anti-tank guns among the assault formations for Operation 'Lion'. If this could be achieved, the chances of a British counter-attack succeeding immediately after the Germans had landed would be remote: furthermore, a rapid riposte leading to a breakout would be simplified and accelerated.

The plans take shape

Planning for 'Lion' progressed well under the goading of the Luftwaffe and Army enthusiasts and was held back only occasionally by Kriegsmarine scepticism. Von Waldau and von Stülpnagel competed in ingenuity to overcome difficulties and, as was the way with élite General Staff officers, instigated a series of technical investigations into ways of overcoming the problems of transportation. Because of the Kriegsmarine's alleged inertia, both the Army and the Luftwaffe began to explore methods of their own to ship troops and equipment across the Channel. Meanwhile the Kriegsmarine simply selected the types of ship and inland waterway barge (*Schiffs* or *Prahms* as they came to be known) deemed most suitable for the tasks envisaged. Each of the three Services thus assembled its own invasion fleet (with an inevitable waste of effort and the construction of an incredible miscellany of craft), while the Luftwaffe was allowed to concentrate on the air lift, hindered only in the slightest by the other two Services, because Goering, who enjoyed the full confidence of Hitler, made a point of dealing direct with the Führer and by-passing OKW, OKH (the Army High Command) and OKM (the Navy High Command) when it suited him.

Jodl's plan gave tacit precedence to the Luftwaffe, though airmen were sparsely represented within OKW by comparison with the Army and Kriegsmarine. Indeed, in the final event, OKW could only formalize what was agreed by the joint services planning committee in which von Waldau held a pre-eminent position.

It was instinctive among the Army's leaders that they desired to launch the invasion on as wide a front as possible, thus providing themselves with the maximum number of options from which to develop alternative directions of thrust. But the primary acceptance by Hitler of Goering's basic requirement for early commencement of the invasion, and the inability of the Kriegsmarine immediately to procure enough shipping for an early broad-fronted strategy, denied them this luxury. They were compelled by Hitler to adopt a narrow-fronted assault in the hope that the surprise and sheer violence of this single descent upon the enemy would establish an instant and invincible local supremacy. Von Waldau went so far as to guarantee the success of the initial airborne landing, if it took place at the shortest possible distance from France and, therefore, well within fighter aircraft cover. In other words, he left OKW no option but to make the attempt somewhere between Hythe and Deal, where the lines of communication were shortest, air protection would be strongest and the turn round of cargo vessels and aircraft quickest. It was almost incidental that the enemy would understood this too, but so sure were the Germans of their superiority that they relied upon gaining a victory by prowess alone.

In any other circumstances a prolonged argument against the narrow front might have been mounted jointly by the Army and

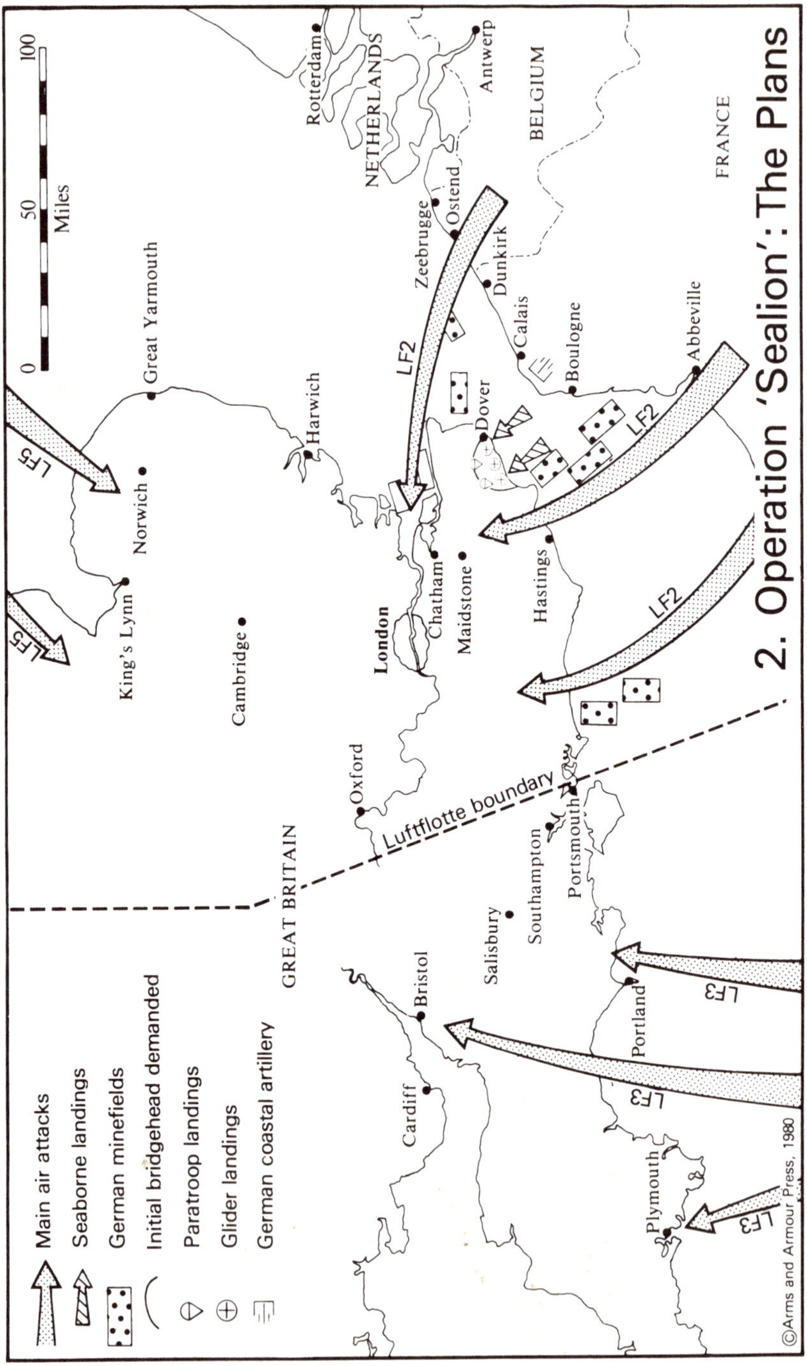

2. Operation 'Sealion': The Plans

Kriegsmarine, but long-standing friendship between General Franz Halder, the Army Chief of Staff, and Admiral Otto Schniewind, the Chief of Staff of Naval Operations, obviated this. Halder had taken a day off, on 25 May, to visit Schniewind in Berlin to discusss the feasibility of Hitler's latest venture. Halder doubted if the British would readily sue for peace and felt sure they would eventually have to be brought to battle in their own land. He came away from the meeting satisfied that, by the beginning of July, the Kriegsmarine could assemble 'A large number [1,000] of small steamers' enough to carry 100,000 men at one time. In fact, far fewer ships were immediately available and the maximum number of men the Navy could undertake to carry in one lift in mid June would be 7,500. But Halder's outline notes for a landing visualised the waters out to mid Channel being dominated by German artillery, ships and aircraft, while 'Artillery cover for the second half of the run across the water and on the beaches must be furnished by the Luftwaffe. Underwater threats [from submarines] can be shut out by net barrages. Surface threats can be minimized by mines and submarines, supplementing land-based artillery and aircraft. Cliffs at Dover, Dungeness, Beachy Head [but] rest of coast suitable for landing . . .' He went on to mention the uses to which the normal, large canal barges, towed by tugs, might be put and 'Dr Feder type concrete barges now under test. Provision in sufficient numbers in July held possible'. Schniewind, for his part, stressed the need of fine weather and smooth water (both of which, indeed, were likely in July) and, of course, the unrestricted use of ports between the River Scheldt and River Seine.[2]

The Halder-Schniewind meeting not only settled an operational pattern and, to some extent, the immediate planning needs of all three Services, but also gave strong impetus to those engaged in preparing the invasion. Halder had felt certain that Hitler would make the fateful decision on the 24th and that, from then on, he would want 'everything done at top speed'. With this in mind, he had briefed von Brauchitsch, and by so doing had generated in the C-in-C that sense of practicability he displayed to Hitler. Pressure on the planners was now increased by Kesselring through von Waldau. Once the former had settled the plan for attacking Dunkirk, he left its implementation to his Chief of Staff, Wilhelm Speidel, and turned to study the problem of mounting the preliminary operations for 'Lion' so as to dovetail them with the inevitable demands which could be expected to support the renewed offensive which was due to commence against France on 5 June.

The Luftwaffe

The Luftwaffe was designed principally as a tactical air force for the support of land forces. It included a few units with experience of attacking ships, but none capable of delivering torpedoes – a technique with which the Kriegsmarine had experimented and achieved barely 50 per cent success. It also possessed a limited capacity to deliver strategic attacks on factories and towns, but was dependent upon daytime attacks for accuracy because the beam navigational guidance system had not yet been fully developed for night use. By day, however, the bomber formations were incapable of adequate self-defence against enemy fighters; they depended therefore upon fighter escorts and their safe radius of action was limited to that of the fighters, little more than 150 miles. In the four weeks which Kesselring knew would elapse before he was invited to begin the subjugation of the RAF and provide the direct support of the invasion, he had to establish his Luftflotte 2 on new airfields (not all of them yet in German hands) within striking distance of England; build up their logistic backing; ascertain the enemy's strength, dispositions and tactical methods; acclimatize his formations and commanders to an entirely new type of operation; and produce a foolproof plan. It was a tall order, but one suited to his talents, frenetic drive and natural optimism.

On the assumption that the strength of the combat formations made available to his Luftflotte 2 on 5 June would be:

200 Long-range bombers (He 111 and Do 17)
50 Twin-engined fighters (Me 110)
20 Long-range reconnaissance aircraft (including some four-engined Focke-Wulf Condors)

and that, in the month to come, this would expand to:—

700 Long-range bombers (including the latest Ju 88)
280 Dive bombers (Ju 87)
550 Single-engined fighters (Me 109)
100 Twin-engined fighters
30 Long-range reconnaissance aircraft,

Kesselring embarked upon a programme geared to a steady intensification of operations both by day and night, aimed at selected targets in and around the coasts of Britain. It was his intention to draw the RAF into battle, sound out the British defences, cause the maximum damage to British ports and shipping, and acclimatize his own men by stages in preparation for the maximum effort scheduled for 9 July. At the same time, Sperrle, whose Luftflotte 3 was already engaged in the preliminaries of the

Right: Eight pages of maps prepared by the Germans for their conquest of Britain. Translations and keys are facing page 33.

A

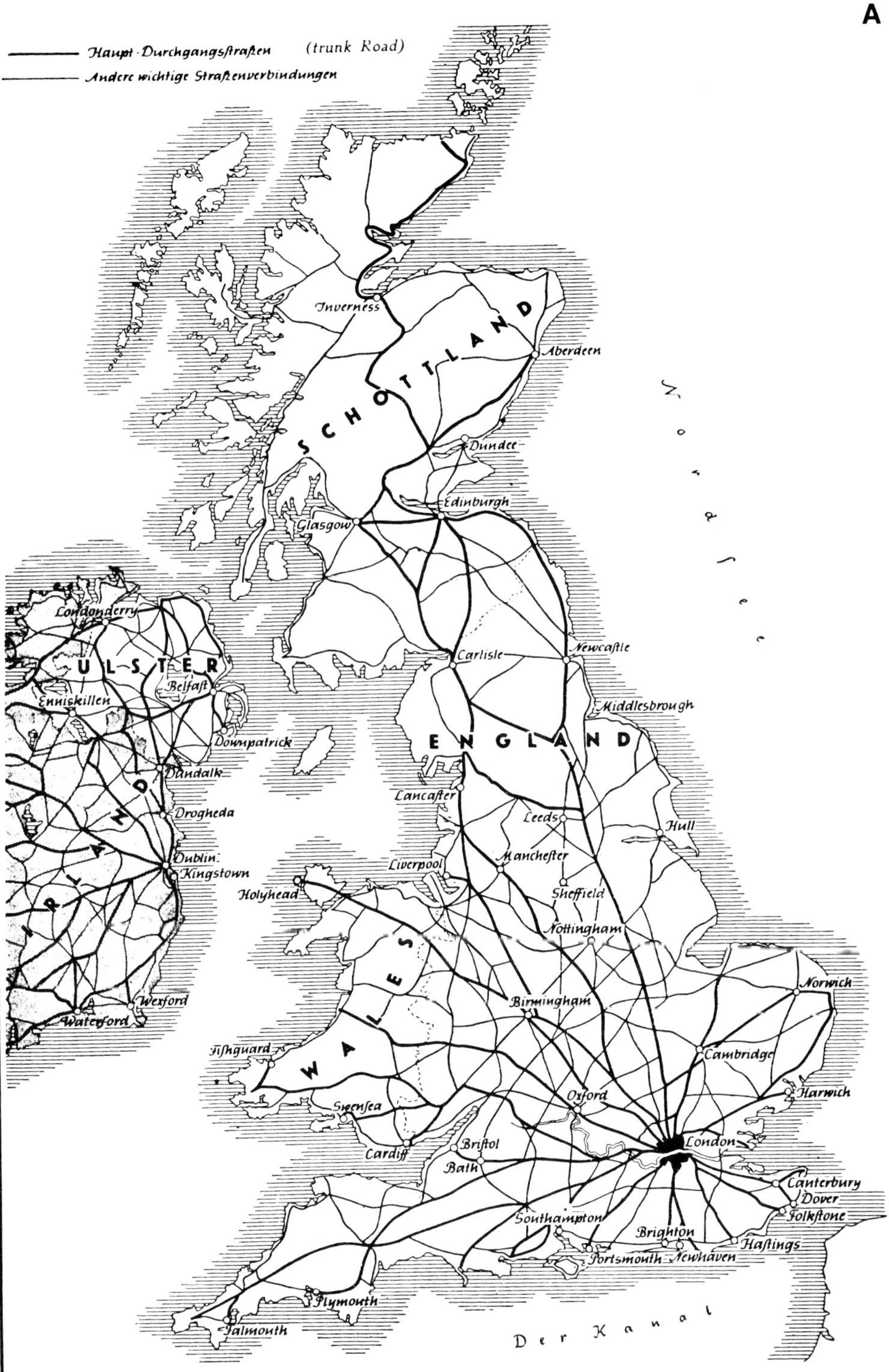

Abb. 10. Die wichtigsten Straßen Großbritanniens

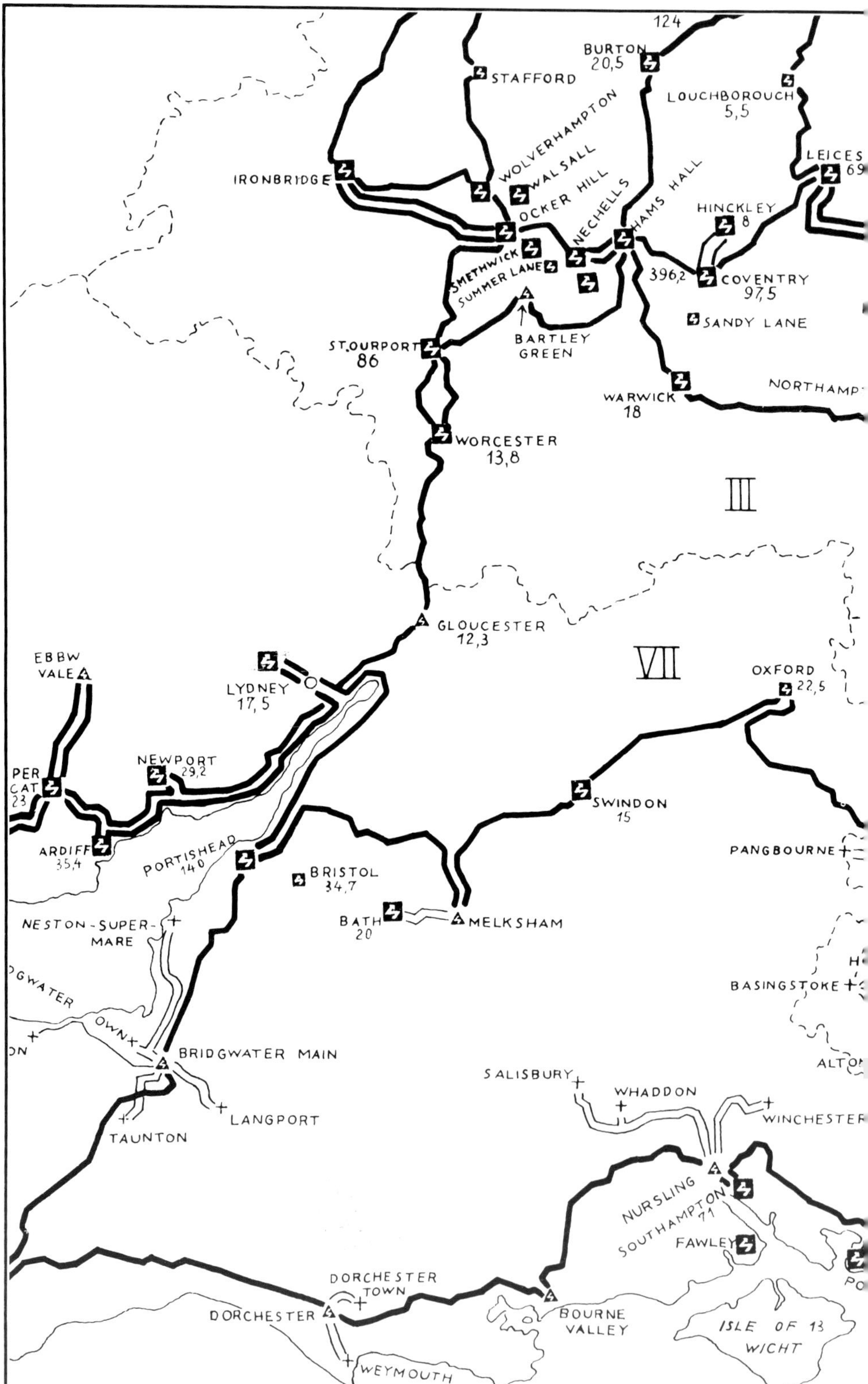

124
BURTON
20,5
STAFFORD
LOUCHBOROUCH
5,5
WOLVERHAMPTON
WALSALL
OCKER HILL
NECHELLS
HAMS HALL
LEICES
69
IRONBRIDGE
HINCKLEY
8
SMETHWICK
SUMMER LANE
396,2
COVENTRY
97,5
SANDY LANE
BARTLEY
GREEN
STOURPORT
86
WARWICK
18
NORTHAMP
WORCESTER
13,8
III
GLOUCESTER
12,3
VII
EBBW
VALE
LYDNEY
17,5
OXFORD
22,5
NEWPORT
29,2
PER
CAT
23
SWINDON
15
ARDIFF
35,4
PORTISHEAD
140
PANGBOURNE
BRISTOL
34,7
NESTON-SUPER-
MARE
BATH
20
MELKSHAM
GWATER
BASINGSTOKE
OWN
ON
BRIDGWATER MAIN
ALTO
SALISBURY
WHADDON
WINCHESTER
LANGPORT
TAUNTON
NURSLING
SOUTHAMPTON
71
FAWLEY
DORCHESTER
TOWN
DORCHESTER
BOURNE
VALLEY
ISLE OF 13
WICHT
WEYMOUTH

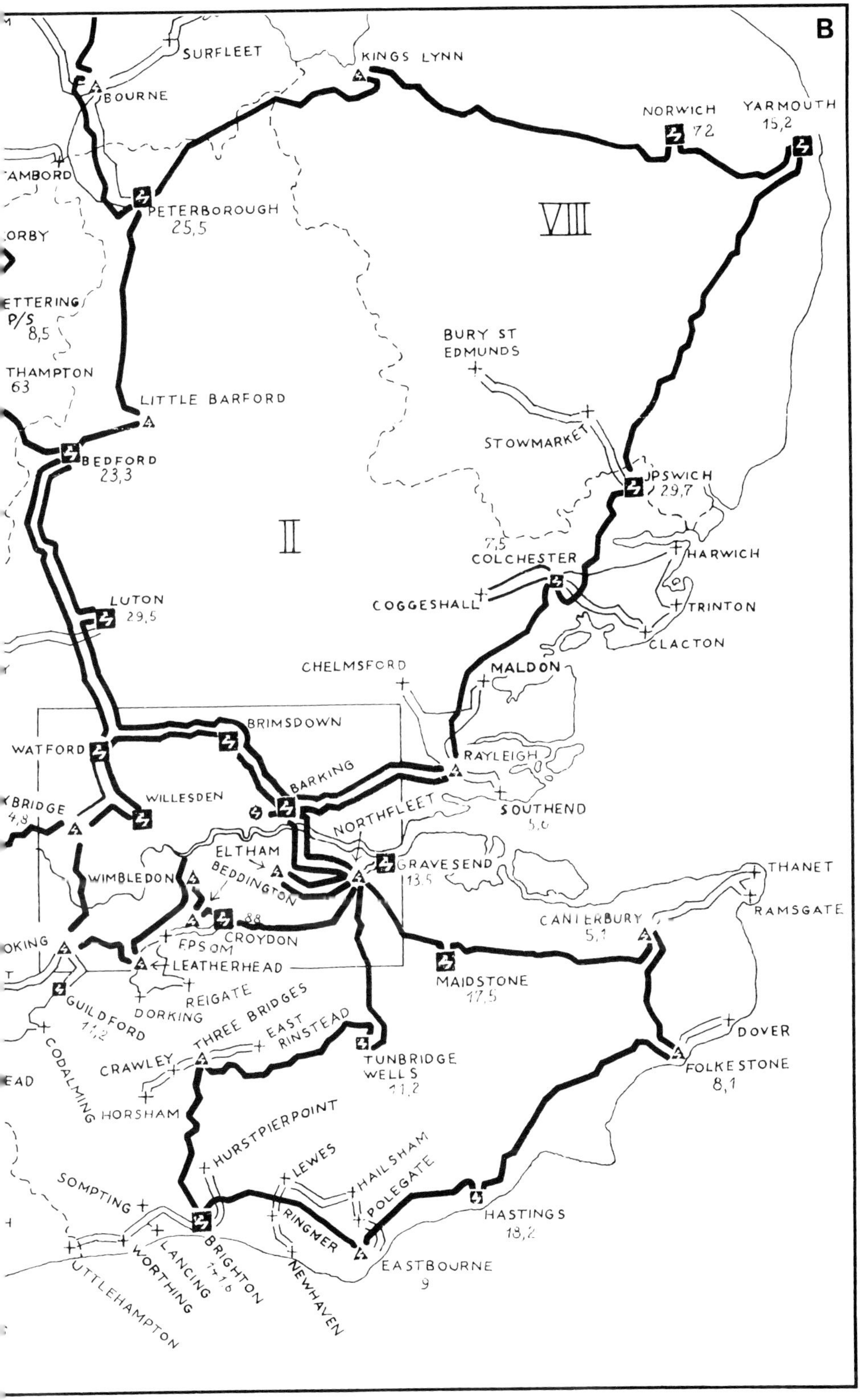
B
SURFLEET
KINGS LYNN
BOURNE
NORWICH
72
YARMOUTH
15,2
PETERBOROUGH
25,5
VIII
LITTLE BARFORD
BEDFORD
23,3
BURY ST EDMUNDS
STOWMARKET
IPSWICH
29,7
II
COLCHESTER
HARWICH
COGGESHALL
TRINTON
CLACTON
LUTON
29,5
CHELMSFORD
MALDON
BRIMSDOWN
WATFORD
RAYLEIGH
BARKING
WILLESDEN
NORTHFLEET
SOUTHEND
ELTHAM
BEDDINGTON
GRAVESEND
13,5
WIMBLEDON
THANET
RAMSGATE
CROYDON
88
EPSOM
CANTERBURY
5,1
LEATHERHEAD
MAIDSTONE
17,5
GUILDFORD
REIGATE
DORKING
THREE BRIDGES
EAST RINSTEAD
TUNBRIDGE WELLS
CRAWLEY
CODALMING
HORSHAM
DOVER
FOLKESTONE
8,1
HURSTPIERPOINT
LEWES
HAILSHAM
POLEGATE
SOMPTING
HASTINGS
18,2
RINGMER
BRIGHTON
EASTBOURNE
9
LANCING
WORTHING
NEWHAVEN
LITTLEHAMPTON
STAMBORD
CORBY
KETTERING
P/S
8,5
NORTHAMPTON
63
UXBRIDGE
WOKING

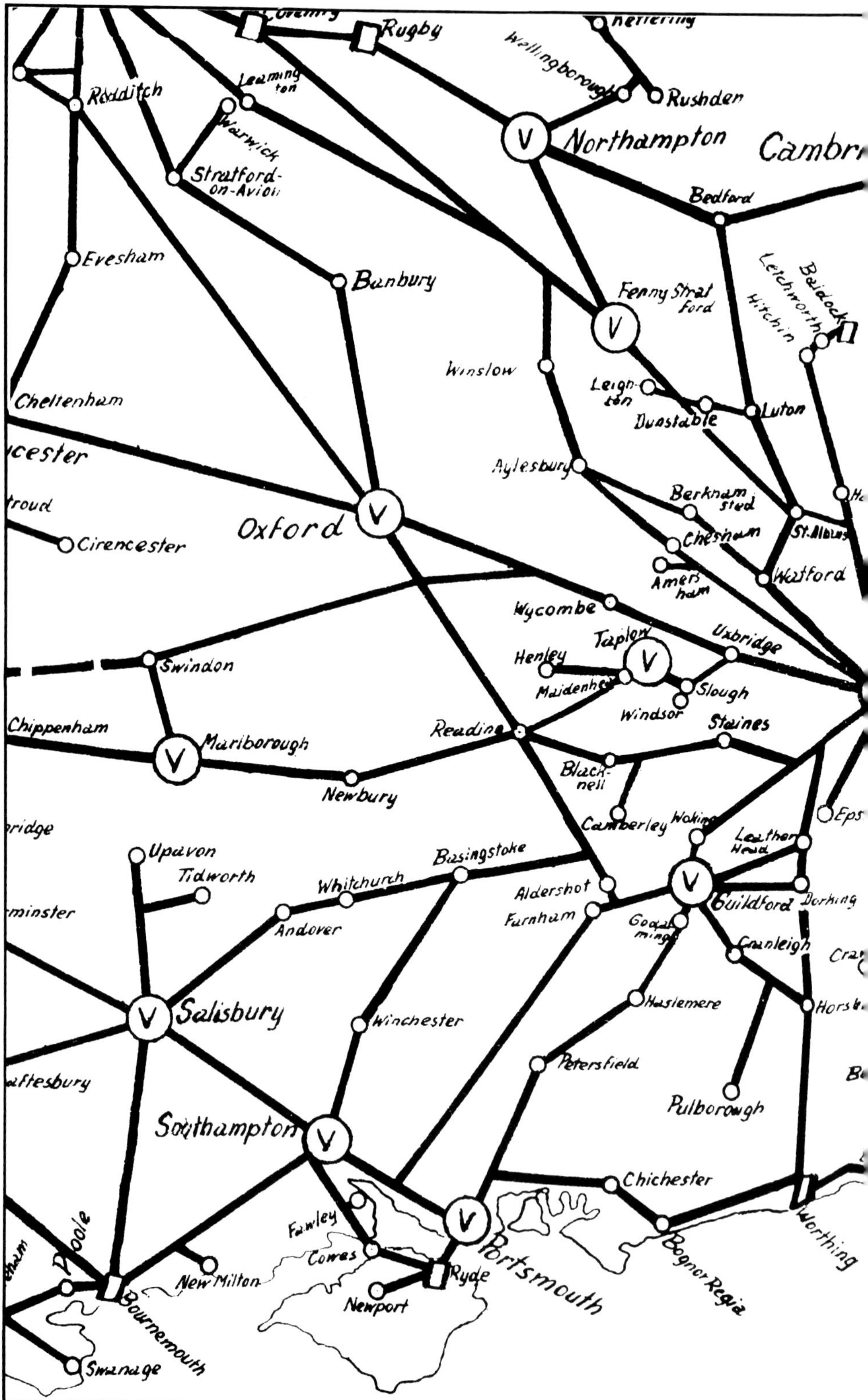

Rugby
Wellingborough
Rushden
Redditch
Leamington
Warwick
Northampton
Stratford-on-Avon
Bedford
Evesham
Banbury
Fenny Stratford
Letchworth
Baldock
Hitchin
Winslow
Leighton
Dunstable
Luton
Cheltenham
Aylesbury
Berkhamstead
Oxford
Chesham
St. Albans
Cirencester
Amersham
Watford
Wycombe
Taplow
Uxbridge
Henley
Swindon
Maidenhead
Slough
Windsor
Chippenham
Reading
Staines
Marlborough
Blacknell
Newbury
Camberley
Woking
Upavon
Leatherhead
Basingstoke
Tidworth
Whitchurch
Aldershot
Guildford
Dorking
Farnham
Andover
Godalming
Cranleigh
Haslemere
Salisbury
Winchester
Petersfield
Pulborough
Southampton
Chichester
Fawley
Portsmouth
Worthing
Poole
Cowes
Bognor Regis
New Milton
Ryde
Newport
Bournemouth
Swanage

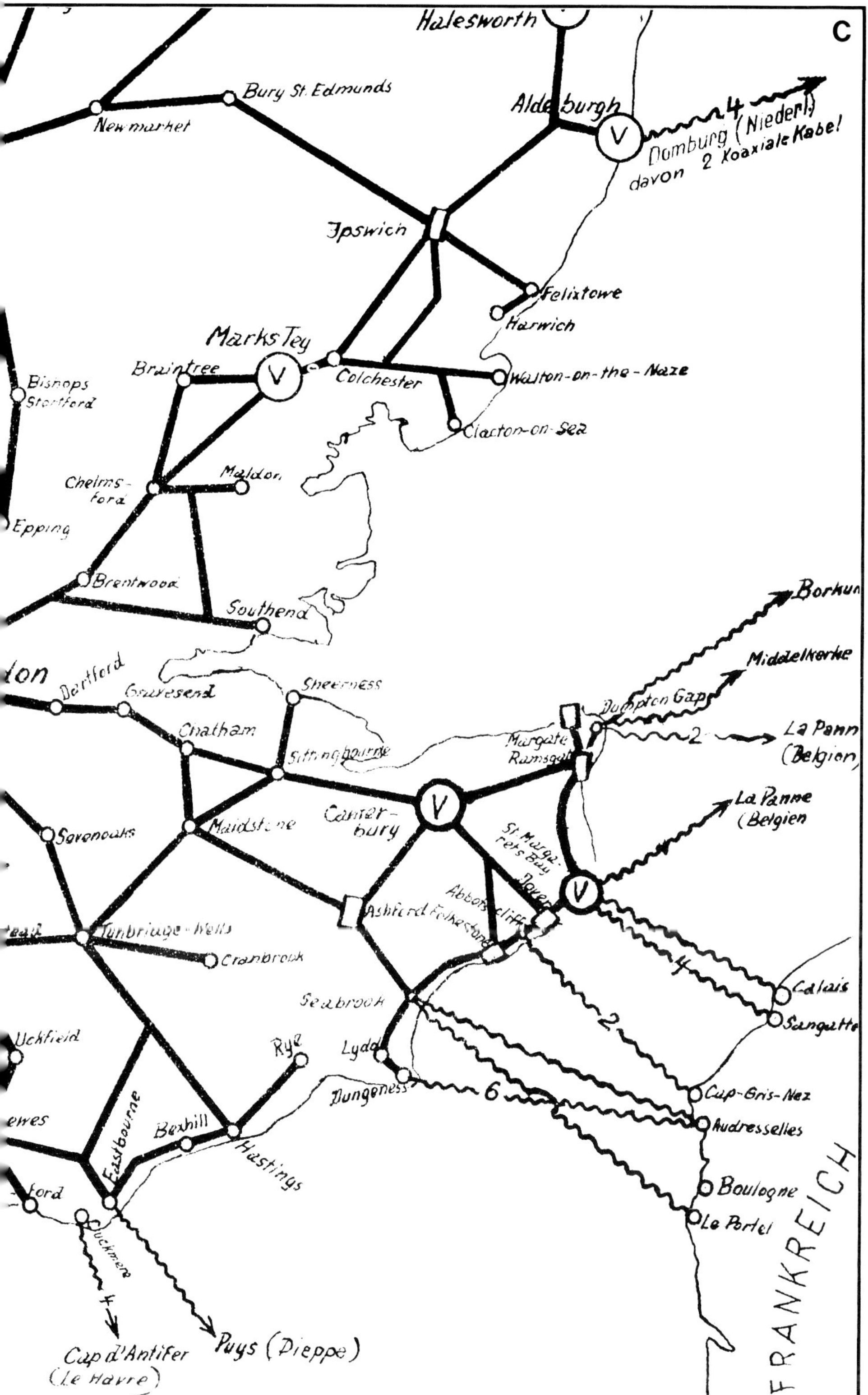
C
Halesworth
Bury St. Edmunds
Newmarket
Aldeburgh
4
Domburg (Niederl.)
davon 2 Koaxiale Kabel
Ipswich
Felixtowe
Harwich
Marks Tey
Braintree
Colchester
Walton-on-the-Naze
Bishops Stortford
Clacton-on-Sea
Chelmsford
Maldon
Epping
Brentwood
Southend
Borkum
Middelkerke
Dartford
Gravesend
Sheerness
Dumpton Gap
2
La Panne (Belgien)
Chatham
Sittingbourne
Margate Ramsgate
Canterbury
La Panne (Belgien)
Sevenoaks
Maidstone
St. Margarets Bay
Dover
Abbots cliff
Ashford
Folkestone
Tunbridge Wells
Cranbrook
4
Calais
Seabrook
Sangatte
2
Uckfield
Rye
Lydd
Dungeness
6
Cap-Gris-Nez
Audresselles
Bexhill
Hastings
Eastbourne
Boulogne
Le Portel
Cuckmere
4
FRANKREICH
Cap d'Antifer (Le Havre)
Puys (Dieppe)

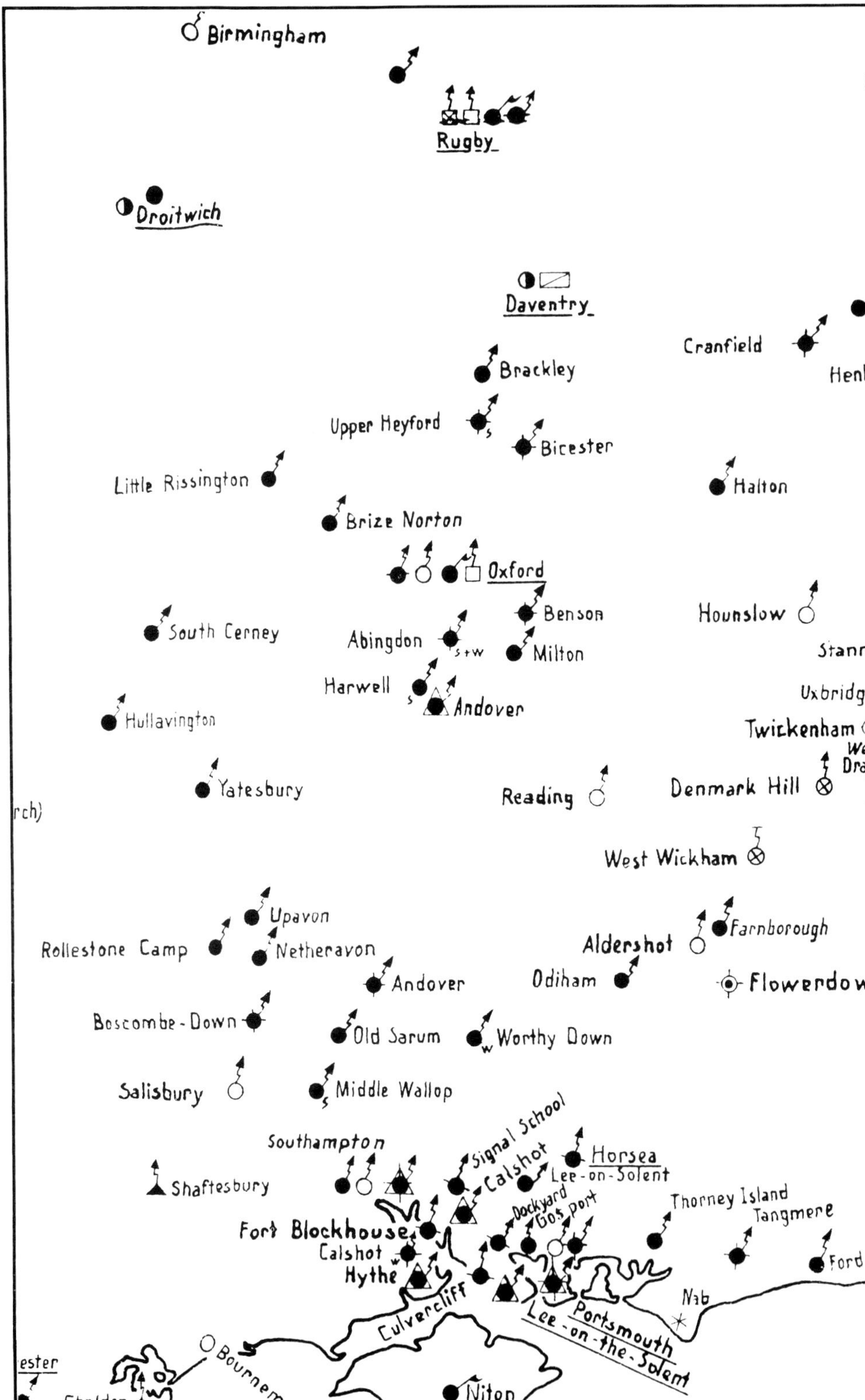
Birmingham
Rugby
Droitwich
Daventry
Cranfield
Brackley
Henl
Upper Heyford
Bicester
Little Rissington
Halton
Brize Norton
Oxford
Benson
Hounslow
South Cerney
Abingdon
Milton
Stanm
Harwell
Andover
Uxbridg
Hullavington
Twickenham
Yatesbury
Reading
Denmark Hill
West Wickham
Upavon
Rollestone Camp
Netheravon
Aldershot
Farnborough
Andover
Odiham
Flowerdow
Boscombe-Down
Old Sarum
Worthy Down
Salisbury
Middle Wallop
Southampton
Signal School
Calshot
Horsea
Lee-on-Solent
Shaftesbury
Dockyard
Gosport
Thorney Island
Tangmere
Fort Blockhouse
Calshot
Hythe
Ford
Nab
Culvercliff
Portsmouth
Lee-on-the-Solent
Bournem
Niton
Chaldon
ester

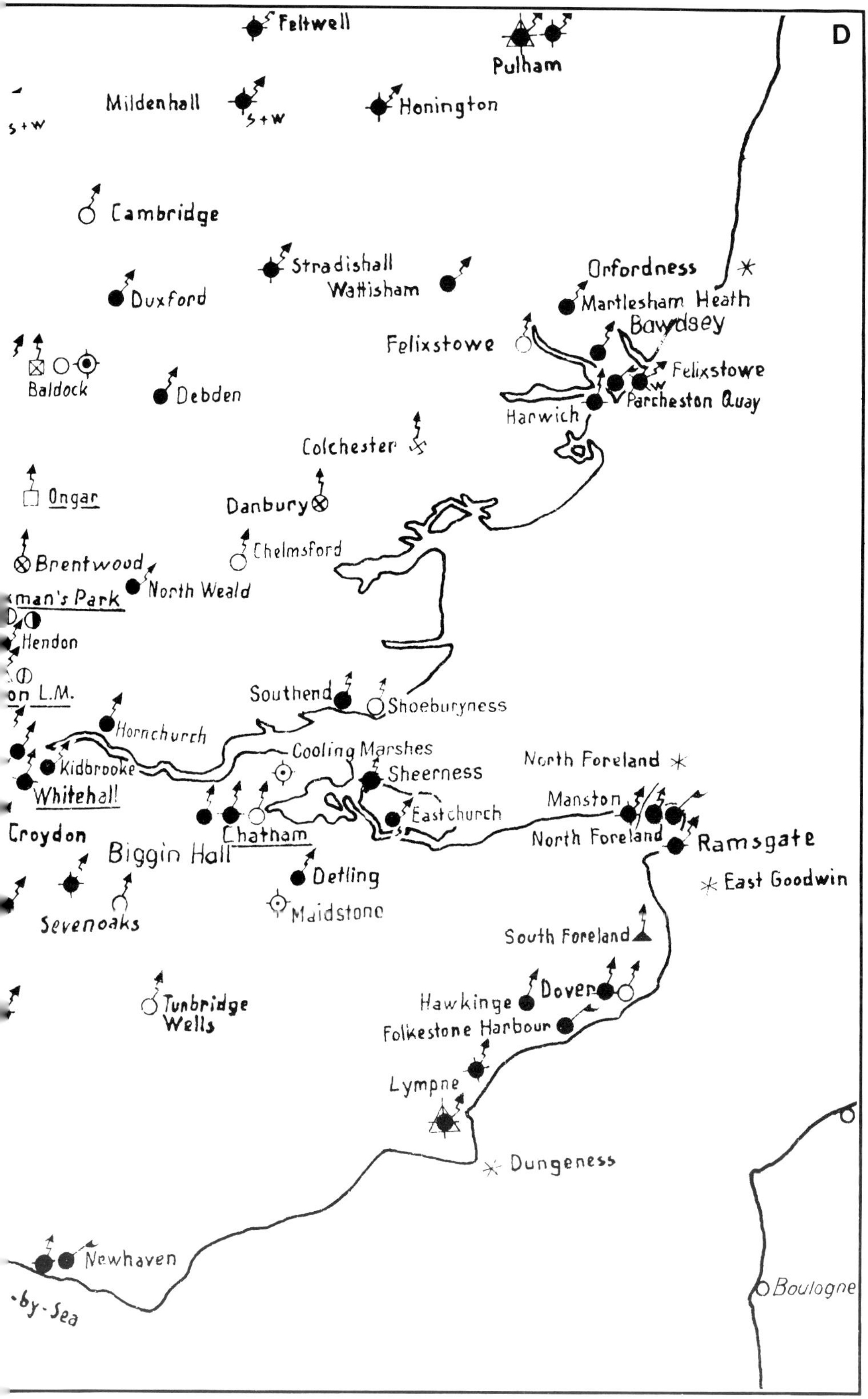

D
Feltwell
Pulham
Mildenhall
s+w
s+w
Honington
Cambridge
Stradishall
Wattisham
Orfordness
Duxford
Martlesham Heath
Bawdsey
Felixstowe
Baldock
Debden
Felixstowe
Parcheston Quay
Harwich
Colchester
Ongar
Danbury
Chelmsford
Brentwood
North Weald
man's Park
Hendon
on L.M.
Southend
Shoeburyness
Hornchurch
Cooling Marshes
Kidbrooke
Sheerness
North Foreland
Whitehall
Eastchurch
Manston
North Foreland
Ramsgate
Croydon
Chatham
Biggin Hall
Detling
East Goodwin
Maidstone
Sevenoaks
South Foreland
Tunbridge Wells
Hawkinge
Dover
Folkestone Harbour
Lympne
Dungeness
Newhaven
-by-Sea
Boulogne

A: Die Wichtigsten Strassen Grossbritanniens = Main roads in Great Britain
Haupt-Durchgangsstrassen = Trunk Roads
Andere Wichtige Straszenverbindungen = Other Major Road Connections

B: Das Kraftnetz des C.E.B. (Central Electricity Board = Elektrizitätsamt) = The Power Network of the C.E.B.
Kraftwerk 1. Ordnung = Major Power Stations
Kraftwerk geringerer Ordnung = Minor Power Stations
Umformeranlage über 132 Kilovolt = Transformers over 132 Kilovolts
Schaltwerk 132 Kilovolt = 132 Kilovolt Substations
Umformeranlage und/oder Schaltwerk unter 132 Kilovolt = Transformers and/or Substations under 132 Kilovolts
Wasserkraftelektrizitätswerk = Hydro-Electric Power Stations
Überlandleitung von 132 Kilovolt = 132 Kilovolt Overhead Cables
Überlandleitung von 66 Kilovolt = 66 Kilovolt Overhead Cables
Überlandleitung von 33 Kilovolt = 33 Kilovolt Overhead Cables
Kabel 132 Kilovolt = 132 Kilovolt Cable
Kabel 66 Kilovolt = 66 Kilovolt Cable
Kabel 32 Kilovolt und weniger = Cable for 32 Kilovolts and under
Leitungen nicht von C.E.B. errichtet = Electricity not installed
Grenzen der Elektrizitätsbezirke = Boundaries of Electricity Areas

C: Fernsprech- und Telegraphennetz = Trunk and Telegraph Network
Erdkabellinie = Underground Cable
Erdkabellinie im Bau = Underground Cable being Laid
oberirdische Leitungen = Overhead Cable
Seekabellinie = Underwater Cable
Fernkabel = Verstärkerämter = Trunk-Cable Booster Stations
kleinere Vermittelungen = Small Exchanges
Schaltstelle = Switchboards

D: Funkstellen = Radio Stations
Funkstellen für zwischenstaatlichen Verkehr = International Radio Stations
Funkstelle = Radio Station
Funksprechsender = Radio Transmitter
Funksprechempfänger = Radio Receiver

Postfunkstellen = Postal Telecommunications
Postfunkstelle = Postal Telecommunications Station
Postfunkstelle (Ultrakurzwellensender) = Transmitter (Ultra-short wave)
Polizeifunkstellen = Police Radio Network
Polizeifunkstelle (Sendestelle) = Police Radio (Transmitter)
Polizeifunkstelle (Empfangsstelle) = Police Radio (Receiver)
Polizeifunkstelle (geplant) = Police Radio Station (Planned)
Küstenfunkstellen und Funkfeuer = Coastal Radio Stations with Beacons
Küstenfunkstelle mit Peilsender = Coastal Radio Station with Mast
Küstenfunkstelle = Coastal Radio Station
Funkfeuer = Beacon
Verkehrsflieger-Bodenfunkstellen = Air Traffic Ground Control
Verkehrsfliegerbodenfunkstelle = Air Traffic Ground Control
Verkehrsfliegerbodenfunkstelte mit Peilsender = Air Traffic Ground Control with Mast
Rundfunksender = Radio Transmitter

Lang- und Mittelwellen / Kurzwellen
= Long and Medium Wave/Short Wave
0,1 — 9,9 Kw
10 — 49,9 Kw
50 — 99,9 Kw
100 — 300 Kw
über 300 Kw

Heeresfunkstellen = Army Radio Stations
Heeresfunkstelle = Army Radio Station
Funkstellen der Kriegsmarine = Naval Radio Stations
Funkstelle der Kriegsmarine = Naval Radio Station
Kurzwellen-Peilstelle = Short-wave Mast
Funkstellen der Luftwaffe = Air Force Radio Stations
Funkstelle der Luftwaffe = Air Force Radio Station
Funkstelle der Luftwaffe (mit Peilsender) = Air Force Radio Station with Mast
Funkstelle der Luftwaffe (mit Sprechfunk) = Air Force Radio Station with Transmitter
Funkstelle der Luftwaffe (m. regelm. Wetterfunk) = Air Force Radio Station with Regular Weather Forecast

final assault upon France, would begin to make ready to operate on Kesselring's left flank as soon as he had completed his present task. On 1 and 2 June, the Luftwaffe launched attacks against communications centres in central France and on the 3rd, bombed the outskirts of Paris. The next day its attacks were switched to airfields as the opening moves of the Battle of France rose to a crescendo – its course to be described in Chapter III. During the night of the 5th, the first tentative flights were made by a few of Kesselring's bombers at a relatively low level over England, causing the air raid sirens to wail in towns and villages and bringing a large proportion of the populace face to face with the throb of foreign engines and the realities of the enemy being actually on their doorstep; learning to live with the Blitz, as they called it. Some bombs were dropped and anti-aircraft guns opened fire, but neither side cared to disclose its full strength or potential, and the Germans were chiefly intent upon practising picked crews in the job of navigating by radio beams transmitted from master stations in Germany. This, the preliminary phase of 'Lion', will be described in Chapter IV.

The Kriegsmarine

Totting-up the resources which might be available to them in mid July, the Kriegsmarine concluded on 1 June that, providing they were spared additional losses in the vicinity of Norway, they might, by extraordinary exertions, assemble in the approaches to the English Channel a fleet consisting of:

- 2 Battle cruisers (*Scharnhorst* and *Gneisenau*)
- 2 Obsolete First World War battleships (*Schlesien* and *Schleswig-Holstein*)
- 1 Pocket battleship (*Admiral Scheer*)
- 1 Heavy cruiser (*Hipper*)
- 3 Cruisers (*Köln, Emden* and *Nürnberg*)
- 10 Destroyers and torpedo-boats
- 34 Escorts
- 30 U-boats
- 20 Motor torpedo-boats (S boats, usually called E boats by the British).

There were also many minesweepers, armed trawlers, and launches available. It was not, of course, a Fleet fit to engage in a general action with the Royal Navy but, aided by the Luftwaffe and supported by coastal artillery in narrow waters, it might just see 'Lion' through.

As has already been mentioned, there were no specially designed assault landing craft in existence, so the land forces would have to be carried in an improvised fleet consisting of small ships, converted barges (*Prahms*), naval vessels and fishing boats. In addition, there were the Siebel ferries developed by the Luftwaffe, driven in some instances by aircraft propellers powered by aircraft engines mounted above the superstructure and carrying 88mm anti-aircraft guns to give accurate fire support during the assault. Raeder gloomily foresaw that the removal of so many civilian craft from their commercial work would lead to a 30 per cent reduction in Germany's important inland shipping traffic, as well as a serious curtailment of fishing. But the work of selecting, hiring and commandeering suitable craft went ahead regardless of the objections. At the same time, repairs began of the ports upon which the invasion would depend for embarkation and the dispatch of supplies. Rotterdam, Ostend, Dunkirk, Calais and Boulogne – none of them in full working order, but not one of them totally unusable – were to be used. Stocks of mines and anti-submarine nets were hauled forward and local defensive barriers were laid. Behind the ports, the chosen Army assault units began to assemble. Everywhere anti-aircraft batteries stood by to protect the ports and vital points.

On 31 May, the planners encountered a tactical difficulty. Whereas the Army insisted that the troops be delivered in an orderly manner to the hostile shore, in combat groups sailing in compact echelons so that they were properly balanced for battle on arrival, the Kriegsmarine could offer no such service. The sailors pointed out that it was asking too much of the captains of ships of unequal performance to keep to a rigid formation and schedule in tidal streams among a maze of sandbanks, wrecks and minefields such as littered the narrow Straits of Dover. They hoped to maintain a steady flow of ships spread over a period of several days, but the Army units might well become disordered prior to landing. The Kriegsmarine would do its best to meet the Army demands, but the Army must plan on the basis of chaos. For five days there was an impasse which was broken when the matter was taken to Hitler who, on 5 June, ruled that the two Services must compromise. He ordered the Kriegsmarine to do all in its power to satisfy the Army's essential demands and he warned the Army to expect unusually severe battlefield frictions. The soldiers should bear in mind, Hitler insisted, that they would not be the first ashore. The airborne troops would have landed already, and the enemy would be distracted. Moreover, the well-tried German system of organization and tactical flexibility, making use of *ad hoc* battle groups, should help to overcome any accidental intermingling of troops on the beach. It would look like 'Formation Pigpile' (*Sauhaufen*), admitted Kommodore Friedrich Ruge, who was in command of the minesweeper and escort forces – but it should work.[3]

The land forces

In Germany, the airborne formations upon which so much depended, had been rested after their exertions in Norway and Holland. Moreover, their potential had been improved so that all three regiments of 7th Air (Parachute) Division were capable of landing efficiently (only two had been ready for Holland). Now they trained hard with the units of Fliegerkorps Zbv, which had been brought up to strength in machines to replace those lost or damaged in the earlier campaigns. By invasion day there would be at least 500 Ju 52 and several four-engined Ju 90 ready, though not all serviceable at once. Alongside the 7th Air Division and the 22nd Air Landing (non-parachute) Division were certain other units which would go into battle by air. Special Unit 800, which came under the wing of the Abwehr (German Military Intelligence) had men able to land by parachute and carry out seaborne raiding; they had been used with indifferent results on 10 May. So too had the men of Infanterie Regiment Grossdeutschland, several hundred of whose members were trained to ride in the remarkable Feisler Storch monoplane which could deliver five assault troopers at a time on landing strips only a few yards in length.

The formations selected for the initial seaborne assault were the 17th Infantry Division and the 6th Mountain Division, the former to go ashore across open beaches to the west of Folkestone, the latter to climb the cliffs between Folkestone and Dover. The mountaineers would have to depend almost entirely on their own skill to reach their objectives, but the men of the 17th would have the assistance of Armour. Already the technique of making the standard Pz Kpfw III and IV tanks wade ashore totally submerged had been mastered. Now the crews of Detachment B of the Panzerwaffe were finding out how to do this on a sloping beach. They would be in possession of 32 fully adapted Pz Kpfw III – a machine which could wade to a depth of 8 metres after entering the water down an extended ramp from a *Prahm*.

Engineer detachments, already well-practised in the launching and navigation of rubber assault boats in the gentler currents of rivers and canals, began to learn how to do it in a tidal stream and through surf. Throughout June and early July, the beaches of the Baltic and of the North Sea and Channel coasts were the scenes of intensive activity as the soldiers and sailors got to know each other's problems and tried to overcome each difficulty as it arose. With the basic skills barely mastered, the skippers of the landing craft selected for the leading assault echelons, began to combine as formations in rehearsals and tactical exercises which showed only too clearly how formidable the problems would be on S Day when it came. Grimly, however, they stuck to the task, working round the clock to eliminate as many of the problems as they could, praying, in some cases, that they might be spared the ordeal. They would never be completely proficient, but the needs of the hour wonderfully concentrated their determination and ingenuity.

Meanwhile, on the headlands overlooking the Channel, and in sites within range of Dover, German artillery began to settle in. For protection of the shore line and the seaward approaches out to about 11,000 yards, stood batteries of 10.5cm Field Howitzers (FH 18). Emplaced a little farther back and tasked to deal with targets out to 11,000 yards were the 15cm Medium Howitzers (FH 18) and nearby, reaching out to about 15,000 yards, 15cm K 18 medium guns and 21cm Mrs 18 howitzers whose task was to protect the invasion fleet in the earlier stage of its journey. Superimposed over this standard layout of German field artillery were to be 29 very long-range pieces (some of them on railway mountings) of 17cm—38cm calibre, whose task would be to bombard the environs of Dover, Hythe and Folkestone, and ships sailing close to the English shore. They could produce a heavy and fairly accurate volume of fire whose effect on civilian morale was expected to be severe.

Behind the Channel coast and reaching back into Germany, the lines of communication were being rapidly improved. Canals that had been blocked during the recent fighting were being cleared to permit the passage of invasion craft to the embarkation ports. High priority was given to the restoration of the railways and the replacement of the many bridges which had been demolished. After that the stocking of supply bases adjacent to ports and airfields could go on apace – and, indeed, the rate of progress was rapid. Also, the recovery of abandoned enemy stores and equipment from the battlefields not only denied them to prospective partisans but proved beneficial to the German logisticians. Local labour made its contribution as the curfew and close surveillance of civilians was relaxed when it was realized that the conquered people had lost the will to fight. A mere handful were resolved to resist; only the Belgians and the Dutch were thinking up ways to hinder the Germans and, most useful of all to the British, transmit information about German activities. Nothing, however, could prevent the Germans solving their logistic problems. By 5 June they were well prepared for the advance to the south, and it would be a mere few weeks before their major supply requirements for 'Lion' were satisfied.

'Sealion' is christened

In the knowledge of the resources which would be provided, it was possible for detailed plans to be laid and disseminated by OKW to enable Busch at HQ 16th Army, Kesselring at Luftflotte 2 and Vice-Admiral Lütjens, the Fleet Commander who would co-ordinate the naval operations, to move 16th Army to England. By 5 June, Hitler had satisfied himself, in so far as he was able, of the feasibility of the Armed Forces' plans and had instructed Keitel to complete the Directive which would authorize the physical preparations for 'Lion'. Much already was in train as commanders and staff took such action as they could to make ready. Two days later, the Führer signed Directive No 16 which, incidentally, renamed the operation 'Sealion'.[4] Its stated intention was 'To eliminate the English homeland as a base for the continuation of the war against Germany and if necessary, to occupy it completely.' It went on to instruct:

1. The Luftwaffe to achieve air superiority over the enemy air force as the essential prerequisite of establishing a bridgehead by the dropping of airborne troops a short distance inland from the places where the Army would come ashore. Thereafter its task would be to act as artillery in support of the Army and the Kriegsmarine, in addition to its rôle of preventing interference with the Lines of Communication.
2. The Army to execute a surprise landing on a narrow front of approximately 20 miles between Hythe and Deal, and then, in order of priority:
   a. Link up with the airborne forces.
   b. Seize control of the ports of Folkestone and Dover.
   c. Extend the bridgehead inland to a line from Rye to Faversham, making particular efforts to gain early possession of airfields to enable the Luftwaffe to operate from them as soon as possible.

3. The Kriegsmarine to:
   a. Transport the Army to its landing areas.
   b. In co-operation with the Luftwaffe, prevent interference with the Lines of Communication.
   c. Open up the ports and transport the follow-up forces to the bridgehead.

Formations taking part were to complete their plans by 7 July, on the understanding that S Day would be 13 July. Logistic support systems would be kept as similar as possible to those normally employed by the Army; the Kriegsmarine participation was that of an extra cog in the machine. It was appreciated, however, that some serious interference with surface routes of supply must occur, either from adverse weather or because of prolonged enemy intervention. The Luftwaffe, therefore, must be prepared to supplement the transport services with air-lifted supplies, the maximum use must be made of captured enemy material and by living off the country, and units must take the minimum of equipment to save space.

The administration of conquered territory, in the first instance, was to come under the jurisdiction of the Army and was to be laid down by OKH. It would be the subject of a special instruction headed 'Orders concerning the Organization and Function of Military Government in England' issued on 1 July.

In order to deceive the enemy as to the timing, objectives, nature and scale of 'Sealion', an elaborate deception plan was devised. The enemy was to be led to believe in the likelihood of several descents against widely separated parts of the British Isles (including Eire), but give the impression that they would not take place until August. As the rest of the French coast fell into German hands, activities in the westerly ports were to be made to appear as intensive as those in the easterly ones – and, indeed, it was visualized that some supply convoys might well use the ports of Le Havre, Cherbourg and Brest once the initial lodgement had been made near Dover. Reconnaissance of the enemy coast line and inland territory was to be widespread and not aimed solely at the chosen beach head. Rumours and misleading information were to be fed to the British Intelligence through diplomatic channels, the news media and any other communication systems that could be used. At the same time, measures were taken so as to suggest a build-up of forces in the mounting area which bore no relation to actuality and instead falsified the agreed date of departure. Above all, the airborne forces were forbidden to send their members outside Germany in order to prevent their being identified by enemy agents in the occupied territories.

To implement the operational aspects of the plan, a joint headquarters was set up in Brussels, adjacent to the headquarters of Luftflotte 2. There, under the overall supervision (or chairmanship, as some called it) of Kesselring, the staffs of Busch and Lütjens co-ordinated their activities. As the din of battle in Norway died away and the Battle of France rose to its final peak, and as German aircraft embarked upon their first serious incursions over the British hinterland, the commanders and staffs who were to conduct the Battle for Britain grappled with problems which, in their experience, were unique and, to some among them, extremely forbidding.

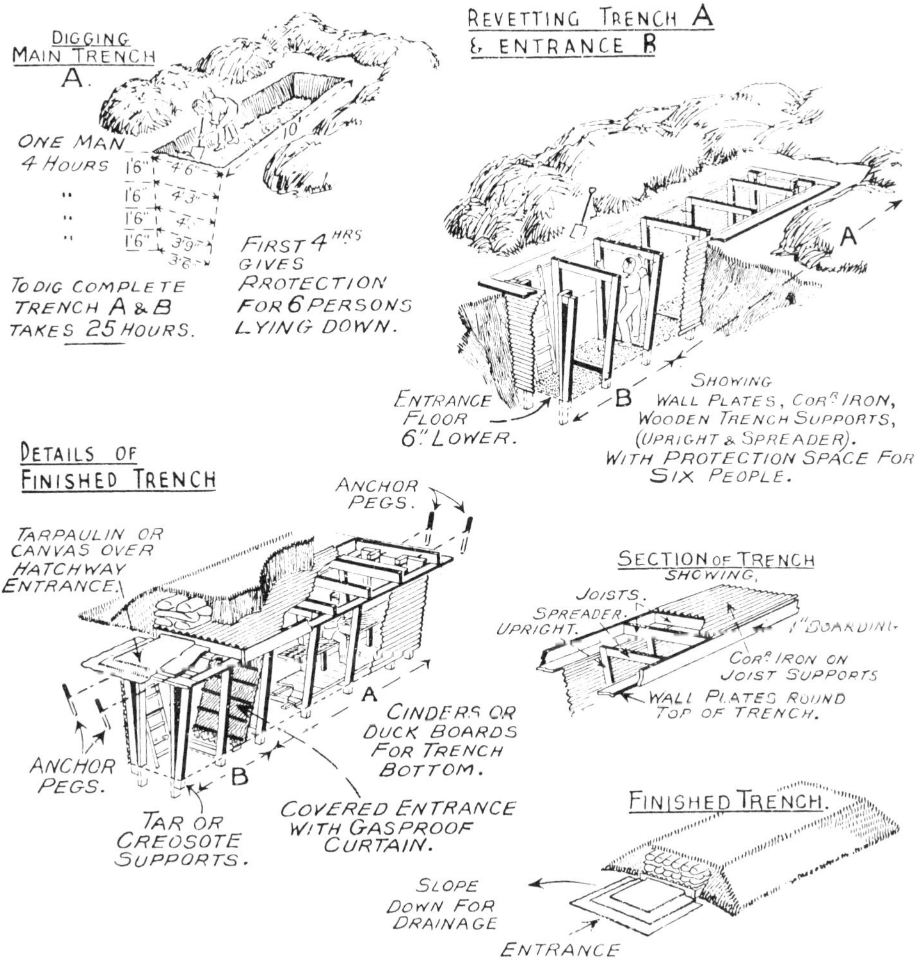

Contemporary instructions to the British public concerning the digging of trenches as protection against German air raids. (Lionel Leventhal Collection)

III

THE TAKING OF WESTERN EUROPE

Battle at sea

Despite fierce bombing by the Luftwaffe and relentless pressure from German mountain troops advancing from the south, combined Norwegian, French and Polish forces managed to recapture the port of Narvik on 28 May. But already it was apparent that this was only a moment of passing joy, for the news of disaster from France left no alternative but to withdraw totally from an untenable position in Norway and concentrate what forces remained for the defence of France and Britain. Accordingly, troops to the south of Narvik were evacuated on the 31st and measures were taken to remove the remaining forces from Narvik itself by 8 June. These preparations did not pass unnoticed by the Germans who were determined to cause as much harm as possible to the Allied Fleet and convoys. The damage inflicted on *Scharnhorst* and *Gneisenau* had been repaired and they, with the cruiser *Hipper*, left Kiel on 4 June in clear weather and steamed north to arrive, undetected by the standing enemy submarine and air patrols, in northern waters on the 8th – demonstrating once more the feasibility of sea power making its presence felt by guile and stealth and showing how easy it might be for a few German ships to appear elsewhere without warning. They found the Allied evacuation in full swing, covered only by cruisers, destroyers and two aircraft carriers, the battleships of the British Fleet having been dispersed on other tasks or sent into dock.

To the delight of the German commander, Admiral Marschall, the British were taken by surprise. Sinking an empty transport and an oil tanker (and letting a hospital ship go) he edged northward and, on the afternoon of the 8th, picked up the aircraft carrier *Glorious* on the horizon, escorted only by a pair of destroyers and without any aircraft aloft. Laying smoke, the British destroyers charged to the attack with torpedoes, but the German ships were equipped with ranging radar and could engage targets accurately through smoke. Within a short while all three British ships had been sunk, but at a price which would impinge upon German hopes of invading Britain. For at her last gasp, the destroyer *Acasta* managed to score a torpedo hit on *Scharnhorst* and severely damaged her, with the result that the German battlecruiser was considerably reduced in efficiency for several months to come, and Marschall was persuaded to withdraw instead of pressing ahead to plunder the Allied convoys. The last troops to sail from Narvik thus lived with much of their equipment to fight another day.[1]

Battle in France

Twenty-four hours after the German squadron sailed out of Kiel, the German Army struck southward into France,[2] eager to expand its already extensive conquests, and confident in its power to do so against an opponent who had squandered his mobile forces. In raids against French communication centres and airfields, the Luftwaffe threw in its dive-bombers with their screaming plunges against the forward French positions from the mouth of the Somme at Abbeville to the area of Rethel. Superimposed upon this bombardment was a pummelling by artillery to soften up French resistance in fortified villages, copses and towns, upon which the French hoped to latch an immobile defence in depth which would hinder, if not stop, the German panzer divisions when they chose to advance. On the left of the German lines stood Army Group A (von Rundstedt) with Panzer Group Guderian as its principal striking force; on the right, Army Group B (Generaloberst Fedor von Bock) with Panzer Group Kleist in which was to be found XIV, XV and XVI Panzer Corps containing between them six out of the ten available panzer divisions. Great emphasis was placed upon seizing the Channel coast with the utmost speed, and on this flank the dive-bomber attacks were heaviest. But to begin with, along the entire Allied line, resistance was staunch. At last the French fought in earnest – but too late. Like maggots in ripe cheese, the skilfully handled German battle groups ate their way through the outer crust of the defences until, on the morning of the 7th, the 7th Panzer Division, in Generalleutnant Hoth's XV Panzer Corps, erupted into open country and, by nightfall, had shot forward 37 miles in the direction of the River Seine until it stood only 25 miles from Rouen.

Elsewhere it was much the same story as the French Army, bereft of a mobile reserve, began to crumble and allow the German

3. The Collapse of France, June 1940

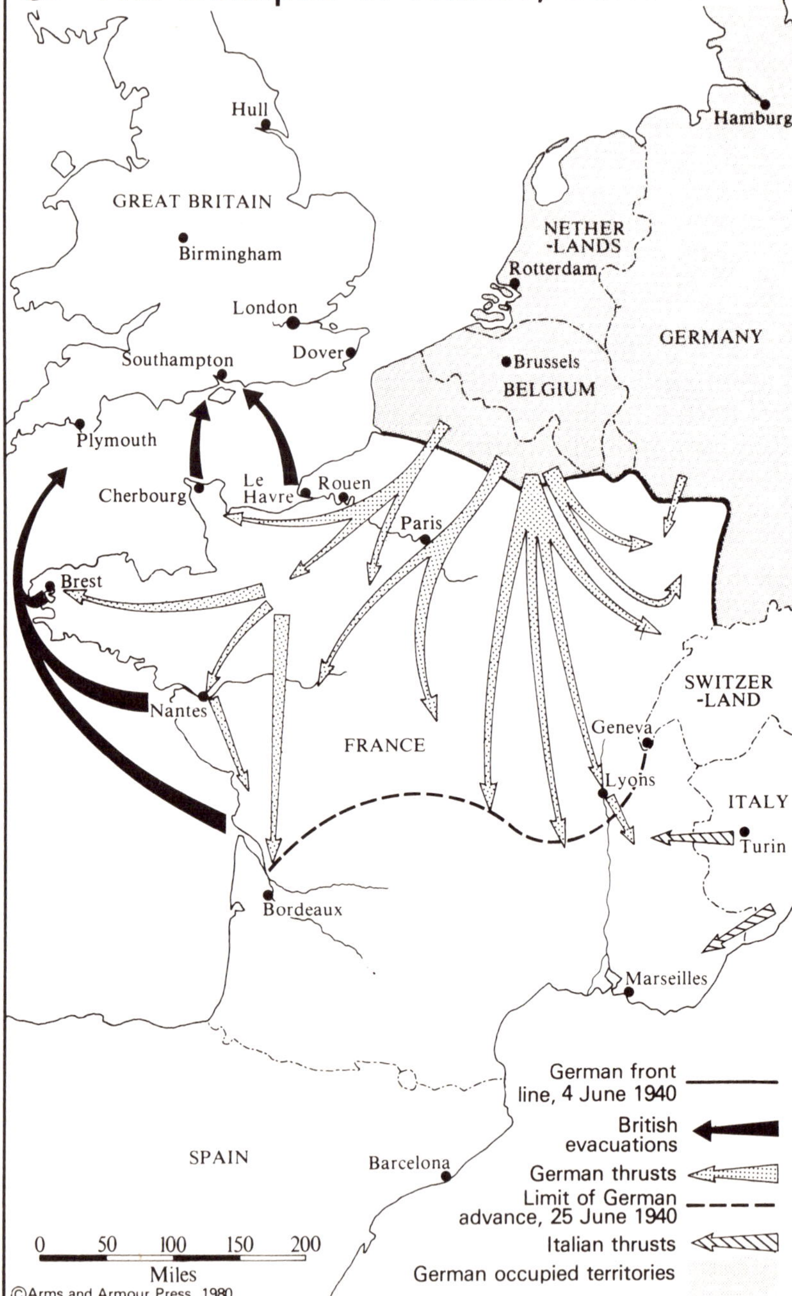

armour, followed by the mass of marching infantry divisions, to surge southwards. Refugees clogged the roads; towns and villages were in flames; the civil administration was on the verge of collapse. In some places, as the British and French troops withdrew, the enemy moved freely among them and were mistaken for friendly troops. Quite frequently the German presence was genuinely welcomed by the French populace, who wanted nothing more of war. In the confusion scarcely anybody noticed that, after the first 48 hours of the offensive, the dive-bombers practically vanished from the scene; according to plan, they had been withdrawn in readiness for the preliminary stages of 'Sealion'. For the rest of the campaign high-level bombers and low strafing fighters, almost totally unopposed by the air forces they had obliterated, carried on the air bombardment. There was no longer any question, on the part of British soldiers and airmen, that they could withstand the German onrush, hard though Churchill would try to sustain French resolve by promises he could not fulfill. From 8 June onwards, it was a question, for the British, of saving as much as they could from the wreck in order to reinforce their defences at home. For the next two weeks a race took place between the Germans and British to seize ports where re-embarkation would be possible – even though the final decision to withdraw the British Expeditionary Force as a whole was delayed until the 15th.

The first leg of this race was won by the Germans when 7th Panzer Division, swinging north from Rouen on the 10th, surrounded the French Tenth Army and the British 51st Highland Division at St Valéry-en-Caux before the Royal Navy, hampered by thick weather and mismanagement, could rescue more than 3,000 men. Further along the coast, however, things were better arranged as fleets of British transports worked feverishly to take off men and matériel – above all, tanks and guns which were in desperately short supply at home. Because 7th Panzer Division had been fully engaged at St Valéry, sufficient time was given at Le Havre to evacuate 11,059 British troops, most of whom were taken to Cherbourg, which in its turn, would have to be evacuated when Rommel approached on the 18th. Whenever the British ships appeared, so too did the German bombers, and remorselessly the losses mounted as more transports were sunk and more of the priceless destroyers damaged. But from Cherbourg, St Malo, Brest, St Nazaire and La Pallice, the 52nd Division, the 1st Canadian Division and what remained of the 1st Armoured Division were brought home. From other ports, too, along the Atlantic coast, the remnants of British, French, Belgian, Polish and Czech forces were picked up, the last ships returning on 25 June. At the same time, units of the French Fleet, including its two newest and uncompleted battleships (*Richelieu* and *Jean Bart*) were removed as British demolition parties did whatever they could to damage or destroy vital port installations.

Italy enters the war

On 10 June, the Allies sustained another heavy blow. In Rome the Italian Dictator, Benito Mussolini, stood up to announce, to the acclaim of his supporters, that Italy had entered the war to liberate Savoy, Nice and Corsica and that she was at war with France and Britain. Not that his army was to make much impression on the French in the Alps when they attacked on the 20th. Nor did his navy put to sea against the combined strength of the French Fleet, in the Western Mediterranean, and the British at its eastern end. Mussolini sought profit without risk and hoped the Germans would help him to it by their victory, the assumption being that the French would surrender within the week and the British, hopelessly out-numbered, shortly after. On 10 June, indeed, the French Commander-in-Chief, General Weygand, informed his Prime Minister, Paul Reynaud, that an armistice was necessary. Reynaud told him to fight on and appealed to President Roosevelt for help from the USA which was not – could not be – forthcoming. As disaster followed upon disaster, and as the Germans drew closer to Paris, which fell on the 14th, Weygand's wish became irresistible and Reynaud resigned. His place was taken on the 16th by the revered Marshal Pétain who formed a new government and immediately sought terms of the Germans. On the 22nd, an armistice was signed with Hitler at Réthondes where, in the same railway carriage in 1918, the French had imposed a similar indignity upon the Germans. To two nations who had become accustomed throughout the past two centuries to the swings of defeat and victory, the reconciliation of pride with reality was easier than it might be for the British who, since 1782 in North America, had become unaccustomed to total defeat.

Britain on her own

Britain was on her own because Reynaud's attempt to transfer the French Government to North Africa and continue the fight at Britain's side had failed. Already Churchill had declared his government's determination to fight on, 'If necessary for years, if necessary alone,' but its capacity to do so was severely limited, the weight of forces poised against it terrifyingly immense. Although he told Parliament that his professional advisers 'were confident that there were good and reasonable hopes of ultimate victory',[3] that in no way meant that they believed invasion could be prevented or defeated. Indeed, some form of airborne attack was expected daily and the balance of naval power gave reason for deep concern. Forces which once had been friendly or neutral now took on a hostile look at the very moment when the destroyer flotillas were being attenuated by their exertions off the French coast. The revolutionized naval situation on 22 June could be evaluated like this:

1. The Home Fleet (Admiral Sir Charles Forbes) was weaker than at any other time since the previous winter. (Its exact position will be described in Chapter IV). That the German Fleet had also been weakened was some consolation, of course, and next day this weakness would be heightened when the submarine *Clyde* would put a torpedo into *Gneisenau*, escorting the damaged *Scharnhorst* to Germany from Norway, thus temporarily removing (without the British knowing it) Germany's two most powerful naval units from the balance sheet.
2. The Mediterranean Fleet (Admiral Sir Andrew Cunningham) was incapable of defending the length of the Mediterranean Sea. With the neutralization of the French Fleet, Malta was exposed and there was nothing left of value based upon Gibraltar. Furthermore, there was a worrying uncertainty as to the eventual intentions and destination of the French Fleet, some of whose units were in British ports, some in Toulon and many of its most powerful vessels at Oran. Admiral Darlan, the Minister of Marine, had given solemn assurances that it would not fall into German hands, and the amended terms of the Armistice satisfied this condition. But its existence in full fighting trim as a potential threat of great magnitude could not be ignored by the British. As a result, it was considered essential by them to reinforce the Western Mediterranean and, at the same time, take measures to guarantee the neutralization of the French ships under British, not German, control. With this intention in view, a further dispersion of British naval power away from their Home Stations was deemed necessary. The battlecruiser *Hood*, the battleships *Resolution* and *Valiant*, the aircraft carrier *Ark Royal*, two cruisers and eleven destroyers were ordered to sail from Britain to Gibraltar on 27 June. Called Force H, these ships were placed under the command of Vice-Admiral Sir

British Warships Involved

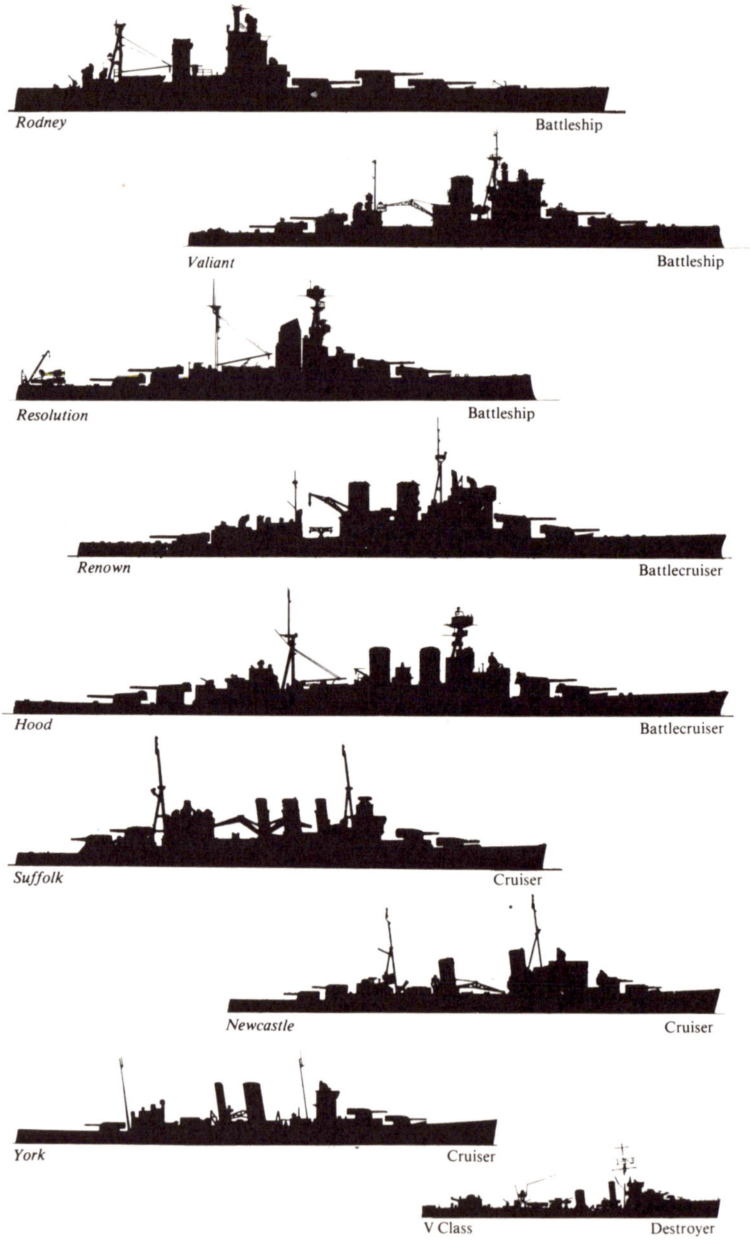

James Somerville, and were free to act in the Western Mediterranean, in the Atlantic or, if the need arose, could rapidly reinforce the Home Fleet and intervene in the English Channel. They thus constituted a vital strategic reserve divorced from the immediate threat of German attack, but capable of exerting widespread influence.

3. The entire strategic picture had undergone a revolution now that the Western European seaboard from North Cape to Bayonne was in German hands, and the threat that Spain, under the Fascist dictator General Franco, might at any time throw in her lot with Germany and Italy. From now on, German naval and long-range air forces would enjoy unchallenged access to the Atlantic without the need to run the gauntlet of the narrow seas surrounding the British Isles. They could break out through the foggy expanses of water in the north and come and go almost as they pleased from Brest and the Biscay ports. Britain's life-line to the West was endangered as never before in her history, at a time when the link with the West and with the rest of her Commonwealth for the provision of food, war materials and reinforcements was most vital. Under these circumstances the importance of maintaining an adequate anti-invasion naval patrol had to be balanced with the need to protect the shipping in her Western Approaches from the depredations of surface

British Warships Involved

	Hood	*Valiant*	*Repulse*	*Renown*	*Rodney*
Type	Battle-cruiser	Battleship	Battle-cruiser	Battle-cruiser	Battleship
Displacement (tons)	42,100	30,600	32,000	32,000	33,950
Speed (knots)	32	24	29	29	23
Armament					
Main	8 x 15in	8 x 15in	6 x 15in	6 x 15in	9 x 16in
Secondary	12x5.5in	8x6in	20x4in	20x4in	12x6in
	8x4in	8x4in	–	–	6x4.7in
Torpedo tubes	4	–	8	–	2

	Resolution	*Newcastle*	*York*	*Suffolk*	V Class
Type	Battleship	Cruiser	Cruiser	Cruiser	Destroyer
Displacement (tons)	29,150	9,100	8,390	10,000	1,100
Speed (knots)	22	32	32	31.5	34
Armament					
Main	8 x 15in	12 x 6in	6 x 8in	8 x 8in	–
Secondary	12x6in	8x4in	4x4in	8x4in	4x4in
	8x4in	1x3.7in	–	–	1x2pdr pom-pom
Torpedo tubes	–	6	6	–	5 or 6

raiders and U-boats. All of this had to be faced at a moment when the Navy was stretched to the limit because of the recently sustained losses in battle.

As the days passed, Intelligence of enemy movements, though sparse to begin with, began to percolate to the British. The interrogation of refugees and servicemen who had escaped at the last moment from the German net produced information which told of a significant build-up of German supplies and aircraft on the airfields of Belgium and Northern France. The radar stations which formed the so-called Home Chain of Britain's air defence could sometimes detect large formations of enemy aircraft as far inland as Amiens. The Photographic Reconnaissance Unit of the RAF, under the control of Air Marshal Sir Frederick Bowhill, gleaned what little it could from pictures taken by the eleven special photographic aircraft, then in service (of which only three were the excellent type C Spitfire of medium range) and from returning Bomber Command missions. By night the approaches to the island were patrolled by small ships and Coastal Command air patrols, while the men on watch on the cliff tops scanned anxiously, when the moon was bright, to catch, if they could, a first glimpse of approaching enemy craft. But little, except British convoys, moved by sea, and the coastal watchers strained their eyes in vain. Instead the night skies, as well as those in daylight, were filled with a rising volume of sound from aircraft engines as Kesselring's air fleet steadily raised the tempo of its operations. Day by day and night by night, as S Day of 'Sealion' grew closer, the air battle came to override all thoughts and to act as a warning to the British Chiefs of Staff that the moment they feared might be nigh. For, although the Navy persisted in its original appreciation that the enemy might, in favourable conditions, land a few thousand men from small, fast craft between The Wash and Lands End, all looked on

German Warships Involved

	Admiral Hipper	*Nürnberg*	*Köln*	*Emden*	*Schlesien*	*Carl Galster (Z20)*
Type	Cruiser	Cruiser	Cruiser	Cruiser	Old Battleship	Destroyer
Displacement (tons)	14,240	6,000	6,000	5,400	13,040	3,418
Speed (knots)	32	32	32	27.5	18	38
Armament						
Main	8x8in	9x5.9in	9x5.9in	8x5.9in	4x11in	5x5in
Secondary	12x4in	8x3.5in	6x3.5in	3x3.5in	10x5.9in	4x37mm
Torpedo tubes	12	12	12	–	–	8*

*Plus 60 mines.

German Warships Involved

Admiral Hipper Heavy Cruiser

Nürnberg Cruiser

Schlesien Old Battleship

Köln Cruiser

Emden Cruiser

Carl Galster Z20 Destroyer

this as 'a most hazardous undertaking'. The sailors really concurred with the Air Staff who believed that a seaborne invasion was 'not a practicable operation of war' unless RAF Fighter Command (Air Marshal Sir Hugh Dowding) were first defeated.[4] In other words, a victorious air campaign by the Germans was absolutely essential, and who would now deny that? Although overt signs of an accumulation of hostile ships and men were not yet to be detected by the British in or near the French ports, the overture to such a battle was already being played.

Right and overleaf: British propaganda (in three languages) designed to discourage the would-be conquerors. A generalised translation would be as follows. (Lionel Leventhal Collection)
WE MARCH AGAINST ENGLAND (a popular German song of the time).

I. Before the Invasion

1. The sea is vast — cold — rough.
2. How many more times must we do disembarkation drill?
3. Do you think that we will ever reach England?
4. Do you think we will ever return from England?
5. When will the next English raid take place? Today, in the morning, at midday, in the afternoon, in the evening, in the night.
6. Why doesn't the Fuhrer travel with us?
7. Our petrol store is still burning!
8. Your petrol store is burning again!
9. Who has cut the telephone lines again?
10. Have you thrown my comrade into the canal?
11. Can you lend me a belt — a lifejacket?
12. What do you charge for swimming lessons?
13. How many invasions must I take part in to receive the Iron Cross, 1st Class?
14. 7-8-9.
15. We leave for England!

II. During the Invasion

1. The sea crossing — the storm — the mist — the high wind.
2. We are seasick. Where is the bucket?
3. Is that a bomb — a torpedo — a shell — a mine?
4. Attention! English motor torpedo-boats — destroyers — cruisers — battleships — bombers.
5. Our boat has capsized — sunk — burnt — exploded!
6. Our squad — our section — our company — our battalion — our regiment is going under!
7. The others — the whole division — the whole — the army corps too!
8. Another boat is beginning to sink.
9. Where is our fleet — our air force?
10. The sea smells of petrol here!
11. Even the sea is on fire.
12. Look how well the captain burns!
13. Karl — Willi — Fritz — Johann — Abraham — burned to cinders, drowned or cut to pieces by the propellers.
14. We have to turn back!
15. We are sailing against England!

III. After the Invasion

1. We have had enough!
2. They are still in hospital.
3. Where did you catch that cold — that lumbago — that pneumonia — that nervous breakdown?
4. That is all that is left of us.
5. Where can one consult the list of dead and missing, please?
6. What does England really look like?
7. There was a German fleet once.
8. There are a great number of English air raids.
9. When is the next invasion taking place?
10. It must take place the 1st, 15th, 30th January, February, March, April, May, June, July, August, September, October, November, December, 1941, 1942, 1943, 1944, 1945, etc.
11. Not me! Not you! Not him! Not us! Not them! But perhaps you?
12. We sailed against England!
13. We want to go home!

N.B. Every German traveller to England will receive a free pocket dictionary on arrival at the prisoner-of-war camp.

DER KLEINE INVASIONS-DOLMETSCHER

PETIT MANUEL DE CONVERSATION POUR L'INVASION

TAALCURSUS ZONDER LEERMEESTER VOOR DUITSCHE SOLDATEN

I. Vor der Invasion

1. Die See ist gross — kalt — stürmisch.
2. Wie oft müssen wir noch Landungsmanöver üben?
3. Ob wir wohl in England ankommen werden?
4. Ob wir heil zurückkommen werden?
5. Wann ist der nächste englische Luftangriff? Heute morgens; mittags; nachmittags; abends; nachts.
6. Warum fährt der Führer nicht mit?
7. Unser Benzinlager brennt noch immer!
8. Euer Benzinlager brennt schon wieder!
9. Wer hat schon wieder das Telefonkabel durchgeschnitten?
10. Haben Sie meinen Kameraden in den Kanal geworfen?
11. Können Sie mir eine Schwimmweste — einen Rettungsring — leihen?
12. Was kosten bei Ihnen Schwimmstunden?
13. Wie viele Invasionsfahrten brauch' ich für das E.K.I?
14. Sieben — acht — neun.
15. Wir werden gegen Engelland fahren!

I. Avant l'invasion

1. La mer est vaste — froide — houleuse.
2. Combien de fois encore devrons-nous faire des exercises de débarquement?
3. Pensez-vous que nous arriverons jamais en Angleterre?
4. Pensez-vous que nous reviendrons jamais d'Angleterre?
5. Quand le prochain raid anglais aura-t-il lieu? — Aujourd'hui, dans la matinée, à midi, dans l'après-midi, dans la soirée, dans la nuit.
6. Pourquoi est-ce que le Fuehrer ne vient pas avec nous?
7. Notre dépôt d'essence continue de brûler!
8. Votre dépôt d'essence a recommencé à brûler!
9. Qui a encore coupé notre ligne téléphonique?
10. Avez-vous jeté mon camarade dans le canal?
11. Pouvez-vous me prêter une ceinture, — une bouée de sauvetage?
12. Quel prix prenez-vous pour les leçons de natation?
13. Combien d'invasions dois-je faire pour recevoir la Croix de Fer de 1ère classe?
14. Sept — huit — neuf.
15. Nous partirons pour l'Angleterre! (Qu'ils disent.)

I. Vóór de invasie

1. De zee is groot — koud — stormachtig.
2. Hoe vaak nog moeten w'exerceeren om 't landen op een kust te leeren?
3. Zullen we ooit in Engeland komen?
4. Zullen we heelhuids wêerom komen?
5. Wanneer komt de volgende Britsche luchtaanval? Heden — morgen, middag, namiddag, avond, nacht.
6. Waarom reist de Führer niet met ons mee?
7. Ons benzinedepot staat nog steeds in lichter laaie!
8. Uw benzinedepot staat alweer in lichter laaie!
9. Wie heeft onze telefoonleiding nou weer doorgeknipt?
10. Heeft U mijn kameraad in de gracht gesmeten?
11. Kunt U mij een zwemvest — een reddinggordel leenen?
12. Hoeveel kost het om bij U zwemmen te leeren?
13. Hoe dikwijls moet ik aan een invasietocht meedoen om het IJzeren Kruis te winnen?
14. Zeven — acht — negen keer.
15. Wij zullen gauw naar Engeland varen! (Plons! Plons! Plons!)

II. Wahrend der Invasion

1. Der Seegang. — Der Sturm. — Der Nebel. Die Windstärke.
2. Wir sind seekrank. Wo ist der Kübel?
3. Ist das eine Bombe — ein Torpedo — eine Granate — eine Mine?

II. Pendant l'invasion

1. Le gros temps — la tempête — le brouillard — la violence de l'ouragan.
2. Nous avons le mal de mer. Où est la cuvette?
3. Est-ce une bombe — une torpille — un obus — une mine?

II. Tijdens de invasie

1. De deining — de storm — de mist — de orkaan.
2. Wij zijn zeeziek. Waar is de kwispedoor?
3. Is dat een bom — een torpedo - granaat — een mijn?

4. Achtung! Englische E-Boote—Zerstörer—Kreuzer — Schlachtschiffe — Bomber !
5. Unser Schiff kentert — versinkt — brennt — explodiert !
6. Unsere Gruppe — unser Zug — unsere Kompanie — unser Bataillon — unser Regiment geht unter !
7. Die Anderen — die ganze Division — das ganze Armeekorps auch !
8. Schon wieder geht eins unter !
9. Wo ist denn unsere Flotte — unsere Luftwaffe ?
10. Hier riecht die See so nach Petroleum !
11. Hier brennt sogar das Wasser !
12. Schauen Sie, wie schön der Herr Hauptmann brennt !
13. Der Karl — der Willi — der Fritz — der Johann — der Abraham ist verkohlt — ertrunken — von den Schiffsschrauben zerfleischt.
14. Wir müssen umdrehen !
15. Wir fahren gegen Engelland !

4. Attention! ce sont des vedettes lance-torpilles — des contre-torpilleurs, des croiseurs des cuirassés — des bombardiers anglais !
5. Notre bateau chavire — coule — brûle — fait explosion !
6. Notre escouade — notre section — notre compagnie — notre bataillon — notre régiment est englouti (*ou* engloutie) !
7. Les autres — toute la division — tout le corps d'armée — l'est (*ou* **le** sont) aussi!
8. Un autre bateau est en train de couler.
9. Où est notre flotte — notre aviation ?
10. La mer empeste le mazout, ici!
11. Même l'eau brûle ici !
12. Regarde comme notre capitaine brûle bien !
13. Charles — Guillaume — Frédérique — Jean — Abraham est carbonisé — est noyé — est déchiqueté par les hélices.
14. Il faut faire demi-tour !
15. Nous partons pour l'Angleterre. (Tant pis pour vous !)

4. Pas op ! Britsche E-booten — torpedo jagers — kruisers — slagschepen. — bommenwerpers !
5. Ons schip kapseist — zinkt — brandt — vliegt in de lucht !
6. Onze groep — afdeeling — compagnie-bataillon — regiment verdrinkt !
7. De anderen — de heele divisie — het geheele legercorps verdrinkt ook !
8. Daar zinkt weer een schip !
9. Waar is onze vloot — onze luchtmacht !
10. Wat stinkt de zee hier naar olie !
11. Hier staat waarachtig het water in brand!
12. Kijk eens hoe mooi de kapitein in brand staat !
13. Karel Willem Frits Johan — Abraham is verkoold — verdronken — tot pap gemalen door de schroeven van het schip.
14. We moeten omdraaien!
15. Wij varen gauw naar Engeland. (Arme bliksems !)

III. Nach der Invasion

1. Wir haben genug !
2. Sie sind noch immer im Lazarett.
3. Wo haben Sie sich den schönen Schnupfen — den Hexenschuss — die Lungenentzündung — den Nervenschock — geholt ?
4. Mehr ist von uns nicht übrig geblieben.
5. Bitte, wo kann man hier die Totenlisten mal einsehen ?
6. Wie sieht England eigentlich aus ?
7. Es gab einmal eine deutsche Flotte.
8. Es gibt sehr viele englische Luftangriffe.
9. Wann findet die nächste Invasion statt ?
10. Am 1., 15., 30. Januar, Februar, März, April, Mai, Juni, Juli, August, September, Oktober, November, Dezember — 1941, 1942, 1943, 1944, 1945 . . . usw.
11. Ich nicht ! Du nicht ! Er nicht ! Wir nicht ! Sie auch nicht ! Aber *Ihr* vielleicht ?
12. Wir fuhren gegen Engelland !
13. Wir wollen heim !

Zur Beachtung : *Ein englischer Taschendolmetscher wird jedem deutschen Englandfahrer bei seiner Ankunft in einem englischen Kriegsgefangenenlager unentgeltlich ausgehändigt werden.*

III. Après l'invasion

1. Nous en avons assez !
2. Ils sont encore à l'hôpital.
3. Où avez vous attrapé ce beau rhume — ce lumbago — cette pleurésie — cette commotion cérébrale ?
4. Nous sommes les seuls qui nous nous en soyons tirés.
5. Où peut-on consulter la liste des tués et disparus, ici, s'il-vous-plaît ?
6. Pouvez-vous me décrire l'Angleterre ?
7. Il y avait une fois une flotte allemande.
8. Il y a un très grand nombre de raids anglais.
9. Quand la prochaine invasion doit-elle avoir lieu ?
10. Elle doit avoir lieu le 1er, 15, 30 janvier, février, mars, avril, mai, juin, juillet, août, septembre, octobre, novembre, décembre — 1941, 1942, 1943, 1944, 1945, etc.
11. Pas moi ! Pas toi ! Pas lui ! Pas nous ! Pas eux ! Mais peut-être vous ?
12. Nous sommes partis pour l'Angleterre !
13. Nous voulons rentrer chez nous !

N.B. Un manuel de conversation en langue anglaise sera distribué gratuitement à chaque envahisseur lors de son arrivée au camp de prisonniers en Grande-Bretagne.

III. Na de invasie

1. Wij hebben er tabak van !
2. Zij liggen nog steeds in het hospitaal.
3. Waar heb je die mooie verkoudheid opgeloopen — spit — longontsteking — zenuwstoring ?
4. Dat's alles wat er van ons over is.
5. Kunt U mij ook zeggen waar ik de verlieslijsten kan nakijken ?
6. Hoe ziet Engeland er eigenlijk uit ?
7. Er was ereis een Duitsche vloot.
8. Er zijn veel Britsche luchtaanvallen.
9. Wanneer is de volgende invasie ?
10. Op den 1 sten, 15 den, 30 sten Januari, Februari, Maart, April, Mei, Juni, Juli, Augustus, September, October, November, December — 1941, 1942, 1943, 1944, 1945, enzoovoorts.
11. Ik niet ! Jij niet ! Hij niet ! Wij niet ! Niemand van ons ! Misschien jij wel ?
12. We wilden gauw naar Engeland !
13. Wij willen naar huis !

N.B. Iedere Duitsche reiziger naar Engeland krijgt een Engelsch zakwoordenboekje cadeau, zoodra hij in het krijgsgevangenkamp is aangekomen.

IV

BRITAIN AGAINST THE WALL

A nation in tension

When German aircraft began regular, nightly incursions over Britain on 5 June, their presence acted both as a shock and as a stimulant, besides a reminder to the populace that they no longer lived in an island. The inactivity of nine months' 'phoney war' since September 1939 had led the British to dismiss the fears of wholesale death and destruction from aerial bombardment which had been prophesied before the war. That winter the scale of Civil Defence measures had been criticized as over-insurance. Now, with talk of imminent invasion on everyone's lips, the appearance of men wearing LDV arm bands and calling themselves 'parashots'; the drone of hostile aircraft, the bark of guns and the whistle and bang from an occasional bomb, they were prone to exaggerate and merge these manifestations of alarm into a mixture of despondency, panic, resolution, incredulity and euphoria when in danger.

By mid winter, at least half of London's population had dismissed the likelihood of air raids so that, come June, over a third of the Capital's households had not bothered to take air raid precautions except to comply with the compulsory blackout at night. Desperation now replaced complacency as feverish measures were taken to give protection against blast and fire. Only one in four knew how to deal with an incendiary bomb. Few shelters were designed for prolonged occupation and a large number were quite inadequate in every respect. Many people who had been evacuated from the cities in 1939 had returned home in the belief that the cities were well protected. Indeed, even as the guns were beginning to fire, there were those in rural areas who contemplated moving into the cities. The noise of war began to take its toll of people's nerves because of loss of sleep in addition to the onset of fear. Disruption of a 'normal' life bred inefficiency and low morale for which the existing Civil Defence arrangements were unready.[1]

4. The Defences of Great Britain, 30 June 1940

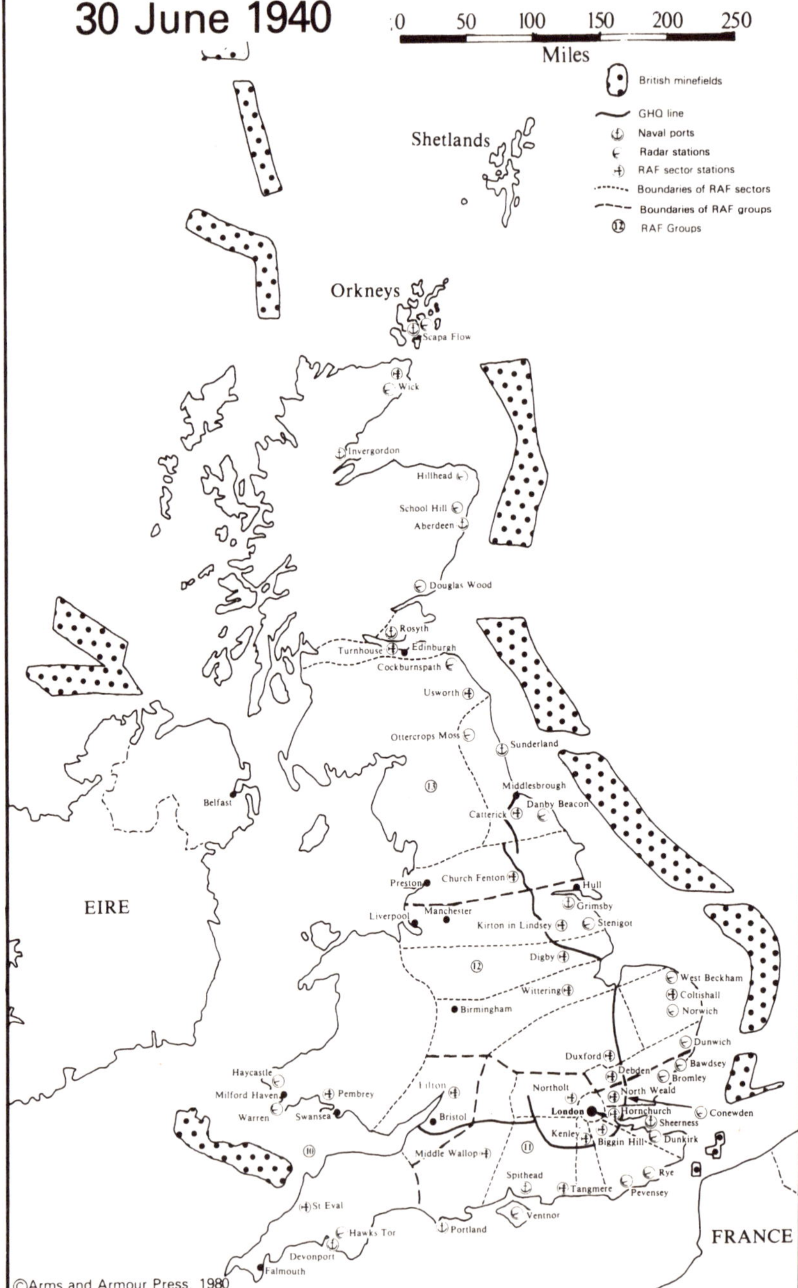

The underlying feeling of panic was to be detected among the residents in the area of Dover and Folkestone which was declared a Defence Area and made subject to compulsory evacuation if required. As the stauncher members of the community turned to caring for the men returning from Dunkirk, to manning the ships and docks, strengthening the ARP defences and patrolling the countryside and clifftops at night on the look out for paratroops, those of faint heart began to leave. There were many vehicles with plenty of petrol available. Some furniture vans were making four trips a day to the rural areas and numerous houses were soon left abandoned and locked up. Even as instructions were received to evacuate compulsorily 60 per cent of the school children from coastal towns between Great Yarmouth and Hythe, the mayors of Dover and Folkestone (J. R. Cairns and G. A. Gurr) were pleading with their townsfolk to show greater resolution and to stay put. Bankruptcy stared these towns in the face as the cross-Channel trade died overnight and industry moved out. Dover Council resisted a request by the Regional Commissioner for the South East (Sir Aukland Geddes) that it should nominate nine councillors to stay behind in the event of invasion. 'What,' asked Clr. John Walker, 'would the Empire think if Dover Council did not stand firm?'[2]

If the populace had been aware of the extent of the dangers confronting them and the frailty of the nation's defences, they might easily have given way to defeatism. As it was, Churchill's intoxicating leadership kept them on an inflexible course striving towards survival and ultimate victory. But already Churchill and his advisers were worried by the direction of the enemy's air effort. From 5 to 19 June, thirteen airfields, sixteen factories and fourteen ports had been attacked. None had been severely damaged, even though the enemy flew at the relatively low average altitude of 10,000 feet, and suffered the loss of eleven aircraft. Casualties were light despite a few bombs on outer London, the worst being nine killed in Cambridge by a single attack.[3] But evidence was accumulating of German possession of a sophisticated radio beam device called *Knickebein* which would permit the Germans to drop bombs within 400 yards of any point in the country. Some of the German flights, as has already been explained, were intended to develop the skills of picked crews in its application.[4]

A false lead

Reports were accumulating of intensive enemy activity in and about the North German and Dutch ports. From neutral sources

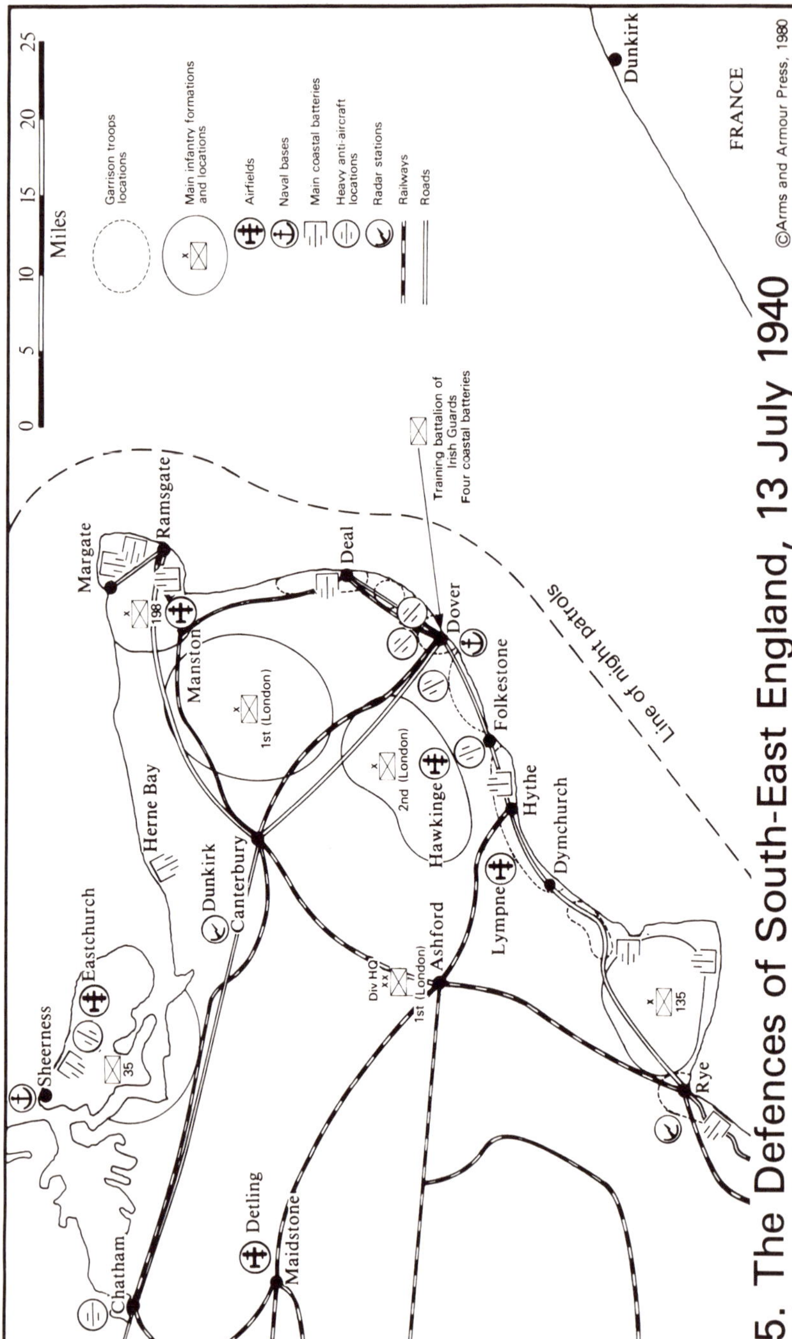

5. The Defences of South-East England, 13 July 1940

and travellers leaving Germany, as well as through diplomatic channels, the first hints of the enemy's intentions began to filter through. As yet, its size, direction and timing were obscure, but from a signal by Kesselring on 24 May, in which he gave his views upon the 'Lion' proposals, it seemed possible that an airborne landing might be expected at any moment. But as June went by without clear corroboration, and also without any sign of airborne troops, fears of a parachute attack receeded to be replaced by a firm conviction that a full-scale invasion must be expected in August. British plans to defeat this assault were governed, of course, by the extremely limited resources at their disposal, and the deployment of those resources was guided by the overall military appreciation of where the main enemy blow might fall. In the absence of positive evidence showing the presence of enemy transport aircraft or shipping close to the Channel ports, but in the knowledge that considerable traffic (much of it assumed to be of a commercial nature) was using the German and Dutch ports, the initial conclusions drawn by the Intelligence Staffs adhered to the traditional opinion, which had been revived in the autumn of 1939 (when the chances of an invasion were rumoured), that East Anglia would be the main objective. Even as German preparation became noticeable along the Channel coast, the General Staff Intelligence (X) Branch at GHQ Home Forces noted on 30 June: 'East Anglia seems most likely because it is further removed from our main fleet base.'[5]

The overall deployment of naval and army units, therefore, matched this threat, priority being given to the protection of the eastern sector of the country rather than the south-eastern part where the enemy actually intended to make his attempt. Forces had also to be kept in readiness should the Germans try to take over neutral Eire – a nation which steadfastly refused British protection, but one which figured as a target in the German deception plan.

The Navy prepares

The Royal Navy based its first line of defence upon cruisers and destroyers, preferring to retain its battleships and aircraft carriers at a distance in readiness to intervene only if major German units put in an appearance. By 1 July its major units in home waters were deployed as follows:

Scapa Flow	2 Battlecruisers, 2 Battleships, 3 Cruisers, 9 Destroyers
Rosyth	2 Cruisers

Liverpool	1 Battleship	
Iceland	1 Aircraft Carrier 7 Destroyers	on escort duties
Tyne	1 Cruiser, 12 Destroyers	
Humber	3 Cruisers, 7 Destroyers	
Harwich	9 Destroyers	
Sheerness	1 Cruiser, 3 Destroyers	
Dover	5 Destroyers	
Portsmouth	5 Destroyers	
Western Approaches		
	1 Battleship, 3 Cruisers, 23 Destroyers[6] on escort duties	

Distributed around the island while engaged upon the escort of coastal traffic and as mobile vedettes, there also were some 1,100 lightly armed trawlers and small craft which would give warning of an approaching enemy, but make little or no contribution in a fight.

The low proportion of strength allocated to the defence of the Straits of Dover could be attributed not only to the belief that this area seemed less threatened than those to the north, but also to the appreciation that such a narrow stretch of relatively shallow water was highly unsuitable for the manoeuvring of major naval units, besides being well within range of enemy guns and bombers. The minefields which had previously been laid to protect the trade routes to France were now of greater value to the Germans than the British, forming as they did the foundation of the mined corridor they eventually intended to create in those waters. Efforts by British minesweepers to clear the mines were resisted by aircraft and by fire from the Pas de Calais, although the laying of fresh minefields close in shore and the floating of booms across the harbour mouths was completed without delay. Likewise, the reinforcement of the existing coastal batteries defending the ports and the Straits of Dover was soon implemented, but the desire of Vice-Admiral Bertram Ramsay, the Flag Officer Dover, to instal long-range guns for use against the enemy in France, could not be met immediately. A single 14in naval gun was known to be available and was being made ready.[7]

The Admiralty's plan depended upon timely intervention by local naval forces which had been forewarned by early information from regular nightly destroyer, MTB and Coastal Command aircraft patrols watching the enemy ports. It also was hoped to receive warning from 'Listening craft' fitted with Asdic, and from an inshore line of drifters and motor boats equipped with radio, flares and rockets. Initially, it was intended that those destroyers closest to a threatened sector would attack at once, in the hope of forestalling a landing. If that failed, a major effort would be postponed until substantial forces of cruisers and destroyers, under the maximum cover from fighter aircraft, could be concentrated. In the most favourable circumstances an interception might be made within a few hours – even, with luck, a few minutes. A strong concentration of cruisers and destroyers from Sheerness and Harwich could deploy in the entrance to the Channel off the North Foreland within two hours, and five hours later these could be reinforced by warships from Hull. Only if the major German units put to sea would the battleships intervene,[8] a decision which reflected the reluctance of seamen to manoeuvre big ships in a confined space. In essence, therefore, the Admiralty plan, while hoping for the best, made no guarantee that the enemy would not get ashore unchallenged.

An army at its weakest

Much therefore depended upon the Army, but Home Forces under the command of General Sir Edmund Ironside, though replete in manpower, was desperately short of equipment. Ironside's first aim, as he saw it in the immediate aftermath of Dunkirk, was 'to prevent the enemy from running riot and tearing the guts out of the country . . .'[9] His plan, which was designed to fulfill the demands of the Chiefs of Staff, was presented to them on 25 June. It was based on a succession of stop-lines beginning at the coast and covering a so-called GHQ Line of anti-tank obstacles guarding Bristol, the Midlands and London, construction of which had not yet started. Inland, too, lay the armoured and semi-mobile formations upon which everything was staked, to deliver a decisive blow should the enemy obtain a firm purchase ashore. Delay was the best that could be expected at the stop-lines, where most of the 786 field guns were deployed, or at the GHQ Line, where the bulk of the 167 anti-tank guns were to be posted. But the mobile forces were enfeebled, consisting as they did in Lincolnshire of the 2nd Armoured Division (which had but 178 light tanks instead of its entitled number of 213 medium and 108 light tanks), and in Surrey of the 1st Armoured Division (newly returned in disarray from France) with only 9 medium tanks. By the end of June, the latter formation would be raised to 81 mediums and nearly 100 lights and, at the same time, would take under command the 1st Tank Brigade with its 90 heavy Matilda tanks – instead of the 180 its establishment warranted[10] – and, at a fraction of its full strength, would become the most powerful striking force in the British Army.

Defence of the south-east of England was the responsibility of XII Corps (Lieutenant-General A. Thorne) and the key sector in Kent where the Germans planned to land was occupied by the 1st (London) Division (Major-General C. F. Liardet). Thorne considered that the landing was more likely to come between the Graveney Marshes and Dover than to the west of Dover. He therefore laid down the Corps Line running from the Marshes to Dover through Canterbury, a system which, for much of its length, followed a railway track and for only a small proportion of that distance could be said to incorporate natural features which provided a significant obstacle. Liardet's triple intention was to defend the beaches, be prepared to occupy the Corps Line and also to be ready to attack the enemy east or west of the Corps Line. The resources at his disposal he called 'ludicrous'. 1st (London) Division had been designated as 'motorized', a derisory title as it stood at the end of June. Since its mobilization in September 1939, nearly all its vehicles were still those which had been requisitioned from civilian firms. Some of its strange assortment of vans and lorries still bore their original merchants' names, and its troop transports were civilian coaches which, in happier days, had taken holiday makers to the seaside. In May, its motor-cycle reconnaissance unit had been removed and sent to its doom in the last-ditch defence of Calais, the motor-cycles then being given to 1st Armoured Division.

On 5 July, Headquarters Royal Artillery of 1st (London) Division, under Brigadier J. Price, controlled 34 pieces of field artillery and 12 assorted guns endowed with a speculative anti-tank capability. They were composed and located as follows:

Unit	*Guns*	*Location*	*Tasks*
64th Field Regiment	2 x 13pdr 8 x 4.5 Howitzer 4 x 25pdr	Richborough	Support either 198th Brigade or, with the 25pdrs and 4.5in Hows, 2nd (London) Bde.
90th Field Regiment	2 x 13pdr 4 x 18pdr 4 x 25pdr 4 x 4.5in Howitzer	St Nicholas at Wade	Support either 198th or 1st (London) Bde.
113rd Field Regiment	2 x 18pdr 4 x 4.5in Howitzer	Whitstable	Support 1st (London) Bde.
C4 Mobile Battery	2 x 12pdr 2 x 3pdr	Godinton	
C5 Mobile Battery	4 x 4in	Godinton	
X Static Battery	4 x 4in	Nr Ashford	

They were short of ammunition, had not fired practice shoots for some time, and had more guns than suitable vehicles to tow them.

As for the infantry, they spent most of their time digging and sandbagging static defences and spent little enough time exercising or firing their weapons, there being a dire shortage of ammunition for the latter purpose. 198th Brigade held the coast line of the Isle of Thanet; Deal Garrison, consisting mainly of 3,000 Marines, were in the line on either side of that port; Dover Garrison, composed of a miscellany of local units, covered the sector between Dover and Folkestone; Shorncliffe Garrison had the stretch of coast from Sandgate to Dymchurch Redoubt; and 135th Brigade (detached from 45th Division) the line from Dymchurch to Midrips. 1st (London) Brigade provided the mobile reserve in the north, while 2nd (London) Brigade lay to the southward, including the task of counter-attacking the airfields at Lympne and Hawkings, which Fighter Command intended to evacuate when enemy pressure became heavy. This deployment, concentrated in the north and diluted in the south, left the door wide open to the Germans' intended descent. It would be outflanked immediately if the coastal defences fell.

Interwoven with Liardet's infantry, however, was a fairly formidable array of coastal and anti-aircraft artillery. Two 9.2in guns in the Citadel at Dover could reach half-way across the Channel. Four old 6in guns (with a range of only 12,000 yards) and two batteries of modern 6ins (with a range of 25,000 yards), which had composed the pre-war armament, augmented the defences. To these there were now added, spaced along the coast, a number of Emergency Batteries consisting of 4in and 6in guns (manned by sailors and army gunners) which once had been mounted in ships during the First World War. From improvised emplacements and with 100 rounds each (of which they were told no more was available) they were instructed to fire at 'big game', engaging small craft only if they were in large numbers. For night illumination, searchlights were also deployed. Quite the most versatile and modern artillery weapons in the area were those belonging to Major-General F. G. Hyland's 6th Anti-Aircraft Division, which was responsible for the guns defending the approaches to London, as well as key ports and airfields. In the region of Dover and Folkestone, Hyland had placed 18 of the latest 3.7in guns (which also had a powerful anti-tank capability if the gunners chose to make use of it), plus a few First World War 3in anti-aircraft guns, some modern 40mm Bofors, four 20mm Hispanos and many machine-guns. Normally these guns fired from prepared emplacements, but all were given a secondary, mobile rôle and were issued with what little anti-tank ammunition was available.

The beach defences, apart from the artillery, amounted to a thin infantry screen, with scarcely any mines and only a few strands of wire to hamper enemy tanks and infantry. Inland, Liardet's mobile companies and platoons were spread widely at nodal points whence they hoped to mount local counter-attacks against such vital places as the Manston, Hawkinge and Lympne airfields. Only one battalion (1st London Rifle Brigade) could be spared to counter-attack both Hawkinge and Lympne. The road-blöcks, shared with the LDV, merely introduced a check to road movement and a watch over lonely places for paratroops. Armed chiefly with shotguns, trained only in the most rudimentary way and prone to report the slightest unusual occurence as a hostile act, these enthusiastic volunteers made movement by darkness a perilous occupation. On the night of 3/4 June alone, there were four cases of people being shot dead in Britain for allegedly failing to answer a challenge.[11]

At the root of the British weakness was a dire shortage of weapons and inadequate factory production to make good the deficiencies. Field-gun production ran at about 50 guns a month, infantry and medium tanks at a mere 100.[12] If, at the end of May, the Chief of Staff had sombrely to admit that 'Should the Germans succeed in establishing a force with its vehicles in this country, our armed forces have not got the offensive power to drive it out,' they were not much better off at the beginning of July. Everything worked on a hand to mouth basis. Improvization was the watchword, training was restricted by lack of ammunition, and hope stood supreme. And just to make matters difficult, the supply services continued to perform their duties at this critical moment as in the manner of peacetime; meticulously they insisted upon requisitions being tendered as 'by the book' – either that or the supplies stayed in their depots.[14]

Air power – the main element of defence

The RAF alone had the weapons and the long-prepared system which offered hope of coping with this unimaginable situation. Since 1915, when enemy aircraft first dropped bombs on Britain, a comprehensive organization of command and control had evolved, in which observation posts, manned by the Observer Corps, and linked by land-line and radio to communication centres, provided the vital information upon which the fighter and anti-aircraft forces depended for exerting the maximum economic influence. Moreover, since the Luftwaffe was first formed, radio interception stations had monitored and assessed the profusion of signals sent by its aircrew under training and, latterly, on operations. Not only was detailed information of its Order of Battle known, but its operational procedures were also understood and it was often possible to obtain warning of raids by listening-in to the aircraft frequencies. Furthermore, since 1938, the observation posts had been powerfully supplemented by the installation of primitive radar locating equipment (called Chain Home (CH) sets) which, although having a 300 per cent factor of inaccuracy, could at least give warning of the approach of aircraft flying above 3,000 feet from a range of about 150 miles. The gap beneath that altitude had to be closed by ground observers, since the latest beam type CHL (Chain Home Low) sets had not yet been installed and the first was not expected to be ready until about the end of July.[15] RAF Fighter Command, under Air Marshal Sir Hugh Dowding, had its headquarters at Stanmore in north London and controlled four Fighter Groups, the Observer Corps, the Radar Group and Balloon Command (which flew barrage balloons over important targets to deter low-flying aircraft), while exercising operational control over Anti-Aircraft Command (Lieutenant-General F. Pile). Under each Fighter Group were the Sectors controlling, by radio, the movements of aircraft operating from airfields within the Sector, each Sector Control being located at one of the airfields. To the largest Group, No 11 (Air Vice-Marshal K. R. Park), fell the task of defending south-east England; on 18 June, its seven Sectors controlled between them some 36 twin-engined Blenheim fighters (with but a limited combat worthiness) and rather fewer than 200 Spitfire and Hurricane, single-engined fighters. On his western flank lay No 10 Group and to the north No 12 Group, each of which, if time and circumstances allowed, could send fighters to his assistance. In the extreme north, No 13 Group looked after the rest of England, Scotland and Northern Ireland. All the Groups and several of the fighter squadrons were below strength in men and machines, as well as in spare parts. On 4 June, there were only 36 Spitfires and Hurricanes ready for issue from the Aircraft Storage Units. But production of fighters, in response to stirring exhortations from Churchill and the drive of Lord Beaverbrook, the recently appointed Minister of Aircraft Production, had risen sharply. It had been 265 in April, 325 in May and in June it was to be 446,[16] a contribution which largely restored the losses of May, but which threatened to be wasted due to an acute scarcity of trained pilots. In relation to an authorized establishment of 1,450 pilots, Fighter Command could call on fewer than 1,200 in mid June (although some 60 were about to be transferred from other commands)[17] while only some six a day were coming from the training units.

The system of radio control, linked to radar early-warning, offered substantial economies to set against the heavy German advantage in numbers, and the Germans themselves had been made aware of the technical qualities of the Spitfires during the fighting over Dunkirk. In addition, they were impressed by the evidence of the RAF's radio command and control of fighters in combat, and of the radar chain which they discovered as soon as they had set up monitoring equipment near Calais in May. It was a shock to find that the British were so far ahead of them. They had nothing so good as the radio system and their radar was inferior to that of the British. The best contribution they could apply to the electronic warfare of the day was a single Freya radar station at Wissant, to locate British convoys as they sailed to and fro in the Channel.

As for the British bombers' capacity, they suffered by day, as did the Germans, from the serious risk of operating without escort, and a chronic inability to find and hit targets by night, unless these were within short range and well defined on the ground. In the event of imminent invasion it was intended that RAF Bomber Command concentrate on enemy shipping in ports and in transit. For the time being, priority was given to attacks on the German aircraft industry and airfields. Throughout June, Wellington, Hampden, Whitley and Blenheim aircraft roamed across the occupied territories and over West Germany, scattering bombs without doing the slightest damage worthy of the effort. It had not yet been realized that dead reckoning and astral navigation were completely ineffective under wartime conditions, and the British, who had found it hard to believe that the Germans possessed an accurate beam navigation system, naturally did not have one of their own.

If everything would depend upon Fighter Command in the air, this was not to say that Dowding was worried only about that dimension. He was concerned, too, about the vulnerability of his airfields, which were quite inadequately defended by anti-aircraft guns and, in many instances, almost unprotected by troops. In a few places, Local Defence Volunteers were incorporated into the perimeter defences, but for the most part, since the Army was principally engaged in developing its lines of static defence, RAF ground staff had to be given arms (when they were available) in the hope that they would make a stand if the enemy arrived. At the best, however, only rifles and a few machine-guns comprised the defence of the airfields, even of those closest to the coast.[18]

The people at war

Fully occupied in dealing with a mammoth task, the fighting Services had little time to consider the nation's plight. Factory workers, too, engaged in a twelve hour, seven day week, enjoyed few moments for contemplation, while an army of helpers in other kinds of work came home at the end of the day to go on patrol with the LDV, stand watch with the ARP, the AFS (Auxilliary Fire Service) or the Police Reserve, drive ambulances and attend for duty with the WVS (Women's Voluntary Service) or the First Aid workers, or serve in any one of a hundred different occupations. With the Home Office at the centre, but with tentacles out to the other Ministries such as Transport, Health, Food, Works, Labour and Pensions, the civil defence of the nation rested upon the traditional committee system functioning through massed voluntary service controlled by a relatively small core of paid, full-time officials. But an ARP Controller, upon whom the welfare of a large district might depend, was often a town clerk, whose training in emergency work was minimal and whose psychological attitude and that of his staff was far removed from the demands of quick, militaristic decision making. A Chief Constable might sometimes control the ARP, but he was not necessarily in tune with local government departments whose methods tended to differ from his more authoritarian approach. An ARP Post might be manned by a full-time Head Warden whose job it would be to recruit, train and direct the volunteer wardens and messengers within his boundaries. Before the collapse of France, it had been difficult to recruit sufficient manpower; afterwards, and as Kesselring's bombers droned overhead, volunteers flocked in and could only be given rudimentary training within the few days available. Every one felt the need to become involved and a great many of the most patriotic appointed themselves as personal guardians of the nation's security, with the result that the slightest suspicious act, such as flashing a light in the blackout or speaking with a mildly foreign accent, could lead to rumours and reports of the presence of the dreaded Fifth Column.[19] On 31 May, when the sign-posts were being removed in order to hamper parachutists in finding their way about, Vice-Admiral Ramsay, deeply involved as he was with the evacuation from Dunkirk, had received a sufficient number of alarmist reports as to cause him to inform the Admiralty of numerous acts of sabotage in the Dover area such as communication leakages, fixed defence sabotage, and second-hand cars purchased at high prices and left parked at convenient places – none of which could be substantiated.[20]

No one could be sure how the undisciplined civilians would behave when confronted with the terror of bombing and by the appearance of a hostile army on English soil for the first time in many centuries. Because refugees had blocked the roads and delayed the movement of troops in France, strict orders were issued for the British not to leave their homes but to 'stay put'. Yet already the early minor air raids of June had caused ripples of movement among distraught people. Since it was so difficult to know how well the untested professional RAF defences would work, no one could be sure what would happen with a ramshackle voluntary one. It was by no means certain if communications or the distribution of food could be maintained. Starvation or a breakdown in the health services might rapidly cripple the closely packed cities. As it was, industrial production was being affected already by the nightly air raids, and the deficiencies of some local councils under stress and strain were being exposed. But when, on 19 June, the Chiefs of Staff recommended a large transfer of civil control to the eleven Regional Commissioners (who had been appointed at the outbreak of war to ensure the smoother running of the administrative machine during abnormal conditions) the Cabinet declined to approve.[21] Hesitating to alarm the population and anxious not to upset the elected hierarchy, the Cabinet took the risk of a breakdown by permitting the existing, complex local government arrangements to continue.

The first test would come when Kesselring's exploratory operations would give way, on the 19th, to large formations arriving in daylight.

V

THE TESTING TIME

Kesselring probes

To the anxious watchers on British coasts and in the CH radar stations, the enemy air activity which materialized overhead shortly after first light on Wednesday, 19 June, looked similar to Kesselring's probings of the previous fortnight. Blips on the radar screens revealed a few individual aircraft approaching at the higher altitudes; radio messages from auxiliary craft at sea reported others coming in at low level, beneath the radar beams; and then the Observer Corps posts began telling of individual twin-engined aircraft making low-level runs over the beaches, apparently engaged in close reconnaissance – as indeed they were. The Germans, now within less than a month of launching their invasion, were extremely short of good Intelligence and it was of prime importance for them to photograph as many target areas as possible, as well as the intended landing places. The controllers at No 11 Group's Sector Stations had already 'scrambled' a few flights from Biggin Hill, Manston and Hawkinge, the scale of their effort severely limited by Park on instructions from Dowding, who was aware, through interpretations of Luftwaffe radio traffic, that initial activity might be small. Throughout the battle, Dowding was to read the enemy's high-level orders with care, although he could not always place complete faith in what they told him. On this occasion he was right. Most engagements were isolated and took place out to sea. Here and there, a Do 17P long-range reconnaissance aircraft might fall smoking or dive to the safety of the clouds or low-lying morning mist. Occasionally the distant burr of octuple machine-guns could be heard as Spitfires and Hurricanes closed for the kill.

But at 0600 hours, the attention of the radar operators was attracted by an unusually large number of blips, representing a massing of aircraft over the Pas de Calais, such as they had not seen since the busy days of the Battle of France. Soon it became apparent that these formations were on course for the Straits of Dover where, at that moment, a convoy was passing westwards escorted by an armed trawler and two destroyers. From the fighter airfields, squadrons on Readiness were sent up while others took their place. For the past fortnight, as Dowding's units recuperated, they had been accustomed to dealing with only small enemy formations and had suffered a few losses. This looked bigger. Within twenty minutes the fighters, clawing madly for height, saw above and ahead of them layered formations of Me 109s and 110s, ranged above a formation of 26 Do 17 bombers which were in the act of lining up to aim at the convoy below. At once the British fighters were involved in a furious dog-fight and at a disadvantage in numbers and tactical position. As they tried to get at the bombers, the German fighters plunged on them from above. Fresh formations joined in as reinforcing RAF squadrons were vectored to the scene by their Controllers, and the back-up staffels of Luftwaffe fighters arrived to cover the retreating Dorniers. A whirligig of aircraft cavorted across the sky, plunging to the lower altitudes and down to sea level as the formations broke into a mosaic of individual combats. Bombs churned the sea's surface, a small merchant ship blossomed to a hit among rising columns of water, and began to settle. The air battle strayed over Dover harbour where destroyers in the harbour and anti-aircraft guns on the cliff-tops joined in, firing against friend and foe alike. Crippled and damaged aircraft were lurching to earth, followed here and there by drifting parachutes. Then all became quiet; as explosively as the fight had begun, it rolled away into silence as the contestants dived for home to refuel and replenish ammunition for the next contest. This was but the overture to the spreading scheme of heavier attacks which Kesselring had devised. By striking at shipping he hoped to draw the RAF into battle in air space of his own choosing, close to his own bases where his own machines were at an advantage. By concentrating on destroying Spitfires and Hurricanes he intended to ensure the success of 'Sealion' and effectively prevent Dowding from increasing the strength of Fighter Command in the aftermath of the Battle of Dunkirk.[1]

The direction and nature of the preliminary operations were not only associated with the primary need of winning air supremacy. They were employed also to delude the British Intelligence Staffs by accustoming them to accept, as routine, certain activities which were directly related to the subsequent launching of the invasion. For example, the regular movement of German coastal convoys and of air traffic into the French airfields was made to appear as like customary commercial and logistic operations as possible. Meanwhile, the rising intensity of movement was also geared to suggest a culmination in August. In the same way, Kesselring's raids against convoys and ports formed part of the deception plan. While endeavouring to cause the maximum amount of damage and attain an ascendancy over the British, he was anxious, too, to avoid alarming them thoroughly, preferring to encourage them to fall into a sense of false security. But here he failed. The Chiefs of Staff had no difficulty in recognizing accentuated activity, particularly when it was drawn to their attention by Ultra translating Enigma signals into plain language. Furthermore, and as a quite unexpected benefit to the British, the German air raids gave valuable and much needed practice to the Civil Defence Services by revealing several fundamental weaknesses in local organizations and beginning to accustom the mass of the people to the nature of Blitzkrieg in its milder aspects. Gradually, the novelty of disturbance began to wear off and people started, for example, to see the virtue of taking cover instead of standing about to watch the action.

As part of Luftflotte 2's own programme of acclimatization, it systematically rotated its units so that as many crews as possible could gain experience of a technique for which the Luftwaffe was not specifically designed – that of strategic bombing. The scale of attack built up as more units became operational on newly captured airfields, and as aircraft from Sperrle's Luftflotte 3 were withdrawn from support of the Army in the dying days of the Battle for France. They took up position on Luftflotte 2's left flank in the region of Brest and Cherbourg. At the same time, Luftflotte 5 started to probe deeper into Britain from its distant bases in Norway, intending to pin British fighters to the defence of the northern sector of the British Isles. Day by day, the narrow-fronted raids which opened against the Dover area on 19 June were expanded until major raids were being mounted along the entire southern and eastern coastline. Small, sporadic incursions, chiefly by night, penetrated inland in search of key installations, such as the Rolls-Royce engine plant at Derby and any other factory deemed important to the aircraft industry.

The rapid enlargement and intensification of the offensive caused Dowding acute concern. On the afternoon of the 19th there was a further attack on the same convoy that had been attacked in the morning, and a supplementary raid by 12 Ju 88s against an east-ward bound convoy off Newhaven. In the evening, this second convoy was dive-bombed as it entered the Straits. On each occasion RAF fighters were drawn into adverse combat situations over the sea. Me 109s and Me 110s, handled with great skill by their pilots. who were flying on what were known as 'free chase' missions which enabled them to operate independently in indirect support of the bomber force, caught the Hurricanes and Spitfires at a disadvantage. Losses sustained by the RAF were 12, all of them fighters, but only two pilots were killed. The Luftwaffe lost 15 aircraft of which only 8 were fighters (with only one pilot missing), the remainder being an assortment of reconnaissance and bomber aircraft and a single He 115 seaplane which was hit by anti-aircraft fire while on a night minelaying mission. These exchanges were not in the RAF's favour proportionately.

Battles of the convoys

On the morning of the 20th, in the immediate aftermath of the usual night raids and the first-light reconnaissance missions, a convoy off the North Foreland was heavily bombed, and this time with greater effect than on the previous day. For the first time, Ju 87 dive-bombers were used and two ships were sunk and a destroyer damaged. A few hours later, more Ju 87s, in conjunction with high-level bombers, attacked another convoy off Portland, again with some success. Above and among the bombers, opposing fighters sought each other in combat, and losses mounted as the comparative combat effectiveness of the aircraft involved became clearly defined. There was little to choose between the Spitfire and the Me 109, the latter of which was superior to the Hurricane which, in its turn, was superior to the Me 110. Of the German bombers, the Ju 87 was easy meat (they lost 8 this day) and the Do 17s and He 111s (which had appeared over Portland) were vulnerable if caught unescorted. Likewise, the best of the German bombers, the Ju 88, was also vulnerable if caught by fighters. Everything hinged upon the struggle between the Me 109s and the Spitfires and Hurricanes, and again, this day, the balance of losses was in the German favour; they lost only 3 Me 109s, while the British lost 5 Spitfires and 6 Hurricanes with half the pilots killed or wounded. Extremely gratifying to the British was the high rate of interceptions it was proving possible to make, and this performance was improving as the radar operators and controllers gained in experience. To the crews of German reconnaissance aircraft attempting to slip through on their own, it was disconcerting to be caught so frequently. Out of nearly 100 such missions that day, some 30 per cent turned away when spotted, 40 per cent had to dive for cloud cover when chased; and 30 per cent were either shot down or badly damaged. The best long-range reconnaissance results were obtained by missions which were intermingled with raids when it was discovered that the British early-warning system often lost track of individual aircraft. Despite a number of successful sorties, however, the Germans were dissatisfied with the information at their disposal; thus far, they knew far too little about the composition of British coastal and inland defences.

Of crucial importance, too, was the minelaying campaign, prosecuted by sea and from the air with great determination by the Germans, who even flew these missions on the two nights between 19 and 30 June when weather precluded other flights. But although laying could be performed by surface craft by day in waters covered by their own air and artillery forces, and dropped into hostile areas by night, it was never possible entirely to prevent enemy counter-measures and keep him bottled-up in port. British destroyers at this time dominated the narrow seas in the fewer hours of darkness, and made life perilous for the layers, while minesweepers braved air attack to complete the daily cleaning of the 'swept channels' along which convoys moved. Hence the process of establishing the mine barrages intended to shield the flanks of the invasion was curtailed. A great deal devolved upon aircraft as minelayers, but they could drop only a minute proportion of the mines needed – though with a high degree of accuracy. Yet minelaying paid, not only in the damage caused, but also in the inhibiting effect it had on operations by coastal forces. A destroyer out of Sheerness was badly damaged and, every now and then, an armed trawler or some other ship would be blown up. Moreover, three more destroyers were damaged by bombing off Dover as the Luftwaffe gained much needed experience in this sort of work. These were losses that the Admiralty would not be able to sustain.

To Dowding, at the end of June, the situation looked bleak. Although the production of fighters had risen dramatically and his men were holding their own in equal combat, too many engagements were taking place to the enemy's advantage. The loss of scarce pilots began to exceed the rate of replacement. The enemy, on the other hand, was showing no signs of wilting and, indeed, he had a massive reserve of pilots, output of 1939 standing at between 10,000 and 15,000 a year, well in excess of requirements. His shortage, in fact, lay in an insufficiency of aircraft; while

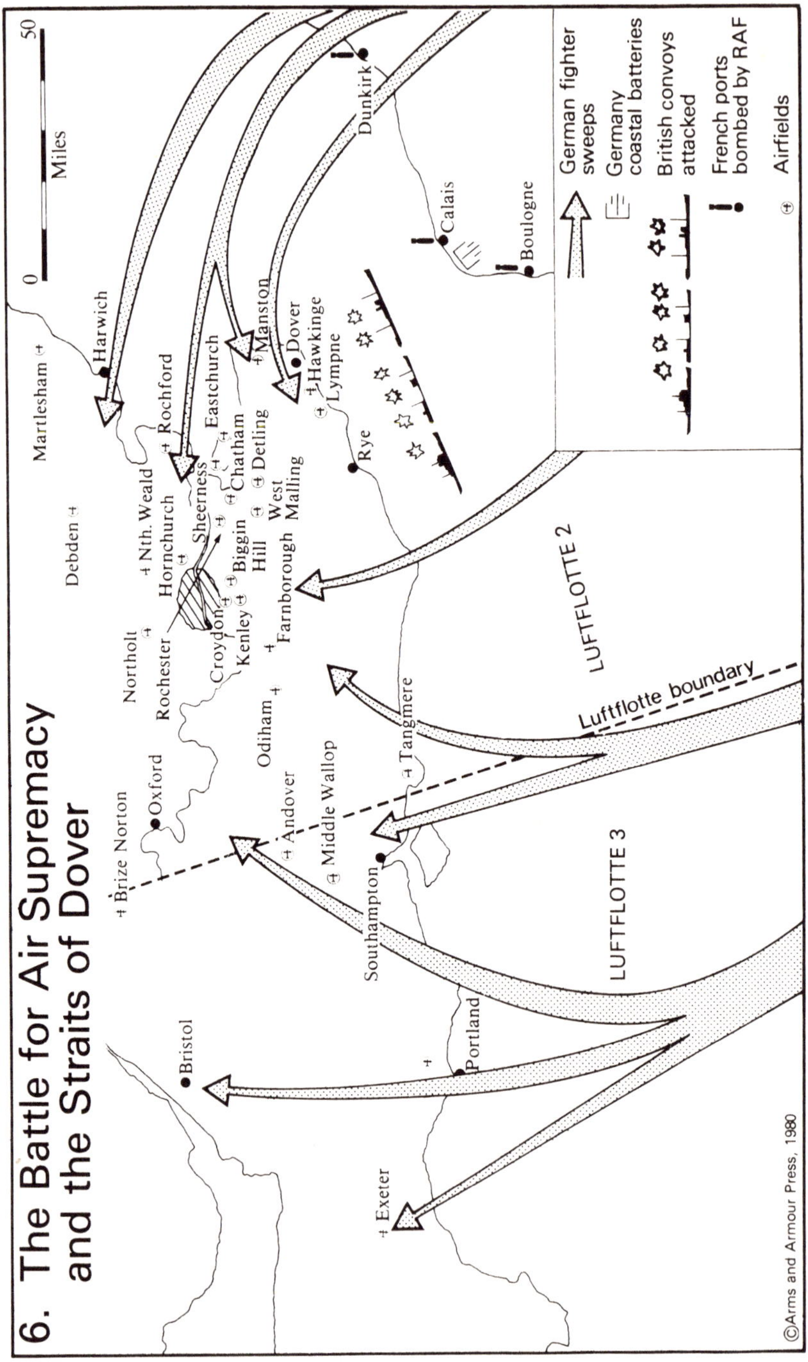
6. The Battle for Air Supremacy and the Straits of Dover
0
Miles
50
Harwich
Martlesham
Debden
Nth. Weald
Hornchurch
Rochford
Eastchurch
Manston
Dover
Hawkinge
Lympne
Rye
Chatham
Detling
West Malling
Sheerness
Biggin Hill
Farnborough
Kenley
Croydon
Rochester
Northolt
Odiham
Oxford
Brize Norton
Andover
Middle Wallop
Tangmere
Southampton
Portland
Bristol
Exeter
Dunkirk
Calais
Boulogne
LUFTFLOTTE 2
LUFTFLOTTE 3
Luftflotte boundary
German fighter sweeps
Germany coastal batteries
British convoys attacked
French ports bombed by RAF
Airfields
©Arms and Armour Press, 1980

British Intelligence credited the German industry with the production of about 1,500 aircraft a month, and the Luftwaffe with an operational strength of some 5,000, the actual figures, respectively, were nearer 725 and 2,000. The true figures imposed restraints on Goering, of course, but those produced by Intelligence were inhibiting to Dowding who was just another victim of the misleading picture presented by his own side (see page 53 and Historical Note 5, Chapter IV). For Dowding had yet to restore the number of fighter squadrons to the 52 reckoned essential for the defence of Britain. Lack of an Air Sea Rescue Service also meant that pilots shot down at sea stood a lower chance of survival than the Germans who were picking up their men in white-painted He 59B seaplanes under cover of the Red Cross – a practice which was frowned upon by the British who soon began shooting down these aircraft after the Germans ignored diplomatic warnings.

The Admiralty's insistence upon keeping open coastal trade forced Dowding to position squadrons near the coast, on Lympne, Hawkinge and Manston airfields, in order to give immediate protection to the convoys. Usually, however, these aircraft could not gain sufficient height in time to intercept the raiders from altitude, while they themselves were often 'jumped' by well-positioned German fighters which had the initiative. The airfields, too, were vulnerable. On 27 June, a lone Ju 88 on a low-level photographic mission, skimmed across Hawkinge without receiving a single shot in its direction – and this was by no means an isolated incident. Low-level missions were hard to detect, as both sides knew. On the 28th, Dowding asked the Admiralty to cease running convoys by day in order to take the strain off his fighters – and, incidentally, to help the Admiralty conserve destroyers. But Churchill objected to this admission of weakness and a decision was postponed.

The Channel guns open fire

Shortly after dawn on the 29th, a few minutes after the sirens in Dover and Folkestone had given warning of the approach of the early morning reconnaissance sortie, there was a loud explosion near the Langdon Battery overlooking Dover harbour. Those who had not already retired to the shelters and the deep caves, which had been prepared by the local council before the war, were caught in indignant surprise. For already the people who had refused to leave Dover and nearby towns had become quite used to living under fire, more so, indeed, than any other community in Britain. They now knew what it meant to be shocked for five minutes after a bomb had fallen, how recovery took place during the next two hours to be followed by a longer period of euphoria at recollection of the incident; and what it was like to return gradually to normal in a state of pride at having overcome the traumas of fear – except that, in their case, incidents piled quickly one upon each other so that the stages of emotional change tended to overlap. This particular explosion sounded different and aroused interest because there was not an aeroplane to be heard. Three minutes later, when there was another bang down by the harbour, it began to dawn upon those better educated to the sounds of war that they were under shellfire from France,[2] while the real experts deduced, as shell followed shell in salvoes of four at regular but quite lengthy intervals, that the Germans were engaged upon systematic ranging of their guns against the harbour. At once the destroyers which had, as usual, spent the night on patrol, put back to sea to join a convoy of 18 merchant ships, escorted by another pair of destroyers, which was approaching and which, the radar plots warned, might be the target for enemy bombers.

What happened now had a profound and perhaps decisive effect on the outcome of 'Sealion'. As dive-bombers plunged upon the ships off Folkestone and the attendant fighters brawled nearby, the guns at Boulogne and then those at Calais, turned their attention to the convoy, gouts of water leaping into the air as shells and bombs burst. A destroyer was seen to disappear amid the spouts and emerge with her guns firing, but on many of these pre-war destroyers the guns could elevate to only 45° and therefore were practically useless against dive-bombers coming in at a steeper angle. The flotilla leader, HMS *Codrington*, was not so lucky, however. She was caught and sunk by Ju 87s as she was clearing harbour. And this was but the overture to a day in which the fighting spread the length of the Channel and the naval forces suffered. Near Portland a naval escort was slightly damaged, and off the Suffolk coast a formation of He 111s sank another destroyer. The day's work cost the Luftwaffe 15 bombers, a seaplane minelayer and 9 fighters, but in return the Germans destroyed 15 British fighters and two of Blenheim light bombers on reconnaissance near the Belgian coast. When the casualty returns had been completed, it no longer made sense either to the Air Ministry or the Admiralty to persevere with sailing in daylight in the Channel. Lucrative targets had to be denied the enemy, the RAF saved from fighting at a disadvantage and the Straits of Dover abandoned by shipping during the longer hours of daylight, leaving these waters to the Royal Navy for the night hours.

Issued by the Ministry of Information in co-operation with the War Office and the Ministry of Home Security

Beating the INVADER

A MESSAGE FROM THE PRIME MINISTER

IF invasion comes, everyone—young or old, men and women—will be eager to play their part worthily. By far the greater part of the country will not be immediately involved. Even along our coasts, the greater part will remain unaffected. But where the enemy lands, or tries to land, there will be most violent fighting. Not only will there be the battles when the enemy tries to come ashore, but afterwards there will fall upon his lodgments very heavy British counter-attacks, and all the time the lodgments will be under the heaviest attack by British bombers. The fewer civilians or non-combatants in these areas, the better—apart from essential workers who must remain. So if you are advised by the authorities to leave the place where you live, it is your duty to go elsewhere when you are told to leave. When the attack begins, it will be too late to go ; and, unless you receive definite instructions to move, your duty then will be to stay where you are. You will have to get into the safest place you can find, and stay there until the battle is over. For all of you then the order and the duty will be : " STAND FIRM ".

This also applies to people inland if any considerable number of parachutists or air-borne troops are landed in their neighbourhood. Above all, they must not cumber the roads. Like their fellow-countrymen on the coasts, they must " STAND FIRM ". The Home Guard, supported by strong mobile columns wherever the enemy's numbers require it, will immediately come to grips with the invaders, and there is little doubt will soon destroy them.

Throughout the rest of the country where there is no fighting going on and no close cannon fire or rifle fire can be heard, everyone will govern his conduct by the second great order and duty, namely, " CARRY ON ". It may easily be some weeks before the invader has been totally destroyed, that is to say, killed or captured to the last man who has landed on our shores. Meanwhile, all work must be continued to the utmost, and no time lost.

The following notes have been prepared to tell everyone in rather more detail what to do, and they should be carefully studied. Each man and woman should think out a clear plan of personal action in accordance with the general scheme.

Winston S. Churchill

STAND FIRM

1. What do I do if fighting breaks out in my neighbourhood?

Keep indoors or in your shelter until the battle is over. If you can have a trench ready in your garden or field, so much the better. You may want to use it for protection if your house is damaged. But if you are at work, or if you have special orders, carry on as long as possible and only take cover when danger approaches. If you are on your way to work, finish your journey if you can.

If you see an enemy tank, or a few enemy soldiers, do not assume that the enemy are in control of the area. What you have seen may be a party sent on in advance, or stragglers from the main body who can easily be rounded up.

Above and overleaf: a leaflet issued to the population by the British Government. (Lionel Leventhal Collection)

CARRY ON

2. What do I do in areas which are some way from the fighting?

Stay in your district and carry on. Go to work whether in shop, field, factory or office. Do your shopping, send your children to school until you are told not to. Do not try to go and live somewhere else. Do not use the roads for any unnecessary journey; they must be left free for troop movements even a long way from the district where actual fighting is taking place.

3. Will certain roads and railways be reserved for the use of the Military, even in areas far from the scene of action?

Yes, certain roads will have to be reserved for important troop movements; but such reservations should be only temporary. As far as possible, bus companies and railways will try to maintain essential public services, though it may be necessary to cut these down. Bicyclists and pedestrians may use the roads for journeys to work, unless instructed not to do so.

ADVICE AND ORDERS

4. Whom shall I ask for advice?

The police and A.R.P. wardens.

5. From whom shall I take orders?

In most cases from the police and A.R.P. wardens. But there may be times when you will have to take orders from the military and the Home Guard in uniform.

6. Is there any means by which I can tell that an order is a true order and not faked?

You will generally know your policeman and your A.R.P. wardens by sight, and can trust them. With a bit of common sense you can tell if a soldier is really British or only pretending to be so. If in doubt ask a policeman, or ask a soldier whom you know personally.

INSTRUCTIONS

7. What does it mean when the church bells are rung?

It is a warning to the local garrison that troops have been seen landing from the air in the neighbourhood of the church in question. Church bells will *not* be rung all over the country as a general warning that invasion has taken place. The ringing of church bells in one place will not be taken up in neighbouring churches.

8. Will instructions be given over the wireless?

Yes; so far as possible. But remember that the enemy can overhear any wireless message, so that the wireless cannot be used for instructions which might give him valuable information.

9. In what other ways will instructions be given?

Through the Press; by loudspeaker vans; and perhaps by leaflets and posters. But remember that genuine Government leaflets will be given to you only by the policeman, your A.R.P. warden or your postman; while genuine posters and instructions will be put up only on Ministry of Information notice boards and official sites, such as police stations, post offices, A.R.P. posts, town halls and schools.

FOOD

10. Should I try to lay in extra food?

No. If you have already laid in a stock of food, keep it for a real emergency; but do not add to it. The Government has made arrangements for food supplies.

NEWS

11. Will normal news services continue?

Yes. Careful plans have been made to enable newspapers and wireless broadcasts to carry on, and in case of need there are emergency measures which will bring you the news. But if there should be some temporary breakdown in news supply, it is very important that you should not listen to rumours nor pass them on, but should wait till real news comes through again. Do not use the telephones or send telegrams if you can possibly avoid it.

MOTOR-CARS

12. Should I put my car, lorry or motor-bicycle out of action?

Yes, when you are told to do so by the police, A.R.P. wardens or military; or when it is obvious that there is an immediate risk of its being seized by the enemy—then disable and hide your bicycle and destroy your maps.

13. How should it be put out of action?

Remove distributor head and leads and either empty the tank or remove the carburettor. If you don't know how to do this, find out now from your nearest garage. In the case of diesel engines remove the injection pump and connection. The parts removed must be hidden well away from the vehicle.

THE ENEMY

14. Should I defend myself against the enemy?

The enemy is not likely to turn aside to attack separate houses. If small parties are going about threatening persons and property in an area not under enemy control and come your way, you have the right of every man and woman to do what you can to protect yourself, your family and your home.

GIVE ALL THE HELP YOU CAN TO OUR TROOPS

Do not tell the enemy anything

Do not give him anything

Do not help him in any way

The Royal Navy pulls back

Dowding had his way. Convoys in future would be reduced in number and would make the passage past Dover only at night. The interception of raiders would be concentrated upon their incursions overland to avoid the perils of fighting over water. At the same time, the Admiralty unwillingly withdrew its destroyers from Dover and sent them to join those at Portsmouth.[3] This, as the delighted and optimistic Kesselring was quick to point out, was a tactical victory of the utmost importance. The removal of the destroyers and the noticeable reluctance, next day, of RAF fighters to engage, presented both the Luftwaffe and the Kriegsmarine with the opportunity to do as they pleased in daytime in the Straits. Above all, it permitted German shipping to move at will, for their surface minelaying to be extended by day at a greater distance from the French coast, while U-boats and aircraft concentrated upon planting the fields in British waters and for them to harass British minesweepers. It meant also that, while the gathering of shipping for the invasion was as yet imperceptible to the British (whose reconnaissance was severely hampered by German fighters and guns), the likelihood of its coming had been more convincingly imposed on British minds and with it the realization that, no matter how forewarned they might be, the chances of preventing it were reduced by the brute strength of the enemy.

Closely though the rest of the world was scrutinizing the lessons from the First Battle of the Straits of Dover, as this series of interconnected confrontations is now called, it was by no means unconscious of significant events taking place in the Mediterranean. After Italy had completed her lustreless campaign against southern France (which had been brought to an end by the Armistice without achieving noticeable results) it had been expected that the Italians would turn their full offensive capabilities against the British. Instead, the boot was on the other foot, for it was the British who tackled the Italians, lightly bombing their factories in Milan and Turin, putting up a staunch defence of Malta with three obsolescent Gladiator fighters at Malta against ineffectual air raids by Regia Aeronautica, maintaining a well-displayed presence at sea to the discomfort of the Italian Fleet (which mostly stayed in port) and harrying Italian land forces in East Africa and on the frontier with Egypt and Cyrenaica. The fighting was never heavy, but nowhere could the Italians claim the initiative. Therefore, Vice-Admiral Somerville's Force H, which assembled at Gibraltar on 1 July, had its hands free for operations elsewhere.

Tragedy at Oran

Something had to be done about the French Fleet where it lay, largely in ports controlled by the Vichy French Government or, in lesser numbers, in British controlled harbours. As June went by and the German threat to Britain seemed to grow, the neutralization of this potent naval force became essential, if only to ensure freedom of action for British naval units against an invasion, apart from the daunting prospect of these ships later being used by the Germans in their own interests. Even if the British Government had been aware of Admiral Darlan's instructions to his captains never to let the warships fall into German hands, it could not have rested easy. Cheerlessly, it was decided by the British on 27 June to take pre-emptive action. On 3 July they moved, taking almost bloodless charge and disarming two old battleships, eight destroyers and three submarines in Portsmouth and Plymouth while neutralizing, also, a battleship, four cruisers and three destroyers in Alexandria. At Oran, however, where the best operational units of the French Fleet lay (including their two most modern battlecruisers), Somerville's request to Admiral Gensoul for a peaceful surrender was rejected and here, in accordance with his orders and previous warnings given, he opened fire. In this dolorous action something far more important and harmful than a battleship sunk, a battlecruiser crippled, besides smaller ships seriously damaged and the loss of over 1,000 French sailors' lives occurred. French feelings were deeply wounded and the nation's sympathy for Britain was forfeited with the immediate consequence of the bombing of Force H at Gibraltar and the breaking off of diplomatic relations on 5 July. But American public opinion, as well as that of many other neutral nations, was favourably influenced by what was recognized as an unwelcome and painful decision bravely taken by the British, and a bold expression of their determination to fight, might and main, for survival regardless of the risk to past and failing alliances. Despite traditional sentiments of sympathy for France, US public opinion veered closer to Britain's side at this news. At the same time, the British Admiralty heaved a sigh of relief, satisfied that its forces in the Mediterranean could now concentrate upon cleaning up scattered Italian ships at sea while ensuring the enemy Fleet did not venture freely out of port.[4] If the First Battle of the Dover Straits had been a set-back, the opening phase of the Mediterranean campaign represented a positive gain for the British.

VI

ASSUMPTIONS AND PLANS

Jeschonnek puts on the pressure

By good fortune, Hans Jeschonnek, the Luftwaffe's Chief of Staff, had arranged to visit Kesselring at the latter's command post on the cliffs at Wissant on 30 June, and he had asked Sperrle of Luftflotte 3 to join them there. Looking out over the Channel at the cliffs of Dover as the air battle raged in the distance, they discussed current progress in their preparation for the invasion. Rather to their surprise, Kesselring had little to show them in the way of combat. A convoy had gone through during the night, but early morning reconnaissance had shown that shipping was giving a wide berth to the Straits of Dover and being diverted elsewhere. Free-chase missions by fighters had also faded away after they had come to blows with British fighters over Hythe, for the British had displayed an unusual disinclination to pursue the Messerschmitts home – as previously had been their habit. Indeed, General W. Martini's radio monitoring service had overheard the RAF controllers ordering their pilots to break off the engagement. It was now necessary, Kesselring asserted, to find fresh targets the enemy would feel bound to defend. But this, as Jeschonnek pointed out, could put the British under such pressure that they might come to expect the invasion at an earlier date than the Germans wished them to do. Within a couple of days, no doubt, the cat would be out of the bag when the main stream of German shipping began to flow towards the western invasion ports, but in the meantime every avoidance of alarming the enemy was a contribution to the achievement of surprise.

The Luftwaffe's leaders had also to take into account the current state of balance in the air war. The efficient way the British fighters were being committed to battle and the existence of locating radar sets, which were better than their own, interested without worrying the Germans unduly. They tended to underestimate the effect of the system of control they could hear, believing it to be localized and not integral to a centralized organisation. And although the Germans realized that they were outmatched in this one aspect of technology and technique, they were also satisfied that the British Early Warning arrangements had defects. Their low-flying aircraft often got through undetected and sometimes the Fighter Controllers were heard in confusion, sending desperate counter-orders after things had gone wrong when, quite frequently, the expert German fighter leaders had outmanoeuvred their adversaries. They knew that, despite relatively heavy casualties among their bombers, the exchange rate in fighter casualties stood in their favour and that the achievement of surprise and superior numbers at the point of contact was more to their advantage than that of their opponents. Free-chase missions were proving effective, although it was hard to persevere with these when the bomber pilots complained plaintively to Goering, who tended to side with them, and ask that the fighters abandon the free-chase and fly instead as close escorts to the bombers.

All were agreed that it was essential to draw the RAF into major actions as a preliminary to the opening of the major assault on its airfields planned for 9 July, but Sperrle's suggestion, that the airfields be attacked immediately, was overruled purely on the grounds that the deception plan might be compromised. Jeschonnek proposed, with Kesselring's concurrence, that the attack on shipping be delivered henceforward on the widest possible frontage, and directed also against the naval ports, in particular Devonport, Portland, Portsmouth, Sheerness, Harwich and the Humber where the destroyers were known to berth by day.

Although to Dowding and his Group Commanders the change in the enemy pattern of operations was not immediately perceptible next day (the 1st), it was soon apparent that their opponents were in more deadly earnest than ever. After what looked like the customary build-up of a morning raid over the Pas de Calais, radar plots began to proliferate from Lands End to Kingston upon Hull. Within 20 minutes of their starting to close in, the largest air battle of the campaign had broken out on a wide front, with small formations of German bombers making for the naval dockyards while fighter packs ranged both close at hand and on wide sweeps, the latter endeavouring to forestall the British fighters as they clambered for altitude. A jumble of plots covered the controllers' tables as Fighter Command found itself stretched. And while the balance of losses, both in this onslaught and those which followed, was like that of the previous day, it was disconcerting to find that

The German High Command in debate. Standing, left to right: Jodl, von Brauchitsch, Raeder and Keitel; seated, back to camera: Goering, Hitler. (Author's collection)

eneral Sir Edmund Ironside, Commander-in-Chief of the British Home Forces. (*Illustrated*)

Sir Dudley Pound, the British First Sea Lord. (*Illustrated*)

Air Marshal Sir Cyril Newall, British Chief of the Air Staff. (*Illustrated*)

Air Marshal Sir Hugh Dowding, commanding RAF Fighter Command. (*Illustrated*)

bove left: A typical Chain Home radar station to detect aircraft at long range. The tall towers are the ansmitters; the smaller ones are the receivers. (Imperial War Museum).
eft: An Englishman's idea of invasion, June 1940, as shown in *Picture Post*. A highly optimistic solution, is was unlikely to work.

MH 9893

Above left: Winston Churchill inspects some rudimentary defences. (Imperial War Museum)
Left: A British 3-inch anti-aircraft gun on a First World War chassis in London. Mostly of use only against low-flying aircraft, their noise did help to stiffen civilian morale. (Ian V. Hogg)
Above: Kesselring directing his air fleet from his 'Holy Mountain' at the Pas de Calais. (Kesselring)

Above: A 9.2-inch gun of the Citadel Battery, Dover. It gave little protection to its crew. (Ian V. Hogg)
Above right: A 6-inch gun of the Langdon Battery, Dover — a first objective for the German glider troops. (Ian V. Hogg).
Right: The cliffs at Dover, from a contemporary German military topographical guide to England, *Bildheft England insgesamt.* (Lionel Leventhal Collection).
Below: A typical emergency beach battery — 4-inch gun with only 100 rounds per gun. (Ian V. Hogg).

Above: A German 28cm long-range gun, capable of harassing British convoys and giving support to the landings. (Ian V. Hogg)
Below: Folkestone under fire.

the enemy bombers had several times reached their targets. Small ships had been damaged at Hull, Harwich and Devonport, and a destroyer was hard hit at Sheerness. At Portsmouth, in particular, extensive damage was inflicted on the dockyard facilities and in the nearby town. Sheerness had escaped harm when the raiders were driven off, but an enterprising He 111 Staffel had bombed RAF Station Hornchurch and caused extensive damage to buildings and some aircraft on the ground at this important Sector Station.

To the British, the inference drawn from the air fighting on 1 July was of a shift in the weight of attack from the Straits of Dover to East Anglia, to add conviction to the appreciation that it was here the main enemy invasion would be made. German minelaying that night in the Thames Estuary, and an attack by S boats, cruising in silence in the darkness of a moonless night, on a convoy off Southwold reinforced that contention, particularly when aircraft of Coastal Command returned from patrolling between the Hook of Holland and Ostend to say they had seen a number of small craft entering the mouth of the River Maas.[1]

Doubts in the Kriegsmarine

By this time, the German plans, incomplete though they may have appeared to many of those deputed to execute them, had reached an advanced state. A lack of confidence within the Kriegsmarine remained, but for the time being the attempt to block 'Sealion' had been abandoned, if only because the danger of an operation, forced on them against Raeder's will, demanded every effort to mitigate its worse effects. Without the support of the other Services, whose enthusiasm was waxing, Raeder could not defy Hitler, who was adamant. So the sailors doggedly went about their duties of assembling the motley collection of *Prahms*, drifters, tugs and ferries before sending them by sea and inland waterways to the assembly ports, commencing on the evening of 1/2 July. Ahead had gone minesweepers and escort craft such as the fast, armed R motor boats and the armed trawlers with their backing of destroyers. Rotterdam and Antwerp were first to harbour the fleet, then successively Ostend, Dunkirk and Calais, followed at the last moment by Boulogne on 10 July. Thus the impression imparted to the British, that the West Country and the south-east coast were not seriously threatened, was maintained to the last.

The main fighting elements of the Kriegsmarine were divided into two wings. That to the westward comprised 15 U-boats and ten destroyers whose task was to harass British attempts against the western flank of the invasion. The eastward wing was the strongest, consisting of six U-boats and the remainder of the major surface units: they were to escort the invasion fleet, hold off the Royal Navy units in the North Sea and provide such bombardment facilities as they could spare during the actual landing. From the start this looked too tall an order, for they would be outnumbered in every department, their existence in peril the moment they cleared the shoals off the Belgian coast after leaving Antwerp. The sole comfort lay in being able to read about 30 per cent of the British Admiralty's Fleet ciphers (which they had been doing for some time past) and therefore to know sufficiently what countermeasures the enemy contemplated.[2]

How to provide fire support at the moment of landing caused much concern. It was realized that this was the moment of maximum peril, and that even a weak enemy, who was not under fire, could wreak havoc during disembarkation. The cross-Channel guns would make a contribution and engage British guns, but their rate of fire and accuracy were neither all-destructive nor suppressive against the landing sites, upon which they would finally play just prior to the assault. All that the Kriegsmarine could offer in the way of heavy fire support would come from the 11in guns of the old battleships *Schlesien* and *Schleswig Holstein*. It was Lütjens's idea to position them, aground if necessary on the Varne, to act as floating batteries for the dual purpose of supporting the landings and helping to deal with enemy ships approaching from the north.[3] Inevitably, the programme of direct fire support was of an improvised nature, provided by ex naval and artillery pieces mounted on *Prahms* and other shallow draught coasters, and supplemented by the Luftwaffe's 88mm guns on the Siebel ferries whose task it also was to deposit those guns on the enemy shore once a lodgement had been made. Practice had demonstrated the impossibility of producing accurate fire from small ships against pin-point targets. It was cheerfully hoped that the noise would simultaneously frighten the enemy while encouraging the German troops; destructive effects would be a bonus.

Reservations among the generals

Nobody on the German side underrated the British fighting spirit. From experience, the commanders and staff of Generaloberst Gerd Von Rundstedt's Army Group A (which had overall responsibility for the land operations) expected a tough fight and realized that they could not rely on simply cowing the enemy. Believing that the most potent bombardment force actually needed to destroy the enemy during the opening phases of the attack would have to be bombers, particularly dive-bombers, they were uncomfortably aware that these aircraft were proving extremely vulnerable to British fighters. Therefore, von Rundstedt insisted, it was essential that the air be totally cleared of RAF fighters before his troops stepped ashore.

Confidence among the airmen

The Luftwaffe's plan was governed by a timetable which was geared to the optimum conditions of tides and light, although it was capable also of accepting slight variations to fit in with variable weather conditions. On 1 July, S Day stayed fixed at 13 July and, therefore, the moment for the all-out assault on the RAF airfields, which was programmed for S minus 5, was set for 8 July. By then, it was assumed, the RAF fighter strength would be sufficiently depleted to permit the initial strike against radar installations and the forward airfields to be executed against relatively light opposition. Thereafter it was intended to tackle the inland airfields and, progressively, like a creeping artillery barrage, destroy by S minus 1 (12 July) the roots of RAF power, making it impossible for the British to mount serious resistance in the vicinity of the coastal belt. On S minus 1, therefore, operations would enter their next phase; while pressure would be maintained against Fighter Command by means of harassing raids on airfields and by fighter sweeps, the preponderance of the bomber effort would be switched to softening-up the selected beachhead zone by attacks against known targets between Dover and Dymchurch, which had not been allocated to the Channel guns, as well as against the defences of Manston, Lympne and Hawkinge airfields.

The leading echelons of 500 transport aircraft carrying the airborne divisions to their dropping zones would take off from their bases and link up with the force of DFS 230 assault gliders and their tugs, which had been assembled secretly on an airfield in France. Simultaneously, the 150 Fiesler Storch monoplanes would rendezvous with their passengers at an airfield close to Lille. The tasks of the airborne troops, upon whom the establishment of a bridgehead chiefly depended, were to seize dominating ground immediately adjacent to the beaches selected for seaborn assault, to knock out the known coastal battery positions and quickly take possession of fields from which transport aircraft could land and take-off. Bearing in mind that the landing of troops amidst heavily defended areas during the invasion of Holland had been costly in machines and men, Generalmajor Putzier (the overall airborne commander) decided that, except in the case of special *coup de main* parties, the main assault would avoid such well protected places as airfields and, instead, land nearby and capture them on foot. Remembering, too, the possibility of the parachute units becoming scattered by attempting to seize too many objectives simultaneously, he decided to concentrate on two main sectors and capture them by the sheer mass of one parachute regiment arriving on each, while the third regiment was brought forward into France, but held back in reserve. Special missions by gliderborne infantry and engineers would attempt to repeat their performance of 10 May, when they had knocked out the Belgian forts of Eban Emael. They would try to land on top of the Langdon and Citadel Batteries on either side of Dover, and deposit infantry on the cliff tops near Aycliff and above Lydden Spout so as to dominate the beaches below. 19th Parachute Regiment would land on the wide open spaces between West Hougham and Hawkinge and from there move to the aid of the glider troops, mount an assault on Hawkinge and develop air-strips from which Ju 52s could operate. 20th Parachute Regiment would drop behind Hythe, in the triangle Newington. Sene Golf Course and Sandling Station, and seize the ridge overlooking the long sweep of open beaches between Sandgate and Hythe, so as to take in rear the beach defence, cut the main A20 road from the west and threaten Lympne airfield. It was then intended to bring in 21st Parachute Regiment to any one of these localities, and for 22nd Air Landing Division to be brought in by stages from airfields in France to the vicinity of Hawkinge with a view to advancing in the direction of Canterbury to the north and capturing the Postling – Elham ridge. Everything possible was to be done to confuse the enemy. Dummy parachutists were to be scattered over a wide surrounding zone and parties from Infanterie Regiment Grossdeutschland were to be landed in Storches on the northern periphery of the main airfield to occupy communication centres, cause confusion and disrupt the movement of enemy reserves. Of particular concern to this group was the immediate elimination of anti-aircraft guns, which had already been pin-pointed as the prime defenders of Hawkinge airfield. But a plan to send in special raiding parties, from the Abwehr's Special Unit 800, to prevent blockships being sunk in the entrances to Dover harbour was cancelled when it was noticed that the British had already begun this task of denial.

Formation 'Pig Pile'

From the outset it was realized by the Germans that foul weather and severe tidal conditions could disrupt the seaborne assault, even if it still remained possible to fly in the airborne echelon, and even if the enemy resistance were beaten down to a minimum. The handling of small craft, many of them inherently unwieldy, would be difficult in any conditions. Under enemy fire and in the hands of inexperienced seamen, who had been granted scanty time for training and rehearsal, the prospects of chaos were immeasurably greater. The survival of the seaborne divisions in Generalleutnant Heinrich von Vietinghoff's XIII Corps depended on the determination of the sailors in getting their craft ashore, and the hope that, in the turmoil, a sufficient number of soldiers would bind themselves into knots of aggressive resistance to win room for the succeeding waves of troops to assemble, prior to advancing boldly inland. Although the maintenance of strict orthodox formations was the aim, Ruge's belief that Formation 'Pig Pile' would prevail was never far away from the thoughts of both planners and executants.

High water on Saturday 13 July would be at 0459 hours, nearly two hours after first light. To take advantage, therefore, of the weaker neap tidal streams at this moment, it was felt desirable to fix S Hour (the time at which the assault troops would touch the beaches) at 0430 hours. This would permit 1½ hours of daylight for a heavy artillery and air bombardment of the beach defences, and would be timed about an hour after the paratroops had landed (scheduled for 0315 hours, at S minus 75 minutes). These arrangements would allow the naval convoys to cross the Straits through previously swept channels in comparative darkness. They also gave scope to postpone the operation by three days should the need arise. Preceded by minesweepers and escorted by destroyers, S boats and coasters, the heterogeneous convoys of German beach assault craft were intended to arrive within two miles of their destination, where they would form up for the final run in. Both the 6th Mountain Division (Generalmajor Ferdinand Schoerner), on the right, and the 17th Infantry Division (Generalmajor Herbert Loch), on the left, planned to land on a two-regimental front, each with a leading wave of 650 men, who would be carried close to the shore in minesweeper fishing boats before transferring to fast rubber storm boats powered by outboard motors. Close behind would follow a second wave of similar size, but carried in motorized *Prahms*. In this second wave, along with motor coasters and Siebel ferries, mounting 37mm anti-tank guns, 75mm field guns and 88mm dual-purpose guns, would sail the special *Prahms* with extending ramps, carrying the deep wading tanks whose task was to appear out of the sea within a few minutes of the leading infantry going ashore.

The logistic survival of the Germans would depend very much on their ability quickly to clear a wide and deep bridgehead into which supplies and reinforcements could be delivered, safe from British observation and direct fire. The oft repeated watchword to the assault troops demanded: 'Clear the beaches and drive for the heights,[4] – then link up with the airborne forces.' But it was also vital that they rapidly capture ports if the momentum of the advance was to be kept up, for both beach and air supply might well have embarrassing limitations.

Von Vietinghoff, with General Busch's full approval, instructed 6th Mountain Division to swing right immediately after landing, so as to surround and capture Dover without delay, and take possession of the high ground on either side of Temple Ewell, astride the A2 main road. 17th Infantry Division was to link up with the paratroops near Hythe, prior to advancing left to capture Lympne airfield. It was also to complete the capture of Folkestone and reinforce the airborne soldiers as best it could in securing the high ground between Lyminge and Elham where a line of anti-tank guns was to be emplaced as a bulwark against the expected tank counter-attacks. To the rear of these objectives, the bridgehead could be consolidated by each division's second echelon, by the arrival of 9th Panzer Division (on S plus 1) and the build-up of supplies by ships through the captured harbours. Once that had been accomplished, mobile operations could be aimed northwards on S plus 2 (15 July) with a view to seizing east Kent.

One among several imponderable contingencies particularly worried the German planners – the weather. Goering insisted on four days' good weather as a prerequisite to opening the major air offensive. Equally important to him on S Day would be reasonably clear visibility and light breezes for the fly-in of the airborne formations. For the same reasons, Raeder and von Brauchitsch demanded smooth waters so as to give their forces a sporting chance of reaching the shore intact. But short-range weather forecasting, let alone long-term estimates, were always a gamble by the German meteorological branches, because the basic information at their disposal was sketchy. Apart from random reports from neutral ships, and the sparse information gathered daily by long-range flights over the Atlantic by Focke-Wulf Condors, there was little upon which to base accurate forecasts. Quite often surprise developments took place with the weather, causing radical last minute changes of plan, particularly for the Luftwaffe which depended very much on reasonable visibility to find its targets and return safely to base.

The Intelligence battle – the German view

Since, prior to the outbreak of war in September 1939, it had not been the prime intention of Germany to come to blows with Britain, low priority had been allocated to the gathering of Intelligence or to the planting of agents within the British Isles. The RAF's fighter and bomber strength was known with some accuracy, but not the shortage of pilots. Luftwaffe Intelligence did not rate the RAF's operational capability very high, dismissing the bomber force for its inaccuracy as of 'nuisance value but [it] will in no way be decisive' and seeing the fighters as inferior to the German fighters. 'The Luftwaffe,' it was declared, 'is clearly superior to the RAF as regards strength, equipment, training, command and location of bases.'[5] And yet it was in some respects ignorant of its adversary, being unaware of the actual function of the various airfields it had located, and in the dark about the nature and efficiency of the fighter control system.

Rather similar conclusions could be drawn about the Germans' knowledge of Britain's land defences. They knew there were grave deficiencies of weapons and they were aware of the whereabouts of the central reserves and the coastal crust units. From this they deduced that the British had abandoned the idea of holding the coastal strip and would pin their hopes upon the mounting of a counter-attack with unified forces after the Army had landed. Of the beach defences they knew little, although aerial photographs were beginning to show where a few major works were in progress. They knew of the pre-war coastal battery sites, and had acquired, from recent experience, a detailed knowledge of anti-aircraft gun sites and their zones of fire.[6] Four agents, sent in by sea, had been captured before they could transmit information, but a certain amount was being gleaned from foreign journalists who had been given permission by the British Ministry of Information to take photographs along the 'invasion coast' (to the indignation of some British journalists who were denied such facilities).[7] Nothing the Germans found out led them to fear that the narrow-fronted assault which they had adopted would lead to disaster – unless, that is, things went badly for them at sea.

The deployment of the major units of the Royal Navy was also well known to the Germans, and from this they could quite accurately work out the strategy and tactics which might be employed once the direction of the invasion had become plain to the Admiralty. In other words, they visualized local interceptions in the early stages of the invasion being contained by their own light forces in the approaches to the Straits of Dover, and, thereafter, a much sterner battle against heavier units converging on the danger area – a threat which would be hard to contain even if the Luftwaffe measured up to its promises. Raeder planned to bring his cruisers and a pocket battleship (*Admiral Scheer*) from the Baltic to Wilhelmshaven on S Day minus 2, with a view to using them against the British light forces in the first phase of the battle. If the *Gneisenau* could be patched up in time, she would be sent against the British cruisers. 'After that,' Raeder bleakly remarked to Schniewind, 'It will be in the lap of the Gods, but I do not expect to welcome home many of our ships if the British battleships are brought south from Scotland. It might have been different if both *Scharnhorst* and *Gneisenau* had been fit for action.' By way of compensation, therefore, Raeder had to be content with deception measures, by the transmission of false radio signals to give the impression that both battlecruisers were fit for action and posed a deterrent, therefore, to the precipitous movement of British battleships against the Straits of Dover.

Meanwhile, the advantage of adopting the narrow instead of the broad-fronted approach were becoming daily more apparent to the German Naval authorities. With fewer craft and a smaller expanse of water to guard, the mining and escort problem was simplified and minimized. Also it made possible the elimination of towed *Prahms* from the assault; those would have been needed, despite their clumsiness, if the broad front had been adopted. Crewing was strengthened, and fewer inexperienced seamen were included. A smaller minelaying and minesweeping task placed a lighter load on the relatively few special vessels available; Ruge became increasingly confident that he could carry out his task, providing the preliminary operations were started on S minus 8 (they began, in fact, before that). With towed craft out of the reckoning, the problems of getting the unwieldy invasion fleet through the canal locks, through the harbours and out to sea was likely to be easier and quicker; furthermore, average speed of convoys at sea was raised from 3 to between 4 and 5 knots. As a result, the landing units on the longest voyage (Ostend to Dover) would take only about 14 hours to make the crossing and, therefore, loading need not begin until the morning of S minus 1, if they were to sail that afternoon in order to make landfall at sunrise next day. Those ships sailing from Calais and Boulogne, therefore, would not have to put to sea until last light, while those which put to sea earlier in daylight might easily be passed off as a routine commercial convoy.

The British remained miserably uncertain about German plans. Their air reconnaissance discovered only the most meagre information, much of it at a stiff price in aircraft as the German air defences improved. Few agents were properly established and their means of communication across the Channel were tenuous. A certain amount of German radio traffic, including a mass of talk between aircraft, provided useful information, particularly with regard to the orders sent out every evening to Luftwaffe units detailing operations for the next day, and the pre-raid testing of radios. But the operational instructions enabled Dowding to form only an outline picture of what was in store, and to take counter-measures of a general nature. For, in their approach to battle, the German commanders of the lower echelons had a habit of introducing tactical variations which could not be foreseen – even by those who had issued the original orders. In any case, only scraps of German long-term schemes could be heard over the air because the vast majority of planning took place in conference and through the passing of papers by hand and down land lines of communication. Ruefully, British Intelligence admitted that, until the first barges were detected moving towards Dunkirk on the night of 1 July, they had no inkling that an invasion might be imminent – and even then they steadfastly declined to draw positive conclusions from the first invasion convoy sightings.

At that moment, British Naval Intelligence held the view that at least 60 per cent of any invading fleet would have to come from the German ports, leaving only 25 per cent from those where it actually was coming from. On successive days, GS I (x) at GHQ Home Forces reiterated its conviction that the main invasion fleet must come from the Baltic ports, and on 11 July declared that 'The increase in shipping in Rotterdam and Amsterdam increases the potential threat to our coast north of the Thames. It also means that a part of the effort previously expected from the Baltic may now come from these ports.' The Prime Minister persisted in his belief that 'It will be very difficult for the enemy to place large, well-equipped bodies of troops on the east coast of England . . .' and that it would be 'Even more unlikely . . . that the south coast would be attacked.' The Chiefs of Staff concurred, worrying that the allocation of one third of their available divisions to the defence of the south coast was over-insurance. So, when reports arrived of shipping movements and the gathering of barges in the invasion ports, the Invasion Warning Sub-Committee (which had been set up on 31 May by the Joint Services Intelligence Committee) dismissed them as part of normal trade 'perhaps to alleviate the problems caused by the blockage of canals and rivers'.[8] Likewise, Vice-Admiral Ramsay's Staff at Dover Command suggested that 'some of the traffic might have destinations as far off as Spain or Portugal'.[9] And in the same way, the Invasion Warning Sub-Committee brushed off a report on 1 July that all leave had been stopped in the German Army as 'the sort of thing likely to happen in any Army'.[10] Even if members of the War Office and Air Ministry Intelligence Directorates were far less sanguine, it remained a pernicious manifestation of the Joint Service Committee's misappreciation that the Chiefs of Staff delayed switching the RAF's bomber offensive from economic targets to those directly related to the invasion threat.

Dowding could no more afford to reinforce 11 Group than he dared to put at risk the vital industrial targets of the Midlands by taking fighters away from 10, 12 and 13 Groups, now that the enemy had air bases within easy range of the entire eastern and southern seaboards. He had also to pay heed to the Intelligence estimate of a greater threat to East Anglia than south-east England, and be careful not to be deflected into committing too high a proportion of his sparse forces in defence of a subsidiary sector. At this stage there was no chance of his destroying so preponderant a foe: he had to strive for deterrence through the infliction of disproportionate losses while conserving his strength for the ultimate day of reckoning when invasion came and everything would have to be thrown in. His policy was to employ squadrons in pairs instead of in big wings of four, such as had been deployed over Dunkirk. As a result, his pilots usually fought at a gross inferiority in numbers and more than 200 aircraft were lost between 5–7 July, as opposed to only 125 by the Luftwaffe: moreover, the ratio of fighter losses was RAF 73: Luftwaffe 95. This could not be allowed to continue, especially as it exceeded production.

The battle for the Straits is joined

On 7 July, the Chiefs of Staff at last conceded the likelihood of an imminent invasion and gave orders that enemy shipping now to be seen in the Channel ports was to be bombed as of first priority. In fact, they merely confirmed what had been practised the previous night when, in showery weather, Hampden and Blenheim bombers of Air-Marshal Sir Charles Portal's Bomber Command had struck at Dunkirk and Calais. Observers and newspaper reporters on the cliffs above Dover saw the enemy coastline illuminated by flares, searchlights and gun and bomb flashes, and the stories they wrote tended to discredit the carefully censored, assuaging news of the intensive attacks being launched upon 'The Invasion Ports', as those harbours across the Channel were known to the public. Nobody who saw had any doubt that the real Battle for Britain had begun. All at once, the populace came to sense that invasion was near to hand. On the following night it was announced that the major part of Bomber Command, including its more powerful Wellingtons and Whitleys, had been committed to the attack upon the Invasion Ports and that, in addition, raids had been made on enemy airfields. Omitted from these reports was the fact that these attacks had been relatively ineffectual. It is true that some bombs did find targets, and that thirty or more barges and light craft were sunk or put out of action, but the attacks on enemy airfields were virtually a waste of effort. During the past month the latter had cost 30 bombers, but so rarely did the bomber crews find or reach their targets that they had destroyed only four German aircraft.[11]

Of more deadly portent to both sides was the intervention by the Royal Navy which joined in the bombardment by night, the cruisers and three destroyers from Sheerness venturing out at speed on 7/8 July to rain shells on Ostend and Dunkirk before returning safely to port to avoid the wrath of the Luftwaffe by day. The Kriegsmarine reacted immediately to this not unexpected British aggression. Unable to sail the invasion convoys in safety by night, they dispatched them through the Straits by day, in full view of the British, enjoying as they did the protection afforded by their batteries and air power.[12]

1st (London) Division prepares

On 1 July, with the Channel air battles in full blast, King George VI had visited Folkestone and Hawkinge to see the troops manning the defences, watch the fighters taking off and landing after action and hear the cheers of his people who had stuck grimly to their work and homes. He was accompanied by Liardet, for whose 1st (London) Division the testing time was nigh – and whose deployment was on the eve of adjustment. On 3 July, the division's principal staff officer (GSO 1) had been changed, his successor having hurriedly to learn about the division and its task at the moment its HQ was moving to a new location near Ashford, and just as the 135th Brigade, covering Dymchurch, was reverting to command of the 45th Division.

This major reshuffle of Liardet's forces was intended to make better use of reinforcements as they arrived. Within 2nd (London) Brigade, on 5 July, the 1st Queen's Westminsters handed over to 1st Bn London Rifle Brigade (1st LRB) the responsibility for guarding Hawkinge and Lympne airfields, and themselves moved to Shepherdswell, north of Dover. 1st LRB sent a company to Arpinge (close by the west of Hawkinge) and at the same time was asked by Brigade HQ, to 'consider moving remainder of troops from Horton Park to Sibton Park and Lyminge'. On the 10th, the 35th Infantry Brigade came under command and was sent to the Isle of Sheppey, thus permitting 1st (London) Brigade to relinquish part of its responsibility. But 35th Brigade was in no fit state for a serious encounter with the enemy, having barely recovered from a hammering by Guderian's tanks at Abbeville in May, where it had been employed as a so-called 'digging formation' on lines of communication duties. It had been poorly armed then and was worse off now. Finally, on the 12th, the Training Battalion of the Irish Guards was sent to occupy the Citadel at Dover to defend the Western Heights. Trained and good soldiers as most of its men were, this was only an improvised unit whose arrival in the front line at the last moment would give it scarcely a chance of establishing a coherent defence or familiarizing itself with strange surroundings.[13]

In consequence of these redeployments, the ground defence of Kent was unsettled at a vital moment and, indeed, there had been a diminishment of the mobile forces giving immediate cover to the Folkestone sector. When Churchill visited the area on 11 July he had discovered 'The plight to which we were reduced . . . The Brigadier [2nd Brigade] informed me that he had only three anti-tank guns in his brigade, covering four or five miles of this highly menaced coastline. He declared that he had only six rounds of ammunition for each gun, and he asked me with a slight air of challenge whether he was justified in 'letting his men fire one single round for practice in order that they might at least know how the weapon worked. I replied that we could not afford practice rounds, and that fire should be held for the last moment at the closest range.'[14]

Perhaps it was with this in mind that Churchill minuted Sir Edward Bridges on the 13th: 'I am receiving from various sources suggestions that there should be another day of prayer and humiliation. Will you kindly find out privately what is thought about this by the Archbishop.'[15]

On a more earthly level, the Prime Minister was shocked at an apparent waste of effort: 'I fear that the troops are being used in large numbers on fortifications,' he wrote to Eden, 'At the present stage they should be drilling and training for at least eight hours a day, including one smart parade every morning.'[16] But even as he wrote these lines it was apparent that the time for preparation was almost over and that, any day, the battle, which in the air was reaching its highest pitch of violence, would begin in earnest on the surface.

'We place our trust in the Luftwaffe and the Kriegsmarine'

Three days before Churchill visited the south-east, there had been a top-level conference in Berlin, early in the morning of 8 July, to receive a report by the OKW of the Wehrmacht's readiness to launch 'Sealion' and to designate the actual date when the Luftwaffe would settle upon 'Eagle Day', the commencement of the major assault upon the RAF. During the previous weeks, Hitler had been subjected at intervals to the fluctuating doubts and hopes of his closest advisers, but at all times, although tense with anxiety that he might this time have over-stepped the mark, and yet filled with hope that the British might save him trouble and sue for peace, he had maintained his aim. Admirals and Generals had to come to accept, some of them with fatalistic resignation, the Führer's inflexible determination to take Britain by storm. As a result, the meeting resolved itself into a formal reporting session as each of the Commanders-in Chief pronounced his degree of readiness for the attempt.

To no one's surprise, von Brauchitsch had the fewest reservations. It was easier for the Army, it had ample men and equipment and the state of its training was excellent. 'We place our trust in the Luftwaffe and the Kriegsmarine to deliver us safely to our destination,' he declared, and there were those present who could not help wondering what the reckoning might be if, in the event, the Army found itself sunk at sea or abandoned upon a foreign shore. Grateful as its officers were to the Führer for having restored them to something approaching their previous dignity after the débacle of 1918, there were those within its hierarchy who despised the 'jumped-up corporal' and who railed against every risk he took.

To everybody's surprise, however, Raeder exuded quiet confidence in the outcome. Although he had been heard to say disparagingly to one of his invasion fleet commanders, 'Well how do you really expect to get over to England',[17] the chances of doing so and the favourable reports from officers such as Lütjens and Ruge had rubbed off. Moreover, the apparent withdrawal of British shipping from the Channel and evidence of the damage inflicted on enemy warships encouraged him to hope that, perhaps, the modern air weapon could be substituted for traditional surface forces. So Raeder presented a favourable report. There had been delays in the preparation of the landing craft, there were shortages of self-propelled *Prahms* as well as of escort craft, and extremely unfortunate was the lack of big ships to hold off a determined foray by the Royal Navy, which all knew must come. But there were sufficient reserves of *Prahms* to replace such losses as might be expected from bombardment of the mounting ports, and there seemed no reason to doubt that a lodgement would be made on the opposite shore – providing the weather was kind. 'I would say go,' concluded Raeder as Keitel and Jodl on OKW's behalf gave an almost audible sigh of relief.

His eyes shining, Hitler turned to Goering: 'And what of the Luftwaffe?' he asked.

'Führer,' announced the Field Marshal, 'The Luftwaffe is ready and to-day, as a result of the operations carried out during the last three weeks, there are signs of collapse on the part of the enemy. I can confirm that, providing the weather holds good for four days, the work commenced will be completed. When our airborne divisions take off they will be supported by bombers and fighters which will be free to concentrate upon attacking ground targets. By then the enemy fighters will no longer be in a state to intervene in any strength'. The Field Marshal braced them all by his robust assurance. It mattered not, at this moment, that he held the opinion that 'Sealion' must not disturb or burden the Luftwaffe operations: as things stood, this loosely expressed opinion of his meant the same to them all. Goering spoke again: 'Only one thing remains to be fixed, my Führer – the date for Eagle Day. What can the weather forecasters tell us? Can we rely upon there being four or five days of good flying weather before us?'

'And, for that matter, can we be sure that those good days will be followed by several more with smooth seas?' interjected Raeder.

Jodl read the lastest forecast which had just been prepared. It was reasonably optimistic, even though minor troughs of low pressure were thought to be approaching from the west. Outside the sun shone although over the Channel that day it had become dull with showers developing – none of them bad enough to curtail flying.

'Then I too would say go,' said the Führer, who had satisfied himself before the conference that the conditions fulfilled the minimum required by all three Services. 'Let Eagle Day be tomorrow the 9th, and S Day for 'Sealion' Saturday the 13th.' Then, as if to emphasise his realization of the perils that lay ahead, he pronounced to his Commanders the words which had already been included in his Special Order for S Day to the Nation and the Wehrmacht:

'In the accomplishment of so crucial an enterprise as we are embarked on and upon which the fate of Europe, of Germany and probably the World hangs, great risks have had to be taken and, if necessary, high sacrifices made. Historic issues must be faced without flinching in the service of the cause we support.'

VII

DAYS OF THE EAGLE

The Battle of Britain opens – 8 July

Notwithstanding the confidence with which Goering spoke at the meeting in Berlin on 8 July, when the decision to go ahead with 'Sealion' was taken, he was aware of misgivings among his subordinates grappling with the British over southern England. A night bombardment of the invasion ports by the Royal Navy had taken place which neither the Luftwaffe, nor the Kriegsmarine nor the coastal batteries had been able to prevent. Then there had been a shocking incident at dawn on the 7th when RAF Blenheims from Bomber Command had struck by surprise at Haamstede airfield catching a Staffel of Messerschmitt 109s as they were taxiing out to 'scramble' to their own defence. Seven aircraft were destroyed or seriously damaged, three pilots killed and three wounded, resulting in this unit being withdrawn from operations.[1] The previous evening, Kesselring and his senior commanders had studied the latest combat reports and found that, not only was enemy resistance well sustained, but it was enhanced by an improved percentage of interceptions. German formations were being tackled well out to sea and this, Martini, the Head of Luftwaffe Signals, attributed to radar detection. Most of the radar stations had been plotted by his direction-finders and by photographs, so he now pleaded that they should be destroyed. Already Jeschonnek had authorized Kesselring to do this when he was ready.[2] Now it was decided to attack them on 8 July, the day before 'Eagle Day' which, it was expected, would be the 9th.

Intensive reconnaissance activity throughout the 7th and 8th was, in itself, fair warning of the approaching climax; 200 sorties were flown by the Luftwaffe over southern and eastern England, intermingled with widespread bombing and strafing throughout the hours of daylight.[3] Of prime importance were the strikes at 0900 hours on the 8th, against the CH radar stations at Conewden,

Dunkirk (near Sheerness), Rye and Pevensey, by the élite Operational Proving Unit 210, which specialized with its Me 109s and 110s in hitting pin-point targets. Each attack, taking the defenders by surprise and meeting no opposition, was delivered with extreme accuracy so that, for the time being, only Dunkirk stayed on the air. Likewise, an attack against Ventnor station a few hours later by Ju 88s put it off the air for the next three days. Within a few hours, some of the stations were back on the air,[4] but holes had been punched in the British Early Warning System, and these Kesselring and Sperrle exploited. Covered by free-chase missions, waves of German high-level and dive-bombers launched heavy raids on shipping in the Thames estuary, off Portsmouth and near Portland. Simultaneously, low-level attacks against Lympne and Hawkings airfields by Ju 88s, which arrived totally undetected (as they would have done whatever the state of the CH radar), carpetted both airfields with bombs, destroying buildings as well as several aircraft within the hangars. For a time both airfields were out of action and the bomb craters, even when filled in, thereafter continued to make operations from the grass strips hazardous. But these attacks, devastating as they were, bore only slight comparison with the one against Manston three hours later. This was led at low level by Operational Proving Unit 210, backed up at high level by Do 17s, and caught several fighters on the ground or about to take off. By a miracle only one Blenheim night fighter was destroyed and a few Spitfires slightly damaged, but the harm to ground installations and the morale of the station personnel could not be dismissed as an irrelevance. Both would suffer again and again as, in the days to come, attack followed attack. The fact remained that, for the remainder of the 8th and part, too, of 9 July, these three coastal stations were entirely or partially out of service.

The air fighting of the 8th also produced its heavy toll of casualties to aircraft (destroyed and damaged) and to aircrew:[5]

	RAF	Luftwaffe
Fighters	31, 19 pilots killed, wounded or missing	27, 18 pilots killed, wounded or missing
Bombers	16	21

This rate was proportionately entirely in the German favour, although there was disquiet when it was reported by Martini that the British radar was once more transmitting. Quite wrongly it was concluded that installations such as these could not easily be knocked out, and so they were omitted from the list of targets prepared for the 9th – 'Eagle Day' – a bizarre omission when it is remembered how important these installations were to the efficiency of Fighter Command. Indeed, the entire German plan for what was intended, after all, as a stunning blow to the RAF, contained irrelevant objectives. For one thing, although airfields were principal targets, those attacked, with two exceptions, were not those directly connected with fighter operations: this could be put down to faulty Intelligence. For another, there was no immediate attempt to follow up the successful attacks on Lympne, Hawkinge and Manston, all three of which were important because they belonged to Fighter Command. And there was a facile diversion of effort permitted in that dockyards were left on the target list, admittedly as secondary targets.

Eagle Day – 9 July

In variable visibility, which worsened as cloud built up throughout the morning, the first free-chase German fighter missions of the day preceeded the appearance on Fighter Command's plotting boards of three distinct masses of enemy aircraft. The plots on Park's left flank were seen to be approaching as if to strike east Kent, but continued towards London up the Thames estuary. The centre block came in over Bognor and, for a moment, it was feared that the fighter station at Tangmere would be the target; instead these aircraft too moved inland, making, in fact, for RAF Station Odiham (an Army Co-operation field) and the Royal Aircraft Establishment at Farnborough. Meanwhile, off Portland, the plots resolved themselves into a Kampfgeschwader (KG) of Stukas with the aim of attacking shipping and acting as a diversion from the other raids.

Only the attack in the east made a pronounced impression. 74 Do 17s from KG 2 met weak fighter opposition as they skilfully wove through the deepening clouds to their target at Eastchurch airfield. Their bombs landed squarely on target and caused extensive damage to the operations block, the hangars and the ammunition stores, besides destroying a Spitfire and five Blenheims. For the rest of the day this airfield, used by two fighter squadrons, was out of action. Sheerness was also hit and some small ships damaged, but the detached portion of KG 2 which was responsible had parted from its fighter escort so that, when caught by RAF fighters, it lost five Do 17s with an equal number damaged. Elsewhere, the fighting and the bombing became scattered. A few Ju 88s from KG54 broke through to Odiham without doing much harm and they, in retreat, dropped bombs all over the place including a few on Tangmere airfield. Off Portland, the Stukas damaged an escort vessel and sank a trawler, but fled with Spitfires and Hurricanes in hot pursuit.[6]

In better weather after lunch, the Luftwaffe's performance looked more impressive. Over 250 Ju 87s and 88s, along with Me 109s and 110s, approached from Cherbourg with the intention of bombing Middle Wallop (a Sector Station), Andover and Warmwell airfields. Detected early and intercepted with commendable precision, only a few raiders found their target and the Messerschmitts were caught at a disadvantage by the RAF fighters. Bombers suffered badly and the German fighters failed to score many kills themselves as they fled. However, a swarm of German bombers broke through to their secondary target, Southampton, and extensively damaged the port and some factories as they roared over the Solent. Yet they might have done better, for they passed by the most important target of all in that area, their Intelligence officers being completely oblivious to the fact that the large factory of Supermarine was engaged in the manufacture of Spitfires.

More effective in maintenance of the aim in the crucial fighter war, were the attacks by Luftflotte 2 against Rochford and Detling (Coastal Command) airfields. Although only a handful of bombers found the former, they caused considerable damage to installations and runways, while Detling caught the full blast of a hail of bombs from Ju 87s which hit the station's messes when airmen were going to the evening meal, destroyed 22 aircraft – all of which had an anti-invasion rôle – demolished all the hangars and cratered the runways.

'Eagle Day' had fallen far short of its high-sounding title and grandiose aims. Instead of stunning Fighter Command by strokes to the heart and brain, it had hacked at limbs and sometimes missed even them. Fighter airfields and radar installations had been given time to recover. Command of the German formations had been too flaccid with the result that, confronted by opposition, there had been a marked tendency to head for secondary targets instead of persevering with the destruction of the key, primary ones. At the same time, Fighter Command was dissatisfied that several large enemy formations had wandered as they chose without being brought to battle. And if the results of combats, when they took place, were favourable, it could not be said that the scores for the day taken as a whole were anything upon which to be congratulated, as the following table of fighter and bomber losses amply illustrates:

	RAF	Luftwaffe
Fighters	26, 10 pilots killed, wounded or missing	33, 17 pilots killed, wounded or missing
Bombers	45, including those on the ground	40

The RAF bomber losses, so rarely mentioned in British accounts of the Battle for Britain (which tend to speak only of their fighter losses while boasting of the number of German bombers destroyed), were heightened by a disastrous daylight attack by 12 Blenheims on Stavanger airfield against a reported heavy concentration of enemy aircraft. Instructed to abandon the mission if cloud cover fell below 70 per cent, they continued in clear skies and were pursued by Messerschmitts on their way home (having, as at Haamstede on the 7th, caught the Germans by surprise). Eight bombers failed to return and the other four were badly damaged.[8] In expenditure of aircraft both sides were exceeding rates of replacements, but the German reserves seemed likely to out-last those of the British; in the matter of reserve air crew, however, the Germans had no worries while the British were hard-pressed, their replacements being quite inadequate to restock a meagre pool. For these reasons, if no others, Dowding awaited the next day's fighting in trepidation.

The second day – 10 July

To his surprise the Luftwaffe did not resume its massed tactics on the 10th. Instead it indulged in repeated raids against airfields and communication centres by several small formations, covered by fighter sweeps. They gave the Controllers little trouble; with plenty in hand they were able to gear their response in appropriate strength to a nuisance. Lacking concentration, the Germans forfeited the defensive powers inherent in large formations. These tactics, which had proved efficacious in France, once the main opposition had dwindled, were the products of German miscalculation allied to the British failure on the 9th to press home their interceptions, added to the exaggerated claims of 80 British aircraft shot down and to misreading of the damage to targets.

Nevertheless, surprise attacks by small, well-led formations did inflict damage out of all proportion to the effort employed – as Manston discovered when Operational Proving Unit 210 visited it again and left hangars, dispersal areas and three Blenheim night fighters in ruins, for the loss of two Me 110s shot down by ground fire.[9] On the other hand, three He 111s which penetrated well into the Midlands to bomb the fighter Maintenance Unit at Colerne, missed the numerous Hurricanes parked on the airfield. Nowhere was the damage so bad as at Manston, but Middle Wallop, Tangmere, Hawkinge, Eastchurch and Hornchurch each received their small ration of bombs, and on each there was damage and temporary disruption which was sufficient to increase the strain on Fighter Command. At the end of the day, the commanders of both sides had good reasons to reconsider their position, although the relatively light casualities (compared to the previous day) gave no indication that a turning-point had been reached.

	RAF	Luftwaffe
Fighters	17 (6 on ground), 4 pilots killed or wounded	10, 7 pilots killed or wounded
Bombers	12 (6 on ground)	17

The third day – 11 July

Dowding sensed that there was a serious change impending. Those Luftwaffe orders which were read by Ultra told him that a massive operation was in preparation for the next day, 11 July, one which would cross the English coastline at many points between Newcastle-on-Tyne and Exeter. He therefore chose this moment when, in his estimation and that of Park, certain squadrons in 11 Group were exhausted, to bring south some fresh squadrons to replace the tired units. The wisdom of this move is open to criticism, because many of the veteran pilots withdrawn were hardly more weary than their opponents, and those who survived had become, within a few weeks, deadly killers in air combat. And veterans, as might have been discerned by examination of combat results, were almost the only pilots who shot down opponents in any numbers: about 90 per cent of all kills were, in fact, scored by only 10 per cent of the pilots engaged, and many 'green' pilots never or rarely fired their guns in action. But Dowding's front-line strength wore a sickly look. 11 Group still could not put more than 200 Spitfires and Hurricanes in the air to meet formations which could be three times that number, and the luxury of drawing upon a reserve from neighbouring Groups was frequently denied it, either because those Groups were themselves involved on their own front or because there was insufficient time in a fast moving battle.

Despite the optimism of their Intelligence officers, the Germans were none too pleased either. It was obvious to the pilots that the enemy resistance was as hard as ever, and to their leaders that their blows were not reaching the essential targets to help win air

British Aircraft Involved

Wellington I Bomber

Whitley Bomber

Hampden Bomber

Blenheim IV Bomber

Spitfire IA Fighter

Hurricane IIA Fighter

superiority before S Day – which was only three days away. As yet, the surface forces of the Wehrmacht could be guaranteed neither the immunity from air attack they demanded nor the bombing support they desired. With these things in mind, Goering issued trenchant orders that, on the 11th and 12th, it was the enemy airfields which were to be saturated, without the softer option of dropping bombs on secondary targets. Two days had been wasted and they would be hard-pressed to be ready on the evening of the 13th to commence the softening-up of the designated beachhead in readiness for the landing next day. At the same time, Goering called a conference for the 11th at Kesselring's headquarters in Brussels, with a view to thrashing out tighter procedures and making better use of resources. Rather late in the day it was appreciated that techniques which had stood the Luftwaffe well against the weaker forces of Poland, Norway, Holland, Belgium and France, were unsuitable against a maritime power such as Britain. There was even doubt in Goering's mind whether it was wise to continue with 'Sealion' at present – but this attack of cold feet he kept to himself, particularly since it contradicted the resounding claims he was retailing to the outside world about the victories his airmen were winning over England.

For the British, the 11th was climactic. During the night, He 111s had roved purposefully inland, finding their targets accurately by the use of 'Knickebein', lowering industrial production by their mere presence and keeping people awake. And the targets they managed to hit in the Midlands were the ones connected with the aircraft industry they sought – the Nuffield Spitfire factory at Castle Bromwich and the Bristol Aeroplane Works at Filton. It was discouraging, too, that the customary early morning enemy

British Aircraft Involved

	Hurricane IIA	Spitfire IA	Blenheim IV
Type	Fighter	Fighter	Bomber
Speed	308mph	362mph	285mph
Combat radius	210 miles	158 miles	563 miles
Crew	1	1	3
Armament	8 x mg	8 x mg	2 x mg
Bomb load	–	–	1,000 lb

	Wellington I	Whitley	Hampden
Type	Bomber	Bomber	Bomber
Speed	235mph	230mph	265mph
Combat radius	1275 miles	1250 miles	995 miles
Crew	5	5	4
Armament	4 x mg	5 x mg	6 x mg
Bomb load	4,500 lb	7,000 lb	4,000 lb

reconnaissance missions came and went without loss, and that several small formations of Ju 88s, which swept in low, took coastal airfields totally by surprise. Manston, Hawkinge, Lympne, Tangmere, Warmwell and Exeter all had visitors and, in varying degree, emerged with their efficiency impaired. Quite apart from the wrecking of support and maintenance services, the early morning cratering of the grass hindered operations by the fighters when they arrived later in the day. This was but the overture to the really heavy attacks which came in mid-morning against selected coastal airfields which, in their turn, would be leap-frogged when attacks were made later against inland fighter airfields. Well supplied by now with detailed knowledge of the area of fire of the defending AA guns, Ju 87s, protected by a top-cover of Me 109s, flew past Dover from the east, before turning west to dive on Hawkinge and Lympne, while Me 110s carried out yet another low-level strafing of Manston. Fortunately for the RAF, only a few Spitfires were on the ground at Manston while fighters from the other airfields were already aloft. But again the damage and cratering was heavy and once more the bombers got in and out without suffering badly, the waiting Me 109s dropping on the British fighters as they moved in to attack the bombers. Most serious of all – and quite by chance – one bomb severed the main power cable supplying the radar station at Rye, with the result that this set was off the air for the rest of the day, tearing an even wider gap in the early warning chain, situated as it was on the

German Aircraft Involved

	Messerschmitt Me 109E	Messerschmitt Me 110	Heinkel He 111	Dornier Do 17
Type	Fighter	Fighter	Bomber	Bomber
Speed	348mph	326mph	252mph	255mph
Combat radius	205 miles	340 miles	600 miles	466 miles
Crew	1	2	5	5
Armament	3 x 20mm 2 x mg	2 x 20mm 5 x mg	5 x mg	4 x mg
Bomb load	–	1,100 lb	7,165 lb	2,205 lb

	Junkers Ju 87B	Junkers Ju 88	Junkers Ju 52	Storch
Type	Bomber	Bomber	Transport	Liaison
Speed	238mph	280mph	178mph	109mph
Combat radius	245 miles	848 miles	930 miles*	119 miles
Crew	2	4	3**	2
Armament	3 x mg	5 x mg	2 x mg	4 x mg
Bomb load	1,102 lb	7,935 lb	–	–

*Range. **Accommodation: 12 paratroops or 18 troops

German Aircraft Involved

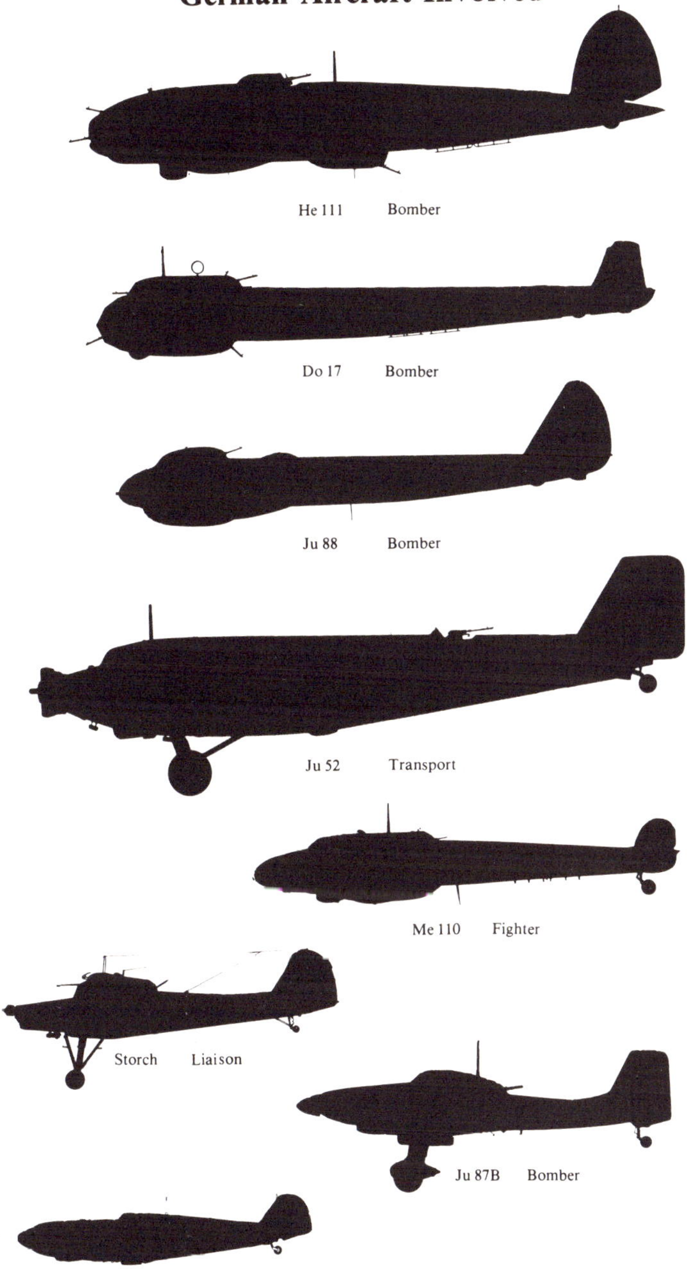

flank of Ventnor which was still out of action. For the next few hours, indeed, most of the south coast was bereft of its early warning facilities.

Dowding's attention was now attracted northward as the long expected attack from Scandinavia appeared on the plotting tables. Goering, encouraged by Intelligence Branch estimates that only 300 fighters remained to the RAF and that these had all been moved to the south, had authorized a two-pronged raid on north-east England; one by 65 Heinkels, escorted by 35 Me 110s, the other by unescorted Ju 88s. Their targets were airfields. With sufficient radar warning of the approaching raids (but not the slightest help from Ultra), five squadrons of fighters from 13 Group found it easy to intercept the Heinkel group far out to sea, to defeat their escort and treat the bomber formations so roughly that they jettisoned their bombs without hitting a single worthwhile target. Without loss, the RAF destroyed fifteen German aircraft here, and were no less successful against the Junkers 88s to the southward, shooting down ten of the fifty raiders which, nevertheless, pressed home their attack with great courage to hit the airfield at Driffield near Hull where they destroyed ten Whitley bombers on the ground, besides wrecking hangars and administrative buildings. Heavy though the German losses were and discouraging as was the impact of the British resistance to the Luftwaffe commanders and crews (who were beginning to wonder if it were possible to defeat the RAF) the outcome of this attack was by no means entirely in the British favour. Its launching re-emphasized to Dowding the need to retain a strong presence in the north, and the losses it inflicted on Bomber Command were blows against the anti-invasion force. Furthermore, it kept Fighter Command at full stretch on a day when it was completely denied respite elsewhere.

No sooner were the heavy morning raids on the coastal airfields over than, once more, Ju 88s and Me 110 bombers were skimming at low level across the Channel in an endeavour to catch Spitfires and Hurricanes engaged in refuelling on the ground. They were unlucky at Manston and Lympne, but at Hawkinge and Warmwell managed to shoot up and bomb the dispersal points, bringing about the loss of six fighters and such important pieces of equipment as bowsers. Naturally enough, the morale of the ground crews began to sag and, inevitably, aircraft maintenance became more difficult so that serviceability rates fell into decline. Squadrons in 11 Group which, in the opening stages of the battle had gone aloft with 12 aircraft, now did well to raise 10, and had on strength only an average of 16 pilots instead of 19 as before. But so long as the inland Sector Stations, which carried out the bulk of the routine servicing at nights, remained intact there was little fear of a general collapse, and 12 Group's squadrons, by comparison with those of 11, remained fresh and strong.

Spending the afternoon recovering from their morning efforts, Luftflotten 2 and 3 gathered for a maximum effort in the evening, in the meantime keeping the RAF pilots in a state of tension by random fighter sweeps and hit and run raids shortly before tea-time. A singularly successful operation by Operational Proving Unit 210 ravaged the buildings of RAF Martlesham; while destroying only one bomber on the ground, it came and went without loss, put the airfield out of action for two days, and its Me 109s shot down three fighters in combat. It was teams of weary RAF fighter pilots who came to Readiness and were successively scrambled to meet the enormous evening raid which began to build up over France and Belgium at about 1700 hours, spotted only fragmentarily by the surviving Hawks Tor and Dunkirk radar stations.

The assault was phased to begin in the west, where Sperrle sent his dive-bombers against Portland as a feint, and then rise to a climax as successive waves of aircraft roared inland to strike at Worthy Down, Middle Wallop, and, a few minutes later (when it was hoped that the mass of RAF fighters would be drawn to the west), over East Kent to strike at Redhill, Biggin Hill, Kenley, Eastchurch and Rochester. This was intended by the Germans as a master-stroke. Inevitably a considerable number of RAF squadrons were sent to deal with the initial attacks in the west, while inadequate early warning denied Park sufficient information of the main attack due to fall on his left flank. Dowding could take comfort from the fact that the feint attacks were expensive to his enemy and did only light damage to their targets, but his paucity of numbers was made all too plain when the mighty German attack in the east broke through all along the line. Between 1830 and 1930 hours the skies above Kent, Sussex and Surrey were tormented by combat as the German formations rolled in. The fact that they often missed their way and hit the wrong airfields was incidental. Eastchurch and West Malling (instead of Biggin Hill as intended) each received a pounding, along with Rochester, where the Short factory which was building the new generation of four-engined Stirling bombers, was hard hit. Croydon too (instead of Kenley as intended) was plastered by Operational Proving Unit 210, with no harm to the fighter squadrons there, but severe damage to factories making aircraft and repairing Hurricanes: the one redeeming feature was that this élite unit was caught on the way out by defending fighters and severely mauled with the loss of seven machines, including that of its redoubtable leader. But the free-chase fighters which covered the entire operation caught the struggling and out-numbered RAF fighters at a disadvantage in the raid's aftermath, and completed their task by indulging in low strafing of all manner of targets on their way home. To rub it in, as the day drew to its painful close, the coastal fields of Hawkinge and Lympne were once more attacked while, as of routine, the minelayers took off after dark to pursue their deadly sowing on the flanks of the intended invasion area. Next morning the troops would begin to embark for the great adventure.

Casualties for the 11th had been by far the highest yet in the air battle over Britain.

	RAF	Luftwaffe
Fighters	47, including 8 on the ground, 28 pilots killed or wounded	36, 12 pilots killed or wounded
Bombers	15, including 11 on the ground	54

Disquieting as these losses were to the Luftwaffe's bomber units (such a high proportion of which had been sacrificed in the ill-conceived foray across the North Sea), they were quite as disturbing to Dowding. It would have looked even worse if he had known that only nine Me 109s had gone down and that the bulk of the enemy fighter losses were among the more vulnerable Me 110s. As it was, he could ruefully reflect that the 28 fighter pilots lost to him represented about 30 per cent of his reserve of these priceless young men, whose powers of resistance were being ruthlessly sapped and who, in their sacrificial attempts to kill bombers, were losing ground to the German fighter arm. At this time, an average of only six pilots per day were rated fit for introduction to action[11] – a figure far below that available to the Germans. The state of mind among Fighter Command pilots may, perhaps, be summed-up by this extract from a letter written by one of them before he turned in to snatch a few hours disturbed sleep that night:

'I never believed that the day would come when the need for sleep became so overwhelming and the chances of getting it less likely. The squadron has been airborne five times to-day and on two of those occasions fully engaged. We have lost three pilots and four aeroplanes and, for all the wonderful claims of nearly 200 enemy aircraft shot down, it seems to make no difference. Still they come on and everywhere you turn there is a Messerschmitt above.

And we have been lucky. So far they have left our airfield alone. How long can this go on? How much more weary can one become? And when do we become so tired that it is no longer possible to fly with any chance of doing the right thing or of shooting straight if one is fortunate enough to get the enemy in one's sights? And how long will it be before the enemy or just plain error makes an end to it all?'

The pilot concerned was one of those who, a few days later, died in flames.

The set-back

These ugly facts about the situation were to be driven home to the British next day, the 12th, when the Luftwaffe returned to the charge, sent in by leaders whose motivations bordered on desperation. This had to be the master-stroke if they were to be able to support the surface forces in their landings on the Kent coast. But as the assault was renewed with unrelenting fury and evidence of success began to reach the German commanders, disquieting news of another kind filtered its way back to OKW, where the confirmation of the 13th as S Day was pending. Reports from the meteorological offices told of 'fronts' moving in from the Atlantic, with the promise of lower visibility, rain and stiff breezes rising to a peak in the early hours of the 13th – the very moment when both the airborne and seaborne troops would be approaching their dropping and landing zones.

Once more Hitler listened to his Service Chiefs giving their estimates of the latest position on the Channel coast. The Army, said von Brauchitsch with pride, was ready. The Kriegsmarine, reported Raeder, was as ready as ever it was likely to be in the circumstances, but an operation which already hung on the lip of disaster, due to the narrow margins of error upon which it was founded, must fail if adverse weather ruffled the Channel while the small craft were at sea. With all the persuasion at his disposal he counselled delay – by only 24 hours, perhaps, and especially since calmer weather was predicted after midday on the 13th. He remarked afterwards to Schniewind that he had not expected to have his way, for Hitler's mood looked forbidding. But he was saved – very much to his surprise – by Goering. Prior to the meeting, the Feldmarschall had listened sympathetically to Jeschonnek's interpretation of the weather forecast and he had agreed that, in marginal conditions such as those to be expected, the airborne troops might be scattered and be unable to find their objectives – let alone capture them. He had spoken on the telephone, to Kesselring, and from him gathered that another 24 hours grace to enable the Luftwaffe to exploit its successes of the previous day, and subsequently pay much closer attention to targets in the invasion area, would be more than welcome. Kesselring stated, in fact, that he would have asked, in any case, for a postponement. The poor results achieved on 'Eagle Day' itself had set the programme back by at least 24 hours – as already he had warned Goering on 10 July. So Goering sided with Raeder and, requested that S Day be postponed until the 14th.

Hitler was impressed. He asked Jodl what might be the consequences of a delay and received from Jodl's deputy, Warlimont (who had planned the invasion's schedule),[12] a detailed explanation. The immediate effect would be to halt embarkation, with a possible forfeiture of security and the further exposure of men and ships to enemy bombing. Apart from that, Warlimont declared, a postponement by one day might prove advantageous on the beaches. On the 14th, as opposed to the present date of the 13th, the troops, by coming ashore shortly after first light to allow time for the airborne operation to take effect, would arrive $1\frac{1}{2}$ hours before high tide, when the tidal streams were at their weakest (about 1 knot) and seamanship, therefore, least under strain. It would mean the soldiers would have to cross a slightly longer stretch of beach, but this might not be so prohibitive as it sounded since the beach, particularly at Hythe, was steep and the distance involved short.

As was to be expected, von Brauchitsch expressed doubts; he had no desire to expose his soldiers to aimed fire at the water's edge for any longer than necessary. Raeder, on the other hand, concurred with Warlimont and took the opportunity to congratulate the soldier on his grasp of a sailor's problems.

'Then,' announced Hitler, 'S Day is set back for 24 hours and will take place to the original timetable on the 14th – dependent, that is, upon a favourable weather forecast being presented to us at this time tomorrow.'

Nobody, it seems, asked what might happen if the outlook still appeared unfavourable.

The fourth day – 12 July

One consequence of postponement which Warlimont had not foreseen when he gave his assessment, was the flurry of radio signals generated by the imperative need to tell lower formations of the change in timing. There was scarcely an out-station which did not need to know. And so, throughout the morning of the 12th, British interception services became aware of a dramatic increase in traffic and a certain repetition in the style of messages being passed. Ultra translations also began to reveal phrases and code-words which, until then, had been unheard or rare. When combined with a study of the latest air photographs, which showed small but significant changes in the position of craft in the Invasion Ports, and linked to the mounting violence of the air offensive, the likelihood of an imminent invasion became even more pronounced to the Chiefs of Staff. At midday, as the Luftwaffe was bending all its efforts to attack England, three special and highly perilous flights were made in broad daylight by the RAF to photograph the ports. They flew into a storm of gunfire and the attention of Messerschmitts galore. Only one, badly damaged with two of its crew wounded, returned, but the photographs it had taken revealed beyond any doubt that part of the invasion fleet had taken steps to put to sea, even if the majority of craft were still tied up. Moreover, an unusual amount of equipment was to be seen at or close by the docksides. If the invasion was not due this day, said the Chiefs of Staff to Churchill that evening, it may be expected within the next 48 or 72 hours. But they held back the precautionary code-word for invasion – Cromwell – because, as yet, there was insufficient reason to plunge the entire nation into alarm.

The first round of air attacks upon Britain on the 12th may be described as an intensive repetition of the episode of the previous day, with the exclusion of any attempt to raid across the North Sea.[13] Good if, at the outset, cloudy weather, gave ample opportunity for the bombers to put into practice that morning what they had intended to do the previous evening – heavily bomb Biggin Hill, Kenley, Hornchurch, and North Weald besides making lighter attacks on other airfields which had been visited in the past, with particular emphasis on Tangmere which previously had escaped serious attention. Massed raiders fanning out over Essex, Kent, Surrey and Sussex mostly found their targets – although a number were either fended off by the defenders or forced by interior navigation to bomb secondary targets. All three Sector Stations were hit, however, Kenley receiving a particularly hard knock which destroyed its Control Room and, for 18 hours, disrupted its controlling function. Hangars, too, were wrecked so that yet another impediment was placed in the way of maintaining aircraft serviceability. The greatest damage of all in the morning was done to the Sector Station of Tangmere, where Ju 87s, followed by Ju 88s and skilfully escorted by Me 109s, deluged the airfield with high-explosive bombs to bring about the destruction of nearly all the principal buildings as well as some 24 fighters on the ground. At the same time, seven Ju 87s went for Ventnor radar station again and once more put it off the air. The loss of ten dive-bombers in these raids, heart-rending though they were to the German formation concerned, were to prove well spent, for Tangmere was of little use during the next vital 48 hours, and Ventnor was deemed as likely to be out of action for the next seven days.

Other raids, spread wide so as to confuse the defenders, found lucrative targets on a number of airfields. Naval aircraft with an anti-invasion rôle were destroyed in their hangars at Lee-on-Solent. Frequently, while the big raids were attracting the controllers' full attention, two or three bombers might slip through undetected, and, in the case of the two Ju 88s which approached Brize Norton in Oxfordshire with their wheels down as if to land, achieved completed surprise with devastating results. This pair raked the hangars and destroyed 35 training aircraft plus eleven Hurricanes undergoing maintenance. As this harrowing day drew to its close, the RAF grimly counted its losses at nearly 100 aircraft of all kinds (the exact figures will never be known), and was compelled to admit that the enemy was getting on top. Although many fighters were still 'scrambling' into the air in sufficient time to make interceptions, a disturbingly large number were failing to get aloft early enough to be guided into action. The reasons were manifold. For one thing, the early warning system was crumbling. For another, 60 per cent of the pilots lost were the most experienced, and their replacements were neither up to the standard required to shoot down the enemy nor sufficient in numbers. Dowding was being forced to fill the gaps with men he considered unready, and to use three Polish and a single Czech squadron, all of which operated under some difficulty because of language problems. Now that the threat of invasion was imminent he could no longer call on the other Commands to transfer pilots to Fighter Command, for they would be needed in their primary rôles. Finally, the wastage of aircraft was twice that of production and the stock of Hurricanes and Spitfires had dwindled to only 63, with production running at about 14 a day.

Not counting losses on the ground, the ratio of losses to strength employed still ran in favour of the Germans:

	RAF	Luftwaffe
Fighters	26, 18 pilots killed or wounded	29, 20 pilots killed or wounded
Bombers	8	31

On the brink – the fifth day

To the Germans, however, losses such as these were lowering their reserve of operational aircraft to a dangerously low level. There were, in the Luftwaffe, senior commanders who viewed these figures, in particular those relating to the bombers, in trepidation. An increasingly vocal handful expressed their dissatisfaction with Intelligence estimates which misled them with tales that opposition was declining, when almost invariably they were met by 100 fighters every time they crossed the English coast. Nevertheless, there were indications that the optimists might be on the right lines. The bombers *were* getting through and their losses on the 12th were fewer than on the 11th. Moreover, they could be satisfied with the performance of the Me 109 fighters which were easily holding their own. Not even Kesselring, the most optimistic of the Luftwaffe commanders, could claim that he had achieved air superiority over the intended invasion area, but he felt sufficiently confident, that evening, to brief Goering along the lines that, given good weather on the 13th and, with it, another day's intensive operations, he could fulfill his rôle on the 14th of delivering the airborne forces to their destination in safety while also protecting and supporting the assault by sea.

'It will be hard,' he said, 'but our fighters' serviceability is still 75 per cent and they can hold the ring.'

At Kesselring's request, through Jeschonnek, Sperrle was asked to employ his aircraft throughout the ensuing days in pinning down the RAF in the West Country and in making sure that the ships of the Royal Navy were prevented from leaving Plymouth and Portsmouth in order to threaten the western flank of the invasion fleet. At the same time, Stumpff's Luftflotte 5 was to mount, from Scandinavia, just enough effort to dissuade the enemy from making an unchecked diversion of forces from north Britain to the south. On both flanks, minelaying was to be maintained at maximum intensity, with particular emphasis upon the placing of mines in the known, half-mile wide channels which were daily swept by the British in order to keep the sea lanes open, and which now were crucial to allow warships to rush unhindered to any threatened point. At the same time, aircraft were instructed to make a special point of strafing minesweepers whenever the opportunity arose, one Staffel of Me 110s being given this work as its primary task. Kesselring intended to cleanse the air space between Rye and the North Foreland of enemy fighters and, on the evening of the 13th, as the invasion fleet headed for its destination and the airborne troops prepared to enter their Junkers 52s and gliders, to project an all-out aerial bombardment at key positions near Dover and Folkestone and communications centres a few miles inland.

The German weather forecast said that, towards the end of the 13th and on into the next 48 hours, the prospects were good. Indeed, throughout the night of the 12th/13th, the winds which had risen to whip up a choppy sea, would begin to die away and the right conditions for a substantial air attack on the 13th were assured. So when Hitler met his colleagues that morning the last valid reason for withholding the decision to go had evaporated. The transcript of this fateful conference merely quotes routine reports and the Führer as saying, 'Let "Sealion" start tomorrow.' But those who have reminisced upon that scene have left behind a fairly unanimous impression of men in agitation. There had been a long pause, after Goering, the last to give his affirmative had spoken, before Hitler said his piece.

> 'Only now,' wrote Raeder in his private diary, 'did it seem that the enormity of what he had started dawn upon Hitler. I thought I detected a flicker of fear – or was it mistrust – in the eyes which, in previous days, had shone only with a hard and hell-bent wilfulness. Just then I thought – I foolishly dreamed – he might at this last moment recognize the folly of his intentions. But it was only a dream.'

Yet even Raeder felt satisfaction that morning with the auguries as presented to him by reports of the previous night's operations at sea. Once more a British cruiser and three destroyers had ventured out from Sheerness to bombard the invasion ports and this time the laugh had been with the Germans. The cruiser concerned, HMS *Newcastle*, was rounding the North Foreland and approaching her bombarding position when she struck a mine which had been laid only an hour before at dusk. Badly holed, she turned for port, retaining one destroyer as escort and sending the remaining two to complete the mission. The bombardment thus forfeited much of its weight on a night when RAF Bomber Command was putting in its maximum effort all along the Channel Coast (losing six aircraft in the process with many more damaged by furious anti-aircraft fire as they delivered their attacks from a suicidally low level in order to make sure of scoring hits). On the way home, *Newcastle* was torpedoed by an S boat and brought to a standstill, exposed to whatever mischief the Luftwaffe might wreak by daylight. As, indeed, it did when a special Staffel of Ju 87s made deadly practice to sink her at a time when Fighter Command had its hands full elsewhere.

On every one of the 400 airfields throughout western Europe which stood within range of Britain there was feverish activity on the morning of the 13th. Every aircraft which could fly and which had a chance of inflicting damage upon the enemy, was made ready. The final adjustments were being made, too, to the Ju 52s of the airborne force, and those selected to tow the gliders were already preparing to take off for the fields in France where the DFS 230 gliders were assembled.

The full fury of the bombers and fighters was unleashed upon Essex, Kent and Sussex as soon as it was light enough to see the targets. From dawn to dusk there were to be German fighters standing guard over the south-east corner of England while the bombers wrought havoc upon the airfields below. Hornchurch, Manston, Hawkinge, Lympne, West Malling and Detling each received their initial dowsings with bombs and from then on were prey to smaller, follow-up raids which remorselessly reduced them to impotence. Radar stations, too, were attacked between Newcastle and the Thames by a few low flyers, thus lending credibility to those in British Intelligence who still clung to the concept of the main invasion falling upon East Anglia. The RAF fighter squadrons were driven back to defend their inner ring of airfields. Although the Observer Corps continued to give accurate warning of raids once they had crossed the coast, they could not eliminate surprise. Regularly the Germans broke through to be met by fighters deeper inland at the point when they were approaching the limits of their radius of action, putting them at a disadvantage. But the simple fact that the Spitfires and Hurricanes were compelled to adopt a rearward position meant that the Luftwaffe had achieved freedom of action over the coastal belt which now lay at the mercy of unescorted bombers. Life for soldiers and civilians in these exposed districts became distraught as German aircraft returning from inland missions made a practice of machine-gunning traffic on the roads. The slightest movement seemed to attract their attention. People who had the mind to evacuate in the daytime either gave up the idea or took to the roads by night.

Towards evening, when the Cabinet and the Chiefs of Staff were already in possession of sufficient information to convince them that the invasion would probably come within the next 24 hours, the surviving Dunkirk radar station began to report the build-up of yet another massive formation of enemy aircraft over the Pas de Calais. The exhausted fighter squadrons again were brought to Readiness on the inland fields – some of them down to eight machines each, most of them committed to flight for the sixth or seventh time that day. This, Dowding thought, would be the culminating blow aimed at demolishing the Sector Stations, and so take-off was delayed for as long as possible. But he was wrong. Instead of probing deeply towards London, the bombers – many of them Ju 87s – split up into several groups, escorted by fighters, and plunged upon targets which, hitherto, had only received passing attention. Within the space of 40 minutes the railway system and the roads of south-west England were in chaos as bombs were rained on vital junctions – on Strood, Maidstone, Tonbridge, Lewes and Ashford, besides a number of smaller route centres – to bring about the partial isolation of the region which was soon to be a battlefield. This surprise switch of targets delayed the commital of RAF fighters to action, thus allowing many enemy bombers to return home before they could be caught. Running fights broke out all the way to the sea and the Messerschmitts, waiting above, had the best of their adversaries who had descended to lower altitudes in order to tackle the bombers. No less than 18 RAF fighters were lost in this one battle in a day when the casualties suffered by both sides were heartrending – justifying as they did, though, the light-hearted comment of Hermann Goering when, on 5 June, he had envisaged the price which might have to be paid by both air forces in order to make the invasion possible.

	RAF	Luftwaffe
Fighters	65, including 25 on the ground and 32 pilots killed or wounded	31, 26 pilots killed, wounded or missing
Bombers	34, including 16 on the ground	30

After dark, when the bombers from both sides took off upon their routine tasks and as the Kent and Sussex countryside flickered with the fires started by day, the invasion fleet drew closer from ports which glittered by the light of flares, guns and bombs. At this time, too, the German long-range guns began a steady pummelling of Kent, one which was to last throughout a tortured night. By comparison with the cacophany and glare on either side of the Channel, the scenes of orderly intent on the airfields of Germany, where the paratroops filed to their machines, were of an exciting tranquillity made vivid by the beat of hearts stimulated by the thrill of participation in this historic and uplifting moment.

Cromwell alert

It was air photographs and the immediate battle taking place within their sight which convinced the British Chiefs of Staff that the invasion was imminent. Information gleaned from intercepts of Luftwaffe traffic (which was profuse and easier to break) spoke volumes about air raids, but divulged nothing positive about the place and date of the actual landings. The Kriegsmarine's Enigma had yet to be understood by the cryptanalysts and the Army maintained excellent radio security by strict discipline. In London, where there was commendable calm by comparison with the clash of battle and the reigning disturbance spreading across the south-eastern lands, the Chiefs of Staff met at 1720 hours and agreed that full precautionary measures should be taken. The Navy would put to sea with all its available ships that night. The RAF would earmark 24 medium bombers for close co-operation with Home Forces and the rest of its bomber force for employment on special tasks. The Army would come to a state of eight hours' notice and the Eastern and Southern Commands would prepare for what was called 'immediate action'. The civil departments, on the other hand, received no warning. At 2007 hours, a staff officer at GHQ Home Forces authorized the issue of the code-word 'Cromwell' to Eastern and Southern Commands before the outcome of the Chiefs of Staff meeting was known. This sent the troops to their battle stations and placed essential telegraph facilities in the hands of the Army—those, that is, that were still intact after the bombing.

In the excitement of the moment, as the soldiers vacated their billets to occupy pre-arranged defensive positions, it was not surprising that some confusion prevailed and that this was heightened by the least disciplined of the land forces. Upon hearing 'Cromwell' (a precautionary code-word and not intended to mobilize the Local Defence Volunteers permanently) some LDV commanders not only went to their posts, but also ordered the ringing of the church bells, to signal that troops had landed.[14] As a result, the remaining hours of the 13th were spent in an atmosphere of false expectancy which gradually wore off as the night passed and nothing unusual happened. The sound of aircraft seemed no louder than of late, and the guns fired to the same rhythm. By 0200 hours on the 14th, the sense of alertness had passed its zenith and, relaxing their watchfulness, men tended to doze. Except, of course, at the coast, where the noise of battle raged loudest of all.

The troops on the cliffs of Dover remained strictly at the alert. The unprecedented shelling alone ensured that. Preoccupied though they were by the spectacle across the water, their senses also, but slowly, became aware in pauses between the shelling, of engine noise different from that of the bombers. From the other side, shrouded in darkness after the moon had set at 0046 hours, could be faintly heard a strange and swelling throbbing. So intent were the watchers, that few if any heard the faint sigh of wings drifting ominously overhead as, in the glimmer of dawn, the first gliders made their landfall.

Don't throw this away. You may need it badly.

CIVIL DEFENCE

MAKE YOUR HOME SAFE NOW

In an air raid a bomb is unlikely to drop ON your house. But a high explosive bomb may drop NEAR your house.

THE blast of a bomb will shake houses some distance away. Some houses may collapse although not hit by the bomb itself. Flying glass, rubble, bomb splinters and fragments from our own anti-aircraft shells will be hurled about in all directions.

Many people already have Anderson shelters or shelters of other types. If you have *not* got a shelter here are some things you can do to give your family some protection.

OUTSIDE THE HOUSE.—If you have a garden, you can dig a trench. Don't dig a *deep* trench, unless you know how to make one properly. Deep trenches are apt to fall in if the sides are not specially supported.

But a *shallow* trench will give you quite good cover. Dig down about 4½ feet, and with the earth you dig out fill boxes or sand-bags and stack them up to a height of about 15 inches all round the edge of the trench above ground level. If you can get some corrugated iron or old boards, put them over the top of the trench with a few inches of earth on top to keep them in place.

INSIDE THE HOUSE.—The first thing to look for is a place where there is a good thickness of wall to protect you against flying splinters. The walls must be stone or brick—*lath and plaster walls give no protection.*

A small or narrow room is better than a large one, because the roof is more strongly supported. In most houses the best place will be either a basement or a passage with no window, or a room such as a scullery with a small window. If the window faces a narrow outside passage, so much the better.

If your shelter-room or passage has a window, you must protect the window against splinters to a level of at least six feet from the floor level. This can be done in various ways.

If it has a basement window partly above ground, build it in with sandbags if you can get them, but you can do without sandbags. You can use boxes filled with earth; or, if you cannot get enough material to build up your earth wall from the ground, get a wooden table or make a wooden platform (at the level of the window sill), and build up your wall from that level with earth in bags or boxes.

Another way of protecting your window is to nail stout boards inside and outside the window opening, to a height of six feet from the floor, and fill the space in between with pebbles, broken bricks, earth or sand. A wooden frame with wire netting on both sides could be used in place of the boarding if you line it with linoleum or other material to keep the pebbles or earth from falling out.

You can also protect a window from the inside by putting in front of it a bookcase tightly packed with old books or magazines, or by piling up against it old trunks or boxes filled with stones or earth. If you do this, be sure that the boxes are firmly supported, and do not sit where the force of an explosion might topple them on to you.

Don't forget the danger from flying glass. If any part of the window is left unprotected, the best place to stand is close to the wall on either side of the window.

These are only a few hints. You will doubtless think of other ways of using the materials you can lay your hands on. And remember—if you make your own home as safe as possible for your family and yourself you will be helping everybody.

BE WISE AND DO THE JOB NOW.

Basic air-raid precautions as advised by the British Government.
(Lionel Leventhal Collection)

VIII

ASSAULT FROM THE SKY

The Germans take off

To the German glider and parachute troops who climbed aboard their machines that night, the ordeal ahead seemed no more desperate than those they had undertaken at the beginning of the Norwegian and Netherlands campaigns. Intelligent men that they were, they looked the dangers squarely in the face and reasoned that surprise – perhaps not the total surprise their leaders dreamed of – would see them through. After all, they had prevailed in Holland when surprise was lacking, so why not now against an opponent who was reckoned to be on his knees? In hope, but with nerves taut, they flew at 2,000 feet across France and Belgium in an armada routed by radio beacons to the selected dropping zones between Dover and Hythe. It was not long before the pilots began to pick out the coastline ablaze with gunfire. But visibility was clear, and the advanced guard of Ju 52s, towing the gliders, easily found their check-points.

Beneath them, the ships of the invasion fleet butted into uncomfortable seas which enervated the inexperienced passengers. The departure through lock-gates and the narrow, swept fairways outside the ports had gone surprisingly smoothly. Vessels which had put to sea in daytime had no difficulty, but those which had come out of Calais and Dover in darkness had groped their way with an air raid in progress. Some damage was done by the RAF, but none of it serious. Confusion there had been as minesweepers and *Prahms* failed to take up the prescribed formation, and there had been a bad moment when a minesweeper blew up on a mine. Apart from that, the sweeping went well, cutting open channels towards England through the British field where it had not been previously cleared. The craft carrying 6th Mountain Division on the right wing achieved an almost immaculate order before dusk, but those bringing 17th Infantry Division on the left were soon reduced to Formation Pigpile because of the difficulties of leaving port at night, as already mentioned. But at least this amphibious vanguard of the Wehrmacht could heave a sigh of relief that the Royal Navy was nowhere in evidence.

Glider landing

The crews of the nine DFS 230 gliders destined to arrive first on English soil and storm the Langdon Battery, had carefully studied their objective from maps and photographs, knowing full well that if this pair of modern 6in guns were not eliminated immediately, the approaching landing craft would be in dire peril. The methods adopted were like those used to subdue Fort Eban Emael on 10 May. Releasing from their tugs at 3,000 feet, below the radar cover, when 5 miles east of Dover, each glider pilot, meticulously trained to land in darkness, guided by spot lights to within 20 metres of his objective, closed the coast in loose formation.

'I could see the white walls of the South Foreland cliffs, and fires in the town,' wrote Leutnant Karl Hollstein of the leading glider. 'Beyond was the clear outline of the harbour breakwater and silhouetted to the right the four tall radio masts we had been told to look for. To one side another glider loomed up and slid away. Shells from our long range artillery had been falling near the objective, but nobody fired at us as we lined up for the final approach and braced ourselves for the impact. Skimming the cliff-top, our pilot went straight at the square turrets which now became visible. Then we were down, bumping crazily and lurching sideways into what I soon discovered was a heap of barbed wire. Without a moment's hesitation the men jumped clear and flung themselves to the ground as two more gliders rumbled to a halt almost within touching distance. At least we were not alone! I waited while the men collected their weapons, in the meantime verifying that we were, indeed, on top of our target. Somewhere not far off I heard the distinctive rattle from one of our sub-machine-guns. 'Advance,' I shouted, and we stood up to find ourselves, after a few steps, with the guns in front of us. It had been a miracle of navigation.'

Eight out of nine gliders lay alongside the battery, the ninth having veered right and come down among a group of 3.7in anti-aircraft guns whose crews recovered swiftly from their surprise and killed all the Germans within ten minutes. But the pre-occupation of the gunners with this private battle gave the Germans at the Langdon Battery a free hand. Penned within their steel and concrete emplacements, the coastal gunners below ground were only vaguely suspicious of something wrong outside, while those in the open were shot down or rounded up. Within five minutes the area was cordoned off by glider infantry while the engineers, dragging with them $2\frac{1}{2}$ tons of explosives, including cavity charges which, when detonated against the casemates, could penetrate and kill or incapacitate those inside, and set fire to inflammable material. Hollstein's glider had touched down at 0300 hours as the grey of dawn showed in the east. At 0320 hours, the cavity charges and the explosives draped round the 6in guns' barrels began to go off.[1]

With their primary task completed it was time now for the glider men to escape as best they could, skirting round Dover in the hope of joining the main German forces. Yet even now they continued to influence the main blow before it had been delivered, for it was the aggressive presence of these intrepid and victorious soldiers carrying battle deep into the British defences, which sowed seeds of uncertainty among the local defenders while the main German forces made their run in. Half their number became casualties, but their timely neutralization of anti-aircraft guns, which might otherwise have made deadly practice on the paratroops' Ju 52s, was crucial, and they also helped confuse local British commanders who were temporarily bemused by the roar of many scores of aircraft and a plethora of reports of hundreds of paratroops descending in a huge triangle bounded by Dover, Canterbury and Ramsgate. The latter, of course, were the dummy parachutes dropped by the glider tugs as they completed their mission. It would be several hours before the effects of this deception had entirely worn off.

Unable to disentangle fact from fantasy, and chronically sceptical, as a result of recent experience with wild reports about parachute landings, neither Thorne nor Liardet were willing to commit their mobile reserves until the position had been clarified. As they waited the Germans arrived in strength. And as the 7th Air Division began to jump, the countryside rang once more to the peel of church bells as one local leader after another at last saw real paratroops, and this time spread the news with terrifying intonation to a population keyed up by anticipation.

When Hollstein was landing at Langdon, the remainder of the glider force, plus the special Storch parties, were also touching down. Not everywhere did the gliders land with spot-on accuracy. Of the ten meant to land alongside the Citadel Battery, with its big 9.2in guns, one overshot and crashed near the Castle and two

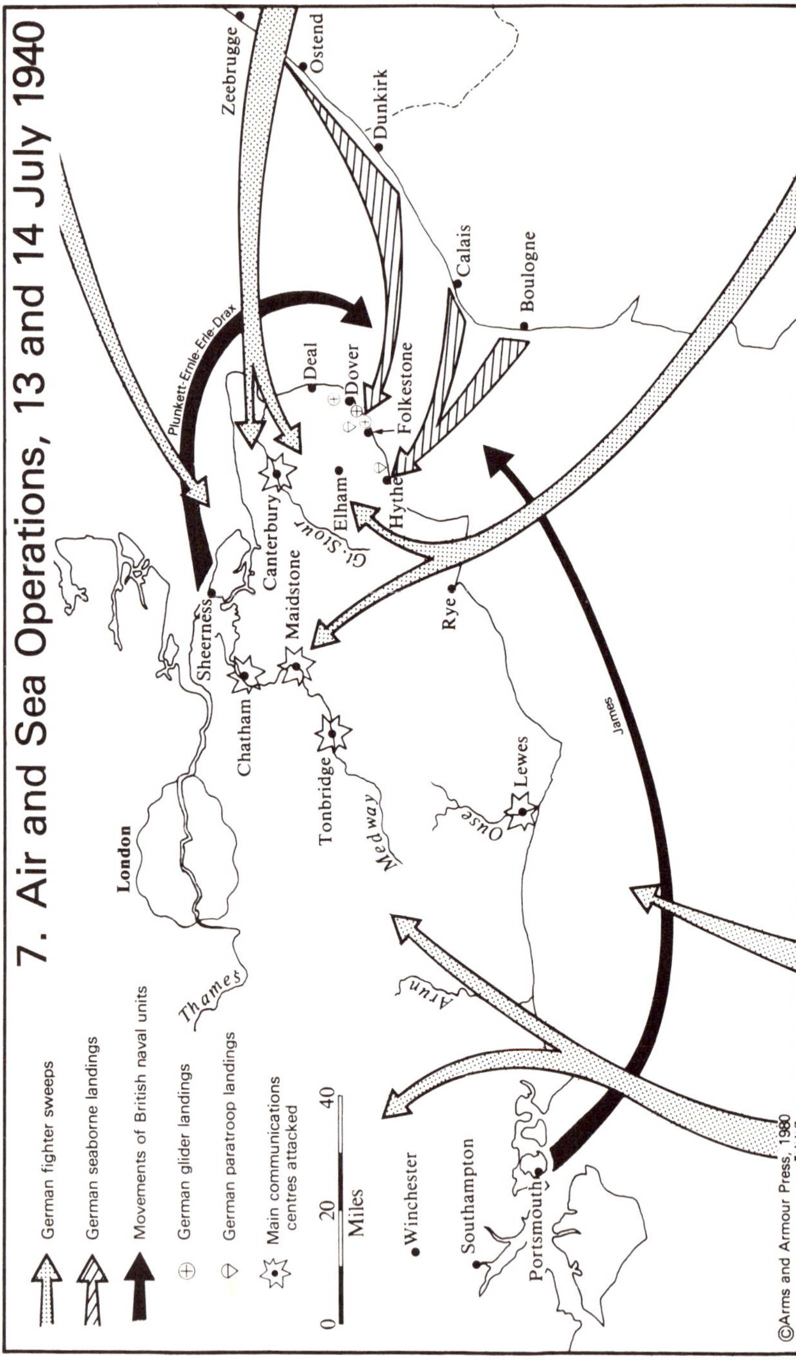
7. Air and Sea Operations, 13 and 14 July 1940
German fighter sweeps
German seaborne landings
Movements of British naval units
German glider landings
German paratroop landings
Main communications centres attacked
0
20
40
Miles
Plunkett-Ernle-Erle-Drax
James
London
Thames
Sheerness
Chatham
Canterbury
Maidstone
Tonbridge
Medway
Deal
Dover
Folkestone
Hythe
Elham
Gt. Stour
Rye
Lewes
Ouse
Arun
Winchester
Southampton
Portsmouth
Zeebrugge
Ostend
Dunkirk
Calais
Boulogne
©Arms and Armour Press, 1980

others came down on the steep slope by the King Lear public house, where the Irish Guards fought back with every weapon to hand. In consequence, the 9.2in gunners were left unmolested, except for those who joined in the local fire fight as gliders landed nearby. But, as on the other side of the town, vital AA guns were diverted from their main task, leaving only the four guns at Farthingloe Farm and the two at Buckland to engage the myriad legitimate targets which were about to present themselves.

Sergeant R. J. Turnhouse of the Royal West Kent Regiment, one of the few survivors from the battle of the cliff-tops, recalls the arrival of the gliders at Aycliff and Lydden Spout.

'My platoon was spread out between the Abbot's Cliff and Shakespeare Cliff railway tunnels and I was about to call them to stand-to when a sort of black shadow seemed to pass close overhead. I thought it was my imagination playing tricks, for we had been shelled all night and had got little sleep. So I called my officer and told him what I had seen. There was by now a commotion coming from the direction of the Citadel and a lot of engine noise, and we were hoping for daylight so that we could properly see what was going on. People were moving about on the open downs behind us and there was rifle and machine-gun fire up by the Citadel, and beyond, in the direction of the Castle. Then there was firing over by Lydden Spout and we began to wonder if the invasion really had begun after all the false alarms with the church bells the previous evening. My officer told me to take a Section and go to Lydden Spout to see what was going on, and so I started out along the cliff path. We had not gone far, and it was getting lighter, when some men jumped out of a patch of scrub and the next thing I knew there was firing and two of my blokes cried out. I ran and went full tilt into a big bloke who lashed out at me. I still had my rifle and I struck him back and he fell. I could see now he was a German, so I shot him as he lay on the ground. They were all around and I could see, too, a number of aircraft which must have been gliders because they landed so silently. At that moment some LDV chaps dashed by shouting there were Germans everywhere and there was nothing to be done. I was on my own and decided they were probably right. So I joined them running towards Dover where I hoped I might be of some use.'

At trivial cost to themselves the German glider troops had, indeed, seized the cliff tops from Aycliff to Abbot's Cliff and in so doing had won command of the beaches below where 6th Mountain Division was soon due to land. The British troops who had occupied the emplacements on this sector had been overwhelmed by sheer surprise. Those few at Lydden Spout who had found time to use their weapons had held out for 15 minutes and performed the duty prescribed by Winston Churchill, 'to take one with you'. But so swift had been the envelopment of the British position that no coherent reports had been passed to local headquarters. Here, as elsewhere, the British commanders could only surmise that the important cliff re-entrants might be in enemy hands, ready for climbing by men coming ashore below.

Even as the final shots of Lydden Spout rang out, and the battle for the Citadel paused while both sides tried to think what to do next, the Feisler Storches were setting down daintily on fields well inland, attempting to deposit the hopeful parties of Infanterie Regiment Grossdeutschland at points whence they could interrupt the movement of enemy reserves. In an arc from Ringwould, in the east, to Barham and on to Elham in the north and back towards the coast at Sellindge, these small ambush and demolition parties did what they could to make their presence felt – and largely failed except by acting as yet another diversionary factor. For the objectives such as bridges and junctions, which they sought to seize or damage were the spots best guarded by troops and LDV and, by now, the British were fully alert, stirred up by the noise of battle resounding from Dover. Some 18 Storches were destroyed as they landed and several more were shot down or damaged as they sought to escape. Other Grossdeutschlanders were hounded to death. Nevertheless, the railway from Canterbury to Dover was cut in a couple of places, as was the one from Ashford, while isolated blocking positions on a few country roads helped delay the transfer of troops belonging to 2nd (London) Brigade.[2]

The parachute landings – West Hougham

Attention, in any case, was now fixed upon the sea front between Dover and Hythe, whence the thunder of aircraft engines in unprecedented volume was predominant in a dawn that was vibrant with noise. Flying low and skimming the beaches, Messerschmitts recommenced the strafing they had left off the previous evening, shooting up everything suspicious near the parachute dropping zones. In their wake came Ju 88s to bomb the known British gun positions and strong points, particularly in the vicinity of Hythe as well as on Lympne and Hawkinge airfields. These came and went unopposed, the RAF fighters inland having yet to leave the ground. But when the RAF did arrive the scene was unlike anything experienced before. Close upon the heels of the bombers and fighters flew the stately mass of Ju 52s, winging their way in three dense streams at a height of 150 feet, each Staffel of 12 aircraft broken into four Vics, each transport with 12 men poised to leap into space at the end of his static line.

Braving the surviving Dover anti-aircraft guns and those of Folkestone, the seemingly endless procession of Junkers cruised ponderously over their dropping zones in the half light, cascading paratroops and weapon containers. Here and there, a crippled Junkers staggered out of formation or plummeted to earth in flames, but the torrent poured through, unchecked, to deliver their cargoes in safety. Tightly bunched for organized combat, each 'stick' hastened to find and broach the containers which held their heavier weapons, reserves of ammunition and radios. Within a few minutes, the flat, open spaces to the north of West Hougham and the west of Capel le Ferne seethed with smocked figures from 19th Parachute Regiment, carrying out the task of consolidation, while the airborne engineers set about clearing the ground to receive the next wave of aircraft which would land with the heavy 37mm anti-tank guns, the mortars and the 75mm field guns together with their ammunition.

The parachute landings – St Martin's Plain

Only to the north of Hythe, where the 20th Parachute Regiment came down, was there a set back. Because it was difficult to distinguish the dropping zone to the north of Saltwood, the leading Staffel commander was a fraction too late giving the signal to jump. The first 'sticks' were thus carried farther north than intended, with the result that those Staffels behind became confused. 2nd Parachute Battalion, which should have landed around Newington, was scattered towards Arpinge and immediately found itself at grips with a company of 1st London Rifle Brigade (1st LRB). Meanwhile, 1st Parachute Battalion found itself dispersed between Sandling and Postling while the 3rd, which was meant for Sene Golf Course, lay dotted across St Martin's Plain, with little more than a company actually on the proper objective. Here, on ground hallowed by successive generations of British infantry, both sides fought for survival.

The CO of 1st LRB, quick as he was to hear where the enemy were landing, drew the conclusion that both Lympne and Hawkinge constituted the enemy objective. Appreciating that there was nothing he could do at once about Hawkinge, he decided, as a preliminary, to eliminate the threat to Lympne, telling his engaged company at Arpinge to hold on while he sent the rest of the battalion to its relief. 1st LRB moved with commendable speed and caught several paratroopers in Postling before they had gathered all their weapons and organized for defence. Securing the village, 1st LRB pressed up hill in the direction of the wood at Postling Wents and Sandling Station. In the wood a company of paratroops had collected and here a fight took place between enraged but inexperienced British infantry and the annoyed, battle-practiced 1st Parachute Battalion – a small arms encounter since neither side yet had artillery support. 1st LRB stumbled into hot machine-gun fire and stopped. The sound of firing attracted more paratroopers to the scene and they widened the defences as the British tried to mount a fresh assault combined with flanking movements. But they were too slow. Within 20 minutes, such numerical and moral superiority as 1st LRB may have enjoyed at the start had dissipated. Suffering heavy casualties, they withdrew to the high ground above Postling to await reinforcements – above all, for their artillery which was still far away to the north – and dug in.

Meanwhile, 3rd Parachute Battalion endured the same difficulties as had 1st LRB. With one company pinned to the ground among the fairways, greens and bunkers of Sene Golf Course, and the rest of the unit assembling under a drizzle of fire from enemy outposts surrounding St Martin's Plain, they were compelled, in an attempt to seize their main objective on the high ground overlooking Hythe, to attack the well-emplaced British before they had possession of their full strength or armoury of heavy weapons. Moreover, they were slow assembling their communications equipment with which to contact the bombers and cross-Channel guns which, alone, might bring to bear the heavy fire support they needed. Their casualties mounted whenever they tried to advance: the defenders of Saltwood Castle, the Club House and Sene Farm were not to be budged. Moreover, these key positions were being steadily reinforced by the Shorncliffe Garrison commander out of his reserves in Folkestone and also from a few sub-units withdrawn from the sea-front between Sandgate and Hythe. But as Major A. J. Stovold put it:

'There we were, guarding the 19th hole, facing inland, with our backs to the sea we were supposed to be watching – well knowing that, at any moment, the Germans might arrive by boat. But what else could we do with such weak forces as were at our disposal? I suppose we all guessed how hopeless it was and that killing as many Germans as possible would not make much difference. But kill Germans we did, and with a will!'

Despite the partial failure at Saltwood, the German airborne troops had gained nearly all their objectives by 0430 hours. Between West Hougham and Capel le Ferne they had, indeed, performed better than the most optimistic among them could have desired. Within 30 minutes of landing, the commander of 19th Parachute Regiment felt sufficiently satisfied to call for the first waves of Ju 52s to land on the air strips being prepared in the midst of his dropping zone. It was a decision not without risk, even though the fields had been cleared of what few obstacles had been in the way. The danger now lay in the air and not on the ground. RAF fighters had begun to appear shortly after the landing, and already six Ju 52s on their way home had been chopped down. But these fighters, in their turn, had been punitively tackled by the Messerschmitts and, for the moment, it seemed reasonable to hope that the sky above could be kept safe for the following waves of vulnerable transport aircraft which, it had always been accepted,would be in peril. It was a calculated risk on the Germans' part, and one taken by Kesselring in the belief that the sheer density of his bombers, fighters and transport aircraft, operating in a relatively restricted area, would saturate the defences.

The RAF strikes back

It did not need the British Chief of Air Staff's insistent directive to make Dowding realize, immediately the report of parachute landings came in, that the time for holding back his fighter forces had passed. Expecting rich pickings among slow Ju 52s, he ordered Numbers 10, 11 and 12 Groups to throw in everything they had. In general terms the Spitfires were to tackle the enemy fighter escorts, the Hurricanes to deal with the transports while even two squadrons of Boulton Paul Defiant twin-seater fighters, which had proved too vulnerable in daylight operations, were committed to the fight. At the same time, the 24 Blenheims of Bomber Command, which were permanently on call in an anti-invasion rôle, were sent up under orders to find and bomb the invasion craft at sea. Thus a potentially mighty collision of air power was set in motion over the Straits of Dover. Within a period of ninety minutes, approximately 3,000 aircraft were to enter an area 30 miles square and 15,000 feet high.

IX

ASSAULT FROM THE SEA

Contact at sea

The crews of the British Auxiliary Patrol boats, lying five miles offshore on the night of 13 July, sensed the enemy's presence in the same way as they habitually apprehended a coming storm in these familiar waters. Before setting sail they had been warned that this might be the night, but they had been told that before. This time, however, an Admiralty assessment stated that the two days on either side of 11 July would be ideal for a German landing in the Dover area. The sights and sounds of battle they had long become accustomed to now reverberated in association with the continual throb of aircraft, but, as this night wore on, they began to detect unusual and unexplained lights in the direction of the French coast. Not until they were turning for home, however, did Joe Barling, skipper of the motor launch *Anne Ducket*, see the bow wave of a minesweeper coming up astern.

'I banged on full speed,' said Barling, 'and shouted to Fred Tompsett to loose off the rockets to let those ashore and the other boats know they were coming. Balls of red tracer started whizzing about as this Jerry ship let rip, but I saw more rockets going up and somehow he missed us and we got away. Then all those big aeroplanes came roaring over – the ones what dropped the parachutists – and some of our boats were burning – and we're bloody lucky to be back at all.'

Some among them were not so lucky, caught as they were by gunfire from the German escorts before they could escape. And some there were whose skippers rounded upon the enemy, hoping, unavailingly with their trivial armament, to do some damage or, perhaps, even to ram a landing craft as some contribution to the defence of their land. In the early morning light the turmoil afloat and ashore became plainer. Citizens who had decided to depart inland were either caught by the paratroops or strafed from the air, but the unruly drivers of civilian cars and lorries who had set off at dusk were already well inland, carrying tales of despair. Here, as in France, the refugees occupied valuable space on the roads, and inadvertently conspired to sap public morale. Meanwhile, the stalwarts who held firm at home and peered anxiously for enemy ships, at last picked up advancing shapes in the wake of the Auxiliary Patrol vessels as they raced for safety. Soldiers stood to arms, while the civilians made for the deep caves, flimsy garden shelters or crouched beneath stairways. Already the scores who had lost their homes, had discovered that a creaking civil administration was unable to provide anything but scanty help. Some found room in abandoned houses; others dwelt in the caves. There was food, for the shops were well stocked, but the failure of gas and electricity supplies brought about by the bombardment made cooking rudimentary. People put a good face on it and braced themselves for the fight, but none dared look much beyond tomorrow as the unknown closed upon them.

To the majority of Germans at sea, with the enemy coast a faint loom, it seemed miraculous that they had come so far without serious challenge. 6th Mountain Division's boats managed to retain good order, but the best that could be said of 17th Infantry Division was that they had conglomerated – but never in the desirable formation. Less fortunate were the minelayers putting down their cargo on the flanks. A few miles off North Foreland, shortly before the moon was down, they attracted the attention and the bombs of Coastal Command aircraft. Close by, Royal Navy destroyers, probing towards Dunkirk in the hope of intercepting the invaders, were attracted to the spot and, illuminating the Germans with their searchlights and with starshell, sank two minelayers at close range. But even as the surviving sailors took to their boats they too were rewarded by the flash and thud of one of their assailants, swerving away, striking a mine which had been laid previously by a U-boat. It was a lucky strike for the convoy carrying 6th Mountain Division, since otherwise it would have soon come under fire. As it was, the badly damaged destroyer was left to limp home and her consorts felt compelled to haul off rather than tarry in a minefield of which they had no information. It was rather the same down Channel. Destroyers out of Portsmouth found and sank a minelayer near Hastings and were, in turn, heavily engaged by German destroyers. Neither side inflicted much damage on the other, and moved apart when the British sought for another way round to the Straits. But both sides also drew apart, each fearing they were about to bump into one of their own minefields. For the Royal

Navy's officers it was not a question of shirking losses at the moment of their nation's greatest peril; it was simply a question of avoiding almost certain destruction without, in return, making the slightest contribution. It was prudent to survive in order to fight later under less calamitous conditions when they could hit the enemy harder and decisively.

In daylight, the British warships, few as yet in number at the crucial point, were compelled to seek shelter from the inevitable air attacks. This was a fundamental condition of the campaign to come, and it left the German sailors free to restore whatever order they could to their advancing flotillas even though the time for assault was nigh. Fortunately, for them, the minesweepers carrying the first wave of storm troops had fared well and were on schedule. Most of the *Prahms* had also kept up, but most of the Siebel ferries had fallen behind and thus could not contribute to the final close bombardment. Everything depended upon the overworked destroyers, T boats, S and R boats to shepherd the assault craft into some sort of formation for the final dash, and also to keep a wary eye open for enemy warships while endeavouring to give what fire support they could against the shore defences. The sight of the two old battleships pushing towards the Varne Shoal may have given heart to the soldiers, but sent shudders down the spines of sailors who understood their vulnerability.

Battle in the Straits

Out of Dover at full speed roared the five motor torpedo-boats, followed by the slow submarine *H 49.* Shore searchlights picked out the oncoming fleet and the surviving guns at Hythe, Folkestone and on Dover harbour breakwater started to fire at their special targets, the German warships. To a prearranged plan, the bigger ships returned fire, while the small, faster ones hastened to lay a smoke-screen shielding the flotillas' exposed flanks. Almost at the same time, those Germans nearest Dover saw the MTBs coming and focussed their attention upon this imminent threat. The air became thick with projectiles, the water erupting with so many shell splashes that neither side was able to make sensible corrections of fire. And piled on top of this scene of chaos, air power added its contribution.

The efforts of four RAF Coastal Command Hudsons, dropping bombs while on their way home from night patrol, became lost in the vast Luftwaffe display as the machines supporting the airborne landings were replaced by those helping the seaborne ones. No sooner was it light than Ju 87s were seen orbitting and diving upon the coastal gun positions. They did well. One bomb landed inside a sand-bagged pit on Dover Hill overlooking Folkestone; more fell close by their targets and distracted the gunners from their primary rôle. To a dispassionate observer, the overriding impression could only be one of a deadly German war machine overwhelming an almost defenceless victim by brute force, efficiency and terrifying finality. The cacophony of engines and explosions, vibrating among clouds of smoke and dust, merely underlined the obvious conclusions. And yet, those out-numbered individuals had something to say for themselves, no matter what the result might be.

'We took off at about 0345 hours from Lincolnshire,' wrote Flying Officer Eric Derwent, who flew one of the 24 Blenheims ordered to attack the invasion fleet, 'and set course round London to the west, hoping to meet the fighter escort which had been promised. No such luck! We kept going, low level over Hastings, with the idea of curling in from the direction of France to take the enemy by surprise before making our withdrawal northwards. Our own guns took pot-shots at us, we frightened off a Do 17 which somehow got in the way, and saw some of our Hurricanes having a go at a couple of Ju 88s over Rye. Soon we saw what we had come for, a whole gaggle of boats and ships of all sorts, sizes and shapes stretching back to France for as far as one could see. There was a lot of flak coming up and no time to pick a target. You just took a clutch of them and aimed into the middle. I saw one of our chaps go smack into the sea. I released my bombs at what looked like a destroyer and then tried to follow my leader out of the flak right down to the wave tops. A couple of ships were burning, but there was also a lot of smoke about from what could have been part of a screen. Somewhere east of Dover, two of us saw some Ju 52s lumbering along, so went for them and I think mine went down smoking. But then we were jumped by Messerschmitts which chased us over Kent where, once more, our own guns fired at us. We were lucky to get home. Four of the squadron did not.'

RAF fighters which had set out to chase transports and bombers occasionally found themselves shooting up invasion craft, but more often than not were engaged in dog-fights with Messerschmitts. Ju 88 pilots, sent to bomb airfields, sometimes found themselves, after dropping their bombs, fending off attacks upon Ju 52 transports. To the men in the German ships it was extremely difficult to tell friend from foe, but the attacks upon them were infrequent, and they saw a great many British aircraft, besides their own, shot down. The shooting of the coastal guns was neither very heavy nor accurate, concentrated as it was upon 'the bigger game', and limited as it was by having only 100 rounds per gun available. All, that is, except the big 9.2in guns in the Citadel which were amply supplied, but also closely beset by enemy airborne troops. They, like the 6in coastal guns, took on the larger enemy warships under the direction of the Fire Controller in Dover Castle. The Controller's aim was to support as best he could the developing attack by the MTBs, and in this respect he enjoyed initial success by securing a hit on a T boat as the MTBs were making their run in. But at the crucial moment he saw, dimly silhouetted to the south, the bulk of an enemy battleship – and that was a target he could not ignore. So the MTBs, shaping course to attack round the German smoke-screen in the hope of geting to close quarters with the craft bringing in 6th Mountain Division, found themselves unsupported and the targets for concentric fire from enemy craft of all kinds. They did manage to launch their torpedoes and had the satisfaction of seeing a T boat cut in half, but before they could close upon the landing craft they were floundering in a storm of shot. Two of the five MTBs were mortally hit, the others broke away, taking such violent evasive action that their own gunners could do little. Only one reached the safety of the smoke undamaged in this, the only effective attempt by British ships to come to grips with the invaders before they landed.

When the moment came for those on board the German assault minesweepers to lower the outboard-motored storm boats, there were few fully capable of carrying out their duties. Seasickness had taken its toll. So the task took longer than expected and the boats, when they did sail for the shore, were filled by pallid occupants who could hardly be described as fighting fit. In the meantime, the Dover guns had sunk three minesweepers and two *Prahms* besides damaging a T boat which, while laying smoke, had tried to out-shoot the shore batteries. This combination of hazards broke up the previously tidy flotilla carrying 6th Mountain Division, so that it approached the shore piecemeal and in disarray. No amount of heavy shelling from the battleships *Schlesien* and *Schleswig Holstein* (which were engaged in a dual with the Citadel battery), or heavy dive-bombing by Stukas, could put right what had gone wrong among the small ships. And in any case, *Schlesien* was hit at an early stage by a couple of 9.2in shells and forced to retire on fire and with one of her main turrets out of action. Indeed things might have gone ill for the men in the landing craft everywhere had it not been for the dive-bombers and, above all, the combined efforts of glider and paratroops already ashore. Shortly after a Ju 87 had scored a hit on one of the Citadel's caissons (regardless of the risk to nearby glider men), a company of paratroopers from West Hougham arrived to seek ways into the fortifications. Once more the defenders were distracted, and increasingly the 9.2in gunners manning the sole surviving piece were hampered as they came under accurate mortar fire.

Check at Hythe

The fact remained that a far larger volume of shell fire was arriving unchecked from France and mid-Channel than was going out under difficulty from Britain. At 0400 hours the German guns in the Pas de Calais had switched, after a pause, from bombardment of the airborne landing areas to a steady fire upon the beaches of west Dover, Sandgate and Hythe. It was inaccurate but persistent, inflicting few casualties, but causing a lot of damage and fires while serving to shake inexperienced troops as they stood to for their first direct confrontation with the enemy. In consequence, German soldiers who were suffering from the ravages of a rough voyage, crawled ashore against defenders quite a few of whom were demoralized by the heavy fire to which they had been subjected.

Oberfeldwebel Franz Maas, in 55th Infantry Regiment of 17th Infantry Division, who was among the first to set foot on Hythe beach, described the event as, 'Something I would rather not repeat. I was among the minority who resisted seasickness. Most of my company had spent the night leaning over the rail, so that when we came to slide the storm boats into the water there were too few of us fit to do the job properly. Several men had to be thrown over the side into the boats and we were ten minutes late casting off. But some of the others were even later and so, instead of driving in as part of a neat assault line, as on training, we made for the shore like a lot of drunken waterboatmen zig-zagging across a pond. All hell was let loose on shore. Houses were burning and I could faintly see some sort of scrap going on along the crest beyond. There was a big gun in Hythe which kept loosing off over our heads, dropping shells among the ships behind us. We touched down on the beach all in one piece, but I had the Devil's own job getting the men out, and some of them just flopped down and lost interest. To right and left I could see storm boats at sea, but precious few on land. We took cover behind the sea-wall which, at this point, was not much higher than the level of the steep, pebble beach. Bullets were flying about and seemed to be coming from some buildings to the left. Some of our men were hit and crying out. I tried to spot the enemy guns, but there was not much I could do except join the others behind the sea-wall and fire my rifle in the general direction of where the trouble came from.'

Rubber boats were carried eastward with the 1 knot stream and deposited in a muddle on the foreshore. For the first ten minutes, while the shaken British infantry began to pluck up enough courage to return the fire, their German adversaries lay comatose and confused behind the promenade. Only when the invaders began to recover their composure and look for momentary ways to improve their situation did the defenders of the Shorncliffe Garrison, encouraged by a falling off in shellfire, also raise their resistance. But as the volume of small arms fire on the beach increased so, too, was the amount of fire augmented from armed coasters and Siebel ferries of the second German wave as they edged in closer. Most of the shooting was wild because the gunners afloat failed to compensate for the pitching of their ships, but its fury made up for inaccuracy and encouraged the prostrate German infantry.

Tanks in action

Armour finally tipped the scales for the Germans when the issue on the beach stood finely balanced. The *Prahms* carrying the wading tanks had elbowed their way through the press of retiring or sinking minesweepers, their captains determined to carry the tanks as close as possible to the water's edge rather than disembark them at sea with the time consuming business of putting down the extended ramps and the additional risks imposed upon the tank crews. 'This we had agreed among ourselves long before,' remarked the tank company commander, Hauptman Werner Appelbeck. 'We reckoned it might even be safer for the *Prahms* to get in under the lee of the shore, quite apart from the advantages to ourselves. One of our *Prahms* had fallen behind during the night and another had been damaged by a shell when we were a mile offshore. But the rest of us stayed together – those sailors really caught the *Panzerwaffe* spirit – and finally dropped ramp on a good, solid beach a couple of hundred metres east of the seafront buildings of Hythe – quite close, in fact, to where we were meant to go. I saw the others climbing out – saw too that the infantry were pinned down. Clearly it was up to us, particularly because we had not suffered nearly so badly from seasickness as had, I gather, the infantry. I suppose it was something to do with the different behaviour of a *Prahm* compared with a minesweeper – or perhaps our morale was better. Anyway, we were fit to fight.'

At 0450 hours, spread out over a frontage of 4,000 metres, some ten Pz Kpfw III tanks, after divesting themselves of their wading gear, began crawling inland. To the relief of their crews there were no mines and only one became bellied in deep shingle. Surmounting the lip of the promenade also presented no great difficulties, but as they did so, guns blazing, the enemy threw everything he had at them. But small arms fire did little harm and the three 0.5in Boyes anti-tank guns, which were the total anti-armour weapons on this piece of coastline, were ineffective against a Pz III at more than 300 metres, even if the gunner managed to hit the target with this unwieldy piece. Fanning out, the tanks systematically located and shot up each British strong-point with their 37mm guns and combed the intervening terrain with their machine-guns. Taking courage from the tanks' success and noticing that the return fire was slackening, the German infantry (upon whom the effects of seasickness were wearing off) began to shift for themselves, to creep forward and fire purposefully at the windows whence shots had come. By 0515 they had secured a foothold in the seafront hotels and buildings of Hythe, had accompanied two tanks across the old Royal Military Canal at Seabrook, and were infiltrating towards Shorncliffe Camp. At the same time, they became aware that there was little or no resistance coming from the high ground ahead, but only from the flanks and, in particular, from Sandgate.

The first martyr

At last, the defenders of Sene Golf Course, had been overcome. They had fought with determination, but weight of German fire power (enhanced by four mortars which the German paratroops had brought up) and the skillful use of ground by their assailants had been too much. The defence of Saltwood also began to collapse as tanks and infantry, working their way into Hythe, found the way open. Shortly before 0600 hours, men of the 55th Infantry Regiment on the left of 17th Infantry Division linked up with a section from 20th Parachute Regiment on the slopes below the golf course. But it was a fateful meeting marred by the sort of incident which can convert a simple battle into a confused disaster. As the German soldiers began to relax and explore the surrounding houses, a 17-year-old youth, wearing plain clothes, graced by a grubby LDV arm band, let drive at a German officer with a shot gun – and missed. His capture in a nearby back garden and his appearance before the officer, together with the aged couple who

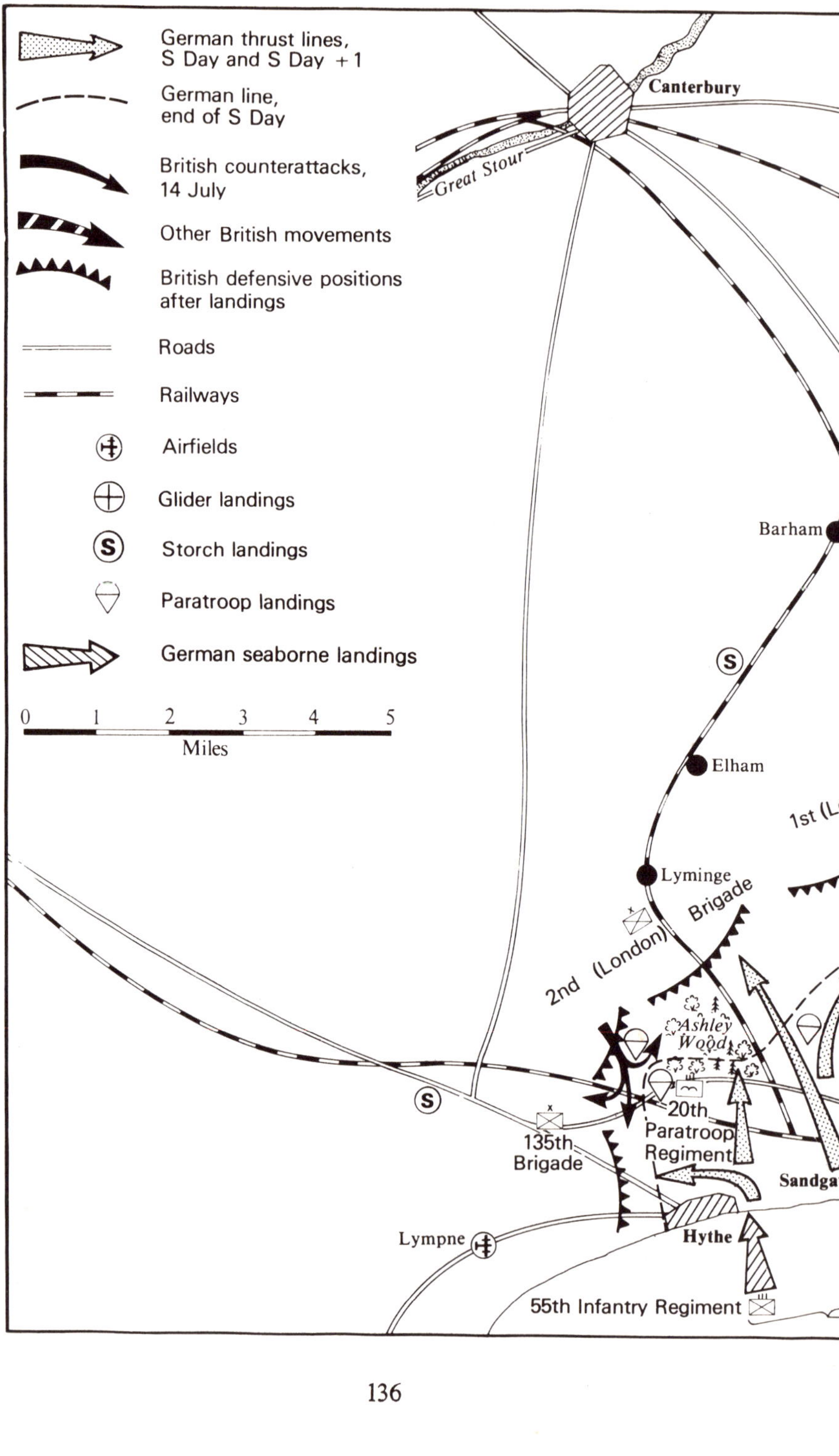
German thrust lines, S Day and S Day +1
German line, end of S Day
British counterattacks, 14 July
Other British movements
British defensive positions after landings
Roads
Railways
Airfields
Glider landings
Storch landings
Paratroop landings
German seaborne landings
0 1 2 3 4 5
Miles
Canterbury
Great Stour
Barham
Elham
Lyminge
1st (L
2nd (London) Brigade
Ashley Wood
20th Paratroop Regiment
135th Brigade
Sandga
Lympne
Hythe
55th Infantry Regiment

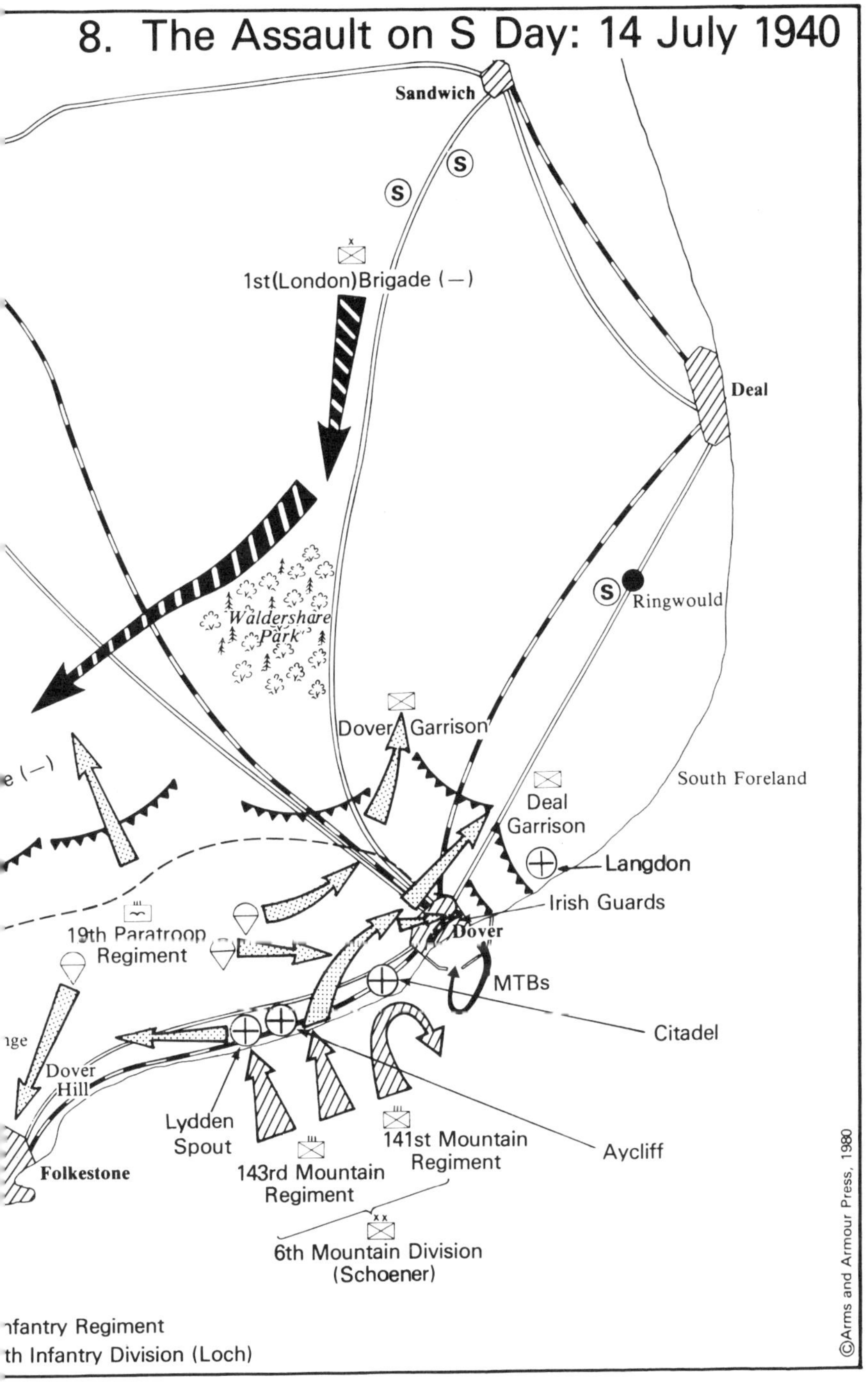
8. The Assault on S Day: 14 July 1940
Sandwich
1st(London)Brigade (—)
Deal
Waldershare Park
Ringwould
Dover Garrison
South Foreland
Deal Garrison
Langdon
Irish Guards
19th Paratroop Regiment
Dover
MTBs
Citadel
Dover Hill
Lydden Spout
Folkestone
143rd Mountain Regiment
141st Mountain Regiment
Aycliff
6th Mountain Division (Schoener)
nfantry Regiment
th Infantry Division (Loch)
©Arms and Armour Press, 1980

lived in the house to which the garden belonged, led swiftly to retribution in the heat of the moment. Charged as *franc tireurs* (whom the Germans for traditional reasons held in dread) the youth and his companions were put through a form of trial, found guilty and stood against a wall and shot. The incident was witnessed by civilians, as well as by soldiers, and word spread fast on both sides – the Germans with anger that the British were prepared to adopt this despicable form of warfare; the British in dismay and sickened at the rough justice meted out. Hatred born and never laid to rest after the First World War, was regenerated with fury as a result of this execution.

Battle of the cliff-tops

With Hythe securely in their hands, 17th Infantry Division, in conjunction with 20th Parachute Regiment, could now expand its sector of the bridgehead, according to plan, in a north-easterly direction. Even though 21st Infantry Regiment, due to a fanatical defence by British troops among the houses and gardens of Coolinge, had yet to penetrate Sandgate and make progress towards Folkestone Harbour, reinforcements could be brought in across the beaches and, with them, field artillery and 88mm guns carried on Siebel ferries. Both Folkestone and Dover harbours were, in fact, already dominated to some extent by the Germans. 19th Parachute Regiment had sent a company to seize Dover Hill overlooking Folkestone and on the way it had captured there the two 6in guns and the four 3.7in anti-aircraft guns. The airborne men who swarmed round the Citadel could actually see into Dover and only awaited the leading elements of 6th Mountain Division to complete the capture of the Citadel and begin the assault on the port.

Disaster under the cliffs

Weakness and disorder had been features of 6th Mountain Division's disembarkation below the Abbot's and Shakespeare Cliffs. A great many craft were missing or badly delayed. Unnerved men of the 141st Mountain Regiment were deposited higgledy-piggledy on the narrow foreshore and left to fend for themselves. The minesweepers and coasters which had brought them were under a raking fire from the Dover harbour guns and from machine-gunners of the Irish Guards along the sea front. Recording his impression of the scene laid out before him, Charles Foster, a freelance journalist, wrote:

'It was a ghastly and yet uplifting sight, reminiscent I suppose of the slaughter our lads had once suffered at Gallipoli in 1915. A fleet of what looked like fishing boats and barges, and a few warships, had sailed in and were being plastered by the guns on the mole. Then outboard motor boats began to appear, driving fast for the shore. Shot and shell which, I suppose, came from the German warships and some rather odd-looking barges, began to whistle about our ears, but without seeming to do much harm. The Irish Guards patiently held their fire until the boats reached the shore and men began to jump or, in some cases, flop out of them. And then every machine-gun and rifle in sight loosed off and the beach was churned to porridge by the bullets, and grey figures were stumbling helplessly and falling in rows. Realizing that the Hun was doomed, I was able to take in the scene at leisure – the small ships burning at sea or trying to escape under smoke, the motor boats close to shore folding up as they were hit, the waves of men withering until none moved apart from the wounded and hapless fugitives who crouched behind what few rocks there were to shield them. After 30 minutes we could cheer and exalt at the massacre of the invader.'

At Lydden Spout it was different. Here the 2nd Battalion of the 143rd Mountain Regiment retrieved 6th Mountain Division's fortunes, because British resistance had been eliminated already by the airborne troops on the cliff-tops who had begun firing at the defenders on the shore below. Mixed up as they were on landing, the mountaineers wasted no time climbing the steep spout. Those least afflicted by seasickness made the first ascent while those below recovered or began gingerly picking their way along the foreshore to seize control of the railway tunnels through the cliffs.

In the space of three hours, a foothold up to 3,000 yards deep had been won along the better part of the coast between Hythe and Dover. The 9.2in coastal guns, in their exposed cupolas on top of the Citadel, were taken in the rear and their gunners shot down at their posts; the Germans occupied the heights and began to ferret into the caverns below. Most of the remaining coastal guns had been wiped out or captured intact, as had been the anti-aircraft guns and the entire Shorncliffe Garrison. Neither the Royal Navy nor the Royal Air Force had intervened to any serious extent, and now the German follow-up flotillas were arriving in a steady flow which gradually dissolved into something akin to Formation Pigpile. But come they did, bringing reinforcements and the elements upon which a logistic service could be constructed and upon which the subsequent development of operations almost entirely depended. Likewise, the transport aircraft were playing their essential rôle, pouring in reinforcements and stores so that the surface supply lines might take care of all.

But the battle as yet was far from won. The Germans had still to take possession of a port, and already British naval demolition parties were busy destroying wharves and cranes. Also, the Royal Navy remained very much in being and had yet to make its effort; and the RAF, frustrated as it had been during the landing, was still to be reckoned with. There was a truculence, too, about the British civilians, let alone the belligerent soldiers, which gave notice that an early collapse of resistance could not be expected. Finally, a threatening weather forecast loomed which cancelled the promise that had sanctioned the start of 'Sea-lion'. In the circumstances, the Germans might have felt justified in saying, as had a British commander on the first day of the landings at Gallipoli in 1915, 'Now you must dig and dig until you are safe'.

Perhaps Ironside, Thorne and Liardet hoped they would, but in the meantime they had to bend all their ingenuity to the task of ejecting the enemy before he was safe, making use of forces whose capabilities were suspect to say the least.

X

THE FIGHT FOR THE BRIDGEHEAD

The counter-thrust

A prime cause of delay in the formulation of British plans throughout the crucial hours of 14 July was the acute shortage of reliable information made available to their commanders. The telephone services, through which the majority of signal traffic passed, were already depleted due to bombing and shelling, and radio networks were limited in number, far from reliable and insecure. It was midday before Liardet, at Ashford, and 1315 hours before Thorne, at Tunbridge Wells, received a clear indication of the nature and scope of the German presence around Dover. Until then Liardet felt unable to issue precise orders to his four brigades which, therefore, with the exception of 2nd (London) Brigade which converged on Folkestone, stayed in their existing locations. Meanwhile, Thorne tried to make up his mind whether to begin the pre-planned withdrawal from the coastal zone or stay for a little longer in the hope of throwing the Germans, with naval assistance, back into the sea. In London, Ironside, hourly pressed for strong measures by the CIGS (General Sir John Dill) and by Churchill, could only pester his subordinates and the other Services for news – and then wait. Radio signals from Ramsay at Dover, via the Admiralty, spoke of continuing resistance in the neighbourhood of the port.

At 1315 hours Liardet had a telephone conversation with Thorne and told him positively that the Germans were well-established between Hythe and Dover, that Folkestone must soon fall and that, to all intents and purposes, the advanced delaying position – the so-called Eastern Curtain – was out-flanked. Thorne, who had long ago dismissed the likelihood of his Corps making a stand,[1] rapidly made up his mind to commence the withdrawal to the GHQ Line that night. In a delayed telephone conversation with Ironside (which was interrupted by a line break) he convinced the

C-in-C that this was the correct course. Dill concurred, but when he told Churchill he drew the Prime Minister's wrath. Churchill had recently become discontent with the GHQ plan to surrender British soil without a stiff fight; and he rejected Dill's plea that to interfere with an existing scheme might well engender uncertainty and confusion. He insisted upon 1st Armoured Division, the best equipped and most experienced armoured formation in existence, being sent at once to counter-attack the Germans, regardless of the CIGS's plea that it would be operating unsupported, on ground with which it was unfamiliar.

'The tanks must thrust through to the beaches and destroy the enemy before he can advance another yard,' declared Churchill, and Dill was unable to withstand him.[2]

This turnabout in Whitehall caused further delay, and prevented Thorne and Liardet from acting upon confirmation of their intentions until 1830 hours. By that time Thorne had acquiesced to Liardet's urgent request that 1st (London) Brigade should be released to cordon off the Germans to the north of Dover and had given permission for the Royal Marines from Deal to shore up the defences which were holding the east flank of the German bridgehead. He also agreed that 6th Battalion Somerset Light Infantry should be taken from reserve in 135th Infantry Brigade in 45th Division and used to reinforce 2nd (London) Brigade in its endeavours to stop the Germans breaking through in the direction of Ashford. Having done what he could to seal-off the enemy holding, Thorne turned to the unexpected task of destroying it, telling 45th Division to do what it could to exert pressure in the direction of Folkestone (well knowing that its offensive power was virtually non-existent) and urging 1st Armoured Division forward during the night in order to strike towards Dover the following morning.

The British counter-offensive – if such it can be called – evolved rather than burgeoned as the product of dynamic and deliberate planning. Thorne cobbled together the elements of an attack which he hoped would begin at dawn on the 15th. The infantry and artillery support was to be improvized by Liardet, whose mobile elements tried hard to establish a firm base upon which the armour could base its efforts. The tank leaders were invited to move across ground of which they were ignorant with the minimum – in some cases, the total lack – of reconnaissance. Everything was done at a pace with which neither the training of the troops nor the foundering communication systems could cope. Meanwhile, the Chiefs of Staff in London were attempting to make arrangements for a co-ordinated naval and air effort, designed to unsettle the German commanders and cut their lines of communication. For the night of the 14th/15th, the Admiralty had already ordered a concentric occupation of the Straits of Dover by ships approaching from the Nore and Portsmouth. The RAF was to give maximum fighter support to the Royal Navy and persist in its night raids upon the invasion ports as well as upon ships at sea and transport aircraft over the Channel. But the RAF was in retreat and operating well below par. Much to Churchill's disgust, Newall backed Dowding's insistence on evacuation of the exposed airfields of Manston, Hawkinge and Lympne; these could no longer operate with any certainty and their skilled men could be better employed elsewhere. The Navy would receive all the help possible, but from a distance and at the expense of the Army for which, in consequence, nothing could be spared.

The Germans consolidate

To the Germans, as the 14th went by and no serious British counter-stroke developed, the expansion of their holdings proceeded with unexpected ease. By nightfall they could congratulate themselves upon seizing all their objectives without serious loss – all, that is, with the exception of Dover. Hythe was securely held, even if attempts to advance towards Lympne had been prevented. The high ground from Postling in a semi-circle through Alkham (including Hawkinge airfield) was largely in their possession, although here and there isolated British parties were making a nuisance of themselves. Resistance in Folkestone had been quelled at last light, after a grim fight among the hotels, the town centre, and the port, where British sailors and soldiers, assisted by the dockers, had fought, unreinforced, to the end. The setback to 6th Mountain Division at Aycliffe had been rectified by the remainder of the division and the paratroops seizing the Citadel (where all effective resistance came to an end late in the afternoon), and by the infiltration of the residential areas of Tower Hamlets and Buckland. At nightfall, the ramparts of Dover Castle were reached and groups of mountaineers were engaged with the Irish Guards in a fierce battle for the port area.

Most satisfactory of all from the point of view of Busch and Kesselring was the almost unimpeded flow of reinforcements which were getting across. It was true that the quantity of men and material finding its way through by sea was relatively small, but it did include a fair amount of transport, a significant number of 105mm artillery pieces and 88mm dual-purpose guns, besides just enough ammunition and fuel to sustain the forces ashore. Also the number of tanks brought in had risen to 50, with more on the way that night. Such was the progress that had been made with clearing air landing sites at West Hougham and, latterly Hawkinge, that a regular delivery of stores by air in addition to two Regiments from 22nd Air Landing Division was taking place. In effect, the Germans had managed to move in something like the equivalent of three divisions before nightfall, giving a clear local numerical superiority over the British. By then, too, the minelayers at sea had made good use of the hours of daylight, while protected by air power, to extend and thicken the barriers screening the flanks of the German sea lanes to Britain. In due course they would have guns pointing out to sea from Britain – some of them captured, some brought in on ferries. A hot reception was therefore being prepared for the Royal Navy's next entry into the Straits, which the Germans, reliably informed by the intercept and decoding of Admiralty signals, were confidently expecting.

Ships versus aircraft and mines

Shadowed by the Luftwaffe and bombed from the moment they left port, the daylight movement of two cruisers and 16 destroyers of Nore Command, under Admiral the Hon Sir R. Plunkett-Ernle-Erle-Drax, and the 8 destroyers of Admiral Sir William James's command out of Portsmouth, boded ill for the sailors, who could forget any hope of achieving surprise. The RAF could, at the most, put only two squadrons at a time over the warships, and these were almost invariably engaged by German fighters soon after their arrival. By sheer weight of numbers, Kesselring and Sperrle drove their dive-bombers through to the ships whose guns used up much precious ammunition long before they came in sight of the Straits. At last light, however, and at the price of a cruiser and a couple of destroyers badly damaged and limping for port, the two British flotillas were nearing their objective. Ahead lay the minefields (which could not possibly be adequately swept by minesweepers which were under persistent attacks by the Luftwaffe), a few anxious German destroyers and 2 U-boats – guarding a patch of water from which the German convoys were scuttling for safety as fast as they could.

Having, therefore, in the first instance, achieved something worthwhile by persuading the Germans to halt their sea traffic, neither British admiral was at all happy about trying to impose a physical and permanent presence in the Straits – even if they could

Above: A DFS 230 glider of the Luftwaffe, carrying a crew of two and eight troops. (Imperial War Museum)
Below: Units of the German invasion fleet put to sea. (Imperial War Museum)

Above: Landing point for the 17th Panzer Division: the beach at Hythe. (Author's collection)

Below: A Panzerkampfwagen III with schnorkel attachment, leaving a Prahm. (Imperial War Museum)

Above: Population on the move: evacuee children. (Imperial War Museum)

Below: A road-block under construction. (*Picture Post*)

Above: A German 37mm anti-tank gun being moved into action. It proved useless against heavily-armoured tanks such as the British Matilda. (Author's Collection).
Right: German infantry searching for snipers. (Author's Collection).

Above: Panzerkampfwagen 38(t) tanks advancing with infantry. (Imperial War Museum)

Below: A German 88mm dual-purpose gun in action in the ground rôle. (RAC Tank Museum)

Matilda IIs of the 1st Tank Brigade "brewing up". (Author's Collection)

reach them reasonably intact. They knew, from experience, the navigational hazards involved in the narrow seas and the perils of mine, bomb and shellfire – let alone from the many wrecks lying about. As if to remind them, German S boats sprang an ambush off the North Foreland and sank a destroyer, and from then on made Ernle-Erle-Drax fight for every mile of his advance. The out-gunned light German craft withdrew on the Straits where bigger guns on their old battleships and on shore could join in. Long-range gunnery by the light of a pale moon and from flares was never accurate, but it generated a wild excitement which wore down both sides. Several unfortunate *Prahms*, tugs and drifters were caught and destroyed, but ample warning had saved the rest which lay inshore on either side of the Channel waiting for the danger to go away – as, hopefully, Lütjens thought it must. But as the British ships began to search for more lucrative targets nearer Dover, a destroyer struck a mine and blew up, followed a few minutes later by another mine strike on the flagship, HMS *Manchester*. At once, the other captains grew wary and gave up the pursuit, preferring instead to prevent movement by a distant presence, and giving vent to pleasure when a report was received from the submarine *H 49* that she had torpedoed and sunk the already damaged *Schlesien*.

As for James's destroyers, one was torpedoed by a U-boat off Selsey Bill, leaving the rest to steam on less one of the destroyers which hunted the U-boat to its death. Off Beachy Head, when forced to manoeuvre by German destroyers and S boats, mines claimed a second destroyer and shellfire damaged a third. And when James learnt that German traffic across the Straits had been stopped and his colleague had retired, he too held back, contenting himself with a brisk gun battle against the German destroyers which hung on his flanks. And so, when dawn broke on the 15th, the British ships were maintaining the blockade of the Straits at a distance and declining to interpose physically at the narrowest point for fear of a catastrophe – as undeniably there would have been in those unswept channels. To Kesselring the British fleet presented a target to be bombed to distraction, while to Lütjens the scale of Kesselring's assault plus incontrovertible indications that the British were reluctant to enter the Straits, was a clear invitation to restart the movement of shipping to and from the Continent.

Despite a deterioration of visibility, damage to the British ships mounted throughout the morning. Although, for reasons which will be described below, the Germans were unable to throw in all the bombers they would have liked, the efforts of their dive-bombers kept the ships at bay, while the RAF fighters, caught up in a furious battle for survival, which will also be described later, were unable to spare the effort to take the pressure off the Navy. In any case, the atrophy of inland communications was nullifying the early warning system, depriving the fighters of any advantage they had once enjoyed. At 1100 hours, with evidence to hand that the enemy had recommenced his convoy sailings and that air traffic was moving to and fro without hinderance, Ernle-Erle-Drax transferred his flag from the *Manchester* to a destroyer, intent upon a despairing dash into the Straits. But a few minutes later this ship was hit by a bomb and her after gun turret wrecked, and news arrived of James having lost yet another destroyer on a mine. Casualties apart – and these were severe enough – there was another factor which compelled the Royal Navy to withdraw its ships: they were running out of ammunition. Left to their own protection against sea and air forces, they used up shells at a prodigious rate which could not long be sustained by destroyers whose magazines, for example, held only 200–250 rounds per gun. In these circumstances, a return to port was compulsory in order, with tired crews, to undertake the laborious chore of replenishment in dockyards which were under air bombardment, or the threat of it, and the efficiency of which was in decline as facilities were damaged and the dock labour force quailed before attack. In plain terms, the Navy was out-matched, suffering losses without achieving commensurate return; finding it impossible to maintain a prolonged presence across the enemy lines of communications in the long hours of daylight, while the shorter hours of darkness (in which it could operate with a measure of safety) were not long enough to permit decisive intervention.[3] For the better part of the day it had to be recognized that the Germans possessed almost free use of the Straits.

While the struggle in the Straits raged, the bombers of both sides made whatever contribution they could – those from the RAF hitting the invasion ports and concentrations of shipping, those from the Luftwaffe attacking the land routes leading to the bridgehead. At the same time, the Germans within the bridgehead worked diligently to re-establish order among their forces which had become intermingled during the landing, and push out their forward defences to give maximum depth and security to the air landing zones and ports. Above all, they concentrated on thrusting northward, from Hawkinge towards Barham, and eastwards towards Deal, while the capture of Dover was completed in the badly damaged port and among the crumbling ruins of the Castle. For their part, the men under command of 1st (London) Division fought with a sense of depair. Deprived of artillery support and woefully short of ammunition of all kinds, quite apart from being insufficiently trained, they could only stand and die, run or surrender when their means to resist had been expended. It was with a tinge of regret that Leutnant Max Groener of the 6th Mountain Division described the last stand by a platoon of Irish Guards in the vicinity of the Dover Train Ferry dock:

'It was obvious to us, as we blasted the area, that the enemy was at his last gasp and that his ammunition was almost spent. But when we called upon him to surrender he answered with ribaldry and two or three rifle shots. And after we had saturated their position again with bullets and brought in a flame-thrower, there were still some who showed defiance. Eventually, and with deep respect, we had to kill every man at his post.'

Dover falls

The Castle fell shortly after first light, the last message from Ramsay striking an heroic note of defiance when the Admiral spoke in person on the telephone to Thorne as sounds of a gun battle could be heard in the background. The port was almost unusable, with block ships in place, cranes and wharves wrecked, and a shortage of experts and labour to put it right. The town itself, however, yielded useful quantities of supplies and vehicles, many of the latter still fit for use despite orders to their owners to immobilize them. Some 60,000 gallons of petrol were found in and about the town and port and this would help tide the Army over its initial shortages until the lines of communication were functioning to capacity.[4] Instructed from on high to improvize and make every possible use of British material and live off the land, the Germans complied with enthusiasm. The sight of even a few of their supply vessels burning at sea was enough to impress the need for economy and encourage pillage as a means to survival.

1st Armoured Division committed

Improvization in the struggle for survival also provided a serious threat to the counter-attack by 1st Armoured Division (Major-General R. Evans) as arranged. This formation had not recovered from the battering it had received in France, and its number of units and vehicles in no way matched its intended establishment and rôle. Instead of two brigades, each of three regiments of cruiser and light tanks, it had three depleted brigades of only two regiments each, each of which was understrength. In the 3rd Armoured Brigade (Brigadier J. T. Crocker), there were 70 fast cruiser tanks of various kinds manned by battle-experienced crews. Ist Tank Brigade (Brigadier D. H. Pratt) was, however, equipped with the much slower, though more thickly armoured, infantry tanks which had given the Germans such a shock at Arras. The inexperienced 8th RTR had 50 of these and the battle-experienced 4th RTR, 32. But the latter had taken over their machines and operational rôle from 7th RTR as recently as 13 July, and, therefore, had had no time to do much work on them. 20th Armoured Brigade (Brigadier E. D. Fanshawe) was equipped with a mixture of light tanks, armoured cars and lorries and therefore was capable of giving only reconnaissance and infantry assistance to the division. The towed 25-pounder guns of 3rd Royal Horse Artillery would give artillery support, but necessarily it would be thin when split between the brigades; moreover, the gunners, like the rest of the Army, suffered from frail communications because of the endemic shortage of radio sets.[5]

Originally it has been intended that 1st Armoured Division, which stood guarding vital points and airfields between the River Thames and Horley in Surrey, should move to its battle zone by rail. But the state to which Southern Railways had been reduced from air attacks put this out of the question. Evans told Thorne that, if the division were required in action near Dover on the 15th, a move on the night of 14th/15th was imperative to avoid attention by the Luftwaffe, and it would have to be by road. He warned that, even if granted the best of good fortune and the least hindrance on the roads, it would be a stroke of luck to effect a concentration at the desired place, and even luckier to launch a properly prepared attack by the afternoon of that day. Thorne, who knew better than Evans the extent to which the roads were already congested, could but silently concur while insisting vehemently that the attack be launched with the least possible delay. It was agreed to execute a two-pronged assault, with 3rd Armoured Brigade on the left making for Canterbury and then driving south-eastwards via Barham to Dover. Simultaneously, 1st Tank Brigade would concentrate in the Lyminge Forest before assaulting the Elham–Lyminge–Postling feature, as a preliminary to re-taking Hawkinge airfield and the West Hougham high ground beyond. 1st (London) Division was to cooperate to the full, to place its meagre artillery in support of the attack, and use its infantry to occupy the ground taken.

In convoy, the best speed cruiser tanks could move was 12mph, while the infantry tanks could only manage 8mph. In the event, these speeds were never achieved in the dark, through the traffic cluttered roads and round the diversions forced by bomb damage. Halts for refuelling and maintenance conspired to delay 1st Armoured Division, as did the refugees whose plight was heart-rending to soldiers who, on the one hand were desperately anxious to throw the Germans back into the sea and, on the other, reluctant to behave brutally to their own people and push them off the road. The fighting men's dilemma was made no easier, as they wended their way through columns of lorries, private cars, bicycles and horse carts, by the appeallingly even temper of the refugees, who had fled on impulse, and who, in many cases, were vehement in their encouragement of the soldiers in their task.

The refugee problem, indeed, was at its height that night. By a mighty effort of persuasion and coercion, the police were beginning to divert them from the main routes. To a large extent, however, the reduction in this migration came about because people began to see that there could be no possible escape if the Germans chose to come their way. Panic began to subside as a will to win was restored, a spirit which was stimulated by Churchill over the radio on the night of the 14th when, in resounding terms, he had reminded his listeners of the nation's duty to the Cause of Freedom and in the service of its past traditions. He had spoken of the stirring fight by the Army and the Navy and had reviled the atrocities which had already been inflicted upon innocent by-standers. He had extolled the sacrifice of the pilots of the Royal Air Force who were 'tearing the enemy bombers from the skies in a pitiless battle for our very survival'. 'Grim will be the news in the days to come,' he said, 'Hard will be the blows we will suffer and grievous the injuries inflicted upon our beautiful and beloved land. But we will persevere, regardless of the cost, until we have won the final victory and thrown the Nazi guttersnipes back into the sea whence they came. Now let every man and woman go forth into battle, armed for the struggle and abandoning all thought of rest – and certainly of life – until our native soil has been cleansed of this foul presence. May God be with you in this sacred task.'

But the Prime Minister already knew that his oratory might be meaningless. The Straits had not been closed by the Navy. Dover and Folkestone had fallen. The RAF's bombers were seemingly making little impression and its fighters were being overborne. When Dowding saw Churchill and Newall at 1900 hours on the 14th it was to tell them that the last of the reserve fighters were being dispatched to the squadrons, but that this could not restore the full fighting strength of his Command which was operating at barely 65 per cent of its essential capacity.

An Intelligence wind-fall

Even as Dowding spoke, the Sword of Damocles was about to fall. That afternoon, the 14th, a party of Luftwaffe officers had landed at Hawkinge to begin making it ready to operate Me 109s. Entering the undamaged, single-storey control building they had found, intact, diagrams and documents which had escaped destruction in the hasty evacuation and which betrayed at a glance the Command and Control system of RAF Fighter Command. Without delay this invaluable information was sent to Kesselring where he conducted the battle from his 'Holy Mountain' overlooking Calais. Laid out before him were clues to the vital part played by the Sector Stations.

'Those airfields,' commanded Kesselring, after a brief examination, 'will be priority targets tomorrow. They must be eliminated immediately and, if necessary, the Kriegsmarine may have to do with a little less help than it wants, and the Army may have to be without bombing support. It will be worth it. If we can destroy the enemy's apparatus of control the campaign is settled!'

Throughout the 14th at Hitler's headquarters, the news coming in from the invasion front looked bad. Ill-tidings assumed precedence in the Führer's imagination (and that of the pessimists on his staff) over good news. Incomplete messages from the threatened left flank formations of 7th Air Division tended to override the far better news from the secure right flank, on the cliff-tops and of the Langdon guns being out of action. Messages telling of the disaster at Aycliffe and the hold-up on the beaches at Sandgate and Hythe rather over-shadowed a calm appreciation from Busch, which indicated that the successful airborne landings probably compensated for setbacks at sea. But what Hitler and Raeder dreaded most was the news that the Royal Navy was loose in the Channel and that the RAF was still making its presence felt.

At midday, Goering had found himself under heavy criticism and pressure. Protest as he might, that the enemy air effort was not preventing the essential plan from working and that, in any case, there were clear signs of a falling-off in resistance, this satisfied neither Hitler nor Raeder, both of whom had always insisted upon total air supremacy as a guarantee of overall success. The announcement from Lütjens that sailings between France and England had been suspended and that heavy losses had been sustained by surface craft, exaggerated as the latter information was, suggested to imaginative minds that a calamity of untold proportions was threatening doom. Goering began to wilt under a barrage of criticism, and it took a memorable effort of persuasion by von Brauchitsch, backed up by Jodl when Keitel wavered, to prevent the Führer giving unpremeditated orders which might easily have stalled the invasion in its tracks. Wrote Jodl:

> 'The Army C-in-C was remarkably calm as Hitler ranted and Goering procrastinated. Remembering how callously Hitler had treated von Brauchitsch in the past, it was a courageous act of his to confront the Führer with coolly reasoned arguments with a political flavour, pointing out that, to call off the battle now, would cause damage of untold magnitude. The Army's confidence would be sapped, he said, and that might have unimaginable consequences beyond even its wide boundaries. I think Hitler recognized the political threat which was being implied – and that sort of angle was rarely lost upon him: he still feared that the Army might rebel. Rather grudgingly, I thought, he agreed to withhold a decision until more information had come to hand. I asked for 36 hours, with the proviso that an immediate study be made into the feasibility and consequences of withdrawal. The Führer would only put matters off until midday the 15th, insisting that by then there must be a marked reduction in enemy sea and air activity. That was the best we could obtain.'

Naturally, as the day wore on and fresh reports began to come in that the enemy fleet (*sic*) was withdrawing, spirits began to revive, but the air battle sounded as if it were as intense as ever and, of course, the news and significance of the discovery about RAF organization did not immediately filter through. So far as Hitler and OKW were concerned, the night watches of the 14th/15th were spent in acute tension and a furious planning session as to how to evacuate the troops already landed in England if Hitler irretrievably lost his nerve next day. Raeder was sure the Royal Navy would return quickly in strength. Goering, himself, began to have doubts if Kesselring could pull it off (and by telephone he pestered the commander of Luftflotte 2 with cajolery and threats), while von Brauchitsch, in consultation with an habitually worried von Rundstedt at Army Group A, kept to himself the worry of what would happen when the inevitable enemy counter-attack on land materialized.

All in all, as S day drew to a close, they were a gloomy group who controlled the destiny of Operation 'Sealion'.

XI

CHECK AND COUNTER-CHECK

Tanks advance

When the weird mixture of tanks, armoured cars and trucks of 20th Armoured Brigade arrived at, respectively, Canterbury and Ashford en route for battle, they found orders awaiting them to probe ahead in order to make contact with the forward elements of 1st (London) Division, as a preliminary to the attack by the tank brigades which had yet to put in an appearance. Unit and sub-unit commanders had travelled in advance of the main columns and by 0700 hours were up among the defenders of the line Womenswold to Stowting, endeavouring to arrange for the projected attack. An hour earlier, the infantry had repulsed German patrols, and the guns of 1st (London) Division were firing desultory shots at parties of Germans which could sometimes be seen on the ridges beyond and attempting to infiltrate into the valleys below. To the sound of air battles and in the knowledge that it must be between three and five hours before all the tanks had reached their forming-up areas, the tank officers laid their plans – and found at the outset that the units of the London Division with whom they were to collaborate, and which had fallen back before German infiltration during the night, had only the haziest idea of the local situation, let alone how to cooperate with tanks.

It came as a surprise to the tank crews that, even in daylight, they were scarcely troubled by air attacks – this despite the spectacular air battles going on overhead. They were, of course, witnesses of Kesselring's all-out attack upon the Sector Airfields, and those few of his aircraft which took the opportunity to fire at ground targets did so only as a diversion from their main occupation of destroying Fighter Command. The 62 tanks in 3rd Armoured Brigade which concentrated north-east of Barham at 1100 hours had completed refuelling by midday. 1st Tank Brigade was secure in Lyminge Forest with 42 tanks a little later, but, due to refugees holding up its supply echelon, was not replenished until 1330 hours. Evans, who was resolved to adhere to its original two-pronged advance, at 1215 hours abandoned the concept of a simultaneous attack and ordered Crocker to move at once, telling Pratt to start the moment he was ready.

Supported by two batteries of 25-pounder guns, 2nd and 5th RTR broke cover and moved along either side of the A2 at their best speed. As they passed through the lines of 1st (London) Brigade they were joined by the 8th Bn Royal Fusiliers and flanked by the light tanks and armoured cars of 1st Northants Yeomanry. Ahead, the smoke from Dover and the surrounding villages rose sadly in the air while a few distracted civilians scurried aimlessly here and there. Not until the tanks topped the Womenswold ridge were German infantry observed in the distance, and some ineffectual mortar and anti-tank fire from small calibre weapons was encountered. Accelerating, the cruiser tanks closed with the enemy and started a panic among some men of 22nd Air Landing Division who were themselves preparing to continue their advance on Barham and Canterbury.

If the British attack had come sooner it might seriously have embarrassed the Germans. As it was, von Vietinghoff's regrouping of formations had proceeded sluggishly due to shortage of transport and the reluctance of divisional and battle-group commanders, who had made spectacular gains with only light forces during the night, to release tanks and guns to each other for fear of exposing their already thin defensive positions to even greater risk. It took some forceful talking by the corps commander to have his way, and it was not until after midday that a centrally-placed armoured reserve of 60 tanks was assembled at Hawkinge, and a line of 88mm dual-purpose guns pushed forward to the outer perimeter of the bridgehead. Things hung by a shoe-string. Some tanks and guns, together with fuel and ammunition, had gone to the bottom under the Royal Navy's guns and through bombing, but a great many more had been diverted in their ships to the shelter of the French coast and were only now in transit again. Although it was the intention to advance and keep the situation fluid on the 15th, most German commanders tended to hold back to establish solid defended localities until truly effective air, artillery and tank support could be produced – as was then far from the case.

Thus Crocker's 3rd Armoured Brigade found itself tackling thin enemy defences which were occupied by jittery men. Air reconnaissance reports about the approach of massed tanks unsettled the Germans so that, when the lightly armoured British tanks did

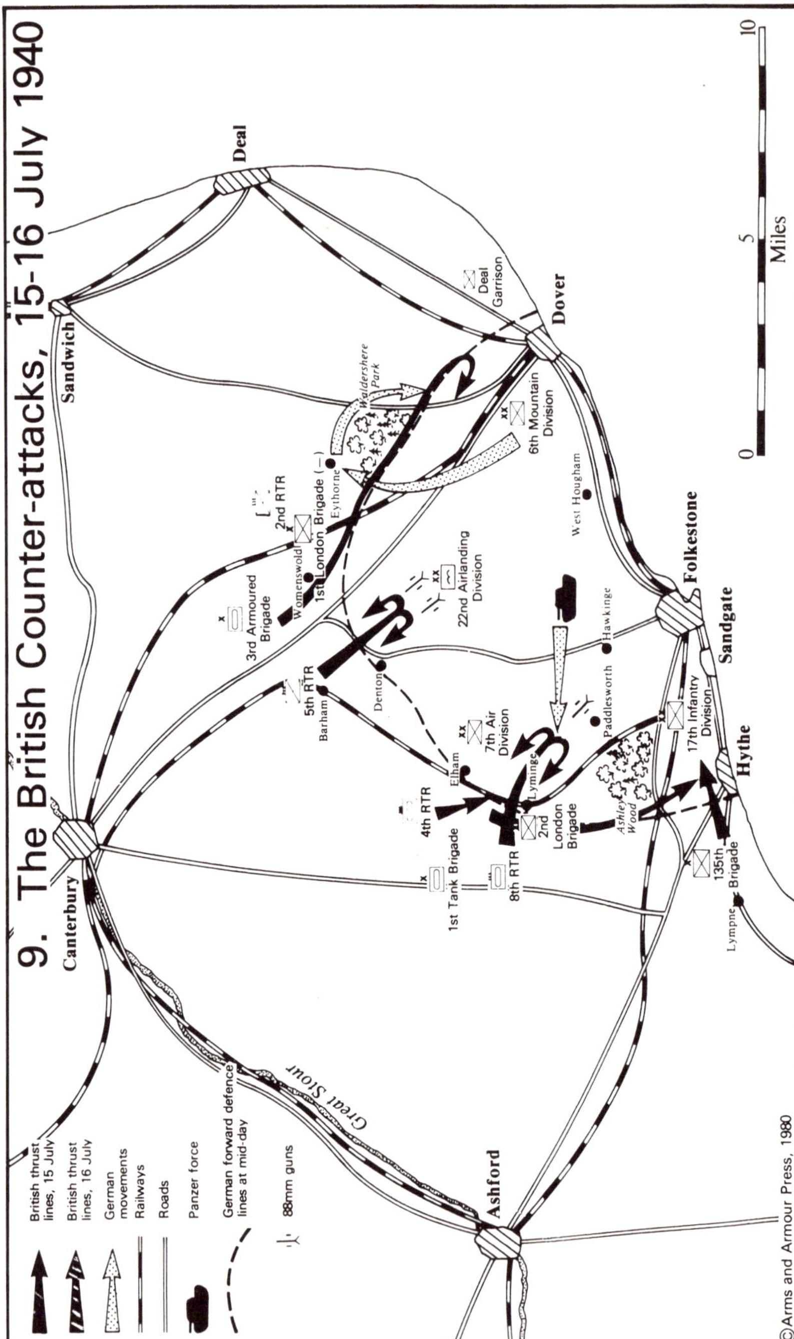

9. The British Counter-attacks, 15-16 July 1940

appear, the 37mm anti-tank gunners were inclined to shoot wildly and give up readily. They scored very few hits and were rapidly by-passed by the British who plunged eagerly in the direction of Dover. Not until 5th RTR, after negotiating the valley south of Barham and nosing through Denton (which had previously received a pre-planned concentration of 25-pounder fire), came out into the open were they checked. But there the 37mm gunners, stiffened in their resolve by the recent arrival of four 88mm guns, stuck it out. When the leading cruiser tank burst into flames and another had its turret knocked off by an 88, the British tank commanders came on more cautiously, feeling the way ahead under cover of dead ground and smoke – but to little avail. Encouraged by their initial successes, the fire of the German guns became devastating. The leading squadron lost half its tanks in a three-minute shoot-up and the advance came to a halt. Attempts to push another squadron round to the west were abortive and costly. Further movement was abandoned in the hope that artillery fire might eliminate these terrifying guns while 2nd RTR applied leverage by its, as yet, unchecked advance on the left.

Aided by some badly-needed luck, and helped by excellent use of the close country to the south-east of Womenswold, where the German forward defences were least well-developed, 2nd RTR cared not, at first, that neither the infantry nor the attached artillery observer failed to keep up. The tanks had it all their own way. Veering to the eastward to avoid the German guns which were known to be defending the high ground on either side of Lydden, 2nd RTR swept through Waldershare Park and headed for Whitfield, wreaking havoc as they went. Germans who were facing east were suddenly told to face north, while guns from the outskirts of Dover were pushed into position above the Buckland Valley and 30 tanks told to move post-haste from Hawkinge to Lydden. It was at this moment that von Vietinghoff also began to receive reports of still more British tanks debouching from the woods opposite Elham and Lyminge, seemingly with the intention of striking at Hawkinge. These, of course, were the heavily armoured Matildas of 1st Tank Brigade, which began their assault in two columns shortly after 1500 hours. They began their advance just as 2nd RTR was starting to hit heavy resistance for the first time near Whitfield and beginning to realize that, due to lack of support, further progress into the built-up areas was improbable. The fire directed against 2nd RTR was of a desperate intensity – the sort which causes superficial damage to machines but which deters men from charging into its midst. Although four tanks

British Tanks Involved

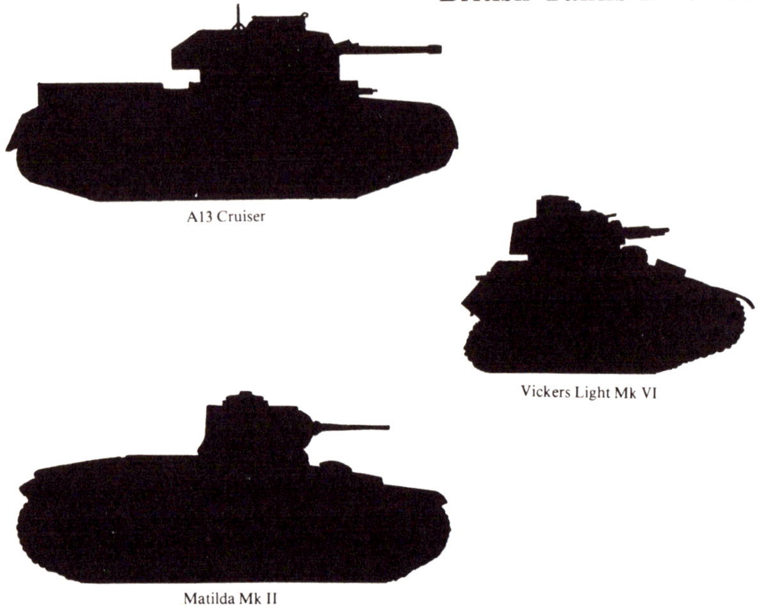

British Tanks Involved

	Vickers Light Mk VI	A13 Cruiser	Matilda Mk II
Weight	5 tons	14 tons	26 tons
Speed	30mph	30mph	15mph
Armament	2 x mg	1 x 40mm 1 x mg	1 x 40mm 1 x mg
Armour (max.)	14mm	14mm	78mm
Crew	3	4	4

entered Guston, little more than two miles from Dover, their commanders felt quite unable to go farther until something was done to give them infantry and artillery help. So 2nd RTR, with the concurrence of Crocker, attempted to maintain a threat to the eastern German flank, while endeavouring to bring pressure to bear against the enemy guns near Lydden in the hope of eliminating the resistance to 5th RTR.[1]

The attack by Pratt's 1st Tank Brigade was less spectacular than that by 3rd Armoured Brigade. Moving at a ponderous and yet inexorable gait, they crossed the valley, brushing aside resistance as they climbed to the crest-line ahead. German 37mm anti-tank gun crews which stayed to fight, saw their shot bounce harmlessly off the Matilda's thick skins. What was more, as the tanks reached their first objective, the crews had the pleasure of finding that infantry from 2nd (London) Brigade were close behind. Four miles away, the enemy landing zones were denoted by transport aircraft landing and taking off. For the first time in its history, the élite 7th Air Division found itself beset by a foe who seemed unstoppable, and even these fine troops began to give ground at a rate which did not meet with their leader's approval. With sinking hearts the German watched the Matildas take possession of the high ground and begin to fan out – some driving due south towards the beaches at Hythe and the others, on the right, making straight for Hawkinge. But at this moment it was noticed, too, that the British infantry were no longer in as close attendance as it had been. They were engaged, in fact, in mopping-up by-passed Germans in the villages and copses. As a result, the tanks of 1st Tank Brigade, like those in 3rd Armoured Brigade, found themselves nearing built-up areas when they were deficient of essential escorts and, equally upsetting, out of touch with their artillery whose observers hung back on the dominant Lyminge feature. Only the light, tracked and wheeled vehicles of the 2nd Northants Yeomanry kept up with the Matildas.

Destruction of the armour

In an arc from Densole to Postling through Paddlesworth and Ashley Wood, 88s awaited their prey, while the score of Pz Kpfw III tanks (whose 37mm guns were useless against Matildas) stood ready at Paddlesworth to counter-attack. Von Vietinghoff went there in person to direct operations, at the same time telling Generalmajor Schoerner, the forceful leader of 6th Mountain Division, to restore the situation in the vicinity of Dover. Von Vietinghoff watched his gunners open fire and saw the Matildas stagger under their blows. To the crews of 4th RTR at Elham, who had experienced this sort of treatment at Arras in May without realizing that it was 88mm guns which were reducing their tanks to scrap, the sensible solution seemed to be to pull back and try to find ways through the dead ground to the north. But this proved difficult and slow. 8th RTR, whose first time in action this was, tried to press-on regardless of the cost, and lost a squadron in ten minutes in front of Lyminge. The rest of the regiment swerved under the lee of Postling Wood, and with the help of 2nd Northants Yeomanry, managed to knock out a couple of 88s and punch a hole in the German ring at the boundary between the 7th Air and 17th Infantry Divisions. Shortly, a few armoured cars and the better part of a squadron of Matildas were crossing the railway near Sandling Station and rumbling towards Saltwood. They had come to grips with German defenders before news of this breakthrough reached von Vietinghoff and prompted him to dispatch ten of his reserve Pz Kw IIIs to the rescue. Yet these arrived when the battle was already decided. German infantry, by firing everything they had at the British vehicles, were able to set fire to kit strapped on the outside of the Matildas and destroy a number of the Yeomanry's thinner-skinned machines. Even so, a solitary Matilda and two light tanks waddled up to the banks of the Royal Military Canal and caused immense alarm and some damage to German troops and equipment on the beaches before a hastily laid mine immobilized the Matilda and the light tanks were knocked out. The handful of light tanks and armoured cars prowling around Saltwood and Sene Golf Course remained a threat but had lost momentum.

As these dramatic events were taking place, Schoerner was leading his divisional reserve (II Battalion 143rd Mountain Regiment) to link up with the 30 Pz Kpfw IIIs at his disposal, prior to throwing them in a north-easterly direction across the A2 road in the direction of Eythorne. The tanks ran straight into 1st (London) Brigade as it was trying to catch up with 2nd RTR, their appearance producing a dreadful effect upon the British, whose anti-tank defence consisted only of anti-tank rifles and the guns of a couple of cruiser tanks which had fallen behind the others. Within 45 minutes, the tanks had been destroyed and the infantry were prisoners or in flight. Schoerner, quick to exploit his opportunity, now sent off his tanks in a south-easterly direction to fall upon the 2nd RTR. Between Eythorne and Whitfield the opposing tank forces collided. Their machines were roughly equal in performance; the German slightly out-numbered but concentrated; the British surprised, spread out, still trying to find a way into Dover. Crocker, who was up with the commander of the 2nd, narrowly escaped capture. As for the 2nd, it fought as best it could after recovering from the initial shock. But gradually its casualties mounted until, shortly before last light, with only eight tanks left in action, orders were received to pull out to the north if they could.

The 1st Armoured Division retained a useful portion of its strength even though it had suffered nearly 40 per cent casualties in machines. As an offensive weapon it was, however, blunted, and prey therefore to the pressures applied by local British infantry leaders who wanted nothing better than to have tanks with them, dotted along the front. Both Crocker and Pratt resisted this strongly, and with some success, but of the machines which survived at nightfall, only a proportion managed to rally next morning in readiness for their next task.

An important victory

Only slowly did it dawn upon the Germans that they had won an important victory. At the height of the battle, von Vietinghoff had sent an anxious signal to Busch in France, stressing the need for reinforcements and, above all, the provision of heavy air support when the British renewed their attack. Busch was satisfied that the Kriegsmarine and the Luftwaffe were doing everything possible to send men and material across and that, with the withdrawal of the

German Tanks Involved

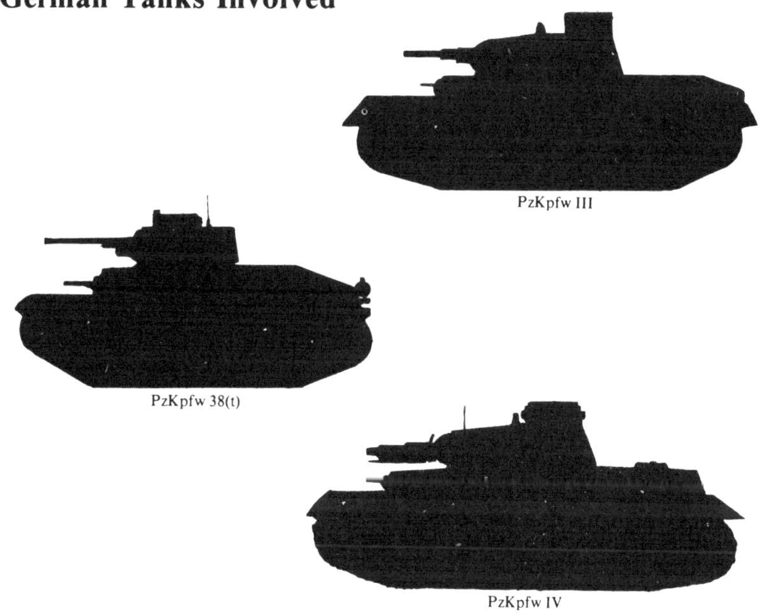

German Tanks Involved

	PzKpfw 38(t)	PzKpfw III	PzKpfw IV
Weight	11 tons	19 tons	20 tons
Speed	35mph	25mph	25mph
Armament	1 x 37mm	1 x 37mm	1 x 75mm
	2 x mg	3 x mg	2 x mg
Armour (max.)	50mm	30mm	30mm
Crew	4	5	5

Royal Navy, the movement of supply ships had recommenced. But he made it clear in person to Kesselring that, no matter how important it might be to complete the destruction of the RAF, that would be pointless if, due to lack of air support, the Army in England was overrun.

Kesselring, who was well aware of how finely-balanced was 'Sea-lion's' future at OKW, was as yet unsure how well his battering of Sector airfields had worked, and was beginning to feel concerned about the state of his Staffeln, all of which were being overworked, was sufficiently impressed to pilot Busch in person to Hawkinge in his Storch. There they were relieved to hear von Vietinghoff put their worst fears at rest with the news that the British counter-attack had been contained. But he thought they would try again, and he explained the paucity of his reserves and how Schoerner had used up his last resources, and lost 20 out of 30 tanks in the fierce tank battle. Busch joined in, saying that the Straits would probably again be closed that night and that, therefore, the Army would be stretched thinner than ever. If more heavy equipment could not be got across, Kesselring must substitute for it with bombing. As a fine and experienced soldier himself, Kesselring was sensitive to his colleague's anxiety. He promised full dive-bomber support next day, taking heart from a message just handed to him which said that the RAF fighters were undoubtedly far fewer in number and that their Controllers were repeatedly 'off the air'. This seemed to indicate that the Sector Stations had suffered.

As indeed they had. The bombing had caught aircraft on the ground, demolished important repair facilities and smashed control rooms and communication links. With their numbers depleted and their control facilities crippled, the fighters lost heavily. As the day wore on, Dowding was forced to tell 10 and 12 Groups that they could no longer depend upon 11 Group and that, in the near future, the whole system of Home Air Defence would have to be put on a different footing. Fighter Command, Dowding said, could no longer provide a shield for British cities if it was also to help the Services in the sea and land battles. In actuality, as he knew, all hope of deterring the Luftwaffe through punishing losses was gone. The RAF, itself, was finding it hard to survive.

The chief limitation Kesselring placed on the use of the dive-bombers in support of the Army next day, was that they should be used only against enemy mobile forces and not in support of local infantry operations. Something had to held back to deal with the Royal Navy if it intervened again in daylight. But it was heartening, when he and Busch flew back, to see below in the fading light, the shapes and wakes of sea transport making for England, and to know that some vital equipment must reach their destination. Nowhere on either flank could be seen any sign of the Royal Navy.

The sense of optimism generated by Kesselring and Busch arrived too late to affect the vital meeting at OKW at 1300 hours on the 15th, when the decision to proceed with or cancel 'Sealion' was debated. By then, a much more complete picture of the situation had been assembled compared to that of the 14th. Furthermore, news of the commencement of the British armoured attack had not yet come through to disturb composure. That the lodgement was well made, if somewhat insecurely based, was no longer in doubt, as von Brauchitsch proudly explained. And both Raeder and Goering were now hopeful. The unexpected reduction in activity by the Royal Navy allayed some of the anxiety, while the hope that Kesselring's attack on the Sector Stations (as yet unassessed in its effectiveness) might finally win air superiority, were factors in favour of continuing. But it was Keitel who made the vital contribution, briefed as he now was about the consequences of withdrawal should it be demanded. The Conference Minutes put his case in a nutshell:

> General Keitel said that under adverse conditions on the sea and in the air it would be even more difficult to evacuate the land forces than it would be to go on trying to maintain them. In point of fact, the existence on English soil of some four German divisions meant that the Wehrmacht had passed the point of no return.

Reader remarked in his diary, with wry amusement, that Hitler seemed to blink at this bare assertion. But he had no adequate reply – 'and so we persevered and carried on worrying.'

XII

THE TRADE-OFF

Counting the cost

Shortly before midnight on 15 July, Churchill was told that 1st Armoured Division had been checked and repulsed, and for a moment it looked as if the Prime Minister's indomitable spirit had been broken. He sat brooding in silence, weighing the consequences before asking searching questions and then addressing his Chiefs of Staff and his closest advisers – Anthony Eden, Sir John Anderson (the Home Secretary) and Lord Halifax (the Foreign Secretary). They must face the future with brutal frankness, he declared, for this heavy blow at the end of a day soaked in bad news demolished all hope of a quick ejection of the enemy. Already Pound had described the difficulties the Navy was having in cutting the enemy's lines of communication, and Newall had stated that, as a result of the perceptive and accurate attacks on the Sector Stations, 11 Group was virtually impotent. On the morrow, Newall explained, Fighter Command would be achieving miracles to put 200 fighters in the air, while Bomber Command could manage about the same number of machines, but these could not operate with any chance of survival except at night. For the first time in many centuries the British would be compelled to fight on their own soil, inflicting severe damage on their homes, hearths, kith and kin instead of those of other people.

Churchill did not flinch once the initial shock had passed. Together with the inner Cabinet and the Chiefs of Staff he thrashed out new directives.

1. The Royal Navy must try again and again, regardless of the cost, to close the Straits. No longer could the Capital ships be held back until the German Fleet put to sea – if it had ever intended to do so. Now, the C-in C-Home Fleet, Admiral Sir Charles Forbes who, until then, had disbelieved the Germans would try to invade,[1] must commit everything.

2. The Army would be permitted to make a 'fighting withdrawal' to the GHQ Line, while deploying strong forces to delay a deep westward enemy encroachment to the vital ports and aircraft factories of Portsmouth and Southampton. At the right moment, another attempt by the mobile forces to cripple the enemy must be made.

3. The RAF must concentrate upon disrupting the enemy build-up by attacking his bases on both sides of the Channel, and by lending fighter protection to the Fleet – even if this meant laying open the rest of the country to unopposed bombing.

4. Regional Government would be augmented with the grant of full powers to Regional Commissioners– acting, of course, within Central Government guidelines. Food shortages, notably in the invaded region, were expected, perhaps over the entire country now that the Channel was closed and the Port of London strangled. The way the police, the AFS and the ARP were to function in the enemy presence was also discussed, but in some confusion. For while there were those who suggested that the civilian Services should cooperate with the occupying power in the interests of the people, and thereby place the police, for example, in the position of discouraging resistance, Churchill thought that 'The police, the ARP and the fire services, etc., should withdraw from any invaded area with the last of His Majesty's troops.'[2] 'We do not,' he said, 'contemplate or encourage fighting by persons not in the armed forces, but we do not forbid it,' adding that the unarmed members of the Services, 'will actively assist in the stay-put policy for civilians. Should they fall into an area effectively occupied by the enemy, they may surrender and submit with the rest of the inhabitants, but must not in those circumstances give any aid to the enemy in maintaining order, or in any other way.'[3] But already it had been found that, under pressure, the people tended to do what they thought best, and the appeals to them to stay-put had been of little avail. News bulletins, which attempted to calm the inhabitants when the enemy was almost in sight, proved derisory. In any case, the German radio was being listened to almost as much as the BBC, and was frequently proving more accurate than the Ministry of Information in reporting the progress of the invasion.

5. The Prime Minister would again plead with Roosevelt for direct military aid such as might actually involve the USA in war.

As had happened so frequently in history, the weather took a hand in operational matters on the 16th, and to a lesser extent on the 17th. The rain which moved up Channel late on the 15th cut visibility and made flying difficult, in addition to hampering work on airfields, particularly in Northern France. The small force of Royal Navy destroyers which again ventured into the Straits found far fewer targets than the previous night, not only because the Germans had cancelled the night passages, but also due to adverse visibility. Minelaying was carried out industriously by both sides, however, and night bombers continued to grope for targets they infrequently hit. Next day, the 16th, to the benefit of the British, the Luftwaffe was prevented from carrying out very many sorties. Hence the Royal Navy could move in greater safety, the RAF was given a chance to recuperate somewhat, and the Army was saved the attention of Kesselring's dive-bombers promised to von Vietinghoff. What was more, Busch's anxieties were stimulated because both naval and air lift of supplies into the bridgehead fell well below expectation and again raised the spectre of a logistics failure. Moreover, Folkestone harbour was operating only at a low level, Dover was still out of action, and the handling of stores across the beaches was as slow as the pessimists had foretold.

Yet it heartened von Vietinghoff when a score of tanks turned up – the vanguard of 9th Panzer Division – and with them two batteries of 88s and a quantity of ammunition and fuel. He still admitted that offensive operations were too risky, but he would feel a lot safer when the situation at Hythe had been stabilized.

Last gasp at Hythe

To Schoerner, who badly wanted to follow up his victory of the previous day, he issued a stern standfast order, and to 17th Division's commander, General Major Herbert Loch, he allocated all the tanks and guns he could spare, together with a crisp instruction, 'to clear the enemy out of Hythe and Saltwood once and for all and then to seize Lympne airport'. The British, however, forestalled Loch, by launching a renewed dawn attack by 135th Brigade, and two troops of 8th RTR's Matildas, and pushing triumphantly through the shattered seaside town, with their left flank companies seizing control of the much fought over ruins of the Sene Golf Club House. Instead of attempting, to gain fresh ground, Loch found himself striving desperately to regain that which was lost and, above all, to prevent the capture, with effects of disastrous potential, of the beaches near Sandgate.

Neither Thorne, Liardet nor the men of 135th Brigade ever knew how close they were to a resounding victory when they reached their first objectives. With the Hythe bridgehead and a dismayed enemy in their sights, it needed only the introduction of the reserve infantry battalion and a few more Matildas to start a rot among the Germans. But at that moment they came under a storm of fire from every weapon the Germans could bring to bear, under the personal direction of Loch himself. At the same time, two of the Matildas were crippled. At that moment, too, Thorne's orders for an orderly withdrawal filtered through, finally to extinguish the brigade commander's instinct to send in his reserve battalion. Sadly the British relinquished the initiative so that, when the Germans turned to aggressive patrolling later in the morning, they saw the British withdraw. By nightfall, they were back where they had started.

The cruiser battle

The destroyer foray into the Straits on the night of the 15th/16th had been the best stop-gap effort possible in the aftermath of the previous night's major operation. That for the night of the 16th/17th, dictated by Churchill's directive, was necessarily much larger and, indeed, the most which could be managed. Bringing his battleships southward to cruise off the Humber, and reinforcing the Nore with six cruisers and twelve destroyers, Forbes ordered Ernle-Erle-Drax to enter the Straits once more, but this time massively to bombard the ports in the hope of stopping the enemy convoys at source, catching those at sea as a bonus. This was the genesis of the Second Battle of the Dover Straits, for, almost from its inception, the Germans were made aware by their code-breakers of what the British intended, and this time Raeder decided to lay an ambush employing the heavy cruiser *Hipper* and the light cruisers *Nürnberg*, *Köln* and *Emden*, backed up by half a dozen destroyers and escort vessels and the coastal artillery and Luftwaffe. Knowing that Ernle-Erle-Drax would bombard Calais first and then shift from target to target towards Zeebrugge, Lütjens planned to time his interception off Gravelines when the enemy would be focussing his attention on the shore. Covered by fighters, which effectively prevented British air reconnaissance, the German warships put to sea from Antwerp at 1700 hours and headed west, close inshore.

They did not sail undetected. A patrolling British submarine gave ample warning to Ernle-Erle-Drax, who deployed in two columns – one, consisting of the 6in gun cruisers *Southampton*, *Birmingham* and *Sheffield*, to concentrate on bombardment, the other with the 8in gun cruisers *Sussex*, *Norfolk* and *York*, to give flank protection to the east, joining in the short bombardment only when convenient. When the British ships opened fire on Calais from 6 miles range, at 2130 hours under conditions of dim light in lowering cloud, it was difficult for their gun-layers, or those of the German shore batteries, to make good practice. Some damage was inflicted in the port, however, and German convoys for England were further disrupted and delayed – but without being completely halted. As the bombarding force steamed eastwards to engage Dunkirk, the cruiser *Sussex* was straddled by 8in shells directed by radar from *Hipper.* At rapidly closing ranges, until the intensifying accuracy of the British return fire made the Germans reverse course, the cruisers fought it out. Initial and, as it proved, fatal damage to the *Sussex*, was soon compensated by hits on *Hipper*, which put her after turret out of action and damaged her excellent fire-control equipment. A torpedo strike by a German destroyer on *York*, which compelled her, down by the head, to limp for home, was achieved at the price of another German destroyer set on fire. In a scene lit by flares from ships and aircraft, the German light cruisers with their 5.9in guns came to the aid of *Hipper* and scored numerous hits on *Norfolk*. Meanwhile, in compensation, *Köln* was hit by a deluge of 8in and 6in shells and blew up.

Ernle-Erle-Drax abandoned the shore bombardment to concentrate on the destruction of the German vessels which were running for the safety of the River Scheldt. He ordered his destroyers to launch a torpedo attack to slow down the enemy, well knowing the risk he was taking of sending these valuable ships into dangerous waters. The Germans were, indeed, trying to lure the British into just such a trap, shaping a course which brought them under the protection of shore batteries and among the complex shoals off Ostend. *Hipper* received another hit from a 6in shell and *Emden* was also damaged, but the British destroyers found it impossible to press home their attack, subjected as they were to a storm of fire from *Hipper*'s secondary armament and the guns of *Emden*, and losing two of their number before they were called off and ordered to cover the British withdrawal to the north to steer clear of air attack.

Forbes, despite the loss of so many ships, claimed this battle as a victory. Correctly, he assumed that the German cruiser force was spent. Shrewdly, and with Admiralty concurrence, he began to query if the inactivity of *Gneisenau* and *Scharnhorst* was involuntary. On the night of the 17th/18th, therefore, he decided to enter the Straits again with cruisers and on this occasion reinforce them with the battleships *Rodney* and *Barham* as the principal bombarding force.

The Luftwaffe takes hold

But already the blows struck on land and in the air by the Germans were beginning to tell. Because Fighter Command was so debilitated and compelled to withdraw inland, the Luftwaffe could operate more or less as it chose except in the few selected areas where Dowding chose to concentrate his aircraft. As a result, the Germans could at last launch unescorted attacks by Luftflotte 5 with a fair degree of safety from Norway against the Fleet in the North Sea, and upon airfields and ports in the north of England and in Scotland. British impotence began to show on all sides, and very much to the surprise, for example, of von Vietinghoff. On the morning of the 16th, he had spent an uncomfortable couple of hours weathering 135th Brigade's attack, suddenly to hear that patrols sent out by his divisions were not meeting serious resistance. Soon air reconnaissance was filling in the gaps of the Intelligence picture with incontrovertible evidence that the British were in retreat, that their Air Force was tottering and their Navy on the eve of a last despairing effort.

Reading these signs at their face value, Goering intervened for the first time since S Day, and instructed all three Luftflotten to concentrate on eliminating warships while retaining sufficient strength to keep the RAF under pressure and to protect the lines of communication with France. Grievous though the Luftwaffe's bomber losses had been, it remained strong and could put into the air 500 long-range and 200 dive-bombers, together with 600 single-engined and 100 twin-engined fighters. And while the aircrews were brought in by the 350 serviceable Ju 52s and Ju 90s which were beginning to feel the strain, the reserves of pilots at hand gave no fear of the effort fading. Indeed, it was noticeable that the attacks on shipping were beginning, at last, to benefit from the extensive practice which had been provided.

Satisfied that they had established superiority in the air and on the land, the Germans feared only for their sea communications and, in some quarters, were mystified that the Royal Navy had not done more. But as one naval officer said to Lütjens, 'There are those among our masters who have yet to understand the power of the mine and the shoal. I say, in all deference, that the Grand Admiral's fears that we might founder in the narrow seas would have been equally as well applied to the enemy.' Nevertheless, the interruption of communications by enemy action and inclement weather, besides lack of a good port, still kept the Army on a tight leash, and deterred the Luftwaffe (due to fuel transportation problems) from stationing as many fighters as it would have liked on Hawkinge airfield. Moreover, the failure to capture more than this one airfield was a source of discontent on the part of the airmen who dearly wished to extend fighter cover inland. The fact remained that, by the morning of the 17th, 9th Panzer Division (whose mobile punch was so important to XIII Corps) was still incomplete with only 100 of its 190 tanks and 50 per cent of its transport ashore. And the four divisions that had landed, and which needed some 1,200 tons per day to sustain a short campaign,[4] were receiving barely this amount and, therefore, were deprived of a contingency reserve. As it was, most supplies were being momentarily hampered by bad weather. Indeed, if it had not been for the heavy losses inflicted on the RAF bombers, their landing grounds between West Hougham and Hawkinge might have been neutralized.

Logistics and public relations

German logistics also languished because of a manpower shortage. Administrative units and plant were delayed in arrival, and efforts to employ British prisoners-of-war and civilians on the Lines of Communication had been discouraging. The populace exhibited to their conquerors a baffling mixture of shock, torpidity, sulkiness and, in a few instances, downright obstructiveness. The OKH instructions, 'Orders concerning the Organization and Function of Military Government in England', unrealistically laid down that 'The able-bodied male population between the ages of seventeen and forty-five will, unless the local situation calls for an exceptional ruling, be interned and dispatched to the Continent with the minimum delay.' But in more pragmatic terms they also decreed that there must be no interference with the establishment of law and order 'as an essential condition for securing the labour of the country'. The Army was permitted to take all it needed so as to live off the country at first and, in the subsequent occupation, the country was to be stripped of everything barring the bare essentials to support survival. The Germans, in effect, would assume powers similar to those they had practised in all the other foreign countries they had occupied since the year 1870. They would impose German criminal law and administrative practices while trusting that the existing authorities would assist in administering them. They demanded at once a rigid censorship, and the immediate surrender of arms and radio transmitters. They would be particularly severe on youths, having learnt from bitter experience that it was they who, in blithe disregard of the consequences, perpetrated the most daring acts of resistance.[5] But, for the first 72 hours, the Germans were in no position to enforce these regulations. A hardening of attitudes on both sides would come, but for the time being the Germans could only turn a blind eye to all but the most blatant acts of British intransigence, and the British began to develop ways of resistance.

The American price

Churchill's cry for help from the USA, which reached Roosevelt on the evening of the 16th, was at pains to disclose matters at their worst. The Prime Minister made no attempt to conceal the state into which the land and air defences had fallen, and to point out that the committal of the Fleet, to what might become an immolatory gesture, was Britain's last hope, if massive, direct intervention by the USA were not quickly forthcoming. Roosevelt was told by Churchill that, if Britain fell, civilisation was at stake and the USA might, in the shortest time, find herself isolated from the rest of the world and, in due course, threatened. The warning found a sympathetic ear in the President, who was acutely aware of the USA's national interest in sustaining Britain. But the case submitted seemed insufficiently persuasive to override the objections to sending units of the US Fleet and the Army Air Corps to Europe. No doubt some among the large US Irish community would have been happy to see their homeland protected; but the pacifist, isolationist lobby was vehemently influential; the Communists (dictated to by Soviet Russia's pact with Germany) likely to be on the Fascist side; and the anti-Semites positively in favour of the Nazi persecution of the Jews. To take over the guarding of Atlantic convoys in order to release British warships to help repulse the invasion was both a political and military gamble. The re-armament of the US forces was barely under way, her armed strength was at low ebb and the expansionist aims of the Japanese forbade any relaxation of security in the Pacific.

Roosevelt, however, feared for the future of the Royal Navy. In a letter on 20 May, Churchill had foretold what might happen if Britain were defeated, '. . . you must not be blind to the fact that the sole remaining bargaining counter with Germany would be the Fleet, and if this country were left by the United States to its fate, no one would have the right to blame those then responsible if they made the best terms they could for the surviving inhabitants.' Lord Lothian, the British Ambassador in Washington, had, furthermore, been instructed by Churchill on 9 June to impress on Roosevelt that, if the Fleet fell into German hands, the risk was that the USA's sea-power would be completely over-matched. 'Moreover, islands and naval bases to hold the United States in awe would certainly be claimed by the Nazis. If we go down Hitler has a very good chance of conquering the world.'[7]

Undoubtedly Roosevelt and his advisers took these warnings to heart, but they could only advance help to Britain at a speed commensurate with public opinion. Perhaps by natural instinct, or possibly because it appealed to the ingrained commercial bent of Americans, Roosevelt put negotiations with the British on a trade footing.[8] Up to this moment, the rifles, guns, ammunition and aircraft, which were still in transit from the USA, had been purchased out of Britain's dwindling dollar reserves. Now, in return for American sacrifices, the President and his advisers sought to extract enormous concessions which would have a crucial effect upon Britain's future political and economic position. Requests for provision of bases on key islands in the West Indies were but a beginning. If Britain was to have a future propped up by the USA, she must expect to come under American domination in so many ways that her independence would be threatened. Scratchily Churchill remarked on the telephone to the Attorney General, Robert H. Jackson, 'Empires just don't bargain,' and drew the implacable reply, 'Well Republics do!'[9] In a nutshell, Roosevelt's price for sending units of the Atlantic Patrol Force to Europe – and only into the Mediterranean in order to neutralize the Italian Fleet so as to allow heavy units of the British Fleet to return to home waters, was the immediate grant of concessions in certain key British territories, with stewardship in others should Britain fall, and a guarantee that the Fleet be saved from total destruction and its surviving units sent to safety.

The Fleet seeks battle

When the Fleet sought battle again in the Straits on 17 July there were positively no thoughts of self-preservation in the minds of its leaders. American intervention, to them, seemed unrealistic and not in the least likely to come in time. Uppermost in their thoughts were enhanced fears of mine, bomb and torpedo, for it was obvious that with the decrease in British counter-measures of all kinds, the Germans enjoyed the freedom to multiply their anti-ship capability. Late in the afternoon off Harwich, the Luftwaffe began the proceedings with a series of tentative strokes which blossomed into full-blooded attacks by large formations as the Fleet drew closer to France. Dowding threw in all the fighters he could muster – about 100 – and their impact was strong in the initial confrontations when the German fighters were operating very nearly at their maximum range. But at the same time, the wide gaps now present in the radar coverage, and the paucity of fighter strength elsewhere, made it easy for small formations of German bombers to slip through and spread havoc among a variety of targets, including airfields, factories and communication centres. The Fleet got away with it almost undamaged, but parts of the rest of the country paid a high price for that immunity. And once the RAF fighter squadrons were compelled to return and rearm at threatened airfields, and the German bombers fiercely attacking the Fleet flew under superior cover from their own fighters, the balance tilted in the German favour.

Damage on the ships accummulated without immediately distracting Forbes from his aim. HMS *Barham* was hit by a dive-bomber but steamed on. At last light, HMS *Rodney* took an unlucky blow on her main range-finder and two destroyers were badly damaged in the same savage raid. But once again it was mines which exacted a serious toll. First *Barham*, then the cruiser *Birmingham* and then yet another destroyer fell victim to these hidden weapons. Only the destroyer was in danger of sinking (as later she did) but the sting was taken out of the bombardment force which, after firing at long range and unobserved into Calais and Dunkirk, was withdrawn, leaving the Germans to sail their convoys almost as if nothing had happened.

Reporting to Churchill on the previous night's activities and summarizing the achievements of the Fleet to date, Pound had to admit that the most his ships had managed to accomplish was the temporary curtailment of enemy activities without in any way severing the lines of communication. The price for so little had been heavy, and he saw no way of improving upon performance. 'In a sentence, Prime Minister,' he said, 'we are using up valuable ships without commensurate return, and destroying the one valuable bargaining asset left to the nation.'

'That,' replied Churchill, 'is not your concern. It is your duty to prevent enemy ships from using the Channel. There must be no backsliding from that if we are to prevail on land.' To which Pound had replied that it *was* his duty to advise the Premier that, with only three fully serviceable Capital ships left in home waters – *Nelson, Repulse* and *Renown* – and the condition to which the cruisers and destroyers had been depleted, he could no longer guarantee that, if *Gneisenau* and *Scharnhorst* put to sea, the ensuing engagement would go the British way. 'It is now essential that the Fleet be reinforced and that, as a preliminary step, Force H be brought back from Gibraltar in order to make its presence felt in the Channel, and nearly all the score or more of destroyers on escort duties in the Western Approaches withdrawn for battle – to the detriment of British mercantile convoys.'

This was advice Churchill could not ignore. Sacrifices, as he knew, had to come to an end sometime, but the question of reinforcing the Fleet at home, to the relaxation of power overseas and the loss of control over the Western Approaches, which were so vital to Britain's economic survival, was immediate. Eventually, he knew, the Germans might send one or both of their pocket battleships raiding in the Atlantic, and step up U-boat attacks. Indeed, at this moment, *Admiral Scheer*, newly out of dock, was on her way to Norwegian waters waiting for an opportunity to break out. The sinking that night of two cargo ships by a U-boat in an inadequately guarded convoy off the Lizard was merely a hint of what might soon come. Churchill and his colleagues turned to consider the need to bring back Force H and then, for the first time, to discuss measures to prolong the war from overseas if British resistance at home began to crumble – a contingency which he had touched on in June, but which nobody had taken very seriously at the time.

XIII

THE CRUNCH

The Germans advance

To von Vietinghoff, it seemed rather too good to be true when the British started to pull back at Hythe on the morning of the 16th, and wellnigh miraculous when this retrograde movement extended along the entire Corps' front. The Kriegsmarine's worries had only recently been transmitted to him by their liaison officer, and there was nothing in his own reading of the situation to make him expect any relaxation on the enemy's part. But, since the British were willing to go, it required neither Schoerner's insistent demand nor a milder request by Generalmajor Graf Hans von Sponek of 22nd Air Landing Division to persuade him to follow. Ordering Schoerner and Loch to reassert steady pressure on the flanks of the bridgehead in order to tie down the enemy, von Vietinghoff ordered 9th Panzer Division (Generalmajor Dr Alfred von Hubicki) to move through 22nd Division, with a view to seizing the high ground around Womenswold prior to striking at Canterbury.

These co-ordinated German attacks, supported by a blast of cross-Channel gunfire, caught Liardet on the hop. He had been hoping to disengage imperceptibly along his entire front that night, and was already thinning out and beginning to withdraw 198th Brigade from the Isle of Thanet. The sudden eruption of massed tanks towards Canterbury in the wake of a short but sharp artillery bombardment, threatened, moreover, to cleave his division in two. Indeed, as the German thrust gathered momentum, a shortage of reports of their progress indicated that his weakened units, ill-supported by artillery and armour, starved of ammunition and served by decaying communications, were being overrun and that he was losing control. Wholesale retirements took place in the northern sector without his knowledge. 1st (London) Brigade was overrun by nightfall; enemy tanks stood in strength only six miles from Canterbury. To Thorne, Liardet recommended that command of the northern flank be assumed by 1st Armoured Division while he, Liardet, conducted the withdrawal of the southern wing, conforming as best he could to the movements of 45th Division on his right as it pulled back to the Romney Marshes. Thorne agreed and, at a stroke, committed his last remaining mobile reserve – 1st Armoured Division – to holding the line and thus dissipating his one remaining mobile, counter-attack force.

Those who could later disentangle from their memories recollections of the night the retreat began, conjured up a picture with the background flash of the cruiser engagement, beyond the horizon out at sea, and the foreground scene of a widening semicircle of fires and arching signal flares which demarcated the advance of the German Army. Never to be forgotten were the jostling crowds of intermingled soldiers and bewildered refugees fleeing before the terror. Unheralded were those who merged in the saga of resistance rather than abandon their life-long homes, or those who opted to fight it out, preferring death to the enslavement they rejected. There were many who saw this as the beginning of the end, and some soldiers of XII Corps, in the north, realized that, if they did not get through to Canterbury that night, they would be trapped in the Isle of Thanet. There was a natural split in British ranks – between those who saw a future in escape and those whose imaginations switched off at the word defeat and saw virtue in struggle to the death.

Von Vietinghoff gave neither friend nor foe the opportunity to relax. Discarding his doubts and fears, he urged his subordinates to gamble in order finally to smash an opponent in disarray. Kesselring and Busch, elated at the prospects, brought Lütjens with them by air on the morning of the 17th, and with von Vietinghoff, laid plans to exploit the excitingly new situation. Lütjens thought that the Royal Navy had, for the time being, shot its bolt (an opinion corroborated within 18 hours by the repulse of the battleships). Folkestone harbour was handling more traffic, Dover would soon be open and capable of accepting small petrol tankers and, if the Army expanded the beachhead, more and more small harbours would become available for unloading. Kesselring was perfectly satisfied that, if the weather got no worse (and the latest forecasts spoke of an improvement), the airlift would be stepped-up to more than 2,000 tons a day. In accord with Lütjens, he promised Busch a flow of supplies which would easily justify the bringing in of another corps – VII Corps (General der Infanterie Eugen Ritter von Schobert), with its 7th Panzer Division (Generalmajor

Erwin Rommel) first ashore. Consideration was also given to extracting 7th Air Division, in readiness for a fresh airborne task, and replacing it with 35th Infantry Division (Generalleutnant Hans Reinhard). But the removal of the airborne troops was deferred until a more convenient moment. For Busch's orders to von Vietinghoff, with von Rundstedt's and Hitler's backing, admitted no weakening in any form. XIII Corps was to stretch itself to the limit in seizing the whole of the Kent coastline with the least delay, and thrusting as close to London as enemy resistance would permit.

Only in the vicinity of Canterbury was a brake placed upon the 9th Panzer Division, and here it was the remnants of 3rd Armoured Brigade which made it possible. As it had been in France, so it now transpired in England; infantry formations without anti-tank guns collapsed before tank forces, sometimes in a matter of minutes. The garrison troops of the Isle of Thanet were herded into the north-east corner once Canterbury had fallen. An attempt to deny the Germans the use of Manston airfield was fruitless. At the other end of the bridgehead, 17th Infantry Division walked over Lympne airfield and, with 7th Air Division on their right, marched on Rye and Ashford. Every now and then there were hold-ups caused by Matilda tanks, and then it took careful manoeuvring by a few Pz Kpfw IIIs and 88s to shift them. But, for the most part, the Germans were able to proceed at their own measured pace in pushing away the light rearguards at the stop-lines used to cover the retreat of 45th and 1st (London) Divisions. And, as Busch watched the arrows lengthening across his map, and news of the repulse of the battleships was given, along with reports of German aircraft making use of the latest captured airfields and a steady rise in the delivery of supplies, his assurance reached bursting-point. 'Now,' he demanded, 'we must risk still more. Forget the need for a reserve of supplies. Let us just have enough to keep in motion the maximum number of troops which can be brought over.' On the 17th he set up his main headquarters in the Castle at Dover and heard with pleasure that the first Staffel of Me 109s would be permanently based at Hawkinge next day, fuelled by petrol in barrels brought in by freighter to Dover.

The catastrophe which Ironside had feared if German mechanized forces became established was already being enacted. The Germans were running riot, as Thorne and Geddes, the Regional Commissioner, made plain. Thorne could only bend with the storm, Geddes, given full powers far too late, could exert hardly any influence at all upon local authorities which were breaking down under the strain.[1] As the Germans drew close to Ashford and

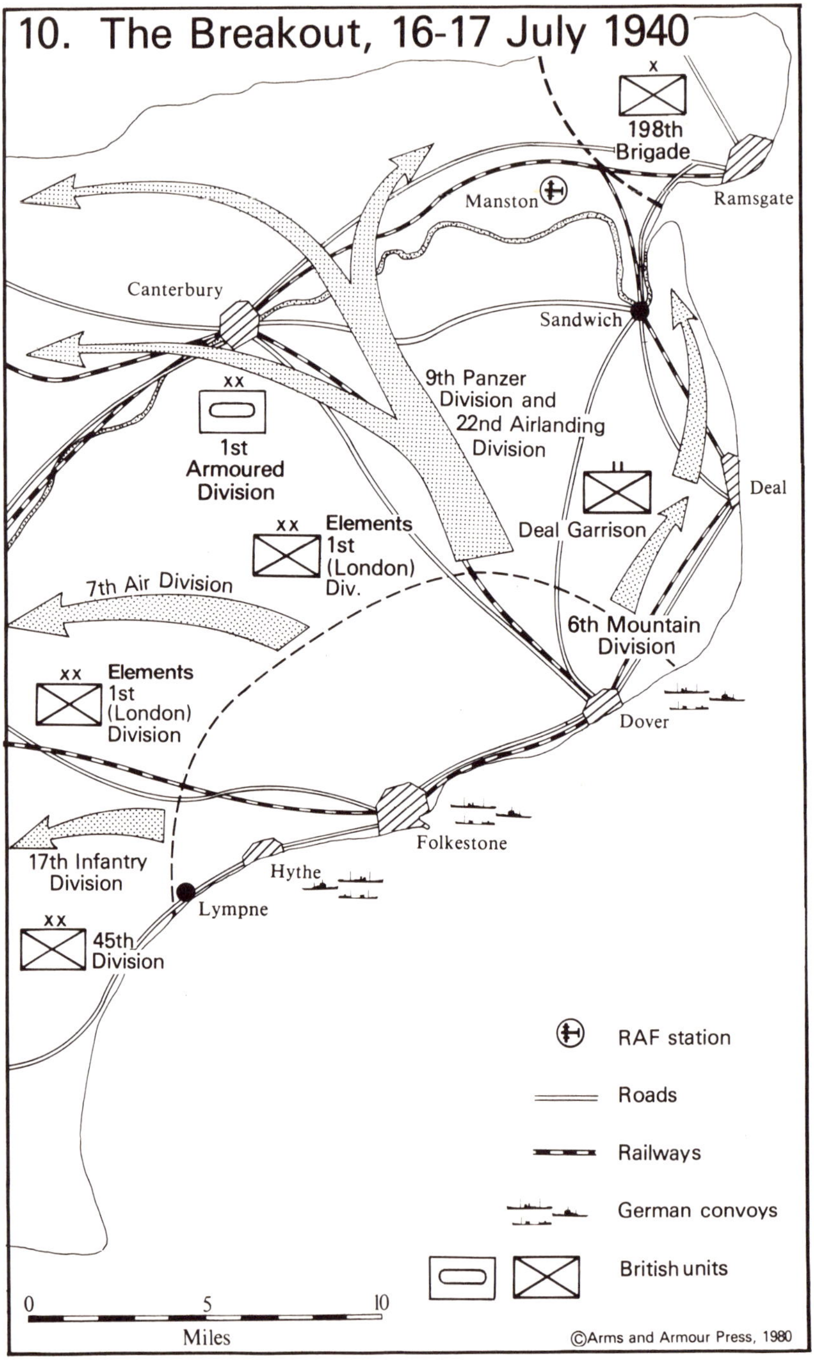
10. The Breakout, 16-17 July 1940
198th Brigade
Ramsgate
Manston
Canterbury
Sandwich
9th Panzer Division and 22nd Airlanding Division
1st Armoured Division
Deal
Deal Garrison
Elements 1st (London) Div.
7th Air Division
6th Mountain Division
Elements 1st (London) Division
Dover
Folkestone
Hythe
17th Infantry Division
Lympne
45th Division
RAF station
Roads
Railways
German convoys
British units
0
5
10
Miles
©Arms and Armour Press, 1980

Faversham, Geddes told Thorne that the administration of law and the distribution of food (two pre-eminent subjects) were collapsing in Kent and that, in due course, it would be every man for himself until the Germans took over. Standing on Wrotham Hill that evening and watching the manifestations of the enemy approach, while Dornier and Heinkel bombers flew unchallenged overhead, Ironside and Thorne had to admit between themselves that even this bastion of the GHQ Line, manned as it was by poorly-armed New Zealanders and Canadians (strong in Canadian artillery and anti-tank guns, but weak in practically all else except fighting spirit) might soon fall. They could see for themselves the columns of dispirited refugees pouring through and knew of the unavailing efforts by the police to stop or divert them.[2] They were aware, too, of the chaos reigning on the roads and railways which was hampering the prompt movement to this most threatened sector of some of the better equipped infantry divisions, plus the less well-armed 2nd Armoured Division, from west and north of London. For, although there was still talk of the threat to East Anglia, Churchill and the Chiefs of Staff had decided to ignore it, appreciating that, whether a landing came there or not, there was no question of denying strong reinforcements to the threatened GHQ Line.

To the Germans, the drive through Kent was like a dream come true, marred only by scattered uniformed British forces and franc-tireurs in civilian dress (sometimes wearing an arm-band with the unintelligble letter LDV upon them) who sprang ambushes and caused, in their view, pointless death and destruction. They took for granted the recalcitrant and surly attitude of the populace, and the older and wiser heads among them deprecated the need to execute franc-tireurs and scavenge the countryside for food and materials to supplement their resources. Acts of suppression and pillage, they knew, would generate a mutual hatred which, bad enough as it already was on the part of the British, might never be assuaged. But their orders demanded a hard line, and the younger, less sensitive officers and men were zealous in imposing strict measures when civilians tried to frustrate their commands. The sense of horror, which had been born in the first 'atrocity' in Saltwood on S Day, spread with every wild rumour. To these would be added the epic of Mayor Jimmy Cairns of Dover.

The Dover martyrs

Cairns was a Tynesider who, at one time, had been a building foreman at Hull docks, and he was the last man to bow to coercion. When the German Commandant at Dover asked him to instruct civilians to assist in the working of the port, Cairns refused point-blank and let it be known publicly that he would only collaborate with the Germans in so far as it affected the normal running of the town. As a result, when the first member of the Gestapo (the Reichsicherheitshauptamt (RHSA)) arrived, he insisted that an example be made. Arresting Cairns as one of a group of hostages taken in reprisal for the sniping of a German soldier as he walked among the ruins of the Maison Dieu Road, the Germans shot the mayor and his companions on the 18th. The execution was given the maximum publicity so as to intimidate the fainter-hearted members of the populace. No doubt some were dismayed, but a great many more were enraged and the anger they felt was broadcast to many parts of the world including the USA.

The news of the martyrdom of Cairns and the other hostages was put to good propaganda use by the British; Churchill swiftly drawing it to the attention of Lothian in the USA, for onward transmission to Roosevelt, as an example of what might be expected wherever the Nazis trod. In the meantime, the deteriorating situation in south-east England made it essential to consider recalling Force H from Gibraltar, regardless of what the Italians might then do in the western Mediterranean. But the velocity and confidence of the German eruption out of their initial bridgehead, when combined with Intelligence of the quantity of men, stores and equipment coming in by air and sea, and the ruthless scouring of the occupied territory for vehicles and matériel, strongly persuaded the Chiefs of Staff that, unless the enemy could be defeated immediately on land, they would become invulnerable, even if the Fleet did manage to establish a permanent presence in the Straits. For at that moment it was evident that Fighter Command would be unable to reverse its eclipse. In trying to guard the Fleet and protect its own airfields, it had suffered additional heavy casualties and was now quite unable even to exert much influence on special occasions, or protect itself. The Luftwaffe was freer than ever to do as it pleased, and its transports could bring in the planned 2,000 tons a day without fear of interruption.

Vacillation in Whitehall

Once more, therefore, the Prime Minister felt compelled, as Commander-in-Chief, to alter his priorities. He concurred with Dill that the defence of the Nation now lay in the hands of the Army, and that the RAF was a spent force whose few remaining units must be conserved for special occasions. So Newall was instructed to save what he could for intervention at crucial moments in the forthcoming battle for London, and to assist the Navy in its final throw to cut the German surface communications. Churchill now decided to bring Force H back from Gibraltar. Negotiations with the Americans were no closer to arranging for intervention by the Atlantic Patrol in the Mediterranean, so the removal of a British naval presence from the western Mediterranean would give the Italians an almost free hand there, regardless of whatever diversionary activities might be mounted by Admiral Cunningham with the Mediterranean Fleet at the other end of that sea.

Pound warned that the intervention of Force H might not have the effect the Prime Minister desired or expected, and was overruled. Newall pointed out that the withdrawal of fighter squadrons into the midlands and north of the country, to save them from destruction on the more vulnerable airfields, would expose the Capital to unopposed raids. But the latter risk was not so severe as it seemed, since Ultra had provided the information that Hitler had forbidden attacks on the city. Therefore it was also agreed that the GHQ Line could be stiffened, where necessary, by the incorporation of anti-aircraft guns in the anti-tank defences of the GHQ Line. For it did not require any imagination to understand that everything hinged upon the holding of that thin and incomplete barrier, regardless of what the Fleet or the Air Force might accomplish.

XIV

THE BATTLE OF THE GHQ LINE

The Busch plan

With remarkable intuition through the fog of war, clarified by unopposed air reconnaissance, the Germans perceived the nature of British intentions and were able to delineate, quite accurately, the configuration of the GHQ Line, with its fieldworks under construction, before their troops reached its outposts. Nothing they saw dissuaded them from adhering to their original plan, with its simple intention to extend the beachhead westwards as the overture to a drive around the western outskirts of London, allied to disruptive penetrations of the industrial midlands. But first the GHQ Line had to be breached and this, Busch calculated, might take a week if he adopted a formal set-piece attack. However, so far as he could judge, after 9th Panzer Division reached the banks of the Medway on either side of Maidstone on the 19th and had watched the bridges blown up in their faces, the enemy preparations were incomplete. It was true that the patrols they sent across the river had been hammered by a storm of fire, but those which returned reported gaps in the defences which might easily be exploited. Furthermore, Busch correctly surmised that the British might actually expect him to close up to the GHQ along a wide frontage, prior to concentrating his forces for prepared blows against one or two selected sectors – as was common military practice. It was, he reasoned, all the more likely that he would achieve maximum surprise were he to dispense with an elaborate set-piece assault and tackle the GHQ Line without assembling the full forces normally demanded.

Elsewhere, the German advanced guards had reached no further west than Cranbrook, progress along the narrow Kent roads among the dense orchards having proved tedious. Neither was the port of Rye yet taken, nor, when it fell, would it ease the German logistics very much. The addition of VII Corps to 16th Army's order of battle could not be implemented overnight, but 35th Infantry Division was landing at Manston (and later at Detling under the nose of the enemy), and therefore it seemed justifiable to try to storm the GHQ Line at Maidstone 'on the run'. In May that year, Busch had been sceptical when Guderian had proposed just such an operations over the River Meuse at Sedan – and filled with admiration when it had come off. Now he was inspired to emulate that masterpiece of military speed and surprise.

Surprise, linked to deception, was to be the essence of Busch's scheme. He aimed not only to conceal from Ironside the pace and direction of his assault, but to actually suggest to his opponent that it was coming elsewhere – away to the west and at a later date – perhaps not until his leading troops had closed up along the length of the GHQ Line at Basingstoke. To avert the attention of myriad informers among the hostile population, Busch withheld the bulk of his assault forces from the environs of Maidstone and ostentatiously harboured his tanks some way to the west, insisting, meanwhile, on the concealment of reconnaissance of the proposed crossing sites over the river and the simulation of maximum interest in a dummy assault beyond Wrotham. He would like to have attacked on the 20th, but 35th Division could not be in position together with sufficient artillery and reserves of fuel and ammunition by that date. It was, he admitted, also worth waiting until the 21st since, by then, 7th Panzer Division would have landed and be on its way to the front, thus immensely augmenting his powers to mystify and out-manoeuvre his enemy along the entire front.

Maidstone in the front line

If, in July 1940, the British Army had been equipped or trained for mobility, it might have had a faint chance of off-setting the German advantages in other respects. Although it became possible, prior to the 21st, to reinforce the GHQ Line with the best equipped infantry divisions and to concentrate some 80 pieces of field artillery, plus 50 (a full 25 per cent of those in existence) of the useful 2-pounder anti-tank guns in the Maidstone sector, the impracticability of withstanding German penetrations, other than locally, was incontrovertible. The infantry divisions would fight where they stood. Only the 2nd Armoured Division, still in East Anglia with its out-classed light tanks, backed up by the handful of surviving heavier tanks from 1st Armoured Division, plus a score of the brand-new well-armoured Valentine tanks of 7th RTR (hurriedly brought down from Scotland), could engage in conditions of open warfare. Naturally, the pause imposed upon Busch prior to making his assault at Maidstone gave the British invaluable breathing-space, and predictably the virtually unchallenged (as well as fore-warned) appearance of Force H off Ushant alarmed Raeder. But as the German Army extended its coastal holdings and tightened its grip on the hinterland, it became crystal clear to Churchill and his advisers that, even if the Navy, substantially reinforced by Force H, *could* take command of the Straits (even for a prolonged period), the strength of the enemy already ashore and his ability to maintain supplies by air made it improbable that he could be dislodged – and most unlikely that the assault on the GHQ Line could be averted. Nothing was more daunting than the relentless unfolding of the German deployment of their battle-groups and patrols, reaching westwards from the banks of the River Medway near Gillingham to the outskirts of Sevenoaks and the approaches to Hastings. Insidiously, an impression of irresistible German power was displayed at the very moment when still more important developments of another kind were impending.

The peace offensive

Hitler and Goering, in a euphoric consultation on the 19th, had drawn the conclusion that the time was ripe to further undermine British resistance by a mixture of psychological and violent assault. The Reichs Propaganda Minister, Josef Goebbels, was instructed to broadcast at once to the British 'an appeal to reason', insisting that, in their own interests, the 'unequal struggle' should be brought to an end. Joachim von Ribbentrop, the Foreign Minister, was told to open peace overtures through neutral countries. In the meantime, the Luftwaffe and the Army, in conjunction with the Abwehr, were to emphasize just how hopeless the British situation really was. The Luftwaffe, some of whose bombers had to be deflected to help Sperrle's 3rd Luftflotte bomb Force H as it steamed northwards, was to bomb selected road and rail targets within Metropolitan London (a reversal of the previous policy), with the dual purpose of contributing to the assault on the GHQ Line and as a demonstration of how vulnerable the Capital now was. Simultaneously, the Abwehr's Special Unit 800 was to take advantage of British weakness to make surprise landings on the flanks of the bridgehead in motor boats, carrying parties of men with folding motor-cycles, to raid military and communications establishments in advance of the main land forces.

London under fire

Anticipated by the British (through Ultra) though the German bombing of the London area was (they were also aware that Luftwaffe doctrine prescribed attacks on important centres of population to precipitate political decisions), the defence which could be offered was meagre. Only two squadrons of fighters were sent aloft to intercept the formations which appeared over the suburbs in large numbers after the regular night raiders had retired to their bases. The heavy anti-aircraft fire on the city's outskirts could do nothing to stem the attacks. Many of the German aircrew tried to hit railway junctions and bridges, but a large proportion of bombs fell on residential areas, causing widespread destruction, many fires and a high casualty rate. Anger, terror and some panic among the people were followed by a deeply rooted sense of what this portended. The rumble of battle which had been growing louder in the distance, now burst loudly upon them. The vast majority in the city stayed to see it through, but a cowed minority began an exodus, the more terrified among them openly expressing the opinion that defeat stared the country in the face. Likewise, the sudden appearance of the German raiding parties, who destroyed power installations and bridges, and ambushed passers-by in the night, redoubled the sensation of alarm and despondency in the rural coastal belt. Unfounded rumours (fed by German radio propaganda) of more large-scale landings encouraged the notion that the enemy was in strength between Selsey Bill and Beachy Head and between Southend-on-Sea and Felixstowe. The intervention of but a few score determined desperadoes (many of whom were promptly hunted down) achieved an effect out of all proportion to their number. They did little physical damage, but their moral impact, magnified in size to that of an Army Corps as at one time gossip said they were, was staggering. Furthermore, they stimulated the zeal of Army and LDV parties at road-blocks whose enthusiasm to clog movement and make life hazardous for ordinary travellers was, in places, unbounded.

In such volatile circumstances the German peace propositions, when they were broadcast by Goebbels, fell on ears which were rather more ready than previously to listen. An increasing number of people began to balance the choice of a prolonged and damaging resistance with the wisdom of surrendering quietly and making the best of a bad job. Only a minority were so infected at this stage. The Cabinet remained steadfast, and the Armed Services, a high proportion of whom had yet to fire a shot in anger, were not in

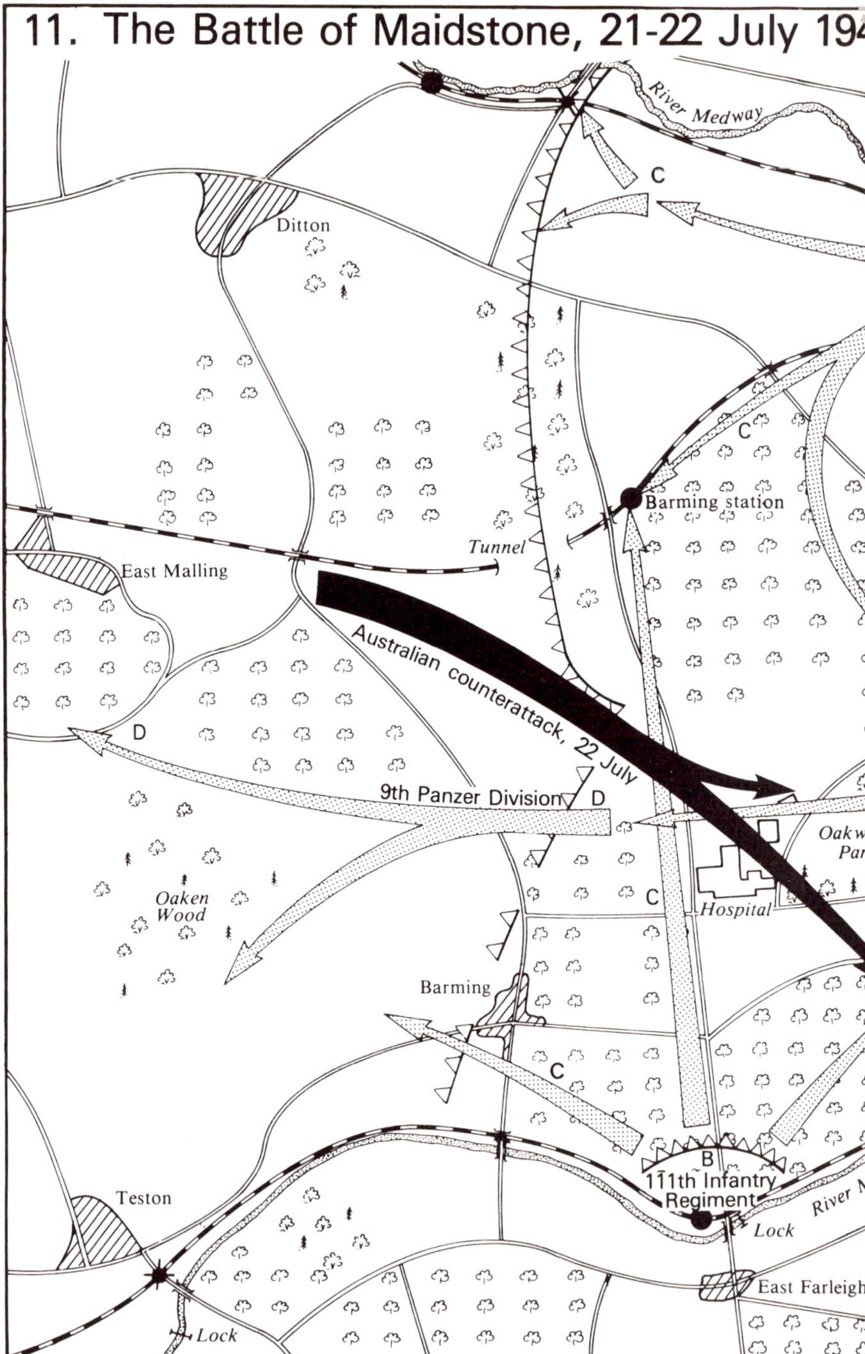
11. The Battle of Maidstone, 21-22 July 194
River Medway
C
Ditton
Barming station
Tunnel
East Malling
Australian counterattack, 22 July
D
9th Panzer Division
Oakw
Par
Hospital
Oaken Wood
Barming
B
111th Infantry Regiment
River M
Lock
Teston
East Farleigh
Lock

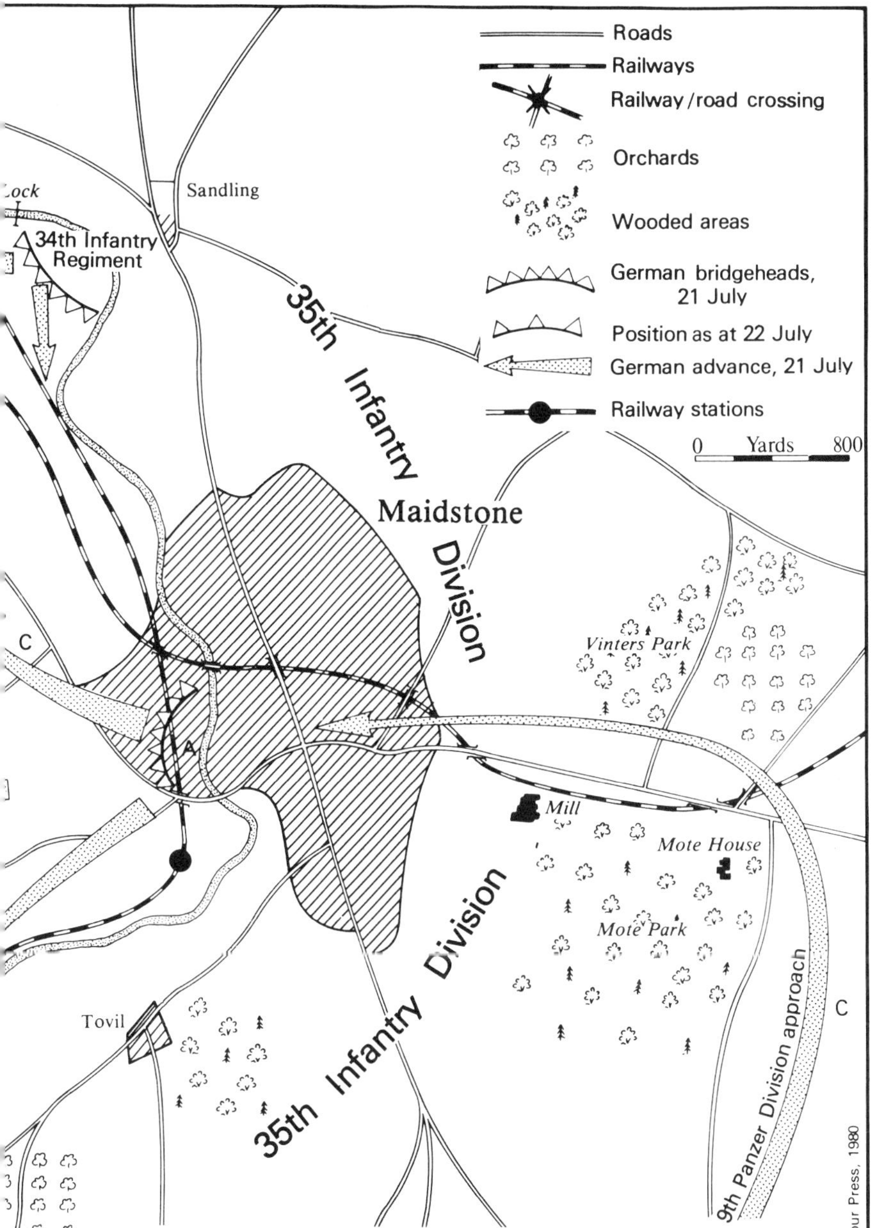

A. Initial attack on 20th/21st.
B. Main attack am 21st.
C. Exploitation by the 35th Infantry Division and the approach of the 9th Panzer Division the night of 21st/22nd.
D. Breakout by the 9th Panzer Division 22nd July.

the least bit ready to give up. But a shaken, helpless unarmed people in the conquered territories was prone to bow before strong-arm methods – and this feeling of impotence deterred the majority from engaging, as yet, in anything more virulent than passive resistance. As the Germans became omnipresent, the incentive to flee or fight evaporated, and people turned to wrestle with the problem of how to survive where they were.

Resistance in its most adamant form was, nevertheless, the keynote of the defence of the GHQ Line. Since immobile troops had few options other than to stand, they met the Germans with an inflexible resolution along the waterways and steep slopes which, for the most part, characterized the Line's configuration. Light German advanced guards found it difficult to brush aside opponents who stuck to their tasks and returned fire with asperity. So 6th Mountain Division mopped up the Isle of Thanet and took into captivity, after a dour 48-hour struggle, the remnants of Deal Garrison and 198th Brigade, 17th Infantry Division, with its score of tanks, dispersed 45th Division (which was innocent of anti-tank guns) and, with 7th Air Division, moved into Sussex. But elsewhere the Germans just contemplated the GHQ Line and the British glowered back.

The battle of Maidstone

The practised fury of a formal German assault by all arms was to be demonstrated by 35th Infantry Division in the bend of the river at Maidstone. Here the division's combined artillery and mortars, augmented by those of 9th Panzer and Kesselring's bombers, were to pulverize a rectangle some 3 miles wide by 4 miles deep. Beginning at last light on the 20th, the bombers began to isolate the battle zone and harass the British gun positions, nearly all of which had been detected. That night, infantry parties crossed to the opposite bank and began to infiltrate the industrial zone in the direction of Oakwood Park. Fierce hand-to-hand combat broke out with New Zealander troops. The Germans were penned against the river but not eliminated, their gunners bringing down a curtain of fire to protect the shallow bridgehead.

Dive-bombers now began to aim precisely at the British gun positions and were in turn tackled by British fighters, called south for what one of their pilots called 'a valedictory gesture'. It was vividly memorable. The Stukas were caught napping and, after their initial assault, lost both in accuracy and numbers before Messerschmitts came to their rescue, and retrieved air superiority.

But this local air success for the British in no way affected the ultimate issue on the ground. Converging crossings of the river near the locks at Allington and East Farleigh were made feasible by the élan of the German infantry of the 34th and 111th Regiments, and by the deadly shooting of 88mm and 37mm anti-tank guns, which had occupied positions in the front line at night, and now fired over open sights at enemy positions on the opposite bank. The intricacies of the struggle which seethed to and fro amid the houses and orchards can be found in the divisional histories, the personal reminiscences of survivors, and the archives of Maidstone Museum. Sometimes called the Verdun of Britain, this is an appropriate title only to the extent that it was the most costly single episode in human lives throughout the campaign. It was not, however, a deliberate act of attrition on the German part and, unlike Verdun, it led to a quick solution – although it is true that the Germans were quite prepared to allow the British to exhaust themselves here if they chose. The British, in fact, had no alternative, knowing that if they were ejected from any sector of the GHQ Line, there was no telling where next they could stand, if at all.

Despite momentary doubts on Busch's part that his ammunition reserves might not satisfy a prolonged duel, furious fighting persisted with heavy casualties mounting on both sides. It was mid-afternoon before troops from the two bridgeheads linked hands near Barming Station, and it would be another 12 hours before the last of the New Zealanders had been cleared out of the loop of the river to allow bridging for tanks to commence. In the meantime, attempts westward were hampered by deadly, though weakening, artillery fire, and a very determined counter-attack by Australian troops at dawn on the 22nd which penetrated to the walls of Barming Mental Hospital before being repulsed. For two hours Busch and von Vietinghoff watched anxiously the development of the battle, the latter going in person to the bridging sites to urge on the Pioneers constructing the bridges. They both offered thanks when the first tanks began to cross at 1400 hours and it was, indeed, the appearance of a few Pz Kpfw IIIs and IVs at Barming which turned the scales against the Australians, who had proved themselves as good in personal combat as the German infantry.

The last tank attack

Throughout the morning, Thorne had deliberated about committing tanks from 3rd Armoured Brigade to throw the Germans back, contenting himself, for the time being, with sending the only available troop of Matildas to help the Australians. The fate of these tanks convinced him of the folly of further involvement within the river bend, where the enemy could bring down converging fire from the opposite banks with devastating effect. 88s claimed two of the Matildas no sooner had they come within sight of East Farleigh. Thorne had no alternative but to pull out from the sack where his men were being destroyed by fire from three sides. A withdrawal to the high ground beyond West Malling commenced that night, as the British centre of resistance shifted to the steep slopes of Wrotham Hill. Thankfully, the Germans followed, boring remorselessly into the outer works of the GHQ Line on a widening frontage, levering aside pockets of resistance which yielded when their means to destroy tanks had been eliminated. Overall, of course, it was the incessant bombing and strafing by an unchallenged Luftwaffe which unsettled the British defenders. Their reinforcements were spotted and ravaged on the way, and their supply became difficult. Scenes of carnage on the roads and in the towns and villages had a detrimental effect on morale. When Ironside passed on Churchill's orders to 2nd Armoured Division (Major-General J. C. Tilly), telling him to move south early on the 22nd and come under command of XIII Corps prior to counter-attacking near Maidstone on 23rd July, Thorne told his C in C that it would be suicide. 'Was not the destruction of 1st Armoured Division enough?' Thorne asked, 'What chance have light tanks with less than ten millimetres of armour got when those with 80 have failed?' But the Prime Minister, replied Ironside, was determined and the hour desperate.

The Germans, moreover, were amply forewarned, and had plenty of time in which to establish a stop-line. Anti-tank guns were installed between Birling and West Malling, outposts established at Offham and Addington, and an armoured reserve placed closely in rear to make security doubly sure. Moreover, 2nd Armoured Division was constantly strafed on its approach march from East Anglia, an onslaught which disrupted its convoys and bewildered a totally inexperienced formation whose induction to battle this was.

Nagging losses had been incurred before the tanks reached their forming-up places. Reconnaissance of the terrain on which they were to fight was sketchy. As it had been with 1st Armoured Division, infantry and artillery support were at a premium and communications deficient. They were urged on by the sheer desperation of the moment and for fear that, if an advance were not immediately forthcoming, Tilly's units would be dislocated before they reached the start line. As Tilly fed his brigades along an axis from Reigate, round Sevenoaks, until they met the enemy, the division tended to drift into action and became embroiled in a series of uncoordinated, individual actions in which small, isolated groups of tanks, manned by dedicated crews, tried gallantly to reach objectives which were not only beyond their reach, but also none too clearly defined. Tanks fell victim to professionally directed anti-tank fire which reduced vulnerable machines to scrap. Before the day was over 2nd Armoured Division was spent and the Germans were coolly measuring up to Wrotham Hill in readiness for assault – seemingly unaware of the deadly blow they had struck.

This was but one disaster in a cataclysmic day. Reports from the west patchily told Ironside of an unhalted German advance. Petersfield was in enemy hands and a strong hostile force was said to be landing along the lengthening enemy held stretch of coast. Most sinister of all was the telephoned information from the Postmaster of Billingshurst, who had managed to keep a line open after the enemy had occupied the town. He spoke of a stream of motor-cycles, armoured cars, tanks, lorries and guns pouring through in the direction of Haslemere. The name of the formation, he said, seemed to be 7th Panzer Division. Within a few hours, Ironside now realized, the enemy fingers which had been feeling their way dexterously along the GHQ Line towards Guildford and Basingstoke, would be clenched into a fist. It was only a mild consolation that the 43rd Infantry Division (TA) (Major-General R. V. Pollock) and the 3rd Infantry Division (Major-General B. L. Montgomery) which, respectively, held the Hogsback and either side of Basingstoke, were among the best-equipped formations under his command, and that the 3rd was regular and battle-experienced. But neither had tanks; the 3rd had but 60 per cent of its entitled artillery; while the frontages each division held were too extended for comfort. By moving 52nd Infantry Division (Major-General J. S. Drew) out of reserve in East Anglia and 2nd Infantry Division (Major-General N. M. S. Irwin) from Lincolnshire, Ironside hoped to provide reasonable depth to a position based on the River Thames. But he was perfectly well aware that these formations, good and relatively strong in firepower though they were, could not do more than delay the enemy. And by taking some formations from the northern and eastern sectors, he left that entire length of coastline unguarded except by divisions as poorly equipped and as immobile as the now almost defunct 1st (London) and 45th Infantry Divisions.

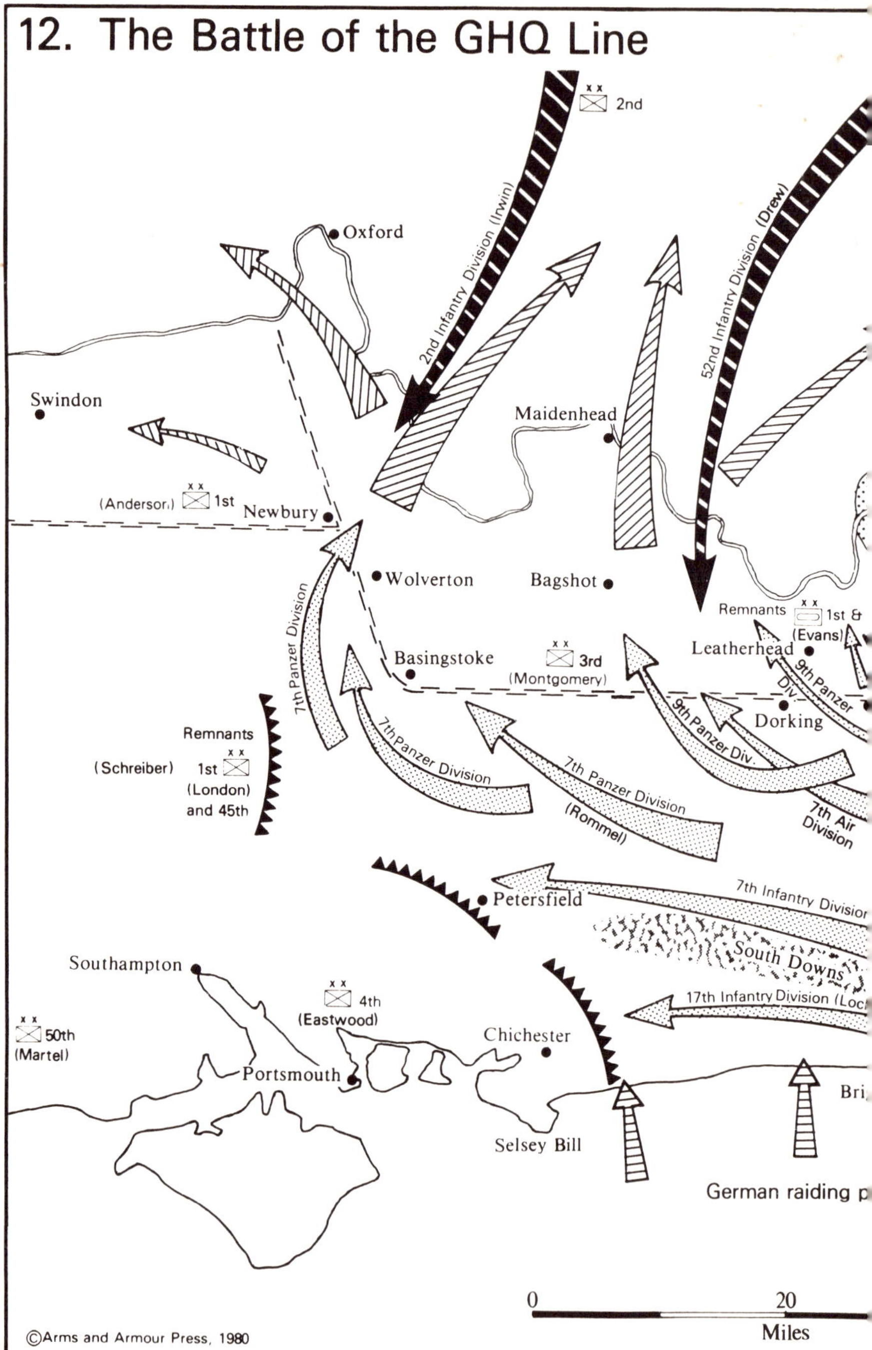

12. The Battle of the GHQ Line

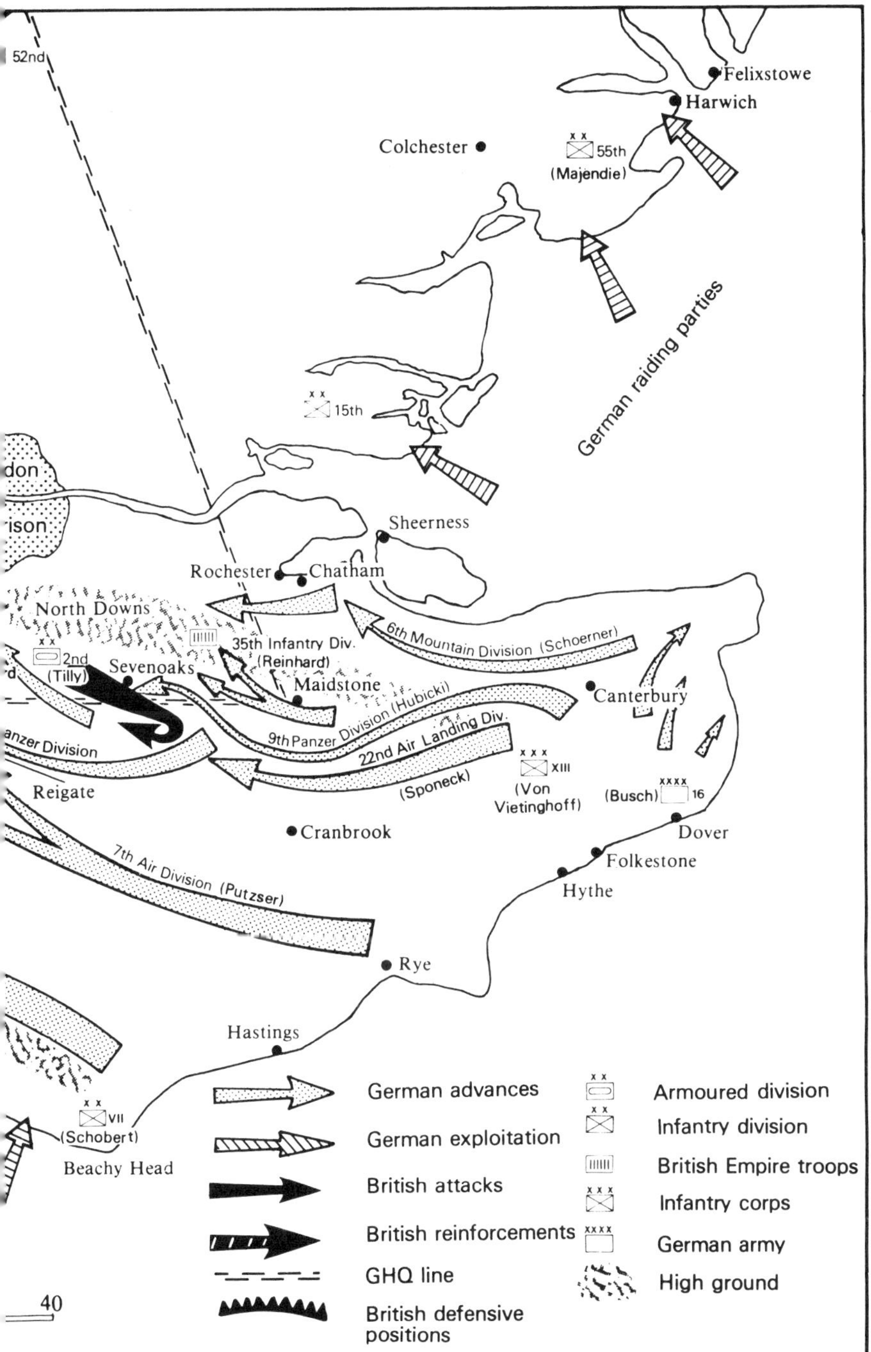
52nd
Felixstowe
Harwich
Colchester
55th
(Majendie)
German raiding parties
15th
don
ison
Sheerness
Rochester
Chatham
North Downs
35th Infantry Div.
(Reinhard)
2nd
(Tilly)
Sevenoaks
Maidstone
6th Mountain Division (Schoerner)
Canterbury
9th Panzer Division (Hubicki)
22nd Air Landing Div.
(Sponeck)
anzer Division
XIII
(Von Vietinghoff)
(Busch)
16
Reigate
Cranbrook
Dover
Folkestone
Hythe
7th Air Division (Putzser)
Rye
Hastings
VII
(Schobert)
Beachy Head
40
German advances
German exploitation
British attacks
British reinforcements
GHQ line
British defensive positions
Armoured division
Infantry division
British Empire troops
Infantry corps
German army
High ground

Force H intervenes

On the 20th, Force H, suffering from the loss of a destroyer, and minor damage to a few units, had dropped anchor at Plymouth where, as it refuelled, it had undergone a continuation of the bombing it had endured ever since it had come within range of Sperrle's aircraft in France. Somerville, its commander, was dubious about the rôle he was asked to play with the force at his disposal. To begin with he decided to detach the aircraft carrier *Ark Royal* from the fleet he would lead up-Channel, since neither the large ship nor its obsolete aircraft could make an impression against the Luftwaffe in narrow waters. So, with the battlecruiser *Hood*, the battleships *Resolution* and *Valiant* (which also presented problems of size), two cruisers and twenty destroyers, he advanced up-Channel on the afternoon of the 21st, just as the Germans were coming to grips with the GHQ Line at Maidstone.

The defences facing Somerville in the Straits were far more formidable than those which had frustrated James and Ernle-Erle-Drax on the 15th, and a diversionary operation by Forbes in the North Sea would in no way distract the Germans from protecting the vital waters between Dover and Calais. For the Germans no longer depended on warships; with denser minefields, guns on both shores and unopposed dive-bombers in plenty, they reckoned they could more than hold their own. In any case, although Churchill, through Pound, had told Forbes and Somerville to 'dominate the Straits and finally put an end to their use by the German fleet and transports', there sounded, for the first time in Churchill's military directives a note of political prudence, 'It is vital to pursue your aim with the maximum resolution, but you should be aware that you hold in your hands not only the fate of the nation, but the last strong card which will enable the Empire to prevail in the struggle to come.' These words, to the Admirals, who were apprised of the political constraints upon the use and bargaining value of the Fleet, had a constrictive effect on their plans. Between the lines they could read that a fight to a finish with annihilation as the final price would no longer be welcomed by Churchill, who was beginning to look around for fresh solutions to Britain's dilemmas.

So both Somerville and Forbes contented themselves with making the maximum impression at the least risk – and that meant keeping strictly within the few swept lanes which remained, venturing into exposed waters only when it was dark or on the rare occasions when fighter cover could be provided. In other words,

Right: Eight pages of pictures from a German military topography handbook of the time.

9. Luftaufnahme des oberen Londoner Hafens.

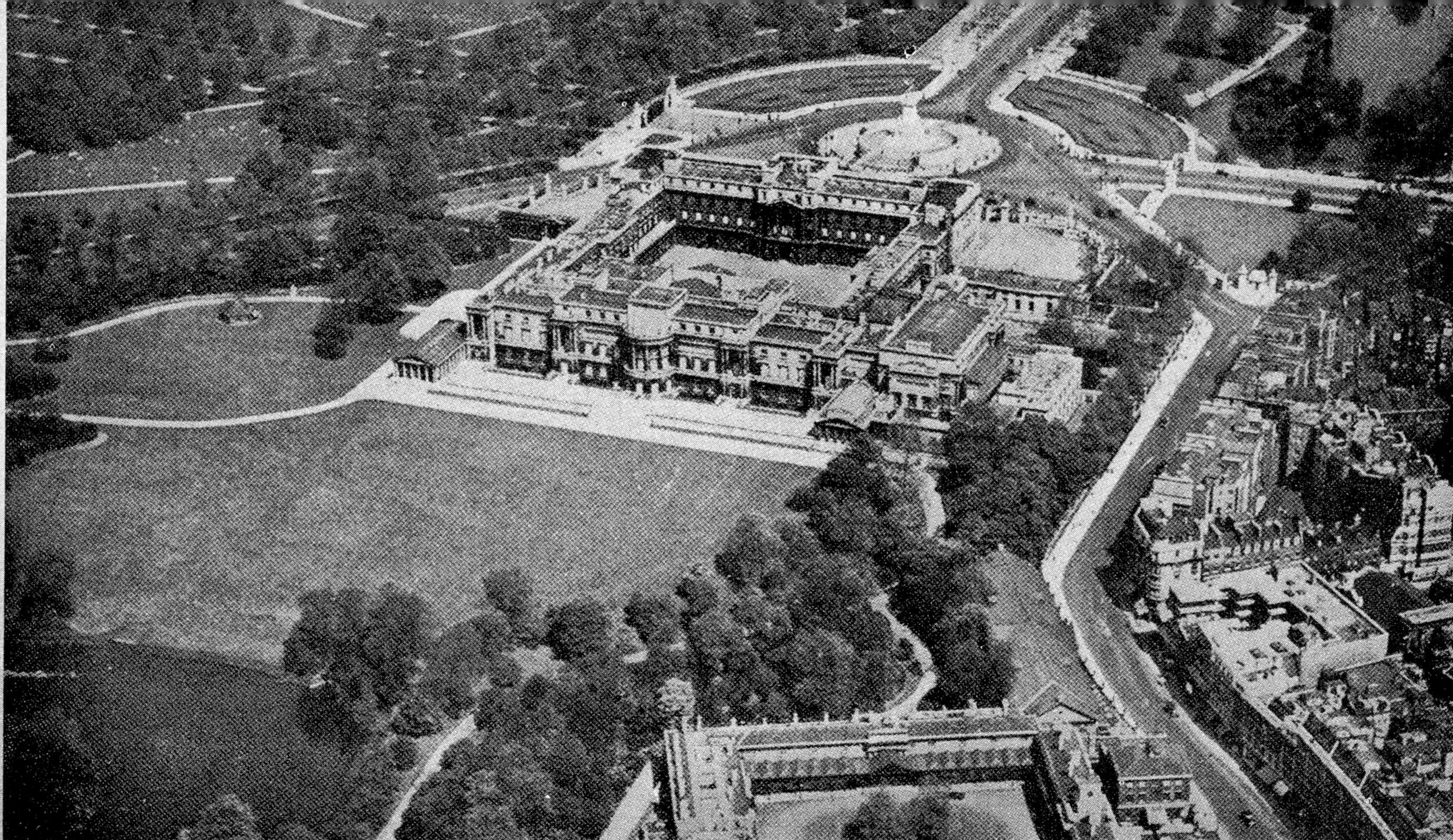

24. Die Residenz.

Gartenfront des Buckingham-Palastes. Links Green Park, rechts St. James Park, dazwischen oben der alte St. James Palast an der Prunkstraße „The Mall"

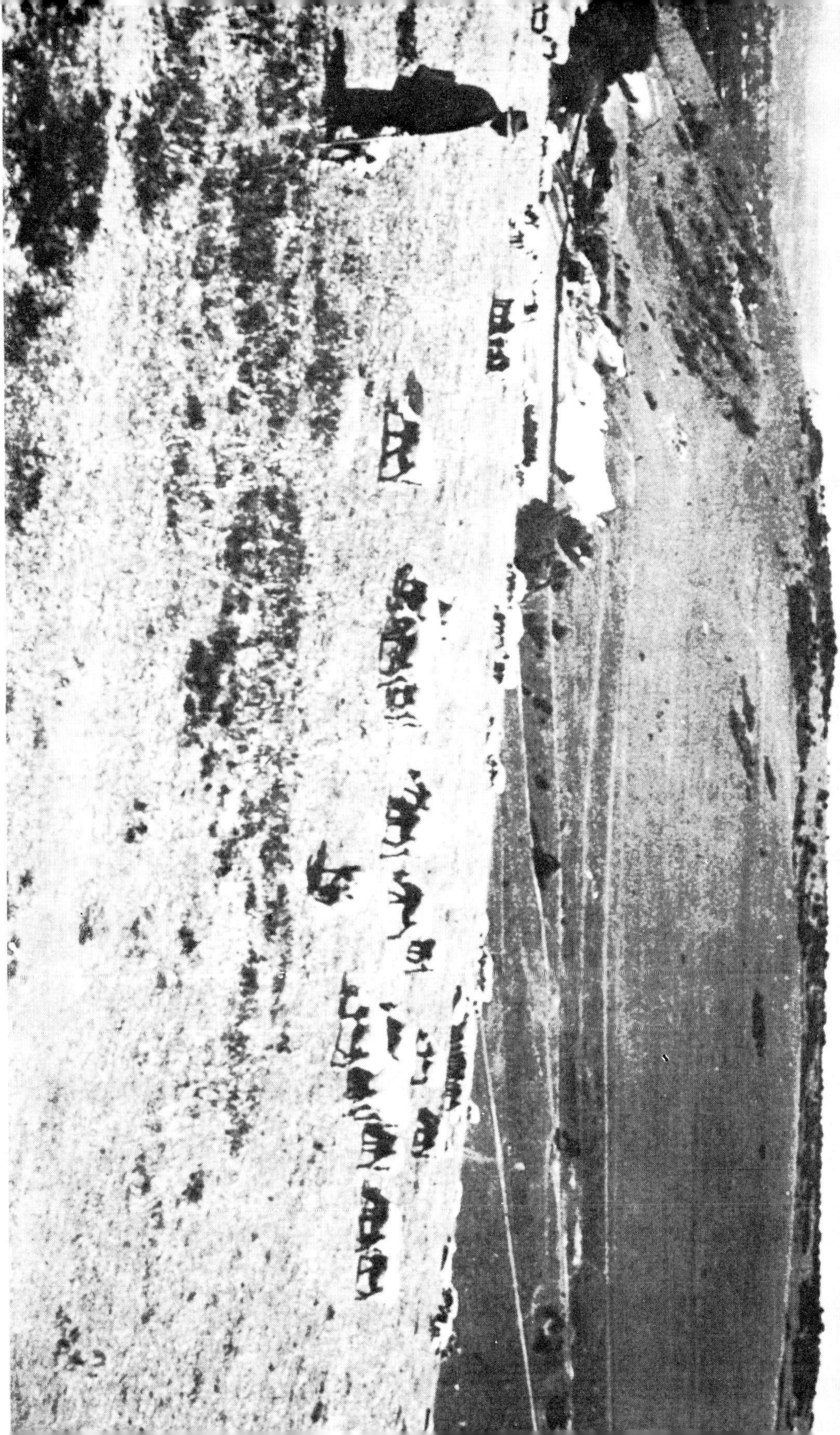

61. Hafen von Folkestone (BB 40).

Blick von NW auf den Binnenhafen (links) bei Ebbe und den Eisenbahnpier.

62. Fernaufnahme der englischen Kanalküste (BB 40).

Infrarot-Aufnahme (Grün erscheint weiß). Vorn die französische Küste ostwärts Cap Gris Nez. Ganz links Shakespeare Cliff, anschließend die Molen des Hafens von Dover. Dahinter die Stadt im Tal (vgl. Bild 63) und rechts davon das Schloß auf der Höhe der Steilküste (siehe Bild 65). Weiter rechts die Kreidekliffküste von South Foreland bis St. Margaret's-at-Cliffe.

63. Stadt und Hafen Dover mit Blick nach Frankreich (BB 40).

Infrarot-Aufnahme (Grün erscheint weiß). Links das Schloß auf der Höhe über dem markanten Taleinschnitt im Dovercliff, in dem die Stadt sich erstreckt und die Bahn (vorne) verläuft. Hinter dem Molenhafen und dem Ärmelkanal die französische Küste (vgl. Bild 62).

69. Themsetal bei Maidenhead (BB 29/34).
Rechts auf der Höhe der Landsitz Cliveden Estate.

they stood off at long range, sacrificed the flexibility upon which sea power depended for its major impact, and fought for most of the time with their hands tied behind their backs, shrewdly suspecting that nothing they could do would affect the final issue. On four occasions they did manage to fire on enemy shipping and they gave several shore batteries a hot time. But the Germans hardly varied their sailing schedules to and from France, and their aircraft, by the weight and persistence of effort (let alone the occasions when they were tellingly accurate), gradually heaped damage on the ships which were virtually deprived of shelter. When Somerville returned to Plymouth late on the 22nd, only *Valiant* among his big ships remained fully battleworthy, the other two capital ships and the cruisers having sustained varying degrees of damage, while two destroyers had gone down and three more were damaged.

Struggle for the North Downs

In a way, the German performance and presence on land in south-east England was a bluff. Only in those places where military operations demanded concentration were they to be seen in strength; nowhere was the bluff more blatant than within the boundaries of 17th Infantry Division, which was spread out over an immense tract of territory. People living in places off the beaten track sometimes did not meet Germans. Indeed, so thin was this division between Littlehampton and Petersfield that Loch declined to advance any further until VII Corps, with its 7th Infantry Division (Generalleutnant Accard Frhr von Gablenz) arrived on the 23rd to share the load on 16th Army's left wing. Nevertheless, although Busch was anxious to avoid any suggestion of hesitation, he sent 7th Panzer Division to make contact with the GHQ Line in the region of Basingstoke, with the firm injunction to its commander, Rommel, that he was to 'withhold from a full-scale assault until 7th Infantry Division had come into line, and VII Corps was pronounced operational'. But Rommel had already won a reputation for disobedience and for taking extravagant risks if he detected weakness in an opponent. Telling his reconnaissance units to make a rapid examination of the enemy defences, and swiftly discovering that the British 3rd Infantry Division was alert and not to be trifled with, he probed westwards to find that the GHQ Line's right flank was refused beyond Basingstoke. Probing still deeper with his tanks on the morning of the 24th in the direction of

Wolverton, Rommel enjoyed one of those strokes of luck which so frequently had come his way in France. His men hit the junction of the strongly-placed 3rd Division with its neighbour, the 1st Infantry Division (Major-General K. A. N. Anderson). At this traditionally weak spot, the 25th Panzer Regiment instantly inserted a small wedge which, as it was driven deeper, began to split the two enemy formations apart.

At the same time, 9th Panzer Division, whose tanks had assisted 35th Infantry Division in a heavily-resisted assault upon the North Downs escarpment at Trottiscliffe, infiltrated its armour among the Empire troops guarding the Pilgrims Way. Before the day was over, they had penetrated to West Kingsdown and were poised to roll up the eastern wing of the GHQ Line. Tanks with bombers had again opened the way and now even the German infantry, who had endured a cruel drubbing from the New Zealanders, Australians and Canadians, began to reap a fine harvest of prisoners. Pummelled from the air and harried on the ground by an assailant who made adroit use of his expert command and control facilities, allied to superior mobility, the GHQ Line began to crumble at both ends. Sensing this, Busch urged von Vietinghoff to throw in everything he had. 22nd Air Landing Division, therefore, began to join in the attack on the flanks of 35th Infantry Division, pushing troops up the Darent Valley towards Offord and feeling for gaps near Brasted and Westerham – one Battle Group leader taking delight in setting up his headquarters at Chartwell Manor, the private home of Winston Churchill. Rarely did the Germans go unopposed, but British courage was insufficient against overwhelming weapons and firepower in the hands of equally staunch and better trained German troops.

The siege of London begins

Vital communication links and centres were falling into German hands and beginning to strangle and distort Britain's internal economy. German VII Corps at Basingstoke cut the direct London rail and road links with Portsmouth, Southampton and the south-west. Already the lines to Bristol and South Wales were being threatened. 6th Mountain Division was in the course of occupying the length of the north Kent coast, thus virtually blocking the Thames estuary to shipping. The naval dockyard at Sheerness was isolated by land, though still holding out. Gillingham, Chatham and Rochester had a cordon around them, depriving the large populace of supplies and stopping production in the factories, including the important Short's works. Recalling the experience of those days in Rochester, Mrs Anne Price wrote:

'I was among those who decided to "stay put" – and, at one time, came to regret it. We had been advised to lay in stocks of food, but neither ourselves nor our neighbours had done much about it. I suppose we did not believe the worst would happen. But on top of the bombing, which destroyed several shops and finally cut off the electricity, we began to find that food in the shops was running out. Taking their chance, people began panic buying. I actually saw them queuing while an air raid was in progress. And then some of the bigger men began throwing their weight about to get to the front of queues and the police, of course, were not to be seen because they were helping control traffic or rescue people from bombed houses. Then rumours began to fly around that the Germans would soon be here and the sight of our soldiers and the LDV erecting road-blocks and putting up sandbags at the town hall and the telephone exchange brought it home to us with a vengeance. Then the shelling began and the mains water supply broke down and at times we could hear rifles and machine-guns. I remember them bringing in a German prisoner and he was all cocky and we booed. But hour by hour things got worse and we couldn't see a way out.'

Indeed, consideration for the welfare of the people worried the Government quite as much as the deteriorating military situation. At all levels from the Cabinet downwards, leaders and administrators, found themselves frequently at a loss to know what to do.

Not that the Germans were free from worry. Von Rundstedt visited Busch on the 24th to reassure himself that the 16th Army was not becoming overstretched. During the French campaign he had fretted perpetually when the Panzer divisions had penetrated far into the enemy rear, constantly fearing a deadly riposte by the French. Now he feared the British. But Busch was able to satisfy him that, touch and go as his logistics were, and thin on the ground though his troops might seem on the map, the situation was under control. Nowhere was the Army exposed to mortal danger. Dover, he pointed out, was at last beginning to handle a useful and increasing volume of cargo. It was his impression that, although the British were determined to resist, they simply lacked the means. Prisoners had been taken who bore the most antiquated arms, and some were defenceless. Of enemy tanks, few had been met since the killing on the 23rd near West Malling, where some 60 had been found destroyed or abandoned on the battlefield. Consenting to Busch's desire to continue with the destruction of the GHQ

Line, von Rundstedt forbade any attempt to penetrate the environs of London. The original concept was to be adhered to. Sixteenth Army, which would be reinforced as speedily as possible, must besiege the Capital while launching disruptive raids in a northerly and north-westerly direction, aimed at objectives whose loss or neutralization were expected to erode British resolution.

Ironside resigns

With the picture of developments at the front anything but complete, Ironside nevertheless came to the conclusion, as the 24th drew to a close, that he had to present the Prime Minister and his closest advisers with the unvarnished truth of defeat. He drove to Whitehall at the height of the nightly air raid, through suburbs which were beginning to show signs of the enemy bombing. Anti-aircraft guns were in action as he approached Westminster, but it seemed to him that the enemy aircraft were flying daringly low above the barrage balloons. He was pleased to notice that fewer refugees seemed to be on the move, and that mainly it was the Civil Defence Services who were out. What fires there were looked as if they were under control, but he was repeatedly passed by ambulances and frequently stopped by jumpy sentries at road-blocks asking for proof of identity. As a result he was late for the meeting with an impatient Prime Minister, a confrontation at which no time was wasted on preamble.

'I have to tell you,' began Ironside, 'that in my judgement, the battle for the GHQ Line has turned against us,' and he went on to outline the progress the enemy was making, set against the loss, on the British Army's part, of 75 per cent of its armour and three of its 25 infantry divisions. He explained that, in endeavouring to the best of his ability to comply with Churchill's insistence on the 'rapid, resolute engagement' of all parties landed,[1] the mobile reserves had been exhausted and dispersed. 'The Army,' he said, when Churchill made a recriminatory remark, 'had not been trained to take the offensive: to create an offensive spirit suddenly, with no mobility, no armour and no training, was impossible'.[2] Taking into account the inability of the Fleet to cut the enemy lines of communication and of the RAF's current incapacity to impede the enemy air effort, it seemed, he added, that the prospects of stopping, let alone throwing back, the Germans had vanished. He therefore, and with a heavy heart, recommended that the time to draw to a close the fatal contest had arrived – and he placed his resignation at the Prime Minister's disposal.

XV

THE HINGE OF DESTINY

The masses of manoeuvre

Winston Churchill accepted Ironside's resignation without hesitation, for he had never reposed much faith in the C-in-C Home Forces, and was anxious to replace him with a younger more dynamic man. General Sir Alan Brooke had distinguished himself in battle in France, but he was not a magician. Instead, as a practical soldier with a character of iron, he was perfectly capable of doing what Dill and Ironside found difficult – standing up effectively to Churchill. The Prime Minister's instructions to Brooke insisted that he should seek to re-establish a solid line of defence so as to prolong the struggle, in order to gain time for American help to arrive and perhaps for a miracle to occur. A quick and keen appraisal of the situation by Brooke instantly destroyed any hope of this, however. Reporting direct to the Cabinet within a few hours of taking over, Brooke bluntly reinforced what Ironside had declared the previous day. A 'mass of manoeuvre', as the Prime Minister liked to term it, no longer existed. Instead, Brooke stated, 'I have only a handful of tanks at my disposal, which might conceivably be capable of a few local and transitory ambushes of the enemy, plus a conglomeration of immobile or, at best, semi-mobile infantry formations, whose fire-power is far below the level required and whose chance of out-fighting the enemy unlikely other than on a local basis. Furthermore,' went on Brooke, 'I have only the slightest contact with some of my subordinate formations since, hourly, the civil communications network upon which I depend is being destroyed. I will do what I can,' he promised, 'but I must tell you that the enemy, with his logistical situation secure and a superiority of at least three to one in armour, is now able to do almost as he pleases.'

This the Prime Minister and Cabinet heard in silence and without contradiction, their discussions at once turning to more realistic political measures than the military ones which seemed to elude their grasp. Long ago in 1938, a previous CIGS, Lord Gort, had told Ironside that if and when the British were defeated in Europe, forces gathered in the Middle East should lay the foundation upon which a recovery could be staged. The Cabinet had now to consider that suggestion as one of a number of possibilities. On the 26th, Churchill's last resistance to a change of policy was overcome when reports of an enemy breakthrough near Basingstoke were received. A body of enemy tanks (Rommel's) had struck hard at night and already were on their way towards the Thames at Newbury with nothing, apparently, at hand to stop them.

Tanks on the rampage

This thrust, of course, was a repetition by Rommel of his breaching of the Maginot Line extension in May. It was a deadly stroke which would soon sever yet another artery out of London – the Great Western railway line to the West and the A4 road – and it occurred as German XIII Corps was continuing to make useful headway on either side of Sevenoaks, with battle groups working their way implacably among the Empire troops and 43rd Division. Indeed, this sector of the GHQ Line was almost entirely in German hands by the end of the day, and with it Biggin Hill airfield. Not wishing to become deeply enmeshed in the suburbia of the outer London towns, von Vietinghoff's commanders, intent as they were upon destroying the enemy forces as they met them, did not mind those who escaped entering the outskirts of London. The German infantry units were told to form a loose cordon round the city's southern boundary, knowing that the people, if they cared or dared, could move to and fro since the Germans were in insufficient strength to erect an impenetrable barrier. 9th Panzer Division, on the other hand, went on the rampage, rolling up the GHQ Line along the crest of the high ground in the direction of Leatherhead and Bagshot, with their distant and ambitious objectives set as far distant as Maidenhead. Frequently they were ambushed by groups and parties of British soldiers, and each encounter produced its toll of casualties and delay. Usually the Germans finished up with more prisoners on their hands than they could comfortably guard, plus a lot of enemy equipment, which, if not promptly gathered in, was liable to fall into the hands of francs-tireurs, as the Germans still called the small bands of British who were being encouraged to form guerilla bands. Throughout the 25th, and into the early hours of the 26th, the 9th Panzer Division made progress. It thus came as quite a shock to them, in the midst of their apparently triumphant progress, when they were suddenly hit, between Byfleet and Chobham, by a fierce counter-attack by British tanks – the combined remnant of 1st and 2nd Armoured Divisions which had been grouped by Brooke in that area in the hope, if nothing else, of restoring a sense of pride by one valedictory blow.

The fighting that day was memorable for one thing: 'This time,' wrote Captain R. Bingley of 4th RTR, 'it was our turn to catch Jerry napping. A bunch of their light tanks and several of their bigger Mark IIIs and IVs came at our Matildas as we were lying back in cover, hull down. We let them come to 200 yards and then let rip with the 2-pounders. There were tanks in flames all over the place and men running. And when the Germans began to shoot back, their stuff just bounced off our armour and made not the slightest difference.'

9th Panzer Division certainly received a shock, their tanks no match for British Matildas and cruisers fighting from prepared positions. But once more it was the 88s, brought into the front line under tank and infantry escort, which turned the scales and drove off the British. Likewise, that same day, 7th Panzer Division, which had broken through on the 25th and, under Rommel's insistent urging, headed north for Newbury, was brought to book. It had reached the River Kennet at Newbury with ease, but had then been delayed by a stiff anti-tank and infantry rearguard from 2nd Infantry Division, which had taken post the previous night. Getting men across in the night and ferrying over the tanks at dawn, the first tank company was unexpectedly ravaged by accurate gunfire from the Valentine tanks of 7th RTR which had been lying in ambush. For a time it looked as if the crossing site would have to be abandoned. Indeed, it took an exploit of personal leadership by Rommel to keep his men facing the enemy while a fresh crossing was made down stream, and decisive flank pressure brought to bear on the enemy to make him withdraw.

Only the bad news reached the Cabinet, red arrows on the maps depicting the enemy making steady progress into the heart of England. The frailty of the German presence did not reveal itself for the very good reason that the meagre information being systematically gathered by the British was extremely slow in transmission through shattered communication systems to the centre. A dark situation was thus made to look even blacker. No matter how tardy the German progress was, or how sparse the British information about their immediate intentions and movements, the evidence from Kent and Sussex left no one in Whitehall in the slightest doubt that the crisis of German supply (if it ever existed) had been overcome. Everything pointed to a substantial increase in the number of administrative units that were operating, and of stores beginning to be accumulated in some quantity. From what could be found out about traffic entering the country through the ports and airfields, it was clear that the single 16th Army (which was all so far identified) must soon be joined by another, and that the Luftwaffe was already in a position to operate a great many more units than hitherto from the several airfields now in German possession. In other words, the Germans must soon be ready to apply redoubled pressure to an already lost British situation.

Time for a halt

Reporting these facts to the Cabinet on the 26th, the Chiefs of Staff felt compelled to admit that, even if a temporary halt were applied to the enemy (and there were encouraging signs that the tank fighting of the previous 24 hours had imposed caution upon the Panzer divisions), the decline in military fortunes could not be reversed. It had become clear that no worthwhile amount of American aid could be made available in time. Indeed, the vast convoy of arms, which had been negotiated in June, had yet to arrive though it was close to port. The members of the Cabinet had no need to ask if further resistance promised success. That day their deliberations had revolved around the blackest of conclusions, so that all the Chiefs of Staff did was to reinforce the collective opinion that a halt must be called. Although Churchill had spoken optimistically of the defence of London being itself enough to consume an enemy army corps, even he was beset by doubts. Sir John Anderson, the Home Secretary, described the privations being suffered by the people of towns already in the German grip. Lord Woolton, Minister of Food, spoke grimly of the famine which must soon come as the Germans throttled imports – a point which was echoed by the Minister of Supply, Herbert Morrison, who reported signs of decline in factory output due to disruption of transport and shortage of materials – quite apart from fears among workers under nightly air attack.

The Lord Privy Seal, Clement Attlee, summed it up when, in measured terms, he balanced the pros and cons of fighting on in Britain, surrendering abjectly, or continuing the struggle from overseas. The other countries of Europe, with the exception of France, he pointed out, had sent their Governments to Britain or elsewhere, so that resistance could be continued. Britain had encouraged them to do so and it was therefore up to her to imitate that example, if it became necessary. For his part, he wished to go on fighting, but he had to recognize that there was no point in bringing down misery on people if, in the foreseeable future, nothing could be gained from it. 'In a siege,' he remarked, 'a moment sometimes comes when common sense, apart from convention, demands that a useless resistance be ended. I am afraid we have reached that moment.' The Prime Minister was unwilling to give way at once. Every ounce of his patriotism revolted against the course his colleagues were contemplating. And when at last he was persuaded to change his mind, and dissuaded from immediately tendering his resignation and that of the Government to the King, it took several hours of exhausting, and at times heated, debate to hammer out what to do next.

A change of government

Common ground was found by agreement that neither King nor Government must fall into German hands. Gallant notions of the nation's leaders battling to the death among the ruins of their cities were discarded in favour of their departure from the country in order to carry on the fight from overseas. At a convenient moment those in highest authority would be evacuated to one of the Dominions or Colonies – Canada pre-eminent as the preferred destination, although this, as it transpired, did not find immediate favour with the Canadian Prime Minister, Mr Mackenzie King. Canada was very proud of the independence she had recently won, and was a country not without differences between its French and English speaking populace. A British Government in Canada could not be allowed to rule and might easily create frictions, although the Royal Family would have been received loyally as 'undoubted King'. Finally, it was resolved that the Government move to the Bahamas – at least to begin with.[1]

The question as to who would govern England as a German puppet was one which the Government felt unable to settle. It was generally expected that Sir Oswald Mosley, who at that moment, along with other members of the British Union of Fascists, languished in prison, would take up the task. As an established public figure, who knew Hitler and Mussolini and who had no desire for war with either country, he was an obvious candidate. On the other hand he had vehemently declared at the outbreak of war that the Fascists 'must not injure our country or help any other power', and, on the 9th May, just prior to the German invasion of Western Europe, he had declared, 'Every one of us would resist the foreign invader with all that is in us.' In Mosley's view, no Englishman would cooperate with a foreign conqueror.[2] Nevertheless, somebody would have to deal with the Germans when they took over, and a large number of people would feel compelled to assist in the administration and survival of the country until a day of liberation dawned. A caretaker or liaison officer was deemed necessary for contact with the Germans once the elected Government departed, as it soon intended to do.

Since nobody of political stature at that moment suggested himself, Churchill sought help from paid or retired servants of the Crown. Neither of the ex-military men held in custody at that moment recommended themselves, if only because they were hardly known to the public at large. In fact only one man immediately on hand seemed to have anything remotely like the qualifications – and he also was an enigma. The intellectual maverick, Major-General (retired) J. F. C. Fuller, who had been among the chief advocates of mechanization in the British Army and who had been close to Mosley among the Fascists, had several qualifications. Through his pre-war activities and his writing he was well known to the public. He was a staunch patriot, sceptical of democracy, anti-Semitic and well known to and respected by the Germans. Whether or not he could operate as a statesman in government harness was obscure, but the fact that he was on good terms with Churchill and had not been imprisoned with Mosley put him in a different category from that of the other Fascists. Be that as it may, Churchill spoke for two hours to Fuller on the night of the 27th, and the upshot was that Fuller, very much against his better judgement, agreed to take on the invidious task of transferring power to the Germans once the Government had left – but not, as he made it clear, 'to do a Pétain'.[3] Once pushed to do something to the detriment of his people, he would resist. Given half a chance to frustrate the Germans and he would fight.

In the utmost secrecy the Government laid its plans. For appearance sake, on the 27th, the announcement was made that it would remain for the time being in London and carry on the fight from there. By that time German spearheads were across the Thames at Reading and Maidenhead and beginning to veer in a north-easterly direction while establishing a defended flank to the west. At the same time, the Royal Family quietly left London, their departure 'to a place of safety', announced the next day. In fact they moved to Chester, whence they could easily be put aboard a warship in one or other of the north-western ports. Unobtrusively, too, the Fleet, while continuing to threaten the German lines of communication and do all in its power to keep open Britain's trade routes, began to station itself for its next rôle. The Government had decided that it must be preserved as the principal instrument of its ability one day to recover the homeland, and as a major piece in its efforts to achieve credibility with the powers – above all the USA – with which it would have to negotiate in maintaining its prestige and influence. The Fleet would, therefore, be needed to assist in evacuating essential personnel and vital items of equipment (such as those connected with deciphering, science and advanced technology) and then proceed to bases from which it could continue to operate against the Axis ports – such as those in the West Indies and the Mediterranean.

A proposal to attempt to maintain a base in Ulster was not rejected out of hand, although the difficulties of doing so for any length of time were fully appreciated. The organization of resistance once the Germans had taken over in Britain was, however, rapidly and cursorily studied. Unlike the Poles and Belgians, for example, the techniques and traditions of this sort of warfare were virtually unknown to the British, except those who had experience of the 'troubles' in Ireland after 1918. And so what little could be done in the short time available was rudimentary. Leadership cells were set-up along with secret arms caches, but a *modus operandi* was scarcely discussed at this stage. Nor could all that much be done to deny industrial capacity to the Germans. As long as the fight was officially on it was impossible to ask people to destroy the factories producing weapons – quite apart from the difficulty of inviting workers to destroy the means of their livelihood. And once Armistice negotiations were set in train, the Germans made it abundantly plain that they would expect the British to desist from sabotage, in 'our joint interests'.

The last act

The negotiations between the two sides were conducted through the mediation of the Swedish Government and made rapid progress. Churchill played for all the time he could get, in order to remove from enemy reach everything possible which might be of value, and to strengthen the outposts of the Empire upon which the future depended. The shipments of bullion, securities and national treasures, which had started on 24 June and which, on 8 July, had employed a battleship, cruisers and four destroyers (which might otherwise have been employed with the Home Fleet) and three liners, was accelerated in order to save everything possible of negotiable value.[4] At the same time, the huge convoy of ships bringing arms from the USA was diverted to the Middle East or turned back to Canada, and all question of direct intervention by the Americans quietly dropped as Churchill informed Roosevelt of the British Government's intentions.

The well-being of the nation began to run down. At the slightest hint of untoward delay in the negotiations which were proceeding at Stockholm, the Germans exacted retribution by bombing selected targets which were of emotional value to the British leaders. Cultural centres of architectural merit were selected for destruction in the hope that this would have an impact on the British ruling hierarchy. So Oxford underwent a sharp attack on the 30th and it was the turn of Cambridge on the 31st, while Eton and Harrow were also meted out their share of punishment, the destruction of a large part of the latter's fabric producing a dolorous effect on one of its most illustrous old boys – the Prime Minister.

While the main body of German troops advanced at a leisurely pace, content to take their time in reducing knots of opposition centred on towns and villages, and anxious to suffer the fewest possible losses now that victory seemed assured, fast-moving motor-cycle and armoured car sub-units infiltrated far ahead, spreading confusion and alarm. Reports from all manner of places – St Albans, High Wycombe, Didcot, even the outskirts of Oxford and of Swindon – lent an impression of an enemy on the rampage, of a foe who could come and go as he chose. Fear was widespread and yet, already in those rearward areas where the Germans had assumed a semi-permanent residence, signs of an accommodation between the people of the two nations were appearing, as had already become apparent in France. The majority of the populace retained their cold rejection of the invaders, but there was an increasing percentage who, when brought into closer contact with German soldiers, began to revise their preconceived opinions. Beneath the stiff exterior and the grey uniform could be discerned signs of humanity and an essential kindness – indeed a yearning by lonely men for companionship and ordinary relationships. It was noted also that, live off the country as the Germans did, they were not now indulging any more freely in pillage than some among the British forces who had shaken off discipline when their units had fallen into disarray. Far more quickly than the traditionalists could ever have imagined, the fundamentals of British social structure began a metamorphosis not all of which was entirely bad.

But the transformation was slow, fraternization furtive and very few of the population would have been happy to witness the highly symbolic event then taking place at Liverpool. For there, on the night of the 31st, the battleship *Nelson* set sail with the Royal Family on board. The secret of their departure had not been kept. The arrival of this great ship at a distance from the heart of battle, at a time when it was known that strange shipments were moving through the Mersey port and when rumours were rife that an end to the war was in prospect, prompted people to speculate. The King was recognized as he drove to the dockside and a crowd began to gather with emotions running high. A sensation of awful foreboding gripped those who witnessed the event. A cheer was raised, but it was one of disbelief and faded almost to a sob. The King and Queen waved briefly and drove on their way, mounting the gangplank quickly to the wail of bosun's pipes. As night fell, the battleship and her escort cleared the river and set sail across the Atlantic. Just behind, Winston Churchill led his Cabinet from London to the comparative safety of Glasgow to await the final news from Sweden before following their Monarch into exile.

Hitler looks to the future

It would be no exaggeration to say that Hitler and his close entourage received the news of their victory as much with relief as joy. The latest of his gambles had come off. The doubts which Raeder had noticed on the Führer's face shortly before S Day had been real enough, and the members of the OKW Staff had good reason to recall the numerous occasions since the 13th when their Supreme Commander had been fidgety with anxiety – particularly when the RAF seemed to be holding the Luftwaffe, and during the hours when the Royal Navy was trying to dominate the Straits. But now that the victory was won and an Armistice on the point of completion, he could relax and, to his closest colleagues, begin to expand on his future designs. Within the space of four months almost the whole of Western Europe had fallen under Fascist rule with Germany as the dominant partner. Soon, no doubt, Gibraltar would be in Spanish hands and Malta in those of Italy, thus expunging the last British holdings on the Continent. The Balance of World Power, as Hitler viewed it, had been upturned. The prospects of a United States of Europe, under German guardianship, a distinct likelihood.

With these thoughts in mind, Hitler redirected his acquisitive gaze eastward. With the western end of the Continent entirely under his thumb and with Britain and France suppressed, the chances of fighting a war on two fronts, if he decided to move against Russia, had been virtually extinguished. 'The USA,' he reflected to von Ribbentrop, 'has neither the strength nor the desire to become involved in Europe. She will accept the New Order and reach an accommodation with us.' As for his latest conquest, Britain, he hoped she would not for too long persist with the resistance that Winston Churchill had announced would continue from overseas.

'Surely,' asked Hitler, 'Churchill cannot believe that with the industrial base and the bulk of the population lost, he can mount a serious effort without the involvement of the USA? And, as I have already said, the USA will not wish to become involved in that way – even though it seems that she is engaged in taking over some of the British islands in the West Indies.'

Until the signing of the Armistice, Hitler was content to allow the Army steadily to strengthen its grip on England, without greatly extending its area of occupation. With London in a state of siege, it seemed unlikely that resistance there could be long prolonged, as the large population consumed its food stocks. It was undesirable to cause further unnecessary damage to industrial plant and ports since it was to Germany's distinct advantage to take over an economy in full working order – particularly if Hitler proceeded with his already hinted aim of invading Russia in 1941. So, although for the time being the Army was allowed to operate its draconian 'Orders concerning the Organization and Function of Military Government of England', it was without any intent on Hitler's part to permit that state of affairs to continue indefinitely. Now that he had won his way, and all immediate threat of outside interference had been removed, he was prepared to show benevolence. In any case, it was clearly in Germany's interests to obtain the collaboration of the conquered nations to prevent the existing deep hostility from plunging into outright resistance. Factory output would be needed along with manpower. The people would have to be fed to enable them to work and to keep them content. The importation of food would have to be maintained – and now that the Royal Navy was apparently vacating the waters surrounding the British Isles and the blockade of Europe was being involuntarily lifted, there seemed no reason why British ports and British ships (if they so wished) should not pursue their traditional commerce. Indeed, Hitler and his advisers at once realized that the absent Churchill Government might find itself in a dilemma if it employed its Navy to blockade its own homeland of 48 million people.

In default of any clear ideas as to how and by whom Britain should be governed, once the Armistice had been signed – the time agreed on 1 August being noon on the 2nd – Hitler welcomed Churchill's announcement that Fuller had agreed to head an interim administration. At least Fuller had won the respect of many Germans for his clear-sighted advocacy of the sort of tank warfare which had gained Germany her victory, and if his inexperience of Government proved a serious handicap, the strings would, in any case, be pulled by Reichs Commissioners who would be appointed to stand behind the puppet British Administration.

These, therefore, were the concepts prompting the methods adopted by the Germans when they acceded in Britain on 2 August. It was an angry and baffled people whom they took under their control, a nation bewildered by the suddenness of its fall from greatness and one which was far from feeling defeated. In some quarters there was resentment at the Government 'leaving them in the lurch' – and the almost traditional recriminations that had been levelled at Churchill at various stages of his career were revived. But, for the most part, there was a deep-seated unwillingless to accept the realities of the situation. Those soldiers and airmen who fought to the bitter end – and some who continued even after the official ceasefire – were perfectly aware of the infirmity of their situation, but stubborn in their rejection of the obvious conclusions to be drawn. From men such as these grew the resistance movement which the authorities had failed to establish in a coherent form before they were swept away. To the sailors, who set course into exile from their native land, the emotional impact, in some ways, was even worse than that suffered by those who stayed. Sent to ports in distant lands, detached by vast distances from their families, their's was a hard and gloomy lot at a time when it was impossible to see what chances there were of reconquering Britain. And as the influence of foreign interests, particularly those of the Americans, became manifest, so would the conflicts of motivation multiply together with an uneasy questioning of the purpose behind their rôle.

These are matters which fall outside the scope of this history. Operation 'Sealion' and the British defence against German invasion duly came to an end at noon on 2 August, less than three weeks after the first German soldier had landed near Dover. Churchill and the Government had departed the night before, and were already on their way to a first stop in Canada at the start of their life and perambulations in the wilderness. In London, Major-General J. F. C. Fuller looked bleakly round an unfamiliar office at Number 10 Downing Street and made ready to meet the first German Commissioner.

AS IT HAPPENED

As history tells us, when Admiral Raeder actually inquired of Hitler on 21 May 1940, whether his previous negative views on the subject of invading Britain had changed, the Führer remained uninterested. And although Goering seems to have expressed initial enthusiasm for Kesselring's scheme (broached at the time of Dunkirk) for an immediate cross-Channel pursuit of the defeated enemy, he soon shelved the notion in favour of an assault by air power alone at a later date. So it was not until early in July that serious thought was given by the Germans to attempting an invasion, and even then it was processed rather half-heartedly by the upper hierarchy who firmly, and with cogent reasons, could not believe that the British would persist in a hopeless resistance.

The prolonged delay in starting to make arrangements proved fatal to the scheme. By the middle of July, at which moment the Luftwaffe was only just beginning to send large numbers of aircraft across the Channel, RAF Fighter Command had not only recovered some of its strength and rebuilt its exhausted reserves of aircraft, but had been given time to carry out an important re-organization of its Groups, and gain invaluable operational experience in minor actions. Moreover, before the end of that month, when far heavier attacks were being made against inland targets, the first CHL Radar Stations were coming into service, making it more difficult for the Germans to achieve surprise by low-level attacks. Therefore, the RAF was able to withstand the preliminary German onslaught in August and remain intact at the crucial moment in September when the German invasion fleet was meant to set sail. But even then it was saved from extinction only because Goering had insisted upon fighting a wholly aerial war and because, at the moment when Fighter Command was rocking on its heels as its airfields were battered by well-directed attacks, he had switched to the bombing of London instead of persevering with the most telling and, perhaps, decisive strategy.

By mid September, however, much else had altered in the British favour. By then, the beach defences were stronger and many Army units had been rebuilt and their mobility so raised that the concept of yielding defence, such as was forced on Ironside in July, could make way in favour of a more mobile and aggressive strategy which might well have destroyed the enemy close to the beaches. Furthermore, the wide-fronted attack, which the Germans would then have been compelled to adopt, would have forfeited the high *proportion* of airborne support such as was possible for a narrow front in July. The far larger numbers of craft strung along the Channel in its length would have been much more vulnerable than the more compact flotillas operating in better weather and, above all, much shorter nights, under close escort and artillery support in the narrows of the Straits of Dover in July. Indeed the whole business of handling invasion craft on the beaches in the deteriorating weather conditions and shorter days of September and October would have been a daunting one.

Readers must judge for themselves if the July invasion would have succeeded. Let it simply be stated that, in the considered appreciation of the British Chiefs of Staff of the day, *that* was the really dangerous period, the one moment when Hitler might have pulled it off. And if he had, the history of the world would have been significantly changed – for who can say what might have happened if Russia had not received British and then American support in the crucial years of 1941 and 1942? And what would there have been to stop the Axis powers dominating large areas of Africa and the Far East, leaving the USA as isolated as so many of her leaders and people desired? And what then might not have happened to create a political environment totally different from the one we now experience.

HISTORICAL NOTES

The political and military backgrounds to this book are founded upon the plans which actually were in existence and they are only varied when inherent military probability demands it. Naturally the German plans have had to be changed rather more than those of the British: to fulfil my terms of reference they would have had to undergo a fundamental alteration. In any case, the Germans had far more options open to them than the British, who were penned-in and weaker than at any time in their history. But the conditions of weather, light and tide which I describe are real and the top personalities are those who were involved. Of necessity, however, I have created fictional characters in the lower stratus of fighting men and civilians in order to inject the realism desired.

In as many instances as possible I have made use of actualities in order to place a cloak of authenticity over this account. To enable the reader to evaluate for himself the feasibility of a German invasion of Britain in July 1940, the notes below may be of assistance, giving as they do the sources from which I drew many of the actual facts, and explaining, for example, when an actuality has been deliberately misplaced in time in order to fit the demands of my theme.

CHAPTER I

1. *The Defence of the United Kingdom* by B. Collier, page 14. My development of this event forms, of course, the starting-point for the fictional side of this book. In fact Hitler showed no interest in invasion at this moment.
2. *Hitler Confronts England* by W. Ansel, page 39 et seq.
3. *Kesselring* by K. Macksey, page 74. A conference similar to this took place on 5 June 1940.
4. *The Rise and Fall of the German Air Force* – Anon, page 75, based on a German directive of 12 July 1940.
5. *The Defence of the United Kingdom*, page 175.
6. Ibid, page 123.
7. *The Ultra Secret* by F. W. Winterbotham, page 34.
8. *The War in France and Flanders* by L. F. Ellis.
9. *The Defence of the United Kingdom*, pages 123–125.
10. *The Second World War*, Vol II by W. S. Churchill, pages 22–23.
11. *The Defence of the United Kingdom*, page 119.

CHAPTER II
1. *The Rise and Fall of the German Air Force*, page 72.
2. *Hitler confronts England*, pages 108–110. In reality this conference between Halder and Schniewind took place on 1 July.
3. Ibid, page 240.
4. In reality Directive No 16 was signed on 16 July 1940.

CHAPTER III
1. *The Naval War against Hitler* by D. Macintyre, pages 41–42, *The War at Sea* by S. W. Roskill, pages 194–196 and *Die Deutsche Kriegsmarine im Kampf 1939–45* by B. Herzog.
2. This account is based on *The War in France and Flanders, To Lose a Battle* by A. Horne and *The Rommel Papers*, edited by B. H. Liddell Hart.
3. *The Second World War*, Vol II, page 198.
4. *The Defence of the United Kingdom*, page 138.

CHAPTER IV
1. Based on various accounts in *Civil Defence* by T. H. O'Brien and *Living through the Blitz* by T. Harrisson.
2. Based on reports in the June and July issues of *The Dover Express* and *The Folkestone Herald.*
3. *The Defence of the United Kingdom*, pages 156–158.
4. *Most Secret War* by R. V. Jones, page 105.
5. Based in general on *Operation Sea Lion* by Peter Fleming, pages 167–172, *British Intelligence in the Second World War* by F. H. Hinsley, pages 159–190 and on various entries in *The Defence of the United Kingdom.* The concept of the East Coast being the likely main target is to be found in various messages and appreciations emanating from British Military Intelligence Branches and from GHQ Home Forces, and adopted by the War Committee in Whitehall. The GHQ Home Forces note referred to here as '30th June' actually was written on 8 September and reflected an opinion never entirely rejected even as the German Invasion craft poured down the Channel. It is apparent from Hinsley that British Intelligence possessed neither the capacity nor the organization and expertise to collect and adequately synthesise the material available in order to draw correct conclusions regarding the nature, direction or date of the impending invasion – a condition which applied almost as equally to the days of September (when the Battle of Britain was actually in full swing) as it did in June and July prior to the opening of the air battle over the Channel. In fact, the Intelligence organizations tended much more to mislead than give constructive guidance. The inhibiting effects of over-estimating of German air strength were another product referred to on page 73.
6. *The Defence of the United Kingdom*, page 440.
7. Information supplied by the Kent Defence Research Group. Work was held up by air raids and the gun had not been delivered by the end of July and only came into action later in August.
8. *The Defence of the United Kingdom*, page 137.
9. Ibid, page 129.
10. Ibid page 130 and War Diaries.
11. This description of the actual defences of Kent at this period is based upon their real state taken from material to be found in the Operational Instructions and Returns of the Formations and Units concerned, relevant

sections of *The Defence of the United Kingdom*, *The Black Cats at War*, *Sealion*, *A Handbook of Kent's Defences* and information gathered by the author from local sources including Town Council Minutes and the press.
12. *The Defence of the United Kingdom*, pages 127 and 128.
13. Ibid, page 125.
14. *The Black Cats at War*, page 18.
15. The description of the development and use of radar is based upon information in *The Design and Development of Weapons*, by M. Postan and others, pages 373–389; *The Defence of the United Kingdom*, various sections, and *Battle over Britain* by F. Mason, pages 91–96 and 124.
16. *The Defence of the United Kingdom*, page 121 and *Royal Air Force* by D. Richards, page 156.
17. *The Defence of the United Kingdom*, page 162 for a general idea of the pilot position.
18. Ibid page 143.
19. *Civil Defence* gives a useful description of organizations and methods. Innumerable other sources have been consulted along with personal recollections of the author who was an ARP Messenger during the 'Blitz' and, for a short time, Private in the Home Guard after the threat of invasion had receded.
20. *Operation Sea Lion*, page 62.
21. *Civil Defence*, page 357.

CHAPTER V

1. The story told here of the air battles over the convoys constitutes compression in imagination of the battles which actually took place between 10 July and 10 August. The weather conditions, however, are those which actually pertained on the dates in question, while losses are close in proportion to those actually suffered by both sides.
2. From reports in *The Dover Express* and from *The War at Sea*, Vol I, page 325. The first shells fell on Dover and Folkestone and a convoy on 12 August, not 22 August as usually stated.
3. *The Defence of the United Kingdom*, page 132. The withdrawal actually took place on 29 July and was due to the danger of bombing alone.
4. This account follows that in *The War at Sea*, Vol I, pages 240–244, amplified by various other references, and took place on the dates given in the text.

CHAPTER VI

1. First signs of the German build-up were not actually apparent until the first week in September.
2. Compiled from *Hitler confronts England*. The information about codes and ciphers come from *The War at Sea*, Vol 1, page 267 and *British Intelligence in the Second World War*, page 141.
3. Ibid, pages 242–243.
4. Ibid, page 279.
5. *Battle over Britain*, pages 612–613.
6. *The Defence of the United Kingdom* and information from local sources.
7. *The Dover Express*.
8. The GS I (x) opinions were actually presented on 8, 12 and 21 September at a time when the intended date of invasion was set for 22 September. The

comments from Naval Intelligence and by Churchill are to be found in *Operation Sea Lion*, pages 169–173.
9. War Diary of Dover Command, 12 September.
10. *Operation Sea Lion*, page 173.
11. Figures in proportion to this are recorded in respect of July and August in *The Defence of the United Kingdom*, page 225.
12. Based on War Diary of Dover Command and *The War at Sea*, Vol I.
13. See Operational Instructions for 1st (London) Division and 2nd (London) Brigade, *c* 5 July 1940 and *History of the Irish Guards* by Fitzgerald.
14. *The Second World War*, Vol II, page 148.
15. Ibid, page 569.
16. Ibid, page 151.
17. *Hitler confronts England*, pages 272–273.

CHAPTER VII
1. This actually took place on 7 August. See *Battle over Britain*, page 212.
2. *The Luftwaffe War Diaries*, by C. Bekker, page 200.
3. *Battle over Britain*, page 237. Adapted from the events of 11 and 12 August which were immediately prior to the actual 'Eagle Day' on 13th.
4. An operation similar to this did take place on 12 August, but included an attack on the CHL station at Dover (which was not ready on 8 July) and did not include an attack on Conewden, which is added here as a likely operation by the Germans in the context of this book.
5. Figures for the losses among RAF fighters and all German types are those for 12 August as supplied in *Battle over Britain*, pages 234–236. Those for RAF bombers are synthetic.
6. Based upon German plans and selected events which occurred during the morning battles of 13 August 1940, but modified in a manner to suit the better weather conditions of 9 July. See *The Defence of the United Kingdom*, pages 184–186 and *Battle over Britain*, pages 237–9.
7. Ibid and based, with variations, respectively, on pages 186–188 and pages 239–243.
8. *Royal Air Force*, page 162–164.
9. *Battle over Britain*, page 244.
10. Although my account of the fighting on 11 July is substantially based on that which actually occurred on 15 August 1940 (see *The Defence of the United Kingdom*, pages 190–197 and *Battle over Britain*, pages 247–264), I have modified certain critical episodes to take account of the imminence of S Day (13 July). The *Luftwaffe* would have behaved differently, as in my imaginary scenario, from the way it actually did on 15 August 1940 when S Day was still a month distant in September.
11. *Royal Air Force*, page 176.
12. *Hitler confronts England*, page 286.
13. Based on the realities of 16 August 1940. See *The Defence of the United Kingdom*, pages 197–199 and *Battle over Britain*, pages 264–273.
14. Based on the actual events of 7 September 1940 as described in *The Defence of the United Kingdom*, pages 223–4.

CHAPTER VIII
1. The German techniques are those described by Oberst Rudolf Witzig in his account of the taking of Fort Eban Emael on 10 May 1940 in

Purnell's History of the Second World War, pages 184–192. A similar operation was carried out in the early hours of 6 June 1944 by British glider troops against the Germany battery at Houlgate in Normandy.
2. A similar operation was attempted in the Ardennes on 10 May 1940. See *To Lose a Battle*, page 185.

CHAPTER X
1. Quoted from *Operation Sea Lion*, page 269.
2. After Churchill had offered 67-year old Marshal of the RAF Lord Trenchard the post of General Officer Commanding 'all land, sea and air forces at home in the event of invasion', on 23 May and Trenchard had refused, Churchill himself had, to all intents and purposes, assumed that appointment. On page 42 of his *Churchill as Warlord*, R. Lewin supports General Sir Alan Brooke in arguing the perils which might have arisen from Churchill's 'impulsive nature and tendency to arrive at decisions through a process of intuition as opposed to "logical" approach'.
3. A similar condition was reached at Dunkirk when the Navy had to abandon the evacuation by day. The extent of losses in this battle can be compared to some extent with those inflicted, at night, by the Royal Navy on the attempted German seaborne invasion of Crete (when the invasion force was largely destroyed by light forces), and RN losses with those at Dunkirk as well as Crete. The German invaders of Crete did not have anything like the support of surface forces as were available to them in the Channel in July 1940, nor were the crossing points so narrow or easy to mine. In consequence, the Royal Navy's problem off Crete was, in some respects, easier and less hazardous at night while appallingly dangerous in daylight from the *Luftwaffe* alone. On balance, therefore, I do not think the extent of losses assumed here are unreasonable and the ammunition problem was *always* severely detrimental.
4. Figure based on official returns to Dover Council showing stocks in July.
5. Strengths and locations extracted from War Diaries.

CHAPTER XI
1. Both 2nd and 5th RTR underwent a very similar experience in France at the end of May 1940 when attacking an entrenched enemy.

CHAPTER XII
1. Quoted from *Churchill and the Admirals*, page 121.
2. *The Second World War*, Vol II, page 576.
3. Ibid, page 581. Cabinet discussions on this issue took place in July and August and produced divisions reflected in these quotes from Churchill's minutes. A clear enunciation of a practical formula governing the behaviour of the civilian Services would appear to have been unlikely in the actual event of invasion. In *Living though the Blitz* page 180, it refers to the reluctance of the Home Secretary, Herbert Morrison, to overrule 'any elected mayor or council, duly appointed Town Clerk or Chief Constable'. No doubt Sir John Anderson would have followed the same policy and each Chief Constable and many of his men would have followed their own dictates.
4. Quoted from *Operation Sea Lion*, page 258.
5. *The Defence of the United Kingdom* page 180, and *Operation Sea Lion*

pages 260–264, and relevant documents some of which are reproduced in this book.
6. *The Second World War*, Vol II, page 51.
7. Ibid, page 355.
8. Summarised in *Churchill as Warlord*, page 37, by reference to the underlying commercial and self-interested approach by the United States in nearly all her principal dealings with Britain throughout the war, with examples of how they operated.
9. This conversation actually took place on 26 July in connection with the exchange of old US destroyers for island bases, and is quoted from *Mr Roosevelt's War* by P. Abbazia, page 94.

Chapter XIII
1. *Living through the Blitz*, page 31.
2. I have based my assessments of the reactions of the civil populace upon the accumulated evidence in *Civil Defence*, *Living through the Blitz* and numerous contemporary documents relating to people's behaviour under stress. To this I have added my own observations of events at the time along with the reminiscences of associates who also experienced the 'Blitz'. As *Living through the Blitz* says (page 32), 'the reasons for [evacuees] coming and going were multiple, complex, highly varied and variable, not justifying simple classifications or fear or compromise, forethought or apathy'. But on page 249, Ibid, there appears a clear simplification by a Manchester woman who said 'We are carrying on because we've got to'.

Chapter XIV
1. *The Defence of the United Kingdom*, page 143.
2. Ibid page 143. To comprehend Ironside's problems and the overall weakness of the British defences in June (which were only marginally improved by mid July) it is sufficient to read Chapter VIII (pages 127–146) of the above reference.

Chapter XV
1. A useful summary of the problems related to what might have happened if King and Government had been compelled to leave the British Isles can be found in *If Britain had fallen* by Norman Longmate, pages 112–116.
2. Sir Oswald Mosley has stated what his attitude and action would have been in his book *My Life*, Chapter 21 and has confirmed this in a letter to the author.
3. Mosley in the letter referred to under Note 2 above says that he cannot conceive Fuller playing the part of Pétain. Anthony Trythall, Fuller's biographer, is more flexible in his opinion, admitting that Fuller had many of the qualifications, that in the summer of 1939 he was under MI 5 surveillance and saying 'I do not believe that he would have advocated or formed a Military junta but a Pétain-like state is a different matter'.
4. See *If Britain had fallen* page 52 and *Operation Sea Lion* page 95.

SELECT BIBLIOGRAPHY

Abbazia, P. *Mr Roosevelt's War*, Naval Institute Press, 1975.
Anon. *German Occupied Britain*, Scott-David, 1971.
Anon. *The Rise and Fall of the German Air Force*, Air Ministry, 1948.
Anon. *1st and 2nd Northamptonshire Yeomanry*, Privately, 1946.
Ansel, W. *Hitler confronts England*, Duke University Press, 1960.
Bekker, C. *The Luftwaffe War Diaries*, Macdonald, 1966.
Bennett, D. *The Handbook of Kent's Defences*, Kent Defence Group, 1977.
Collier, B. *The Defence of the United Kingdom*, H.M.S.O., 1957.
Davis, B. L. *German Parachute Forces, 1935–1945*, Arms and Armour Press, 1974.
Ellis, L. F. *The War in France and Flanders, 1939–40*, H.M.S.O., 1953.
Farrar-Hockley, A. H. *Student*, Ballantine, 1973.
Fitzgerald, D. J. C. *The Irish Guards in the Second World War*, Gale and Polden, 1949.
Fleming, P. *Invasion 1940* (US title and paperback *Operation Sea Lion*), Hart-Davis, 1957.
Harrisson, T. *Living through the Blitz*, Collins, 1976.
Herzog, B. *Die Deutsche Kriegsmarine im Kampf*, Podzen-Verlag, 1969.
Hinsley, F. H. and others. *British Intelligence in the Second World War*, Vol 1, H.M.S.O., 1979.
Illingworth, F. *Britain under Shellfire*, Hutchinson, 1942.
Jones, M. *History of the Coast Artillery in the British Army*, R.A. Institute, 1959.
Jones, R. V. *Most Secret War*, Hamish Hamilton, 1978.
Longmate, N. *If Britain had fallen*, B.B.C. and Hutchinson, 1972.
Lewin, R. *Churchill as Warlord*, Batsford, 1973. *Ultra goes to War*, Hutchinson, 1978.
Macdonald, C. *By Air to Battle*, Ballantine, 1969.
Macintyre, D. *The Naval War against Hitler*, Batsford, 1971.
Macksey, K. J. *Guderian, Panzer General*, Macdonald, 1973. *Kesselring, The Making of the Luftwaffe*, Batsford, 1978. *Rommel, Campaigns and Battles*, Arms and Armour Press, 1979.
Mason, F. K. *Battle over Britain*, McWhirter, 1969.
Morison, S. E. *History of US Naval Operations in World War II, Battle of the Atlantic Sep 1939–May 1943*, Little Brown, 1947.
Mosley, O. *My Life*, Nelson, 1968.
O'Brien, T. H. *Civil Defence*, H.M.S.O., 1955.
Playfair, I. and others. *The Mediterranean and Middle East*, Vol. I, H.M.S.O., 1954.

Plehove, F. K. von. *Operation Sealion, 1940*, R.U.S.I. Journal, 1973.
Postan, M. and others. *The Design and Development of Weapons*, H.M.S.O., 1964.
Richards, D. *Royal Air Force, 1939–1945*, Vol I, H.M.S.O., 1953.
Rommel, E. *The Rommel Papers* (Edited by B. H. Liddell Hart), Collins, 1951.
Roskill, S. W. *The War at Sea*, Vol I, H.M.S.O., 1954.
Ruge, F. *Churchill and the Admirals*, Collins, 1975. *The War at Sea, 1939–45*, Koehler, 1955.
Trythall, A. J. *'Boney' Fuller*, Cassell, 1977.
Williams, D. *The Black Cats at War*, Private, 1955.
Winterbotham, F. W. *The Ultra Secret*, Weidenfeld and Nicolson, 1974.

INDEX

Index

THE FACTS ABOUT CHILD PEDESTRIAN ACCIDENTS

TITLES IN THE FACTS ABOUT . . . SERIES

J. B. Davies and N. Coggans *The Facts About Adolescent Drug Abuse*

B. Gillham *The Facts About Child Sexual Abuse*

J. A. Thomson *The Facts About Child Pedestrian Accidents*

THE FACTS ABOUT CHILD PEDESTRIAN ACCIDENTS

JAMES A. THOMSON

CASSELL

Cassell Educational Limited
Villiers House
41/47 Strand
London WC2N 5JE

First published 1991

British Library Cataloguing in Publication Data
Thomson, James A.
The facts about child pedestrian accidents. – (The Facts About . . . series)
1. Great Britain. Pedestrians. Children. Accidents
I. Title
363.1251

ISBN 0–304–32261–X (hardback)
0–304–32273–3 (paperback)

Typeset by Fakenham Photosetting Limited, Fakenham, Norfolk
Printed and bound in Great Britain by Biddles Ltd, Guildford and King's Lynn

CONTENTS

SERIES FOREWORD

The idea for this series came from an awareness that much of the media hype, and some of the professional practice, relating to major social problems involving children and adolescents was singularly ill-informed. At the same time there was a notable lack of short, accessible summaries of the relevant research data by which people could inform themselves.

Not surprisingly, the conclusions that are drawn from a careful consideration of the evidence challenge many generally held assumptions – at all levels of popular and professional concern.

Bill Gillham

PREFACE

In 1987 over 57,000 pedestrian casualties were reported on British roads, a figure representing 18 per cent of all road casualties and 34 per cent of all road deaths. In spite of the wide media attention given to more dramatic events such as air crashes or motorway pile-ups, the risk of death when travelling on foot is many times higher than when travelling by car or most other modes of transport.

For children, the situation is even worse. Taking into account their relatively low exposure to traffic, a child between the ages of 5 and 9 is at least 30 times as likely to become involved in an accident as the average driver. Little wonder that one road safety researcher has described traffic as 'for children, the plague in modern guise'.

Road accidents are one of the most serious threats to the health and well-being of children: few diseases even begin to stand comparison with them. Yet it is astonishing how lightly we accept such a situation. If a slate blows off a school roof and injures a child, we can expect a substantial local hue and cry. But when 20,000 children are injured on the roads each year, we tolerate this with a degree of stoicism that is completely misplaced.

This book aims to put road accidents into their correct perspective. Beginning with an appraisal of the true scale of the problem, we will examine some of the factors that make children vulnerable road users. We will then go on to assess the extent to which current educational counter-measures help to overcome their deficiencies. Finally, we will take a hard look at some of the ways in which training will have to change if children are to be given a better chance of survival on the roads.

In writing this book, I have stuck closely to the spirit of the 'Facts About' series by trying to give the general reader an informed overview of the problem whilst avoiding too much technical detail. Instead, my aim has been to make the area accessible to readers by providing an interpretation of the data on their behalf. However, for those who wish to pursue the topic further, I have offered some recommendations for further reading. The references incorporated in the text should also enable readers to follow up individual issues that particularly interest them.

Finally, although this book concentrates on children's limitations and how we might try to remedy them, I am acutely aware that this represents only one strand in the effort to reduce pedestrian casualties. It is becoming increasingly clear from studies of driver behaviour, for instance, that drivers are often far from blameless in cases of child pedestrian accidents, although they almost always receive the benefit of the doubt. Far more emphasis should be placed on the driver's role in these accidents and on the implications for driver training.

Likewise, there is currently a great deal of interest in the engineering and urban planning measures that might be introduced to provide an intrinsically safer pedestrian environment. Given that most urban environments appear to have been designed without any thought whatever for the needs of pedestrians, it seems likely that such measures have much to offer in the effort to reduce accident rates.

These approaches are complementary and we should be in no doubt that all three must be vigorously pursued if current accident rates are to be significantly reduced. However, space has not permitted me to address all three in a single volume; indeed, each could easily occupy a book on its own. Nevertheless, if engineering or other measures are to have an effect on accident rates, they must be founded on a knowledge of what pedestrians actually *do* in traffic and of the difficulties they face there. For this reason, the analysis of pedestrian behaviour is in many ways a necessary precursor to the introduction of any measure, be it educational *or* engineering. I hope engineers and urban planners might find the book useful from this point of view.

ACKNOWLEDGEMENTS

The ideas expressed in this book have emerged in the course of long-standing discussion with a number of people. I owe a special debt to Kwame Ampofo-Boateng who, first as a student and later as a colleague, has influenced me as much as (I hope!) I have influenced him. Jim Demetre, Bob Grieve, David Lee and Tom Pitcairn have been a never-ending source of stimulation and debate. Our meetings are seldom less than heated! Likewise Jim Baxter is always ready to argue and debate the issues. By no means least in this list comes my wife, Dana O'Dwyer, who not only supported me in the task of writing but also found time in her own busy schedule to read and re-read drafts of the chapters. I would also like to thank Bill Gillham for editing with sensitivity and tact and for thinking up the whole enterprise in the first place. Finally, I wish to thank Judith Gillham for her detailed and thoughtful preparation of the final version of the manuscript.

Some of the research described in Chapters 5 and 6 was supported by General Accident Insurance and the UK Economic and Social Research Council in the form of a grant to David Lee, Bob Grieve, Tom Pitcairn and myself: I would like to acknowledge this support.

Like all researchers, however, I reserve my most grateful acknowledgement for the many police, road safety officers, teachers, parents and, especially, children who have supported our research and who form the background against which this book was written.

James A. Thomson

1

TRENDS IN PEDESTRIAN ACCIDENTS

In the United Kingdom, accident statistics are compiled from police report forms (known as Stats 19) that record events at the time of an incident. These include characteristics of the road users involved (age and sex); severity of injuries sustained (slight, serious or fatal); movements of the pedestrians or vehicles, where this is known; and a variety of other information such as road conditions, prevailing weather, lighting and so on. Approximately 250,000 such forms are completed annually by the 51 police forces in the country. Each force submits its data at monthly intervals to the Department of Transport, where a master file is compiled and held for analysis. The government uses this information to produce an annual report (*Road Accidents Great Britain*), which surveys the figures for that year and also analyses longer-term trends. Separate figures are reported for Scotland, Wales and the English Regions. Similar information is collected in most countries, enabling us in principle to make comparisons between them, though substantial differences in methods of collecting and analysing data make international comparisons notoriously difficult.

In general, the pattern that emerges from these statistics shows a remarkable stability from year to year. Indeed, even within a localized area police officers often report with disconsolation how reliably they can predict from month to month the number of accidents that will occur, where they will take place and the type of victims that will be involved. To show how consistent such patterns are, we need only consider the UK figures for pedestrian deaths over the last few years. Between 1984 and 1987 (the latest year for which data are available at the time of writing), pedestrian deaths stood at 1,868, 1,789, 1,841 and 1,703 per year respectively. Clearly, the similarities between these figures are more impressive than the differences. The effect is not confined to pedestrians: for example, deaths amongst car drivers over the same period were 1,237, 1,253, 1,340 and 1,327. Even the distribution of accidents over different sections of the population (for example, between child and adult pedestrians) shows a similarly stable pattern. Considering that the population of the UK is more than 56 million, it is quite astonishing how small the annual fluctuations are. This is not to say that longer-term trends are not discernible. However, the stability of the pattern over time and over different sections of the population suggests that some pretty constant factors are at work to produce them. And when we consider that 'accidents' are defined as 'unexpected events whose occurrence may be attributed to chance' (*Oxford English Dictionary*), the stability of the picture from year to year is quite remarkable.

Actually, there is little that is random or unpredictable about accidents and the very name is something of a misnomer. Of course, individual victims will doubtless feel that their misfortune was only too unforseeable and it is not difficult to understand this point of view! Nevertheless, at the level of the population as a whole, the statistical regularities that emerge year after year show that accidents are far from mere acts of fate occurring through unhappy chance. Clearly, consistent factors of some sort are at work to produce these regularities. Probing the statistical pattern is therefore an essential (though by no means unique) starting point for research into road safety as it helps us target the constant factors that underlie accidents. This in turn is a pre-requisite for developing effective preventive measures. For example, if we could show *who* is most vulnerable on the roads, *where* accidents take place, what the *attendant circumstances* tend to be and so on, then we should have a basis for research into *why* these patterns develop. The main aim of this chapter will therefore be to tease out some of the main trends as a prelude to what follows.

ROAD ACCIDENTS IN PERSPECTIVE

In the first place, how do road accidents compare to other sources of morbidity and mortality at the present time? Not long ago disease and infection probably accounted for the majority of premature deaths, particularly in vulnerable groups such as children. The decline in the frequency of diseases over the course of this century is undoubtedly due to improvements in social conditions and discoveries in medical science, leading to better prevention and curative control. Over the same time period, however, accidents have continued to increase and 'whether measured in terms of mortality or morbidity ... represent the most important problem of child health today' (Jackson, 1978, p. 807).

The scale of the problem can be illustrated by the figures for 1987, which show the proportion of all deaths due to accidents for different sections of the population (*Road Accidents Great Britain*, 1988). For young people between the ages of 5 and 24 years, accidents accounted for between a third and a half of all deaths. A similar pattern is apparent in most countries, particularly among the young. For example, accidents rank as the leading cause of death in the 1- to 15-year-old age group in the United States (Jackson, 1978), the UK (O'Shea, Collins and Butler, 1982) and even in developing countries such as Malawi, Kenya and Zimbabwe, where major sources of child mortality such as disease, infection or malnutrition might be expected to overshadow accidents as a cause of death (Marcusson and Oehmisch, 1977). Indeed, only with the onset of early middle age do accidents begin to lose ground, as heart disease, cancer and the other afflictions of advanced industrial societies begin to predominate.

AGE TRENDS IN ACCIDENT PATTERNS

Accidents, then, are clearly the major cause of mortality in the young. However, the pattern of accidents varies quite markedly with age. For example, Kravitz (1973) reported that 91 per cent of the injuries and over half the fatalities to children aged under 5 years occur in the home. However, with increasing age the child is brought into a wider environment, containing previously unencountered hazards. Principal amongst these are the hazards posed by the traffic environment; road deaths are consequently much higher amongst 5- to 14-year-olds than amongst the under-5s. In fact, road accidents are the leading single cause of death to children in highly motorized countries. World Health Organization reports confirm this, showing road deaths as responsible for between a third and a half of all accidental deaths to children under 14 in Europe (e.g. Deschamps, 1981).

The figures for the United Kingdom confirm the trend: in 1987, for example, road deaths accounted for about two-thirds of all accidental deaths to children between 5 and 14 years. Nor does this overall rate diminish as the child grows older: indeed, road accidents represent a larger proportion of total deaths amongst young adults (15 to 24 years) than amongst children. However, a change takes place in the type of road accidents that predominate in these older groups. Thus, while most accidents to young children are pedestrian, vehicle accidents predominate for young adults. For example, Foot, Chapman and Wade (1982) report that in the late 1970s 45 per cent of all deaths in the

15- to 19-year-old age-group resulted from road vehicle accidents. These figures, then, demonstrate quite clearly that accidents in general, and road accidents in particular, pose one of the most serious threats to the health and well-being of children and young adults in the modern world. Indeed, road accidents are the single most important source of mortality amongst children and young adults.

PEDESTRIAN ACCIDENTS IN RELATION TO OTHER ROAD ACCIDENTS

In 1987 there were well over 300,000 casualties on British roads, of whom more than 57,000 were pedestrians. Pedestrians therefore accounted for 18 per cent of all road casualties. The tally is far worse, however, if the seriousness of injuries is taken into account. Thus, while pedestrians account for only 18 per cent of all road *casualties*, they account for 34 per cent of all road *deaths*. This discrepancy occurs because the injuries pedestrians are likely to sustain in the event of an accident are disproportionately severe, due to their relative lack of protection. However, the real vulnerability of pedestrians only emerges when we take their relative *exposure to risk* into account. Numerous factors (discussed in detail in Chapter 2) affect this measure. As an example we must realize that different road users cover varying distances over a given period of time. It is important to take this into account because if the average pedestrian only covers, say, 5 miles in a week whereas a car user covers 500 miles, the two are not equivalent in terms of their exposure to risk. Thus we need to find a method of equating different forms of travel for comparative purposes.

One way of equating the distance factor would be to plot the casualty rates of different road users in relation to a particular distance covered: for example, accidents per 100 million kms travelled. Although not a perfect measure, the Department of Transport uses this to provide a rough index of the relative risks involved in travelling on foot compared with other forms of transport. When distance covered is taken into account in this way, the risk of death to pedestrians emerges as 15 times higher than for travelling by car. The estimate is even higher when some other measures of exposure are used (e.g. Howarth and Repetto-Wright, 1978). Only motorcycling comes out from such analyses as a more dangerous form of transport. Viewed from this perspective, the popular adage that one is safer climbing

Mount Everest than crossing the road seems uncomfortably close to the truth!

WHO IS MOST VULNERABLE ON THE ROADS?

These figures show that pedestrians *as a whole* are a highly vulnerable group of road users. However, for some groups the problem is even more serious because marked age and sex differences mean that some pedestrians are far more likely to be involved in an accident than others. The group that consistently emerges as most at risk on the roads is *5- to 9-year-olds*, whose casualty rate is between four and five times the rate for adults (aged 20 to 59) and has been for many years. The next most vulnerable group is that of *10- to 14-year-olds*, whose casualty rate has traditionally been somewhat lower than that for the younger group. However, a change in pattern has been developing over the last ten years or so, with the accident rate for this group increasing so that since 1985 this group has actually overtaken 5- to 9-year-olds for the first time. This contrasts with figures for all other groups of pedestrians, whose accident rate has either declined or remained stable over the same period. It remains to be seen whether this represents a true change in the accident pattern or is merely a temporary shift. If a true trend, it will have important implications for road safety education both for children within this group and for the 5- to 9-year-olds (who in due course will become 10- to 14-year-olds and need to be prepared for it).

A further noteworthy feature of the accident figures, especially concerning children, is the very marked *sex difference* that emerges. About twice as many boys as girls in the 5 to 9 age-range become pedestrian casualties at all levels of severity. Much has been made of this bias and considerable effort made to account for it. To what extent it is determined by factors intrinsic to childhood is difficult to judge. Certainly it is especially marked amongst 5- to 9-year-olds; however, a sex bias can be found in the casualty rates of every group for whom data are collected (including 0- to 4-year-olds!). We shall return to the factors that might give rise to this pattern in Chapter 3.

Another outstandingly vulnerable group, along with children, is the elderly, especially those aged over 75. Old people are vulnerable not so much because they suffer an especially high accident rate (at least by comparison with children) but because such accidents as they do suffer result in a disproportionately large number of deaths. Fatalities amongst the over-75s actually account for a quarter of *all* pedestrian fatalities. This is due to the relative frailty of elderly people, which means they are less likely to recover from any injuries they sustain than are younger pedestrians.

Which group should be regarded as most vulnerable on our roads at the present time? The comparison between children and the elderly is illuminating from this point of view and shows how careful one has to be in interpreting accident data. In as much as they are most likely to be killed in the event of a collision, the most vulnerable are certainly the elderly. On the other hand, the overall casualty rate for young children is still higher than for the elderly, indicating that young children are much more likely to get involved in an accident *of some sort* than anybody else. This is a notable reflection of just how ill-equipped young children are in terms of the basic skills that are needed to deal with the road environment and how often they get into trouble as a consequence. It also stresses how important education and training in road safety are to this group.

WHERE DO PEDESTRIAN ACCIDENTS OCCUR?

As would be expected, the vast majority of pedestrian accidents (95 per cent) occur in built-up rather than non-built-up areas, though it should be noted that a disproportionately large number of fatalities occur in non-built-up areas. This is presumably because vehicles travel at higher speeds on such roads. What people are doing or where they are going at the time of an accident is, of course, likely to vary a good deal. However, 20 per cent of the accidents to 5- to 9-year-olds occur on journeys to or from school, a figure that rises to 40 per cent amongst 10- to 14-year-olds. This suggests that if road safety research could unravel the circumstances surrounding such accidents and possibly help children establish a maximally safe strategy for the journey, there might be a substantial pay-off.

Within the built-up category, most statistical breakdowns go no further than distinguishing between major and minor roads. This is a pity because various road structures and features also tend to be associated with accidents (see Chapters 3 and 5); to have comprehensive statistical data on these would therefore be extremely useful. However, the major/minor distinction is undoubtedly an important one as the proportion of accidents associated with these categories of road varies with age. For children under 9 years, about 80 per cent of accidents occur on minor roads. Indeed, the majority of child pedestrians are injured in residential areas and up to 60 per cent of them within a quarter of a mile of the child's own home (Grayson, 1975a; van der Linden and Goos, 1975). By early adult life, however, the preponderance of minor-road accidents has gone down to 50 per cent, with accidents on major roads increasing by a corresponding amount. This, of course, reflects the exposure of the different age groups to major and minor roads.

Looking at *where* on the roads accidents occur, it is clear that most of them take place some distance from the nearest pedestrian crossing, that is, in circumstances where the pedestrian is thrown back on his own skills in determining how to cross. On minor roads, where 'official' crossing points are least likely to be found, it is perhaps not surprising to find that young children are most at risk. Again, this stresses the need for young children to be taught good crossing skills for use in such circumstances. In the context of education, it is also important to note that around 40 per cent of casualties amongst under-9s occur where the road is masked by a stationary vehicle. This compares to only 12 per cent for adults. The problem of crossing between or near parked cars is generally recognized by road safety workers as a problem – rightly so, given these figures.

Finally, we commonly assume that the safest place to cross the road is at a pedestrian crossing that has been established for the purpose – hardly an unreasonable supposition given the risk of an accident when crossing elsewhere. It is therefore instructive to note the number of accidents that apparently occur at such crossings. In 1987, 21 per cent of the accidents that occurred to children under 5 on major roads took place on pedestrian crossings. Moreover, even for adults this figure only drops as far as 14 per cent. Precisely what driver and pedestrian behaviour is responsible for these conflicts should be looked at in detail, but it is at the very least sobering to see how safe such 'safe' crossing places actually are.

WHEN DO PEDESTRIAN ACCIDENTS HAPPEN?

In the UK, pedestrian accidents tend to increase during the last quarter of the year (i.e. in October, November and December), though the effect is not very marked. Somewhat fewer accidents occur in January and February, presumably because the weather reduces pedestrian activity at that time. Friday appears to be the worst day of the week for accidents, a finding which correlates with the fact that people walk somewhat further on Fridays. Road traffic is also higher on Fridays than on other weekdays. Nor surprisingly, there are fewer pedestrian accidents on Sundays (4,998 in 1987, as opposed to 10,224 on Fridays).

Pedestrians are 36 per cent more likely to be killed or seriously injured during the hours of darkness than at other times (a slightly smaller effect also holds for other road users). Overall, however, the worst time to be out on foot is between 3 and 6 o'clock in the afternoon, which coincides with schools coming out and the evening rush hour. In fact, around 40 per cent of all casualties between 3 and 4 p.m. are people on school journeys. There is a smaller peak between 8 and 9 a.m., when half of all pedestrian casualties are children going to school. Finally, there is another peak between 11 p.m. and midnight after the pubs have shut, but few of these casualties are children!

Again, these data help us target the circumstances under which children (and other pedestrians) are vulnerable. For the children, the journey to and from school is once again clearly central. Of course, with younger children these journeys probably account for a large proportion of their exposure to the traffic environment anyway, so it is probably not so very surprising that more of them become casualties at these times. On the other hand, it must be assumed that at least some children are accompanied to school by parents or other experienced road users, which presumably should reduce the vulnerability of that group. Also, these journeys are fairly clear-cut in that they occur at fixed times of the day, involve fairly standard routes and are regularly 'practised'. Once again, then, it seems likely that if this area of child pedestrian activity could be targeted, the pay-off in terms of casualty rates might be significant.

THE COST OF ACCIDENTS

The cost of accidents in terms of suffering is such that one hardly feels inclined to lay emphasis on the financial aspects of the problem. On the other hand, it is obvious that accidents cost money and it does no harm to discuss the expense involved in developing and implementing preventive measures in relation to the expense involved in *not* implementing them. For this reason, the financial burden imposed by road accidents should also attract our attention.

The UK Department of Transport estimates the total cost of road accidents on an annual basis and updates previous estimates so that comparative costs over time can be calculated. Coming up with an adequate formula to do this is not easy; in fact the formula used for fatal accidents has recently undergone revision. Among the factors taken into account are the cost of police and medical services; other material costs arising from damage, etc; losses due to lost production; and a 'notional allowance' for the suffering endured by victims and their families. At 1987 prices the cost of a fatal casualty is currently estimated at £500,000; a serious casualty at £15,190; and a slight casualty at £310. The very low figure for slight casualties follows from the minor nature of the injuries and consequent low material costs associated with them ('slight' means a sprain, bruise or cut not judged to be severe, although possibly requiring a visit to a hospital). The figure for serious casualties is based on injuries ranging from severe general shock requiring medical treatment to death occurring after elapse of the critical 30-day period used for defining a fatality. It is therefore an average figure for very wide-ranging costs, which partly explains why the figure looks so low relative to the figure for fatalities. On the other hand, the formulae used for calculating the costs of slight and serious casualties have not yet undergone re-estimation along the lines of fatalities. Research is currently taking place to determine whether this is necessary and it is possible that higher estimates may be used in future calculations.

Whether this occurs or not, the estimates currently used yield, for 1987, the staggering total of £4,990 million. Even looked at in the cold light of economic facts, the cost of road accidents must be judged unacceptable. Of course, the anguish of bereaved families can never be adequately costed.

The aim of this chapter has been to explore the scale of the pedestrian accident problem in relation to other problems threatening the health of children. The evidence leaves little doubt that road accidents constitute one of the gravest health problems confronting children in the modern world. Indeed, it is difficult to think of a single affliction that can compare to road accidents as a source of morbidity and mortality in young children. Yet it is astonishing how easily we seem to tolerate such accidents. We seem almost to regard them as, if not an acceptable facet of the modern world, at least an inevitable one. The rest of this book explores this assumption. Is it, in fact, the case that little further can be done to reduce such accidents? If not, what measures are most likely to pay off? Would significant advances prove possible only if draconian measures were taken with respect to traffic volumes and the like? Or could significant improvements be induced in less dramatic ways through the introduction of sensible urban planning together with appropriate training, properly geared to the skills needed to deal with the road environment? Certainly, the latter are prime areas for consideration. However, advances in the areas of education and planning can only be made if we understand the skills needed to deal with the road environment and the limitations of the child with respect to these. In later chapters, we examine these skills and limitations. First, however, we must look more critically at the statistical methods employed for calculating risk and at how data on accidents are gathered.

2

CALCULATING EXPOSURE TO RISK

PROBLEMS AND LIMITATIONS OF ACCIDENT STATISTICS

Although superficially informative, accident data paint only an imperfect picture and do not really provide an adequate starting point for the design of preventive measures. There are two principal reasons for this. First, accident statistics reflect only approximately the risk that different groups of pedestrians face on the road. Indeed, taken in isolation such data can be positively misleading. In order to gauge vulnerability more accurately, we need to supplement them with evidence from other sources.

Second, while useful in describing basic features of the accident *pattern* (and thereby arming the researcher with a set of questions), the statistics are too crude to be of much use when it comes to understanding what gives rise to the pattern. For example, consider the finding that young boys are twice as likely as young girls to become involved in an accident: this is obviously important information, but what does it tell us about the factors that cause the difference? The statistics merely identify the existence of the problem; they offer no insight into its causes.

The same argument applies even to trends that at first sight seem far more straightforward, like age differences. Again, while showing that young children are more vulnerable than adults, the data do not really help us understand why this is so. It might be argued that the situation is surely clearer in this case and that young children's lack of experience must be the problem. However, this does not get us much further forward unless we can specify more precisely what we mean by 'experience' in the context of safe road behaviour. This is by no means as easy as might first appear. But without a clear perspective on the aspects of experience the child lacks, the road safety researcher has little basis aside from intuition or 'common sense' for designing preventive measures. This is hardly an acceptable scientific basis from which to proceed. Let us now examine the limitations of accident statistics in detail.

EYE-WITNESS TESTIMONY

An initial problem with accident reports is that much of the information on which they are based is necessarily fragmentary and retrospective. To begin with, the police accident report forms are completed after the event and normally by someone who was not actually present. Because they are retrospective, there is always the possibility that important features of the situation may have changed before the police officer's arrival. An ambulance will certainly not wait for the police before removing an injured victim! The vehicles involved are also frequently moved to make way for traffic (although they should not be) and other features, such as nearby parked cars, may change. In wet weather, skid marks and other tell-tale signs may not remain visible either.

To establish events, the police are usually obliged to rely rather heavily on eye-witness testimony. Unfortunately, eye-witness testimony is known to be a poor and unreliable source of information, particularly about events that took place suddenly or unexpectedly. Testimonies are frequently inconsistent and are often influenced by unconscious biases as to what the witness thinks is *likely* to have happened rather than what *did* happen (see, for example, Sheehy and Chapman, 1982).

In any case, there is sometimes no eye witness at all. Of course, reports from victims and drivers can always be obtained but these often make the poorest eye-witness testimonies. Not surprisingly, victims may have little recall of what happened, an effect that will certainly be more marked following head injury or loss of consciousness. In any case, one of the main reasons that the victims probably became involved at all is precisely that they did *not* know what was going on around them; the same may well apply to drivers. Finally, of course, both victim and driver may have an understandable tendency to put themselves in the best possible light. In short, to establish the events leading up to an accident is no easy task. Indeed, police officers will admit that establishing the facts surrounding a road accident can sometimes be more difficult than establishing the cause of a murder! And the former investigation is done with only a fraction of the resources of the latter.

Given these difficulties, it is hardly surprising that Stats 19 report forms stick to the most straightforward and verifiable facts, omitting as far as possible data of a subjective, inferential nature. Unfortunately, this inevitably means that the reports lack the depth of information that might have helped us get at the causal factors underlying the incidents they describe. As it is, the statistics can do little more than show that a problem exists: they say little about why accidents come about.

UNDER-REPORTING PEDESTRIAN ACCIDENTS

Even at this level accident statistics are limited, because only a proportion of them ever get reported to the police. The already rather dismal figures reviewed in Chapter 1 thus actually represent an *underestimation* of the problem. Of course, this tendency varies according to the severity of the accident. As you would expect, very few (less than 5 per cent) road deaths evade the police (O'Donaghue, 1988). On the other hand, definitions of what constitutes a road death can lead to official underestimations, especially in some countries.

Even if we accept that reported road deaths are a fair reflection of the numbers involved, the same certainly cannot be said for accidents resulting in injuries, many of which are not reported to the police. For example, studies of hospital admissions show that police records miss around 20 per cent of accidents where hospitalization was required. Between a third and a half of less serious injuries are missed (Hakkert and Hauer, 1987). For some reason, such underestimations seem to be particularly high in the case of pedal cyclists, amongst whom as many as 60 per cent of 'serious' injuries are not reported to police (Hobbs, Grattan and Hobbs, 1979). The mismatch between police and hospital records seems to be much less marked for pedestrian accidents but is still quite substantial. Clearly, then, official statistics understate the scale of a problem that looks serious enough to begin with.

The reader may wonder if this bias in the accident statistics matters a great deal. After all, the effect is less marked for deaths and serious injuries and surely these are the ones that really 'count?' Indeed, statisticians frequently restrict their discussions to deaths and serious injuries, presumably on the grounds that minor accidents are in some way less important. For the researcher trying to understand why accidents occur, however, restricting the data in this way can be seriously misleading. Accidents occur as a result of errors in dealing with the road environment, *some of which have serious consequences and some of which do not*. It is the existence of these errors that make an individual vulnerable, not the severity of the outcome *per se*. Indeed, errors make an individual vulnerable even if no accident at all has resulted from them (yet!). For this reason, total accident rate is in many ways a more satisfactory measure of vulnerability than the more restricted KSI measure (Killed or Seriously Injured), because it better reflects the *frequency* with which different groups of road user get into trouble on the road. Unfortunately, this measure is the most susceptible to underestimation.

Even if an adequate measure of total casualty rate were available, the fact remains that accidents represent no more than a small proportion of the errors that children actually make (i.e. the ones they didn't get away with). The *incidence* of life-threatening errors may be many times the number of accidents that actually result from those errors. Howarth, Routledge and Repetto-Wright (1974) have calculated that the ratio of potential accidents to actual accidents is at least 10,000 to 1. Moreover, this figure covers only those situations in which a 'conflict' has already developed and where action on someone's part was necessary to avoid an accident. We can expect that in many more cases the pedestrian will get away with his mistake for extraneous reasons, such as there being no cars around at the time. This bias is almost certainly most marked in young children because, as previously noted, children spend most of their time on quieter roads. As a result, they are likely to get away with a higher proportion of the errors they make simply because there are fewer vehicles around to catch them out. The fact that they nevertheless suffer an accident rate four times that of adults underlines their basic lack of preparedness to tackle the road environment.

THE PROBLEM OF EXPOSURE

The main shortcoming of accident statistics, touched on above, is that they do not take into account the *exposure* of different groups to the traffic environment. Pedestrians who spend a lot of their time in traffic, for example, can be assumed to be more at risk than those who never go out. As a result, one would naturally expect the accident rate of the first group to be higher than the second. Similarly, if some pedestrians spend all their time on quiet residential streets with little traffic, we might argue that they are less exposed to risk than other pedestrians whose work or leisure takes them across busy roads. Other factors that will affect exposure are the times of day that the pedestrian is out and about; how far he walks in a given period; the number of roads he crosses; the number of cars he encounters; and so on.

These exposure variables would not matter greatly if everyone were equally exposed to the road environment. However, this is far from the case. Amongst children, the changes in exposure that take place during their schooldays are probably more marked than at any other point in their lifetime, except perhaps old age. To understand the risk faced by children of different ages, then, we need more than the accident rate per 100,000 population: we need a corresponding measure of their relative exposure to the traffic environment and its hazards.

Defining exposure

Unfortunately, it is no mean task to devise a suitable measure of exposure and even harder to estimate scores for different road users on it. Among the more popular measures are distance travelled per unit of time; number of roads crossed per unit of time; and amount of time spent walking over a given period. These are the three principal measures adopted by the UK Office of Population Censuses and Surveys in its major analysis of pedestrian activity carried out in the late 1970s – a study undertaken specifically to derive exposure measures (Todd and Walker, 1980). Three measures of risk were thereby derived: risk per road crossing; risk per kilometre walked; and risk per hour spent on foot. This clearly offers an improvement on the rate per 100,000 population but none of the three measures offers a foolproof index of exposure. For example, two groups of pedestrians may cross the same number of roads in a particular period but unless the roads contained similar volumes of traffic the comparison would not be very meaningful. Comparisons between adults and children would be particularly susceptible to such distortions. 'Amount of time spent walking' and 'distance walked' are not significantly better from this point of view. For this reason, some authors have used 'number of encounters with a vehicle' as a measure of exposure (e.g. Routledge *et al.*, 1974a), which helps overcome the above criticism. But whatever the shortcomings of such exposure measures, they obviously offer a significant improvement on none at all.

The crucial problem with this major census is that it was entirely restricted to adult pedestrians. No estimates of child exposure were made. The study is therefore useless as a means of assessing the risk that children face by comparison with other groups. This is a pity because, as we have already stressed, the changes in exposure that take place during childhood are probably greater than at any other time. Understanding the dynamics of the changing exposure/accident relationship to be found over these years therefore has a potentially enormous role to play in road safety research. It is to be hoped that such large-scale studies will be repeated more comprehensively in the future.

Techniques for calculating a child's exposure to risk

In the absence of information from national surveys, researchers have attempted to estimate child exposure, albeit on a much smaller scale. Amongst the most important studies in this area are those conducted at Nottingham University in the 1970s which have been widely used in road safety research. Routledge, Repetto-Wright and Howarth (1974a, b; 1976a, b) used four techniques for assessing exposure in young children:

- asking parents about their child's travel;
- asking the children themselves what they had done during the previous 24 hours;
- following children home from school and recording their road crossings;
- placing observers at selected sites to note the number of crossings made by different types of pedestrian.

The first three methods would allow some estimate of the *distances* that children travel as well as an indication of the *number of roads* they might be expected to cross. The last method would only permit assessment of the frequency of road crossing by children in relation to other pedestrians and would, of course, be specific to the sites tested (though it might be appropriate to generalize to the *type* of site).

Obvious problems exist in research of this kind: for example, deciding which sites to select for observational purposes; the possible fallibility of children's self-reports and parents' reports of child behaviour. Moreover, following children home from school does not tell us about their exposure at other times. There is also the problem of generalization from such local studies. Nevertheless, it is information of this type that is needed if proper measures of exposure and risk are to be developed.

The findings of such studies are generally that verbal reports from both parents and children tend to underestimate exposure in comparison with observational data. The observational measures correlate highly, however, which is encouraging if we wish to assume the two are measuring the same variable (exposure). Observational approaches also have the additional benefit of allowing quite a lot of extra data to be collected concerning children's road behaviour.

The picture that emerges when accident data are supplemented by exposure data to produce estimates of risk is that the former grossly underestimate the scale of the problem. For example, Routledge *et al.*'s estimates suggest that children aged 5 to 7 are up to 40 times more vulnerable than adults aged 20 to 50. They also suggest that the marked difference between boys and girls is not primarily due to exposure differences. This is important, because it implies that the differences are linked to how boys and girls behave on the road rather than to the fact that boys just spend more time there. Another important finding is that, when exposure is taken into account, major roads are more dangerous for young children than minor ones. By contrast, adults are no more vulnerable on one than on the other. This is consistent with the idea that adults are skilled in dealing with the road (hence busy roads are not particularly dangerous for them). By contrast, children are more vulnerable on such roads because they do not yet know how to behave on them.

A related observational approach has been used by researchers concerned with assessing the dangers posed by particular sites or locations on the road. For example, in an early and influential study, Mackie and Older (1965) looked at the frequency with which different types of pedestrian crossed different portions of the road near pedestrian crossing facilities. The study revealed that the stretches of road adjacent to crossing facilities are areas of high pedestrian accident risk. This finding eventually led to the introduction of the zigzag markings that are now standard features of such facilities (Grayson and Howarth, 1982). The benefits of this kind of exposure study are clear: by observing what pedestrians actually *do* in the vicinity of crossing facilities, problems can be identified. This provides valuable information to researchers that can even locate problems requiring solution. The value of observational studies thus goes beyond merely calculating exposure: they also help identify factors underlying accidents.

In summary, it can be seen that estimating exposure is a serious problem in road safety research and one that has not been fully solved at the present time. As far as children are concerned, however, one thing is clear: accident statistics, severe as they are, actually *underestimate* children's vulnerability. There could be no stronger indication of the severity of the problem.

IN-DEPTH ANALYSES OF ROAD ACCIDENTS

The deficiency of the available information on circumstances surrounding accidents has long been recognized. But how might we obtain stronger data? An obvious starting point would be to conduct deeper, more detailed accident investigations in which quality would be substituted for quantity. As early as the 1960s, in fact, efforts were being made in the United States to obtain richer information through the establishment of Multidisciplinary Accident Investigation (MDAI) Teams, whose job was to submit individual accidents to a far higher degree of scrutiny than could be expected of the normal authorities (Grayson and Hakkert, 1987). At first such studies were conducted by universities and other research institutes but in the 1970s a National Accident Sampling System (NASS) was founded to devise a system for the nationwide sampling of accidents for in-depth analysis. Similar initiatives have been taken in many other countries, though seldom with the same degree of vigour as in the USA.

The advantage of the multidisciplinary approach is that a far more detailed analysis of accidents can be undertaken than would otherwise be possible. For example, behavioural scientists can report on the *human factors* that may be involved; road engineers assess the possible contribution of *road conditions and other environmental factors*; and vehicle engineers examine the contribution of *vehicle design features* to the accident, particularly in relation to the injuries sustained.

The investigation of the 'human element' in this way has, unfortunately, not been particularly illuminating. The conclusion has been reached that 'human error' is certainly a contributory factor in a very large proportion of accidents (70 per cent), with 'failure of judgement' and 'errors of omission' (such as not looking) being particularly common faults (50 per cent and 33 per cent respectively). The latter is especially associated with pedestrian accidents. But these rather global conclusions can hardly be described as profound considering the expense and scale of the operation. More sophisticated models of human errors and their causes are currently being developed by, for example, Rasmussen (1985) and Reason (1985).

Vehicle design features generally receive a lower weighting than human error (involved in some 40 per cent of accidents) and the road environment is identified in even fewer cases (around 30 per cent). Amongst environmental factors, sight or distance restrictions appear to figure prominently (50 per cent). Visual restrictions are also the main vehicle design factor (37 per cent).

The main value of in-depth investigations, then, seems to be in highlighting areas where design improvements might reduce injuries in the event of collision. Whilst this is obviously an important contribution, the approach has been markedly less successful for the behavioural scientist trying to understand what underlies pedestrian accidents. Perhaps the aftermath of pedestrian accidents is simply unsuitable as a source of information about the factors that give rise to accidents, making in-depth investigations little better than standard investigations. By contrast, the aftermath of a vehicle collision leaves far more tangible evidence of design faults and the like, making in-depth analysis more worthwhile.

INTERVIEWS WITH PARENTS AND VICTIMS

A technique that has been used by a small number of researchers is to interview surviving accident victims in an effort to identify the circumstances surrounding their accidents (e.g. Grayson, 1975a; Scottish Development Department, 1989). It is a limited technique because, apart from the fact that victims may not want to discuss so traumatic an event particularly when it is still fresh in their minds, it can be assumed that in many cases they were not aware of all the attendant features in the first place. Moreover, it is quite normal for victims to suffer a short retrograde amnesia for events immediately preceding an accident, especially if head injury or loss of consciousness occurred. One certainly cannot expect their recollection to be more than hazy. As an example, when the author's youngest brother was knocked down (at age 7), he later reported that his injuries were caused by 'boys throwing stones'. There were indeed boys throwing stones at the time and this was, in fact, the reason why he attempted to dash across the street. It is easy to see how events could become confused in his young mind and how such a plausible, but incorrect, account of events might emerge. In fact, he had no recollection of the road accident at all. The example illustrates how vulnerable victims' reports are likely to be as a source of information, especially with younger children. None the less, such information is useful if its limitations are acknowledged and it is supplemented by information obtained in other ways. Some of the findings that have emerged from post-accident interviews are considered in Chapter 3.

OBSERVATIONAL STUDIES OF ROAD BEHAVIOUR

We have already discussed observational studies in relation to exposure estimation. However, these methods are equally useful as a means of investigating how children or other pedestrians behave on the roads (e.g. Heimstra, Nicholls and Martin, 1969; Routledge *et al.*, 1976a, b; van der Molen, 1977, 1983). By investigating behaviour in this way, it may be possible to highlight deficiencies that we may assume would make children more vulnerable. This in turn would give a clear focus for educational countermeasures. Being based on natural behaviour rather than performance on tests and questionnaires, the approach also seems more ecologically valid, making such studies of particular value to researchers.

The observational approach, as we have already seen, involves unobtrusive observation or filming, often in the streets near schools as the children are arriving or leaving. The aim is to look at details of the child's behaviour in relation to road crossing to see how adequate it appears to be. Amongst the measures frequently cited are: head movements (used as a measure of looking behaviour); delay time (how long the child waits before crossing); gap size (what sizes of gap in the traffic are accepted/rejected); number of false starts; whether walking or running; and so on. On the basis of such observations, a picture can be built up of how children of different ages behave on the road. The approach poses certain problems, notably in determining how well a limited selection of observations represents behaviour in general. However, the approach has particular appeal because it is based on what children actually *do* in traffic rather than on what they say they *should* do or on adult suppositions about child behaviour.

The aim of this chapter has been to bring the limitations of accident statistics to the reader's attention, both as a source of information about the risk that different groups of road users face on the roads and as a means of assessing the factors that might underlie accidents. In the first case, it can only be said that the statistics seriously underestimate the scale of the problem. As far as getting at the factors underlying accidents is concerned, a number of techniques are available. More detailed accident investigations, interviews with victims and observational studies of behaviour have been mentioned. This does not exhaust the list, however. Experimental studies of children's abilities, both in the laboratory and the real traffic environment; studies of 'conflict behaviour' (i.e. what happens in cases of near-misses); studies of personality, home and social background; and a number of other techniques – all can be used in the effort to gain a clearer picture of what it is that makes some groups vulnerable on the road whilst others are relatively safe. All these approaches are essential if the causes of accidents are to be understood.

So far, we have only talked about the techniques that can be used to study or assess vulnerability. We now turn to what these techniques actually show that might increase our understanding of that vulnerability.

3
CHARACTERISTICS OF THE VULNERABLE CHILD

We have seen that children are one of the most vulnerable groups of road users, in spite of the fact that they are much less exposed to the traffic environment than adults. Is this because they lack the relevant 'experience'? If so, what experience exactly is it that they need? Are children by nature unsafe road users? Perhaps they are more reckless or impulsive than adults and more likely to take risks. This factor has often been proposed to account for the large sex differences noted in Chapter 1. How much evidence supports such assumptions, however? In this chapter we explore some of these questions in an attempt to build an overall picture of the 'vulnerable child'.

PERSONALITY, SOCIAL AND FAMILY FACTORS

Accident-proneness

A common notion is that there are some people who, for one reason or another, end up having more than their fair share of accidents and mishaps. This raises the possibility that there may be individuals who are 'accident-prone'. Probably all of us have come across individuals who seem to fit this description. However, is there convincing evidence for the concept and, if so, what are the characteristics that render one person accident-prone and another accident-free?

The idea of 'accident repeaters' was first discussed in relation to industrial accidents and does seem to have some validity as a general concept. Amongst the factors that have been suggested as related to accident-proneness are aggressiveness, impulsiveness, emotional instability and low intelligence. However, the concept does not really emerge as a powerful one: that is, other factors seem to be more important. Moreover, Smith and Howarth (1981) argue that such small effects as there are may at least partly reflect people's expectations of themselves or their supposedly accident-prone colleagues. Indeed, one reason why such personality types are more associated with accidents may simply be that they are more exposed to accident situations in the first place. For example, if impulsive or aggressive individuals were more likely to choose dangerous jobs to begin with, this might create the impression that it is the personality factors that underlie accidents when, in fact, they only underlie choice of job.

Is there in fact an 'accident-prone' child? Only one or two studies have looked at this idea, while a few have looked at wider aspects of the child's environment such as family and social class background and have considered how these might have a bearing on vulnerability.

Manheimer and Mellinger (1967) constructed an 'accident liability scale' which they issued to almost 9,000 children. They found that children with high scores on this test were also more likely to be considered active, daring and extroverted by their mothers, characteristics that we might suppose to be related to accident-proneness. Unfortunately, since one of the indices of accident liability was whether the child had already been involved in accidents, one cannot be sure whether the personality characteristics caused the accidents or whether the mothers' ratings reflected the fact that the child had been involved in an accident.

In a later study, the same authors found that children with pronounced 'personality maladjustments' also had a high accident rate. However, this cannot have much widespread explanatory power as the majority of child victims can hardly be said to suffer personality maladjustment! Krall (1964) conducted interviews and doll-play exercises with 5- to 8-year-olds who had an accident record and compared them with other children who had not. She concluded that the accident group were less socialized and more aggressive than the others, attributing this to an authoritarian home background. The evidence for this conclusion was that, in the doll-play interviews, the accident group used more threats, commands and punishments in the games. They also showed more affection and affection-seeking than other children.

Several other studies have suggested that family dynamics may produce characteristics that predispose children to accidents. Divorce or marital discord (Backett and Johnston, 1959); physical or mental illness in the family (Ekstrom, Gastrin and Quist, 1966); poor or ineffectual parental child-rearing practices (Marcus *et al.*, 1960; Burton, 1968); and 'maternal preoccupation' (a term used to cover diverse situations including pregnancy or the fact that the mother had a job;

Backett and Johnston, 1959) have all been suggested. The implication of these studies is that certain types of family dynamics or organization may create aggression or hostility in children which, in turn, may lead to behaviour that is associated with accident involvement.

It must be said, however, that many of these conclusions derive from psychodynamic methods and theory, both of which occupy an uneasy place in modern psychology. Moreover, many of the studies suffer from quite important methodological weaknesses and from a tendency to employ ill-defined or value-laden concepts (Sheehy, 1982). It seems reasonable to suppose that children who are preoccupied with family (or other) worries are more likely to get involved in an accident. Indeed, given the marked distractibility of children (see below) it is not hard to imagine how such preoccupations might have deleterious effects on safety, especially if children are less able to temporarily suspend such anxieties when other matters should come to the fore (like road crossing). Whether family dynamics create more *permanent* dispositions in children is far less clear, however.

Social class background

Several studies have examined the relationship between social class and accident prevalence. Generally speaking, the statistics suggest that children from lower socio-economic groups have a disproportionately large number of accidents of all types (Langley, 1984). Preston (1972), working in Manchester and Salford, found a relationship between road accidents and indices of crowding and social class. Similarly Read *et al.* (1963) found accidents to be commoner in areas of dense, multi-dwelling housing associated with inner-city areas which, in English cities, seem to be associated with lower socio-economic groups. In urban Scotland, many of the lower socio-economic housing areas are concentrated in large peripheral housing schemes developed in the 1960s. Our own analyses of accident statistics in Glasgow suggest that child accidents are very high in such areas also (Ampofo-Boateng, 1987).

However, whilst the relationship between accident rates and social class is fairly clear, it is much less obvious how the relationship should be accounted for. Exposure differences seem likely to partially explain the effects. For example, in inner-city areas we can expect traffic volumes to be high, thereby predisposing children to risk. Similarly, lack of garden or other protected playing spaces is likely to drive children on to the streets where their exposure will again be increased. However, it is possible that there are also behavioural differences between children from different backgrounds that interact with exposure factors. For example, differences in training, parental supervision and so on would also be likely to have an effect. At the present time we do not really know enough to disentangle these various factors. But the fact that accidents can be pinpointed to particular areas should at the very least be of some help in identifying the children who are most in need of assistance, whether in terms of training or other measures such as the creation of parks and recreation areas.

Factors intrinsic to the child

Probably the commonest characteristic attributed to child pedestrians, and one that is often invoked to explain their high accident rates, is heedlessness. That is, children are regarded as rash, careless, incautious and so on, characteristics deemed to lead them more often than adults into dangerous situations. Such factors are almost always raised in court cases dealing with child pedestrian accidents and are frequently accepted by the court as a true reflection of events. Indeed, the claim that 'the child ran heedlessly in front of the car and there was nothing I could do about it' is one of the commonest defences offered by motorists in such cases (Howarth and Gunn, 1982).

Whether this is always likely to be true is very much a moot point but the view certainly fits the popular image of child behaviour as revealed when people are questioned about the causes of accidents. In one such survey, Foot *et al.* (1982) questioned parents, teachers, police and road safety officers on the factors they felt were responsible for the majority of child road accidents. They found 'lack of care', 'impetuousness', 'distractibility', 'unawareness of danger' and similar factors *intrinsic to the child* to be the ones most commonly invoked. Other factors, such as the level of safety education they had received or the degree of care and attention shown by drivers, were considered to be of far less importance in determining accidents.

CHILDREN AS INHERENTLY UNSAFE ROAD USERS

It is true that children can be regularly observed acting in ways that appear unsafe, so it is not hard to account for this popular image of child behaviour. In addition, they frequently fail to adhere to the rules of road behaviour that they have been taught even though, when questioned, they often turn out to know those rules quite well (see Ampofo-Boateng and Thomson, 1990). This has led to the widely held view that children are *by nature* unsafe road users. That is, the attributes that seem most characteristic of childhood (indeed, endearingly so) such as spontaneity, playfulness and adventurousness may be precisely the ones that land them in danger once they venture on to the roads. And because these characteristics seem so fundamentally a part of childhood, it is not a big leap to the conclusion that children must be *inherently* unsafe and unreliable pedestrians who simply cannot be expected to behave in a mature, adult way.

This view has received a good deal of support from several quarters and needs to be considered carefully. Amongst the most important proponents of this point of view is Sandels (1975), whose pioneering research into children and traffic in Sweden during the 1960s in many ways set the scene for later research. Sandels examined, amongst other things, the actual behaviour of children in urban areas both during play and whilst engaged in more purposeful activities such as going to or from school. She also examined children's conceptual understanding of the traffic environment and conducted simple experiments on some of the sensory capacities that appear to be important in dealing with traffic. Her general conclusion was that children below the age of about 10 years simply lack the sensory and cognitive capacities needed to cope with modern traffic. She also suggested that these shortcomings are a natural consequence of the child's age and degree of development. Many people have taken this to mean that road safety education can never be very successful in preparing children for the roads and, indeed, Sandels herself stressed that efforts to reduce child accidents should be aimed primarily at *separating* children from traffic. This point of view would, of course, shift the emphasis from road safety education altogether to other areas such as urban planning.

The view has been reinforced in the eyes of some authorities by the relative ineffectiveness of existing education programmes. Much current road safety education aims at getting children to acquire the right *knowledge* and *attitudes* towards road safety, the idea being that if appropriate attitudes can be instilled, the desired good behaviour will follow. In this, road safety education follows closely the approach adopted in other areas of health education such as drinking, smoking or drug abuse (see, for example, the volumes on adolescent drug abuse and child sexual abuse in this series). In the case of child pedestrians, however, the view is sometimes taken that children are simply too immature to change in this way. For example, it turns out that even though children have quite a good idea of how they should behave on the roads, their behaviour does not match that knowledge. The failure is thus often deemed to lie in the child's 'personality' as well as in his reasoning and judgement. In short, we need to realize that 'kids will be kids' and there is only a limited amount we can do about this.

Is this pessimistic point of view entirely justified? It is true that children do seem to fit the picture to a considerable extent. Yet it is by no means obvious that all accidents can simply be put down to children fooling around, behaving impulsively and generally having a 'poor attitude'. As a matter of fact, when questioned about road safety, children tend to display quite a good attitude. Moreover, it may come as a surprise to learn that researchers are frequently more struck by the *conservatism* children show on the road than by their recklessness. Quite a lot of accidents occur to children who do not appear to have behaved in a thoughtless way. Several authors, for instance, have drawn attention to the fact that accidents quite often occur when children step into the street *after* having looked for traffic (e.g., Grayson, 1975b; Kenchington, Alderson and Whiting, 1977). The interpretation of such findings is that children are either insufficiently skilled in making the visual timing judgements required to determine when the approaching vehicle will arrive or that their visual attention is as yet inadequately trained and they do not 'see' the approaching vehicle even though they looked for it (Demetre *et al.*, 1990). Such findings suggest that not all accidents can simply be put down to 'bad behaviour': they suggest that many arise from a lack of *skill.*

SKILL AND ROAD BEHAVIOUR

Many of the findings that have been interpreted as illustrating the global immaturity of young children may be interpreted as reflecting lack of skill in this way. For example, Sandels observed that children are inconsistent road users, in the sense that their behaviour on one occasion might be quite good, on another appalling. The implication seems to be that the child knew how to behave (hence the good performances) but did not always do so. However, inconsistency from one occasion to another is precisely the characteristic of unskilled behaviour, whether it be crossing the street or learning to play games like tennis or darts. Indeed, it would be strange for a beginner in darts not to hit the bulls-eye occasionally: what makes him a beginner is that he cannot do so consistently. The hallmark of the beginner in any activity is that his performances are all over the place rather than that they are always bad. Similarly, it is very possible that the inconsistency shown by children in dealing with the road environment arises because the child does not yet know how to behave in the many different situations he encounters, rather than because he simply chooses to ignore skills he actually possesses.

The proposal being made here, then, is that children lack the skills needed to cope with the traffic environment. Accidents arise primarily because children do not know *how* to behave, rather than because they *choose* not to behave in a skilled way. This point of view, of course, has major implications concerning current road safety education because it implies that the skills children really need are not being properly recognized and taught.

What exactly are these skills that the child lacks? After all, dealing with the road usually seems a fairly straightforward affair to adults and the reader may wonder what all the supposed difficulties really are. Even some researchers have come close to this view. For example, Rothengatter (normally a very thoughtful writer on road safety) has said that 'in contrast to other forms of traffic participation like driving, bicycling and flying, very few skills appear to be involved in participating in traffic as a pedestrian' (1981, p. 30). This point of view in fact grossly underestimates the sophistication of the skills that experienced road users apply, largely without thinking about them, every day. Let us examine some of these in detail.

THE IMPORTANCE OF PHYSICAL AND MOTOR DEVELOPMENT

One very important reason why young children are so vulnerable on the road derives simply from the fact that they are so small. This has several consequences. In the first place it makes children much harder for other road users to see, especially if there are parked cars or other obstructions close to where they try to cross. It must be remembered that the head of a small child may scarcely come above the level of the bonnet and even if it does, not much else will! Even quite big children are substantially obscured by cars: other obstructions can hide them completely. For the same reason, children cannot themselves see the road properly from such positions, so these situations are doubly dangerous. Not surprisingly, we have already seen that masking by obstacles appears to be heavily implicated in child accidents. Indeed, this is one reason why a recently commissioned government report (Scottish Development Department, 1989) suggested that children may be safer in groups than when alone: a group is more visible than an individual.

Actually the evidence does not entirely concur with the conclusion that children are safer in groups, but as far as visibility is concerned the authors are probably correct. A particularly disturbing finding is that children themselves appear quite unaware of the dangers posed by such roadside situations. In studies carried out by our group at Strathclyde University we have consistently found that children under the age of 9 years think it is quite safe to cross next to obstructions or at other locations where they are 'blind' to the road and will readily choose to cross at such places if offered the opportunity to do so (Ampofo-Boateng and Thomson, 1991). They do not appear to realize that they can neither see nor be seen in these circumstances. The findings have obvious implications both for pedestrian and driver training (see Chapter 5).

A second problem arising from the child's small stature is that the road becomes functionally much wider than it is for adults. This will obviously vary according to the age (and therefore the size) of the child, but 5- or 6-year-olds take paces that are about half the size of adult steps. To see how important this is, imagine how you might fare if roads were suddenly doubled in width! Because roads are effectively wider for children, it follows that for a given speed of movement they will necessarily take longer to cross them. Automatically, then, children are more exposed than adults whenever they cross (unless they run which, of course, they are heavily discouraged from doing). It also follows that they will need larger gaps in the traffic in order to cross in safety, which in turn means they must plan their movements relative to cars that are much further away. Hence extra demands are placed on visual timing skills: that is, on their ability to estimate when the vehicle will reach the point where they would like to cross. Related perceptual skills such as distance perception, velocity estimation and the ability to judge acceleration will also be disproportionately taxed. If such skills are less well developed in children than in adults in the first place (as one would expect to be the case), then it is not hard to see why the road-crossing situation is so much more challenging for them.

Finally, because young children are constantly growing, the calibration needs to be kept up to date. It can be seen, then, that the child's small stature is itself a significant contributing factor to vulnerability on the road. We can also see why developing appropriate perceptual and motor skills is so important.

PERCEPTUAL AND COGNITIVE SKILLS

A range of quite sophisticated perceptual, motor and cognitive skills are required to deal successfully with the road environment. Perceptually, for example, crossing the road requires a lot more than just 'looking': the pedestrian needs to know much more precisely what to look *for* and how to behave on the basis of what is seen. Visual *attention* and visual *search strategies* are thus involved, as is knowledge of the road environment and the things that happen there. Because you need to look in at least two directions (and in three or four directions in the case of many junctions and crossroads), *memory* is also a factor. A particularly important skill is *visual timing*, which also involves distance and velocity perception as well as an ability to relate this information to a knowledge of the time it takes to cross. Finally all this information has to be processed (and in a short time period given the speed with which the road environment can change). The pedestrian's judgement and decision-making processes are thus heavily dependent on a number of primary perceptual and cognitive skills. If these are not properly developed decision-making will almost certainly be inadequate.

Looking behaviour

Obviously children have to look out for traffic in the first place if they are to avoid it. A number of studies have examined the extent to which children do this, for example by means of covert observation or through interviews with accident victims and their families. The results indicate that children frequently step into the street without looking for traffic. They also often fail to look for traffic whilst actually engaged in crossing.

The estimated proportion of children of different ages failing to look varies somewhat from study to study but is nearly always substantial (van der Molen, 1981). In a recent major study involving over 10,000 observations throughout the highly populated central belt of Scotland, for instance, more than 50 per cent of children in the age range 4 to 14 were estimated *not* to have looked for traffic before stepping into the road (Scottish Development Department, 1989). This represents an average figure: younger children were even less likely to look. Similarly Valavuo (1976), when observing children on a fairly busy road, found that only a third of 7- and 8-year-olds made head movements in both directions before crossing (although this figure increased if traffic was actually approaching).

The same pattern has been found in studies of accident victims. For example, Grayson (1975b) estimated that 39 per cent of the child victims he interviewed had not looked at all before crossing, a figure also supported by the Scottish study, whose researchers estimated that 25 per cent of the victims had 'almost certainly' failed to look either way before crossing and a further 12 per cent had 'most likely' failed to do so. Other studies have found partial but inadequate looking strategies: in one direction only, for example. A common error occurring at junctions is that children frequently fail to look for traffic approaching from behind them. They seem to be preoccupied with looking to right and left and fail to realize the importance of checking for vehicles approaching from the rear (van der Molen, 1983). This error occurs even though looking 'all round' is the instruction taught by the Green Cross Code. The failure is no doubt a partial contributor to the high accident rates involving children crossing at junctions.

One might think that all we need to do is to tell children to look more. Unfortunately, it is not that simple. One of the real difficulties, as already mentioned, is that the child needs a clear idea of what to look *for*. It is not just a question of pointing your head in the right direction: it is a question of being attuned to the information required to make appropriate judgements. What this information is seems far from self-evident to young children and one often has the feeling that they do not really understand what they are meant to be doing when told to 'look'. Sometimes, they seem to be merely going through a kind of ritual that involves turning their heads from side to side. We have seen children doing this quite faithfully but at such speed as to have no hope of seeing anything!

Such behaviour illustrates a common tendency of children to apply rules they have been taught in a rather blind and rigid manner without proper comprehension of the purpose underlying the rule. Road safety researchers (and no doubt parents) see this kind of behaviour all too often. Such rigidity is a problem not just in road safety education but in all education. It is especially serious, however, where education programmes favour a rule-based approach to learning, as many road safety programmes do. We shall return to this point in Chapter 5. At any event, it seems clear that just telling a child to 'look' before crossing may have relatively little meaning for small children. Their visual search strategies need to be far more closely directed.

Attention and visual search

Looking before crossing, as we have already stressed, is a long way from picking up the information required to judge whether it is safe to cross. A common finding from studies of accident victims is that they did in fact look before stepping out but somehow failed to 'see' the approaching vehicle. For example, in his study of child victims, Grayson (1975b) estimated that 21 per cent of them had 'looked but not seen' the striking vehicle. A similar conclusion has also been drawn with regard to accidents involving the elderly, as many as 70 per cent of whom fail, for one reason or another, to see the striking vehicle (Transport Road Research Laboratory, 1972). These failures are not due to what the man in the street might call 'eyesight' problems: that is, they cannot be put down to acuity problems or similar visual defects. In fact, the acuity of young children does not differ a great deal from that of adults. Rather, it is their *attention and visual search strategies* that appear to be weak.

Actually, most of us have this problem from time to time. Consider how often you yourself have endlessly scanned a newspaper page for an item you know to be there before eventually seeing it. Or, more pertinent to the present argument, how many times you have looked for cars before crossing the road only to find yourself stepping under the wheels of a bicycle. Somehow the fact of being primed for the cars can make us blind to other vehicles, even ones that are perfectly 'visible'. Such errors, probably attentional in origin, form part of a group of what are sometimes known as 'cognitive failures' and seem to be uncomfortably common. Certainly, most people have little difficulty in finding examples in their own experience.

In children, who have not yet developed the skills, such errors can be expected to be less the exception than the rule. This is consistent with evidence from laboratory studies of children's attention and visual search strategies. For example, studies of children's eye movements as they visually explore objects or scenes show that these are rather inefficient and unstructured by comparison with those of adults (e.g. Vurpillot, 1968). Similarly, when asked to scan pictures or text for particular cues, they take much longer than adults to find them and make more mistakes (Gibson and Yonas, 1966). It would appear that the ability to seek out relevant information from an array is not well developed in young children and one can well see how this might transfer to behaviour at the roadside. Whether the development of such skills can be accelerated through training is not currently known but would seem an appropriate area for research.

Distractibility

Before leaving the issue of attention there is the problem of distractibility to consider. Much evidence points to this as an important feature of child behaviour in connection with accidents. We have already seen that children are guilty of dashing out, often near parked cars or other obstructions, thereby putting themselves at considerable risk. Indeed, this is undoubtedly one of the commonest types of accident: van der Linden and Goos (1975) estimate that 70 per cent of child accidents in Holland are of this type. The behaviour does not seem to happen purely at random. In fact, many such dashes seem to occur when a child becomes distracted by something, often of a social or emotional nature, such as the appearance of a friend on the other side of the street or the arrival of an ice-cream van. Sandels (1974) estimates that factors of this kind are involved in up to 50 per cent of the accidents occurring to children under the age of 10.

This probably corresponds well to people's general impression of child behaviour but is difficult to examine in a systematic, scientific way. However, in one study attempting to create distraction conditions of the sort that the child might experience in the real world, Gunther and Limbourg (1974) gave children a classroom session on road safety and then watched them cross the road to meet their mothers who had unexpectedly appeared (this had been arranged by the experimenters). At the same time, a car was driven round the corner. The authors observed a considerable difference between the children's behaviour when the mother was or was not present: that is, their behaviour was much poorer when they were distracted by the desire to reach her, even in the presence of an approaching vehicle.

In a follow-up study, Limbourg and Gerber (1978) observed what children did when either simply asked to cross the road to an adult experimenter on the other side or asked to collect a hidden toy on the other side, which they had been told they could keep if they found it quickly enough. Again, the standard of behaviour declined substantially in the distraction condition. Such findings suggest that children have difficulty both in sorting out their priorities in such situations and in distributing their attentional resources when they have more than one preoccupation. It is quite understandable that such behaviour should be described as heedless or impulsive. However, it may also reflect immature attentional control. This would make the problem one not just of 'immature personality', but also of skill. Again, it might be possible to improve the latter through appropriate training.

Visual timing

A final perceptual skill to which we should draw attention because of its manifest importance in road crossing is visual timing. Clearly, any pedestrian must have the ability to estimate (accurately!) the time that will elapse before an approaching vehicle arrives at the projected crossing point. He must also be capable of relating that time to the time needed to get across the road: a time which will, in turn, vary according to the road's width. These timing skills are probably of less importance on quiet roads where a pedestrian can simply wait for the road to clear completely before crossing. On busier roads, however, they become central because, if the pedestrian decided to wait until the road cleared completely, he would be waiting all day. To cope successfully with modern traffic, the pedestrian must learn to identify gaps in the traffic flow that are safe to pass through and differentiate them from those that are not. Such skills require various perceptual abilities; notably the ability to perceive distance and velocity, as well as the capacity to integrate such information. It appears from both observations in traffic and laboratory studies that these skills are quite well developed in adults. In children, they are not.

Both distance and velocity perception appear to vary as a function of age (Salvatore, 1974; Zwahlen, 1975) and when asked to use these skills in making judgements about the safety of gaps in traffic, children make many errors compared to adults (e.g. Hoffmann, Payne and Prescott, 1980; Lee, Young and McLaughlin, 1984; van Schagen, 1988). Not until the age of about 11 years does performance on such tasks begin to approach that of adults, although it would appear that it can be improved with training (Young and Lee, 1987).

On the whole, children tend to be very conservative with regard to such judgements. For example, they delay much longer at the kerb than adults and only accept bigger gaps (Lee *et al.*, 1984; van Schagen, 1988). However, there are large inconsistencies in their judgements, both within and between children. That is, some children of the same age show markedly better overall performance than others. This suggests that the skills do not develop uniformly in all children (and, incidentally, suggests that training may be beneficial). In addition, there are quite substantial *intra*-individual differences: that is, a particular child may perform well on some occasions but, on others, make many errors. As such, children's decisions are *unreliable*, as already stressed by Sandels. It means that even if a child is conservative in general, risky decision-making errors are still likely to crop up from time to time. Given the relatively limited development of these perceptual skills and a corresponding propensity in children for distractibility, it is not hard to imagine how the combination makes them vulnerable.

All these findings, then, suggest that young children are not simply heedless, neglectful pedestrians who in other respects are equipped to deal with the road environment. In fact, they lack many of the perceptual and cognitive skills necessary for safe road behaviour. Indeed, in reviewing evidence from laboratory-based studies on capacities that seemed likely to be important to road behaviour, Avery (1974) concluded that there are clear developmental trends on almost all skills involving perception, memory, attention, information-processing, reasoning and decision-making, with younger children substantially weaker than older children or adults. Generally speaking, children begin to approach adult levels of performance around the age of 11 years.

Whether development must follow a fixed path or whether the skills can be improved through appropriate training is, of course, an empirical question. However, there does not seem to be a solid basis for the quite common notion that such capacities are closed to intervention through training. One has only to look at the perceptual and co-ordinational skills that *can* be taught to young children, such as those involved in dance, swimming and gymnastics, to wonder why the improvement of road skills should be immune from training. Of course, success will depend on how clearly we recognize the skills that are required in the first place and on how well individual training programmes focus on these.

BOYS VERSUS GIRLS

As we saw in Chapter 1, by far the most striking feature of accident statistics after the age trends is the strong sex difference that is found. Actually, remarkable sex differences are found for every age group except the over-70s, with males having roughly 40 per cent more accidents than females. However, the sex difference is particularly marked in the vulnerable 5- to 9-year-old group, where boys are about twice as likely as girls to be involved in an accident. These sex differences are extremely stable and one sees the same pattern year after year, not just in the UK, but in countries across the globe. Clearly, we need to try to understand what it is about boys and girls that gives rise to these differences in accident liability.

Exposure

We have seen that differences in vulnerability may sometimes be accounted for in terms of exposure differences: that is, one group may have more accidents than another simply through being more exposed to the road environment. This has also been suggested as a partial explanation of sex differences in accident rates. There is some evidence that boys spend more time playing in the street and are generally out more than girls. For example, on the basis of more than 7,000 observations of boys and girls between the ages of 4 and 17 (both before and during the summer holidays), Chapman, Foot and Wade (1980) found that boys were more likely to use the street for recreational purposes. This effect was most marked for 5- to 10-year-olds, which is certainly consistent with the higher accident rates of boys in this group. Similarly, in interviews with mothers, Sadler (1972) and Newson and Newson (1976) found that mothers were more likely to describe boys as 'outdoor children'. These reports are consistent with the interesting finding that boys have better mental maps of their local neighbourhoods than have girls, supporting the suggestion that they may indeed spend more time in it (Coates and Bussard, 1974). Finally, in one of the few studies that actually attempted to find out what children were doing when their accidents took place, Grayson (1975a) found that more of the boy victims were playing in the street at the time.

However, whilst there seems little doubt that exposure differences of this kind exist, they do not appear sufficient to account for most of the boy/girl differences. To begin with, only a proportion of children's time on the streets is spent in 'leisure' activities. Much of children's contact with the road occurs in the context of going to and from school or in other purposeful activities like running an errand. Foot (1985) estimates that well over half the accidents to young children occur whilst engaged in the latter. And here we run into a problem because the exposure of boys and girls to such journeys is about equal. There is a little evidence that girls may be slightly more chaperoned on school journeys and generally may be subject to slightly stricter control but quite extensive observational studies of the type discussed in Chapter 2 have repeatedly found only minor exposure differences between boys and girls on school – home journeys. Thus, differential exposure to the road environment is not adequate as an explanation of sex differences in accident rates. Clearly, other factors must be involved.

Personality characteristics

A common view that we frequently hear expressed, not just by parents but also by the police, road safety officers, teachers and others, is that boys are more reckless or impulsive; in other words, the factors often raised to account for the behaviour of children in general are considered to be even more characteristic of boys. Moreover, a number of researchers have reached the conclusion that, on the whole, boys are less reliable, less consistent and less safe on the roads than girls (e.g. Sandels, 1975; Finlayson, 1972; Scottish Development Department, 1989).

These conclusions are rather global and subjective, reflecting the researchers' general assessment rather than the results of detailed analysis of child behaviour. However, looking at more specific variables, there is some evidence of safer behaviour on the part of girls. They appear more likely to stop at the kerb than boys and are also more likely to look before crossing. Some studies also report that girls are less likely to run across the road; delay longer at the kerb before venturing out; and only accept gaps in the traffic flow that are large compared to those accepted by boys. Finally, they also appear more likely to use crossing facilities where these are available (see van der Molen, 1981 and 1983, for detailed reviews).

However, it has to be said that not all studies reveal these effects and, where they do, the differences are usually too weak to account for the differential accident trends to any significant degree. The comprehensive studies by the Nottingham group described in the previous chapter, for example, failed to reveal any major behavioural differences between the sexes at all. It is true that these authors did not specifically set out to test for sex differences, but given the large number of observations that were involved and the clear *age*-related differences that emerged, it is the relative *absence* of sex differences that is most striking. On the whole, then, there is some evidence that boys exhibit less safe behaviour on the roads, but this trend seems a good deal less marked than is often claimed.

Perceptual and cognitive skills

The importance of these skills in road behaviour has already been stressed and we should consider the possibility that differences in these capacities may underlie sex differences in accident liability. However, examination of the most relevant of these skills reveals few sex differences. Throughout development boys and girls show a more or less equal sensitivity to different kinds of perceptual information, use similar visual search strategies, do not differ greatly in their estimation of distance or speed and show similar visual timing skills (Maccoby and Jacklin, 1974). In fact, whenever we look at such skills as might be expected to affect vulnerability (and where age effects can certainly be shown), it is again the absence rather than presence of differences that is striking.

These findings are extremely puzzling. In spite of a very marked sex difference in accident rates, it seems these cannot easily be accounted for by exposure, skills or any other likely factor. The truth is, we really do not yet know how to account for these differences.

Risk-taking and confidence

Although any suggestion must be highly speculative at the present time, one possibility that is worth considering is that boys and girls do not *use* their road-crossing skills in quite the same way. Although the perceptual and cognitive capacities of boys and girls are similar as far as basic skill levels are concerned, we can conjecture that, if boys were to *overestimate* their skills relative to girls, this might lead them to tackle situations on the road that they are actually not ready to deal with. By taxing their skills in this way, boys would effectively be guilty of taking more risks than girls. Conversely, if girls approach the road environment with a more realistic assessment of their abilities, their liability to accidents might be correspondingly reduced.

Is there any evidence to support this? One finding that is certainly consistent with it is that boys begin adopting adult road-crossing strategies earlier than girls. We shall be examining adult strategies in detail in a later chapter, but for the moment we may note that the behaviour of adults is very different from the exhortations of the Green Cross Code. Adults do not stop at the kerb as the Code asks: instead they look for traffic whilst approaching the kerb and time their movement so that stopping will not be necessary (Routledge *et al.*, 1976a). They also do not wait until traffic has passed before starting to cross: instead, they step out just before a vehicle passes so that they can 'tuck in' behind it. This has the advantage of maximizing the gap between themselves and the next car in the traffic flow (Lee *et al.*, 1984). Although these strategies are markedly different from the ones road users are taught, they are not really examples of bad behaviour. Rather, many of them are what we might call 'advanced techniques' which, in the hands of experienced road users, increase efficiency in dealing with the road. However, these skills demand highly developed perceptual and motor skills as well as clear judgement and decision-making.

It has been suggested that boys may attempt to adopt strategies of this type earlier than girls and before they are ready to do so. We have already seen that boys are less likely to stop at the kerb than girls, but they are somewhat more likely to look as they approach it, which is in line with the adult strategy. Similarly, their shorter delay times and acceptance of smaller gaps in the traffic flow are also reminiscent of adults. At the same time, *we have seen no evidence of more mature perceptual or cognitive skills in boys to support these advanced strategies.* Findings of this type are therefore consistent with the possibility that boys attempt to adopt adult strategies *too early* and, by overextending themselves, increase their chances of getting into trouble. Moreover, some authorities have suggested that boys are less efficient than girls at extricating themselves from difficulties once they get into them (e.g. Foot, 1985). If this is true, it would not be a big jump to the conclusion that their accident rates should vary accordingly.

This possibility certainly warrants serious consideration, particularly as it has obvious implications for training. However, it must be stressed that the foregoing is speculative and not to be taken as proven fact. Again, we need to stress the surprising lack of clear behavioural differences between boys and girls and always be wary of overstating our case. Nevertheless, it would not be so very surprising to find such differences, because boys seem prone to overestimate many of their abilities while girls tend to underestimate theirs. This correlates with a general tendency of girls to show less confidence in themselves. As an example, if children are told that they did badly on a test (irrespective of whether this is actually true or not), boys are more likely to attribute this to external factors (e.g. they will say the test was very difficult, they were unlucky in the questions that came up, etc.). Girls, on the other hand, are more likely to attribute their failure to factors intrinsic to themselves (e.g. they did not prepare well enough, they were not very good at the subject, etc.). Given these differences in self-confidence, it would perhaps not be too surprising to find boys overstretching themselves on the road and girls showing caution (see Matlin, 1987, for a review of such research).

In addition to such biases there does seem to be a tendency in our society to tolerate risk-taking behaviour in boys much more than in girls and it would not be unusual to find analogues of this in road-crossing behaviour. The effect certainly holds good in driving behaviour. Young male drivers show far higher rates of risk-taking than women, especially during the first three years of driving experience. They also develop a very optimistic opinion of their own skill behind the wheel (Svenson, Fischoff and MacGregor, 1985). Unfortunately, accident rates prove them wrong. Whether the same effects apply to young pedestrians is not known but the possibility certainly seems worth exploring.

At the start of this chapter we asked what were the factors that make children vulnerable to accidents on the road. The main answer that seems to have emerged is that they lack the vital skills necessary to cope with the road environment. Individual personality characteristics, social-class background or family dynamics may all have a role to play in determining how a child will use the skills he or she does possess, but the outstanding fact is how similar children of all types and from all backgrounds are in terms of vulnerability. Only the age and sex of the child seem to be crucial factors.

The question that arises from all this is: can these skills be taught to children so that development is accelerated? What, in fact, is the content of current road safety education? How successful is it in preparing young children to face the road environment? And what alternative might improve on what is currently available? The next two chapters consider these questions.

4

APPROACHES TO ROAD SAFETY EDUCATION

There are two separate elements to be considered in road safety education: 1) the *content* of current road safety instruction and how appropriate it is to the needs of the child; 2) the *methods* by which this content is taught and how successful they are in getting the message across to children of different ages. These issues should not be confused: if a programme fails, it may be that the content was inappropriate. On the other hand, the fault could be in the method by which the content was taught.

THE AIMS OF ROAD SAFETY EDUCATION

Most countries have some kind of national educational scheme, often one that is integrated into the school curriculum (in marked contrast to the UK at the present time). Additional programmes may also be introduced at a more local level as the authorities in different regions attempt to improve on the materials available or otherwise deal with the problems they particularly encounter in their own area. Such schemes vary quite widely with respect to the methods employed but are more unified when it comes to programme content. In the majority of cases, the aim is to provide children with broadly conceptual knowledge about the traffic environment and to instil simple strategies for dealing with the roads.

In the UK the principal strategy has long been the Green Cross Code and, in fact, most road safety education takes the teaching of the Code as its primary goal (Grayson, 1981). We comment on the Green Cross Code and similar techniques in detail below. Numerous methods of teaching this material have been attempted but, in practice, the bulk of road safety education takes place in the classroom in the form of talks by police officers or road safety inspectors from the local authority. These talks vary from the straightforward lecture to much more creative affairs as the officer attempts to win the interest and attention of his audience. The talks might also be supported by visual aids of one sort or another, ranging from picture boards to slide shows, videos or films and by a variety of printed materials. Outside the classroom, of course, further printed materials are available commercially and a certain number of television and radio productions appear from time to time, often in the context of a mass-media campaign. By and large this exhausts the repertory. There is seldom any element of practical, 'hands-on' training and none of the elaborate traffic parks or gardens that have been established in other European countries. The material is almost exclusively verbal: that is, children learn by being *told* what to do rather than by actually doing it. The approach is thus almost entirely centred on the acquisition of *knowledge* and the development of appropriate *attitudes*.

Finally, whatever teaching methods are employed, the most characteristic feature of road safety education in this country is how little of it there actually is. Most road safety inspectors or police officers would have difficulty getting round to a particular school more than twice a year at most and generally have little time with the children when they are there. Nor is there any standard provision for following up their work once they have left the scene: such follow-up work is very much in the hands of individual teachers, who must decide what they can achieve amongst their many other priorities. Any discussion of the possible benefits of existing road safety education must therefore be tempered by a realization of how intermittently and irregularly it occurs. On the other hand, there can be few children who have not received *some* element of road safety education in their school years.

A useful preliminary way of classifying teaching techniques is according to how closely they simulate real traffic experiences. After all, we might well imagine that the closer the education process can stick to the real thing, the better chance of success it will have. The techniques available vary from those conducted in the natural traffic environment, to semi-natural simulations (for example, in blocked-off streets with no traffic), to traffic gardens and the like, where a smaller degree of realism is maintained, to much more abstract mock-ups in the school gym or playground. Finally, teaching might take place in the classroom, in which case there would be no element of realism at all (although slides or films might be used to illustrate traffic situations).

In fact, almost all traffic education in this country takes place in the classroom and it is rare to find training by any of the other methods. At best, children might receive simple instruction in the playground (for example, they might go through the motions of the Green Cross Code, with lines on the ground serving to mark the kerb and road, or a simple pedestrian crossing might be simulated). More elaborate set-ups are almost non-existent. Evaluating the potential of classroom teaching is therefore of some importance.

CLASSROOM TECHNIQUES

Making general statements about the effectiveness of classroom teaching is complicated by the variety of activities that it can encompass. However, there is general agreement that, in spite of widespread use, classroom instruction *by purely verbal means* is a poor way to teach road safety and is certainly inferior to most other methods. At best, such teaching may improve children's *knowledge* about road safety. Unfortunately, such knowledge does not readily generalize to *behaviour* in the traffic environment, as numerous studies have reported (see Rothengatter, 1981, or Ampofo-Boateng and Thomson, 1990, for reviews). Indeed, children whose performance in traffic is very poor have sometimes been shown to exhibit rather good knowledge about road safety (Ryhammer and Berglund, 1980). This lack of correspondence between knowledge and behaviour is the single most serious criticism of classroom teaching as a whole. Even worse, the results of such instruction can actually have negative effects because the increased knowledge the children exhibit when asked questions about road safety can create the false impression that their ability to face the road environment is improving. If this is not the case, then not only is the teaching ineffective; it creates the dangerously misleading illusion of increased competence that is not borne out in practice. The importance of validating knowledge acquisition against behavioural change is therefore crucial.

Verbal methods are only likely to be effective where they focus firmly on the *behaviour* that the child needs to adopt. However, even here there is often difficulty because the language and concepts used may be beyond the understanding of young children, though they seem perfectly straightforward to adults. For instance, in investigating the words and concepts contained in the materials used to teach road safety in Dutch schools, Groos (1977) and Meijer and Vinje (1978) found that such commonly used words as 'pedestrian' or 'pavement' were frequently not understood by young children. Simple concepts often referred to in road safety education like 'left and right' or 'being careful' were also frequently misunderstood. Problems of this kind are common when designing road safety packages. For example, the developers of the Green Cross Code in this country had to make considerable efforts in order to find a wording for the Code that would be comprehensible to young children (Sargent and Sheppard, 1974). Moreover, continuing concern has been expressed about the ability of younger children to understand even the final version. Sheppard (1975) found that nearly one-third of the words in the Code were incorrectly read or not read at all by 20 per cent of children tested in a follow-up study. More important than understanding individual words, verbal instructions are often too general to influence children's behaviour. 'Be careful' is a case in point: what behaviour exactly constitutes 'being careful'? Obviously, this raises fundamental questions about how effective any purely verbal education method can be, particularly in settings where the language is not solidly secured to the objects or behaviour to which it refers. When used in isolation and without the very clearest understanding of the child's conceptual and language difficulties, verbal instruction would seem to be a hazardous technique, particularly with children whose familiarity with traffic is at the most elementary level.

FILM TECHNIQUES

Where the instructor supplements his talks with other material, can this significantly improve the situation? Visual methods of instruction involving videos, films or slide shows have obvious appeal, because of their ability to illustrate material that is difficult to verbalize. It is also well known that such media can be successful in both obtaining and holding children's interest. A number of packages involving this type of material have been put together but few of them have been evaluated (Singh, 1982). Such studies as have been attempted (mainly on an experimental basis) reveal rather mixed results.

In a well-known early study, Pease and Preston (1967) evaluated a road safety propaganda film, *Mary had a Little Lamb*, aimed at teaching children how to use the kerb drill. Although the film was attractive and had a relatively clear-cut objective, when 5- and 6-year-olds were later tested in a simulated road-crossing situation, those who had seen the film were no better at using the drill than children who had not seen it. Moreover the film study raised a number of questions concerning children's ability to generalize from film demonstrations that have implications for the use of visual media in general.

Other film approaches have been somewhat more successful. For example. McKelvey (1978) presented children with filmed shots of approaching traffic in an effort to teach them how to distinguish safe gaps, where crossing could be attempted, from unsafe ones that should not be accepted. McKelvey found that the youngest children showed improved ability to discriminate gaps after training, provided they got plenty of feedback during the training sessions. However, this improvement was not seen in older children. Whether such improvements would transfer to judgements at the roadside was not assessed.

Similarly, Colbourne (1971) used slide presentations to teach crossing behaviour to 7- and 8-year-olds. The children were later tested in a traffic garden and some beneficial effects were found. On the other hand, Nummenmaa and Syvanen (1970) found that, whilst slide presentations increased traffic knowledge in 5- to 7-year-olds, they had no influence on their behaviour in the traffic environment, a finding later replicated for films (Nummenmaa and Syvanen, 1974). However, if the film was supplemented by practical training (the children received roadside training from their parents), there was a marked improvement in the behaviour exhibited in the traffic garden tests. The authors concluded that the practical training on the real roads had been decisive. The role of the films on their own, however, was much more ambiguous.

THE POSSIBLE ROLE OF VIDEO

Similar conclusions must apply to video productions if these are used as a simple alternative to films. However, video offers a flexibility not available to film in that 'local' productions can be made, illustrating, for example, dangers in children's own locality. They may even incorporate the children themselves as subjects. It is possible that material which is targeted in this way may be more effective than 'general' productions. Certainly, the use of video feedback has taken an important place in athletics and sports training. Few studies have systematically explored this approach in road safety, however.

Cyster (1980) reports that video sequences in which they saw themselves and their friends made a considerable impact on primary school children, as shown by their ability to vividly recount details of the recording two or three weeks later. However, one can hardly be sure that it was the road safety content of the production which made the lasting impression! No effort was actually made to determine memory for the specifically road safety features of the video. More encouragingly, Valavuo (1976) used videos of pupils' own road behaviour (they had earlier been unobtrusively filmed) and found some later behavioural improvement. This was not the case for controls who had received an equal amount of conventional instruction, suggesting that the feedback capabilities of video may well be worth exploring. Certainly, the recent use of video feedback by police to demonstrate to drivers their own earlier dangerous behaviour suggests that this can have a powerful impact (though in such cases drivers probably find it in their best interests to perceive their previous behaviour as shocking!).

On the whole, and despite a number of appealing aspects, it is difficult to disagree with Singh's (1982) conclusion that there is really no convincing evidence of substantial benefits following instruction involving film or video material. Certainly, there is no evidence of changes in everyday road behaviour. There is clearly a need for further research before we can seriously argue that such techniques really work. On the other hand, there is enough evidence of potential in such materials, if properly directed, to make the effort worthwhile.

BOOKS AND OTHER PRINTED MATERIALS

By far the most widely used supplements to verbal instructions are books, posters and other printed matter. Although such materials are seldom evaluated at all (Gerber *et al.*, 1977), such evidence as there is suggests that they are not particularly effective, at least on their own. Once again it appears that while such material may increase children's knowledge, such knowledge does not readily transfer to their behaviour (Schioldberg, 1976).

In Britain a major source of printed materials has been the Tufty Club, which illustrates good road sense through the behaviour of an attractive squirrel character. These have been evaluated by Firth (1973), who did find improvement in road crossing knowledge when the books were read to children individually over a two-week period. However, this did not generalize to a behavioural test or to tests using a model set-up. More recently, Antaki, Morris and Flude (1986) found that children trained with Tufty materials did not even exhibit superior road safety knowledge to peers who had not received such training when tested using video and picture cards.

Much of the evaluation work that has been undertaken has also been concerned with establishing that the material can actually be understood by children. This has applied perhaps particularly to poster material, which, by definition, has to use curtailed presentation methods. Colbourne and Sheppard (1966) examined the extent to which children between the ages of 5 and 7 understood the message in a poster designed to discourage them from rushing into the street. It was found that the vast majority of 5-year-olds failed to grasp the message and only about half of 7-year-olds did so. When the poster was broken up into a sequence of pictures, however, the message was much better understood by both age groups. Firth (1973), investigating posters made by the Tufty Club, examined the ability of children to understand what was implied when pictures of street layouts were shown from various viewpoints, such as oblique or 'bird's-eye' views. She found such viewpoints could indeed cause difficulty. A range of other pictorial devices has been found to pose difficulty for young children: for example, the use of dotted lines to convey the path someone might take and other conventional symbolism. Too much inessential detail also causes problems. Such findings illustrate how careful one has to be in designing material of this sort, and, incidentally, stresses how important process evaluation can be (see p. 51).

In summary, none of these findings give much reassurance that books, posters or other printed materials are very effective in improving children's readiness to face the roads. It seems undoubtedly true that their knowledge improves as a result of such material. Unfortunately there is scant evidence of corresponding improvements in their behaviour out on the streets.

BEHAVIOURAL TECHNIQUES

Much less widely used than the above techniques are simulations or practical training of some sort that involves an element of active, behavioural participation by the child. Simulations may take the form of test tracks, traffic gardens or more limited set-ups in the playground, school hall or gym. These might be used to teach children how to deal with specific structures, such as pedestrian crossings. Alternatively, the training might take place in the real traffic environment, in which case more elaborate problems could be tackled. A basic question with any simulation is, of course, the extent to which it successfully imitates the real world. However, the evidence available to date suggests that a behavioural approach using lifelike set-ups is by far the most promising approach to road safety training: the more lifelike the task, the more likely it is to induce appropriate road behaviour.

For example, in an early (unpublished) study Johansson (1967) compared the effectiveness of training in a real traffic situation with training in the school yard and traffic garden. The real training situation proved superior to the other conditions. Sandels (1975) reports two experiments conducted with 6- and 7-year-olds in which the benefits of training in streets closed off to traffic were compared to traffic gardens and schoolyard training. A further experiment compared the effectiveness of street training in relation to classroom instruction. The results showed that training in the real streets was superior both to classroom training and to training in the schoolyard or traffic garden.

Similarly, Saska (1971) found real street training superior to training in a traffic garden, although the latter was superior to controls. Colbourne (1971) also found that traffic garden training was superior to classroom instruction for 6-year-olds although the effect was not found with 7-year-olds. An important additional finding in the Saska study was that the benefits of real world training were much more marked in *younger* children. This would suggest that early training should concentrate on behaviour, with verbal techniques being reserved for more experienced children.

Rothengatter (1984) developed a behavioural programme which he taught to mothers and kindergarten teachers, who later used it to train 5- and 6-year-olds in everyday real traffic situations. He found evidence of some improvement in the children's behaviour as a result, and also found that the benefits were maintained over some months.

These results all suggest that the direct teaching of behaviour in as natural a context as possible may be the best way to improve pedestrian behaviour. This is also one area where printed material may have a role to play. Whilst such material does not seem to change children's behaviour directly, if appropriate courses were available to parents, showing how they might themselves train their children, then it could be an important adjunct to the practical training advocated here. That has, in fact, been an aim of the Dutch group as well as the American Automobile Association (AAA, 1976), who produce similar materials. Unfortunately, no evaluative research on the effectiveness of the latter has yet been done. We return to these approaches in Chapter 6.

EVALUATION STUDIES

How should we go about deciding whether the available methods and approaches work or not? And how might we assess the relative effectiveness of each? Clearly, there is little justification for introducing a measure unless it can be shown to be in some way effective in preparing children to face the roads. Evaluative studies designed to provide such information would seem to be an obvious prerequisite to the introduction of any programme. Yet here we come up against an astonishing paradox: despite a widespread commitment to road safety education hardly any measure introduced at either national or local level has ever undergone evaluation as to its effectiveness. As a result, we know little of the merits of different packages and 'the organizer of a programme for pedestrian safety is usually in the position of having to choose a method on the basis of personal preference or current policy with no indication of whether it will produce the desired effects' (Singh, 1982, p. 71).

This criticism is not restricted to the United Kingdom: with a few notable exceptions, the majority of programmes have received only 'passing' evaluation at best, often at an early exploratory stage. To my knowledge, no studies have attempted systematically to trace the long-term effects of a programme. We thus know hardly anything about the lasting effects of training nor do we know much about the continuing appropriateness or otherwise of programmes that may have been introduced years or even decades before.

How does it come about that evaluation has attracted so little emphasis in this area? The reasons are complex and numerous factors appear to be at work. Moreover, these factors are surprisingly common in many other areas of applied research (see the other books in this series). Many road safety researchers are, of course, aware of these problems and their implications. For example, in a very frank article on the evaluation of pedestrian safety programmes, Grayson and Howarth (1982), both major figures in the field of child pedestrian behaviour, list a number of factors that determine whether or not evaluative research is undertaken and, if it is, the type of evaluation that will be conducted. Apparently, in the early days of road safety research, enthusiasm for the design and introduction of safety measures blunted the judgement that such measures need to be shown to work. Getting programmes off the ground seemed to be the top priority. Where there is a perceived need for the rapid introduction of measures such an attitude might be understandable, but it is at best short-sighted. In the long term it is quite unacceptable. Moreover, there seems to have developed a tendency for evaluative research to attract little prestige or academic status, being regarded as prosaic in comparison with more creative research into the devising of countermeasures. Evaluation was apparently seen as an optional extra that someone else might see fit to conduct. It seems there was little onus on the designers of these countermeasures to back up their creations themselves with hard-nosed demonstrations that they worked. Such attitudes would certainly render evaluative research unattractive to many researchers, whose values tend to be dictated by the character and priorities of the field as a whole. When these priorities are firmly fixed on development rather than evaluation, it can only be expected that researchers will follow suit.

In addition to 'internal' pressures of this kind, there is also a strong political motivation to get road safety programmes off the ground and the interested authorities are often not really willing to hang about waiting whilst researchers in their ivory towers satisfy themselves that particular techniques work. They want something that they can implement right away – preferably yesterday! Where there is a self-evident need for action, it is more than understandable if people are unwilling to delay implementation, particularly if there seem reasonable grounds to believe that a measure will work. Unfortunately, once a measure has been introduced in this way, possibly at considerable expense and perhaps with the good intention that evaluation will be conducted subsequently, as time goes on it becomes less and less attractive to conduct evaluation that may show that it doesn't work and was a waste of money. When yet more money has to be expended for the privilege of financing the research that showed this, the temptation must be strong to let the issue slide. This leaves aside entirely the fact that introducing the programme in the first place represented a public demonstration of confidence in it and that face as well as money is at risk if it is shown not to work. Little wonder that such retrospective evaluation may almost come to be seen as a 'subversive activity that could rock the boat' (Grayson and Howarth, 1982). In such circumstances, 'there is a very human tendency to give potentially unfavourable evaluation a low priority in safety programmes or to give undue emphasis to trivial but apparently favourable results' (ibid, p. 111).

PROCESS VERSUS OUTCOME EVALUATION

The latter tendency to conduct evaluation that puts an adopted measure in the best possible light raises another problem of evaluative research. A common error is to confound two different kinds of evaluation, known as *process* and *outcome* evaluation. The former is concerned with how to organize a programme so that it will run in a smooth and efficient manner: the latter with how well the underlying aims are met. It is by no means uncommon for these types of evaluation to be confounded and for a programme to be justified on the grounds that the process works well. In the case of road safety education, process evaluation would be concerned, amongst other things, with ensuring that the vocabulary and concepts are appropriate to the age-group involved; that the prior knowledge assumed is reasonable; that the programme content builds on previous parts of the programme in a systematic way, and so on. Feedback from the users of the package, from parents and from the children themselves would obviously be important in this, and programmes might undergo quite extensive modification on the basis of such feedback. However, such evaluation is solely concerned with how well the package is designed as a tool and how well it appeals to its potential market. None of this can tell us whether the tool actually *works*. Unfortunately, it is an all-too-common experience that if everyone concerned is happy and if the programme 'seems' to be having an effect, it will have a good chance of implementation. The question 'does the programme work?' is assumed to have been answered when in fact it has not.

ESTABLISHING OBJECTIVES IN ROAD SAFETY EDUCATION

Allied to the problem of evaluation is the problem of deciding precisely what goals the programme is aiming to achieve. Obviously, the ultimate goal is to reduce accident rates amongst children but this is far too general a criterion for evaluating a training programme. Apart from anything else, a reduction in accident rates could only be expected if the programme were introduced on a sufficiently large scale: since the aim of evaluative research is to determine whether such widespread implementation would be justified in the first place, other criteria are necessary.

Determining educational objectives in road safety education is, in fact, a matter of long dispute that has never been satisfactorily resolved. Most road safety education programmes simply do not set themselves concrete objectives in this way (Rothengatter, 1981). Often, it seems to be assumed that if the programme deals with road safety at all it is virtually bound to have beneficial effects. As we shall see, there are no grounds for so uncritical and optimistic an outlook.

How should we determine the objectives of an education programme? Most programmes, where they set objectives at all, have tended to do so at a very general level. Apart from 'reducing accidents', other generally agreed objectives include getting children to 'behave safely' or 'avoid dangerous situations' (Organization for Economic Co-operation and Development, 1981). However, unless there is a clear specification of what these vague terms mean, we do not really know what the child is being taught nor how to assess whether the goals of teaching have been achieved. Unfortunately, when we do try to specify objectives more concretely, there is virtually no agreement at all. Just about the only area of agreement is that children should be taught to look before crossing – a consensus the reader may find less than profound. Even then, there is no consensus as to *where* they should look or what exactly they are looking *for* (Rothengatter, 1981). When it comes to specifying how children should be taught to deal with such common problems as crossing near parked cars or at road junctions, the disagreements are fundamental. Some authorities, for example, argue that children should be taught to avoid parked cars when crossing the road whereas others argue that they should be encouraged to use parked cars as an extension of the kerb, making the distance over which the child is exposed to traffic correspondingly shorter. Similarly, some authorities argue that junctions are dangerous and should be avoided altogether, while others say crossing at junctions should be encouraged since vehicle speeds will be lower there and the situation encourages drivers to be more alert. Obviously, these disagreements need to be confronted before a programme is developed. They also emphasize the importance of solid empirical evidence in confronting such questions: conjecture, supposition or 'common sense' are no substitute in reaching such decisions. Unfortunately, this is all too often the basis on which road safety programmes are designed.

A final problem in formulating objectives is to determine what changes in the child we wish to bring about. Most current road safety education is concerned with the acquiring of knowledge and a conceptual framework for understanding the traffic environment. Inducing appropriate attitudes and values is another common aim.

However, as we have seen, it is by no means obvious that children who can answer road safety questions correctly or who express appropriate attitudes towards road safety when asked about it, will necessarily behave better when out on the road. Whether such indirect education actually works is an entirely empirical question and raises the whole issue of the validity of current road education.

In conclusion, it cannot be said that any of the most widely used methods appear particularly effective as techniques for road safety education. With the exception of the behavioural and possibly video methods, which have been little studied or used, the record is uninspiring. Clearly, a considerable amount of work is needed to determine the most efficient techniques.

However, throughout this discussion there lurks an underlying problem. In the above studies, it is typically assumed that the content being taught is valid and should lead to improvements in road behaviour provided the teaching method is right. But an education technique is only as good as its content. It is therefore essential that the substance of current road safety programmes be considered independently of the techniques themselves before evaluation can properly be made of either: only then can their merits be gauged. We do this in the next chapter.

5

CURRENT ROAD SAFETY EDUCATION PROGRAMMES

THE GREEN CROSS CODE

By far the most widely publicized countermeasures introduced in the UK have been sets of simple verbal rules designed to provide children with a general-purpose strategy for dealing with the road. The earliest of these, the Kerb Drill, was introduced in 1942 but was revised in the early 1970s because of its by then outdated and rather militaristic approach (it used terms such as 'Halt!' and 'Quick march!'). More important, the style of the drill lent itself to rote learning and very rigid application by children, who tended to recite it almost as a talisman for warding off danger (Preston, 1980). This tendency to treat drills as if they had magical properties is an important feature of young children, which will be examined further below. The Drill was eventually replaced by the more flexible Green Cross Code (Sargent and Sheppard, 1974), which has constituted the main theme of road safety education in Britain ever since.

In devising the Code the authors conducted a preliminary study in which a sample of mothers, teachers and road safety officers were asked to indicate the importance they attached to each of twenty different items concerning road safety. When the results were analysed, considerable agreement emerged as to what were considered appropriate priorities, and the Green Cross Code was constructed on the basis of this consensus. The Code was carefully phrased so that the language would be simple and clear enough for young children to understand. Considerable care was taken over this: for example, nearly 300 6-year-olds were questioned at the roadside to determine whether they understood terms like 'traffic', 'kerb', 'pavement', etc. Finally, a set of six main precepts was formulated, each of which was accompanied by supplementary information to enable instructors to elaborate on the basic points. The six precepts were:

- First find a safe place to cross, then stop.
- Stand on the pavement near the kerb.
- Look all round for traffic and listen.
- If traffic is coming, let it pass, look all round again.
- When there is no traffic near, walk straight across the road.
- Keep looking and listening for traffic while you cross.

The Code in its formulated version was tested on a sample of 170 7- and 8-year-olds to see whether they could read it satisfactorily and could go through the steps described in an adequate manner. The conclusion was that children between 7 and 8 years of age would be able to follow the instructions and read the Code without too much difficulty. However, the authors suggested that finding a safe place at which to cross would probably still prove too hard for them. Later studies suggested that younger children (aged 5 and 6) were significantly less likely to benefit from the Code and that a different approach might be required with this age-group (Fisk and Cliff, 1975). We shall return to this issue below.

The precepts of the Code can be justified on the basis of at least some of what is known about child behaviour. For example, the injunction to stop at the kerb makes sense because it has been shown that children are more likely to look if they stop than if they do not (e.g. Heimstra *et al.*, 1969; Limbourg and Gerber, 1978), and looking is obviously the most fundamental of all road-crossing activities. Furthermore, a child who stops is much less likely subsequently to run across the road (Michalik, 1978). Running is greatly discouraged because children have less control over their movements than adults, making them not only more likely to trip but also less able to stop or change direction in an emergency. Finally, the Code instructs the child to look all round (not just to right and left as in the old Kerb Drill) and to listen as well. In fact, the Code was intended to get away from the rote aspects of the old Kerb Drill and to encourage a more open, flexible approach.

It might be felt that the Code is a reasonably comprehensive strategy, which at the very least should keep children's road behaviour along the right lines. However, it was clearly designed to capture only the most essential features of safe road behaviour, presumably with the aim of producing rules that even young children can be expected to understand and use. As such, it is obviously a very limited strategy. For example, it fails to recognize or develop almost any of the skills that were claimed to be essential in Chapter 3. The Code could, of course, be considered simply as *an introduction to road safety for younger children*, to be augmented as the child's age and traffic experience change. Unfortunately, the Code does not represent so much the foundation as the sum total of road safety education in this country. Indeed, young people of 12 or 14 (if they continue to receive road safety education at all) will in all probability be hearing much the same story as when they were introduced to the topic years earlier. By contrast, the approach in some other countries has been to build *hierarchically* on earlier skills so that the training keeps track of the child's needs (see pp. 67–69). Finally, the Code is primarily a *verbal* technique and is taught almost exclusively in the classroom. Doubts about this approach have already been raised. A number of factors converge at the outset, then, to raise questions about the Code's suitability as the main plank of road safety education for the young.

EFFECTIVENESS OF THE GREEN CROSS CODE

Since its launching, the Green Cross Code has been the underlying basis of most teaching programmes and road safety campaigns in Britain and, in the short term at least, was viewed as being rather effective. Morris (1972), for example, saw the Code as achieving four goals. These included a reduction of 11 per cent in child pedestrian accidents over the first three months of the campaign; a demonstrated knowledge of the Code in children (suggesting a possible causal relation); some evidence of improved real road behaviour in children; and a cost-benefit analysis, calculated on the basis of the reduced casualties over the first three months. Such findings encouraged adoption of the Code as the country's main educational measure for improving road safety for the young.

Unfortunately, many of these supposed benefits are difficult to assess because of the confounding effect of other factors. For example, the dip in accidents following the Code's introduction is extremely hard to relate causally to the Code as it was introduced at a time of global energy crisis, which in Britain led to fuel shortages, dramatically increased petrol prices, and sharply reduced speed limits. Any of these factors could be expected to contribute to fewer accidents and, indeed, a reduction in accidents of all sorts was obtained over this period. Whether the dip in child accidents was the result of the newly introduced Code or was merely one aspect of the *overall* reduction of accidents at that time, is impossible to gauge (Sheehy and Chapman, 1984). No control group of children was ever employed to compare the skill of those who had been introduced to the Code with those who had not, so these alternative factors cannot be eliminated. Moreover, the Green Cross Code was launched to the accompaniment of a large-scale publicity drive designed to emphasize road safety. The extent to which the reduction in child casualties was due to the effectiveness of the Code or to the impact of the campaign on the public at large – including possible influences on driver behaviour, for example – is impossible to assess (Grayson and Howarth, 1982). In the absence of properly designed evaluations that include appropriate experimental and control groups, the impact of any one variable is impossible to determine.

In short, we simply have no way of knowing, objectively, if the Green Cross Code works or not. Although the Code received a large amount of quite careful *process evaluation*, as with other attempts at road safety education, it never received a proper *outcome evaluation* that would allow us to determine its success in improving child pedestrian behaviour or reducing accidents.

Most informed opinion seems to have stabilized on the view that the Green Cross Code and similar countermeasures are, at best, having a marginal effect on accident rates with a likely reduction of no more than 10 per cent (Howarth and Repetto-Wright, 1978). This is clearly very modest given the pre-eminence of the Code and the effort expended in promoting it. The modest effect cannot be put down to children simply not knowing the Code because studies show that children know it quite well. Nor is it the case that they simply refuse to adhere to the Code's instructions. In fact, observational studies show that young children are, on the whole, far *more* likely to stick to the precepts of the Code than are adults (e.g. Routledge *et al.*, 1976a; van der Molen, 1983). In fact, *experienced road users, who are many times less vulnerable to accidents, simply do not use the Code at all.* The very reasonable question then arises as to whether the Code teaches what pedestrians really need to know in order to interact safely with traffic. And what is it that experienced road users actually do on the road that makes them safe, if it isn't using the Green Cross Code?

In my view, the major shortcoming of the Green Cross Code (and, by implication, most current road safety education) is precisely that it lacks a clear appreciation of the skills that are needed to deal with the traffic environment. As we have seen, road crossing involves a range of complex perceptual, cognitive and motor skills without which skilled pedestrian behaviour is impossible. Instead of teaching these real skills, current road safety programmes concentrate on instilling the most general rules and guidelines and fail to build on these as the child's needs change. Hardly surprising that the benefits of this approach appear so limited. How, then, should we go about improving on this situation? What should we be putting into road safety education, and how should we design our programmes to accommodate it?

ADULT VERSUS CHILD BEHAVIOUR

One obvious starting-point would be to compare the behaviour of groups who are known to have lower pedestrian accident rates (i.e. adults) with those whose accident rates are high (i.e. children). This comparison might give insight into what the first group is doing that makes it safer, as well as highlighting what the other group is doing that makes it vulnerable. We should then have a clue as to the direction training should take. The overall aim would be to make the vulnerable group behave like the safe group, rather than inducing them to adhere to some notional 'safe' strategy constructed primarily on the basis of adults' opinions.

In fact, the observational studies described in Chapter 2 revealed a number of extremely interesting differences between adult and child road behaviour. However, these differences were probably not what one might have expected. The expectation of most people, and probably of most researchers at the time, was that adults would show 'better' behaviour on the road. That is, they would take more 'care', would not expose themselves unnecessarily to risk and, in general, would act with a 'maturity' that children so clearly lack. Even allowing for the common view that adults often set a bad example, the far lower pedestrian accident rates of adults relative to children would surely oblige even the most cynical observer to assume that adults follow road safety 'rules' better than children. This expectation hardly seems very demanding, given how poorly children adhere to the Green Cross Code in the first place.

In the event, far from behaving more in accordance with the Code's six points (see p. 55), adults are even *less* likely to follow the advice than children. Adult behaviour is simply nothing like that advocated by the Green Cross Code. Adults do *not* stop at the kerb before crossing; they do *not* wait for traffic to pass before stepping into the street; they do *not* walk directly across the road but frequently cross diagonally; they often use the crown of the road as a half-way house, planning how to cross the nearside lane before considering how to cross the farside lane; and they accept far tighter gaps in the traffic than any child would accept (e.g. Routledge *et al.*, 1976a).

Children, on the other hand, are much more likely to stop at the kerb; they delay much longer at the kerbside before attempting to cross; they accept only large (sometimes only very large) gaps; they are more likely to walk straight across the road; and they do not use the crown of the road as a half-way house.

In short, adults do most of the things that the Green Cross Code tells them *not* to do, yet they are still much less at risk on the road than children. How are we to explain this discrepancy? And where does this leave the Green Cross Code if the only road users who use it are the most vulnerable?

The paradox comes about because experienced road users adopt different strategies from those advocated by road safety education. Although completely contradicting the advice of the Green Cross Code, these strategies are not, in fact, examples of 'bad' behaviour. On the contrary, they reflect a great deal of skill. For example, adults do not stop and look for traffic at the roadside because they assess the situation *before* arriving at the kerb. This means they have no need to stop and can cross without kerb delay. The behaviour does not reflect carelessness or incompetence: rather, it reflects skill.

Similarly, the tendency of adults to step into the street *before* a vehicle has passed is a strategy that maximizes the size of the gap into which the pedestrian is stepping. This 'tucking in' is possible because adults look ahead for up-coming gaps and anticipate their arrival by stepping out smartly as the lead car passes. Not only does this effectively 'enlarge' the gap, it also means adults can accept smaller gaps than would otherwise be possible. This obviously makes particular sense on busy roads where large gaps might not often occur.

Children, on the other hand, show none of this anticipation. In selecting a gap, for instance, they do not even consider whether a gap might be suitable until after the first car has passed. By the time they have got round to thinking about it, the gap has shrunk and crossing is impossible. Children miss many perfectly safe opportunities to cross in this way (e.g. Lee *et al.*, 1984). This may also partly explain why children appear so indecisive at the roadside: they realize that they should have had time to cross but before they made a decision the situation had changed: hence the stop-start behaviour that is so commonly observed. The situation is almost bound to be frustrating and one wonders whether some of the 'impulsive' behaviour one sees is the result. The basis of the problem seems to lie in a lack of anticipation, which in turn probably reflects their still rudimentary perceptual and decision-making skills.

By the age of around 11 years, however, children's behaviour has changed and observation shows that most of them have adopted the adult strategy (Routledge *et al.*, 1976a). Notice that this happens completely informally and without any instruction: indeed, adopting adult strategies requires the child to *reject* what he has been taught. Although *everyone* comes to use the more efficient adult strategy, children learn it by themselves, presumably through a process of trial and error on real roads. If they survive they become quite good at it. Unfortunately, the accident rates show that all too many of them do not.

The Green Cross Code, then, is at best a 'starter' strategy which introduces the child to the behaviour needed to deal with the road. It does not provide an efficient strategy, especially for dealing with busier roads, and all children abandon it sooner or later. This would suggest that its suitability for pedestrian needs is very limited.

ALTERNATIVE APPROACHES

What, then, should we be teaching children if not the Green Cross Code? Should we perhaps simply teach them to adopt the adult strategies? Most authorities, whilst recognizing the positive side of the adult strategy, take the view that encouraging children to behave in this way would be hopelessly irresponsible (e.g. Howarth and Repetto-Wright, 1978). Children simply could not be expected to cope with such a sophisticated approach because they lack the underlying skills. Indeed, one of the factors that was raised earlier as a possible explanation of the higher accident rates amongst young boys was precisely that they might be attempting to adopt adult strategies before they have the skills to sustain them. At the same time, current educational strategies are widely recognized as of limited value. So what is the way forward?

It is, of course, unacceptable to start encouraging young children to adopt adult strategies when they do not yet have the skills to support them. But the correct course of action is not to begin telling them one fine day to start stepping into the street through narrow gaps in the traffic. Rather, it should be to provide them with the underlying skills, so that eventually they will be in a position to adopt effective strategies safely. As we have said, at the present time children develop (and test!) these skills entirely on their own and without the benefit of any guidance whatsoever. Meanwhile, we restrict their teaching to the most general rules and guidelines. Surely, this whole approach is misguided. Road safety training must equip children with the abilities they really need to cope with modern traffic: otherwise, they will simply teach themselves, with all the dangers that this must necessarily entail.

A second possible approach would be to analyse the characteristics of advanced strategies, particularly with reference to the skills involved, and then adapt them to what can be expected of children. Once a group of strategies had been simplified in this way, they could be gradually introduced to children in accordance with their changing needs. Of course, the problem would remain of how children would develop the skills to move from the simplified to the advanced versions of the strategies. It therefore seems likely that this approach would have to be combined with skills training. But it might be a useful adaptation to the skills approach particularly if some proved hard for younger children to learn. In many ways, then, these approaches would seem to be complementary.

If a skills approach were to be taken, which skills should we teach and how should we go about it? Some researchers have begun by identifying individual road *dangers* that seem to make children vulnerable and have worked out a practical way of teaching how to overcome them. Another approach, a little more open-ended, is to identify particular *skills* that seem especially important and then train these in children. The idea here is that if the skills are properly learned, they should generalize to a wide range of situations, including ones that have not yet been encountered. Let us consider two skills that can be tackled in this way: visual timing and the ability to select a safe place to cross.

TRAINING OF VISUAL TIMING SKILLS

The first example concerns the visual timing skills, briefly discussed in Chapter 3, which are clearly central to safe pedestrian behaviour. No current road safety programme attempts to teach these: instead, children are simply advised to wait until the road is clear before crossing. This advice may be adequate for the very young pedestrian who, as we have seen, deals primarily with quiet roads where it is practicable to wait for the road to clear. However, on many roads the child would be there all day. Moreover, children have a marked tendency to interpret instructions such as 'wait until the road clears' very literally. We have seen children interpret this so literally that they were unwilling to cross if they could see a car at all. This occasionally included ones that were so far away as to be scarcely visible! This degree of rigidity is not functional and suggests that the children were not just being conservative about safety but were blindly following a rule. It is obvious that at some time they must start crossing in a more efficient manner, accepting gaps in the traffic that are safe to move through whilst rejecting those that are not. We might argue about the *age* at which such training should begin but it is hard to justify ignoring these skills in road safety education.

How might we teach such skills? Visual timing cannot be acquired just sitting in the classroom: it is a *practical* skill and therefore requires practical experience, preferably in a naturalistic setting. Of course, we can hardly ask children to start walking out in front of passing vehicles in order to practise their timing judgements: a safe alternative has to be found.

The pretend road method

One ingenious way of doing this has been developed by Lee and his colleagues at Edinburgh University (Lee, Young and McLaughlin, 1984). Their method is to set up a 'pretend' road in parallel to a real one. The children view traffic approaching on the real road but they cross on the adjacent simulated one. In this way they make genuine visual timing judgements and co-ordinate their movements to that information in a natural way. However, because they do not cross the real road, no harm comes to them if they make mistakes: indeed, such mistakes provide feedback and promote learning. The pretend road, then, is a simple simulation that could be used both to assess timing skills and provide practical training in a realistic but safe environment.

When children were assessed on the pretend road, several findings emerged. Perhaps the main one is that the children tended to be extremely conservative in their judgements, missing many opportunities where they could have crossed in complete safety. Between the ages of 5 and 7, as many as 45 per cent of the gaps that could safely have been accepted were rejected in this way. Adults, on the other hand, rejected only about 10 per cent of such gaps.

In addition to missed opportunities, children also made a number of 'tight fits': that is, they accepted gaps which were too short for safe crossing and which would have put them at risk if they were accepted on the real road. Such tight fits were made on a relatively small number of crossings (9 per cent) which may not seem too bad until you realize that a tight fit may only need to be made once to be fatal. The fact that the children did this on a number of occasions just in the short space of time during which they were being tested (and when they were probably behaving more cautiously than usual to please the experimenter) reinforces this point. The behaviour is thus of some concern.

Finally, the children were also much less consistent in their judgements than adults or older children. This inconsistency was found in the size of gaps they chose on different occasions; in the time they allowed to elapse before stepping out; and in the time they took to cross the road. As we have already noted, such inconsistency is a prime hallmark of the unskilled.

Training visual timing on the pretend road

In a follow-up study (Young and Lee, 1987), the authors developed a training programme, based on the pretend road, which they conducted with 5-year-olds. The substance of the training was simply to give the children feedback, both by allowing them to *see* the results of their actions and by discussing their performance with them. The main result was a marked reduction in the number of missed opportunities, which appeared to occur as a result of improved anticipation of acceptable traffic gaps. That is, the children were looking ahead to assess approaching gaps *before* they arrived. They also stepped out more briskly after the first car passed, thereby increasing the gap size.

It is important to note that the reduction in missed opportunities was not due to the children simply 'going earlier', in a blind sort of way. Had this happened there would not just have been a decrease in missed opportunities: there would also have been an increase in tight fits. However, this did not occur. This means the children were not just learning to take more risks. Rather, they were improving their strategies and skills on the road.

These findings, then, offer one example of how a practical, behavioural approach may hold promise as a means of teaching children as young as 5 years the complex skills that are needed to deal safely with the road. Note that it is very difficult to see how these skills could possibly be taught through verbal rules or, indeed, through any of the other classroom approaches. No one should be surprised about this: after all, whoever learned to drive just sitting at a desk? Wherever practical perceptual and motor skills are involved, it seems unlikely that we will find effective substitutes for behavioural training.

Alternatives to the pretend road method

One drawback of the pretend road method is that it requires access to a fairly wide piece of ground next to the real road where the pretend road can be set up. In many areas this would not be feasible. To address this problem we have recently been working on variations of the pretend road and comparing their efficacy (Demetre *et al.*, 1991). One such variation requires the child to stand by the kerbside and to judge the oncoming traffic from there. The child is asked to go when he judges he could get across the whole street but, unlike the pretend road, he does not actually walk out. Instead he indicates he is ready to go by calling out. This variation has both advantages and disadvantages over the pretend road: on the credit side, the children receive a more natural view of the traffic because they stand right at the kerb, not a whole road width away. On the other hand, they do not actually cross, so quite a lot of valuable experience is lost in this way.

In fact, children's performance appears to be quite similar in the two cases. Indeed, in some ways performance in the 'shout' condition is better. This version may thus turn out to be a simpler and more pragmatic alternative to the pretend road where the latter is difficult to set up. We are currently conducting studies on several such approaches to evaluate their respective merits, as are other researchers (e.g. van Schagen, 1988). Further research on the refinement of such methods certainly seems merited.

FINDING SAFE PLACES TO CROSS THE ROAD

A second example of the benefits of a skill-based approach comes from work developed in our own laboratory at Strathclyde University and concerns the child's ability to find safe places to cross the street. Our concern with this initially arose from an analysis of accident patterns in Strathclyde Region (Ampofo-Boateng, 1987). The analysis led us to suspect that child pedestrian accidents are over-represented at certain types of location on the road such as bends, intersections, brows of hills, obstructions and so on. The common characteristic of the sites seemed to be either that visibility was restricted there; or that traffic might approach from a number of different directions, thereby taxing the child's attention and information-processing capacities. It seemed clear that such places are intrinsically dangerous for pedestrians and should either be avoided, or else dealt with by means of special strategies (Ampofo-Boateng and Thomson, 1990).

However, whether a pedestrian takes appropriate action in such cases obviously depends on whether or not he recognizes the intrinsic threat posed by the sites in the first place. Current countermeasures do not seem to accept this as a problem at all. For example, the Green Cross Code simply instructs the child to 'first find a safe place', which assumes that the child knows how to do this. Moreover, when questioned about the priorities in safety education, parents, teachers, road safety experts and the police all relegated finding a safe site to a secondary level of importance (Foot *et al.*, 1982). But can children, in fact, find safe places to cross the road? Do they even recognize dangerous places when they see them? These questions are fundamental because no matter how well children have mastered the Green Cross Code or the more sophisticated timing skills discussed above, if they try to put them into practice on a blind summit they will be in considerable danger. For this reason, the ability to find a safe place is an essential precursor to the crossing skills that are the main focus of attention in all current road safety education.

To examine this, we conducted experiments in which children were presented with locations that were either very safe or extremely dangerous. We then simply asked them to say which was which. In other experiments, we asked the children in a more open-ended way to find their own routes across the road. We set up the experiments in a number of different ways, such as in the streets near their schools or on table-top models of traffic layouts in the classroom (Thomson, 1989; Ampofo-Boateng and Thomson, 1991). We have now individually tested over 300 children between the ages of 5 and 11 years in this way.

The results reveal a very clear pattern, with 5- to 7-year-olds exhibiting almost no ability to distinguish safe from dangerous places to cross. Only from about 9 years do children begin to appreciate the risk posed by obscured positions where they cannot see the road properly.

We were particularly interested in the strategies that the younger children used to solve this task. If they could see a car somewhere in the vicinity, no matter how tangential, they would invariably argue that it was dangerous to cross. Now this might seem to be just a very cautious strategy that the children were adopting, which may be no bad thing in view of their lack of experience. Unfortunately, if no cars were visible from the position they were currently occupying, the children almost invariably felt it was safe to cross. *They did not seem to realize that many locations are dangerous precisely because cars cannot be seen.* Thus, sharp bends, positions obscured by parked cars or other obstacles, brows of hills and similar positions were normally regarded as perfectly safe places to put the Green Cross Code into practice. Our impression was that the children were very rigidly putting into practice a rule they had been taught, namely 'don't cross if you see cars'. If none could be seen they assumed that none were around and it was safe to cross. Only older children spotted the danger and suggested how they might deal with it, for example, by moving to a safer spot.

These findings suggest to us that young children under the age of 9 years must often be at considerable risk on the road because they do not have the ability to recognize such dangers on the road even if they know the mechanics of the Green Cross Code. It seems to us that this will have to become a much more important priority area in safety education than it is at the moment.

Training children to find safe places

Can these skills be taught? We have recently tackled this question by training 5-year-old children and observing whether their performance could be brought nearer the level of older, more experienced pedestrians. We conducted the training in two ways: either entirely in the real world (in the streets near the children's school) or we combined a small amount of real-world training with practical training conducted on the table-top model (Ampofo-Boateng *et al.*, 1991). The idea in the latter case was to see if a modest amount of real-world experience could 'prime' a classroom technique so as to enable a mixed technique to work. The motivation here was purely practical: class numbers, weather conditions and similar factors might make extensive training in the road environment impracticable. We wanted to know if a combined technique avoiding these difficulties could be shown to work in a satisfactory manner.

Children were trained either individually or in groups and were tested at various stages: (1) prior to training; (2) immediately after training ended; (3) again two months after the end of the programme; (4) and finally, some 8 months later. The large number of post-tests was to establish the long-term effects of training. The results were also compared to those of children who had received no training at all.

The results showed a very substantial improvement immediately after training, with the proportion of 'safe' responses rising from 10 per cent to 70 per cent. This actually placed the 5-year-olds at about the same level as 11-year-old control children. After a two-month lapse, this improvement had fallen to 50 per cent and after eight months it had moved closer to 40 per cent. However, even 8 months after the end of training, their judgements were still closer to those of 9-year-olds than to untrained 5-year-olds. Interestingly, there was no difference between those trained by the combined real-world/model condition and those trained entirely in the real world. On the other hand, children trained individually seem to do rather better than those trained in groups. The latter research, however, is not yet complete.

These findings seem to show two things. Firstly, it is possible to train skills of this type in very young children and in a fairly short period of time. Young children do not seem to lack the basic capacities to benefit from such training: on the contrary, in the 'safe place' training 5-year-olds were performing not far from the level of 11-year-olds, and this after a modest amount of training (only six sessions of about half an hour each, presented at a rate of about one a week). Despite this, quite marked benefits were obtained and many of these were maintained over a considerable period following the end of the programme.

At the same time, it is clear that updating should be undertaken from time to time in order to keep the children's skills 'tuned up'. Given the relatively small amount of training that was necessary in the first place, it does not seem likely that massive amounts of further training would be necessary to hold on to the gains. It would thus seem a pity not to capitalize on such resilience by introducing refresher courses from time to time.

TRAINING TO DEAL WITH SPECIFIC SITUATIONS

An approach that is different from, yet in many ways complementary to, the approach described above has been developed in the Netherlands, where a systematic, long-term programme of road safety training has been under way for a number of years (van der Molen, 1989). This, like the approach advocated here, starts with a systematic analysis of the tasks that the pedestrian faces in traffic. The strategies that experienced pedestrians adopt in order to accomplish these tasks are then examined with a view to defining what the inexperienced road user needs to learn. A difference between this and the skills approach, however, is that instead of attempting to develop the skills directly, they *adapt* the adult strategies to a level appropriate to the skills of young children. These simplified strategies are then introduced at the age when children first start to confront the road situations to which they refer (van Schagen and Rothengatter, 1986).

Four main strategies have been identified to date. First, there is a Basic Strategy (not unlike the Green Cross Code), which is regarded as suitable for introducing to children as young as 4 years old. This is regarded as useful for children who deal mainly with quiet streets, such as are found in residential neighbourhoods, and is sufficiently simple for children to comprehend at any early stage. However, unlike the Green Cross Code, the approach acknowledges that as children grow older they gradually come in contact with a more complex environment for which the Basic Strategy will be inadequate. Accordingly, children of around 5 to 6 years are introduced to two further techniques, one for crossing at parked cars and the other for dealing with intersections, both of which become a problem at around this age. These techniques are elaborations of the basic method, so previous strategies are not undermined by the later ones. A fourth strategy, developed more recently (van Schagen and Rothengatter, 1986), is to teach children how to deal with intersections where there is also a parked vehicle. The latter are amongst the most dangerous of all situations confronting young children (Howarth and Repetto-Wright, 1978). This strategy is taught to children from around age 7.

The Dutch approach, then, involves a number of stages. Firstly, those road-crossing situations that seem to give rise to accidents (and which, it can be assumed, tax the child's road-crossing skills) are identified. These are then considered in relation to the ages at which children are likely to start coming across them. This helps determine when training of the different strategies should begin. The strategy is then designed, taking into account the skills that can be expected in children of the age concerned. The approach is essentially hierarchical, with each stage building on previous ones, and the programme as a whole has coherence because it is based on a relatively clear theoretical and empirical foundation.

This approach has many admirable features, as well as several points in common with the skills approach that has been advocated here. The most important common point is the stress laid on practical training, which is fundamental in the Dutch approach. The training is undertaken mainly by parents and kindergarten teachers, who are themselves trained in using the various methods. Certainly, there is no question of the education being centred around occasional talks by outside speakers to a largely passive audience, as in this country.

In spite of these positive aspects, however, the approach remains susceptible to at least some of the criticisms we have made of other approaches. For example, the Basic Strategy, like the Green Cross Code, does not teach children how to recognize a dangerous place or find a safe one in which to practise the strategy. To some extent this problem is tackled in later parts of the programme where the danger of parked vehicles and intersections is implicitly recognized. However, we have already noted that the ability to find a safe place logically precedes the need for a crossing strategy, because if the child cannot discriminate safe from dangerous places, he will try to apply his crossing routine under dangerous conditions. At the moment, this does not seem to be appreciated in the Dutch system any more than in the British one.

A second issue arising from this work concerns teaching children how to cross at parked cars or intersections. Many authorities are extremely uneasy about training children to cross at such sites: indeed, the advice given in the UK is to avoid such situations and cross elsewhere. This would apply particularly to the car/junction combination, which clearly taxes the abilities of 7-year-olds (van Schagen, 1985).

The Dutch approach, on the other hand, is to teach children specifically how to cross at such locations rather than how to avoid them. There is thus a very controversial aspect to this approach. Our own feeling is that the child must come to appreciate the intrinsic danger in such situations in advance of being offered a strategy to deal with them. Indeed, unless the child appreciates this there is the very real risk of failing to see the point of the strategy.

Nevertheless, a combination of approaches, emphasizing on the one hand the strategies that children are likely to need at different ages and, on the other, the skills that will enable them to move to more efficient adult strategies in a logical and systematic way, seems to hold out most hope for education in the foreseeable future. Resorting to some 'golden rule' that is supposed to work universally is a misguided approach.

6

HOW SHOULD ROAD SAFETY BE TAUGHT?

There can be no definitive answer to so broad and challenging a question, but it is clear that current road safety education lacks some essential components. It is not just a question of incorporating a few new elements into existing programmes: the ramifications seem to go beyond that and substantially change the whole way in which road safety education is viewed at the present time.

BEHAVIOURAL VERSUS VERBAL TEACHING METHODS

The benefits of a behavioural approach to road safety training have been repeatedly stressed in this book, as many of the skills young children need simply cannot be taught by other means. In this, road crossing is no different from any other skill where perceptuo-motor judgements are required. Skiing, swimming, driving or learning to ride a bike all depend on practical experience: no one would even think of suggesting these skills could be learnt just by being told what to do. Yet this is precisely how pedestrians are taught. Meanwhile, the practical experience that does, eventually, turn children into skilled pedestrians is picked up on real roads and without supervision. Little wonder that so many fail to reach adulthood without mishap.

The advantage of practical training is not just that it ensures children will adopt certain behaviours: it also ensures that those behaviours are properly 'tuned' to the road environment. When children learn in the classroom that they should look right and left before crossing, there is the very real danger that all they are really learning is to make certain movements of the head. We have already mentioned the 'ritualistic' way in which some children execute the Green Cross Code. The problem seems to be that, because the movements are learned in a 'vacuum', the children cannot see how these relate to the traffic environment, i.e. to the directions from which traffic might approach them. In fact, children as old as 7 years turn out to have rather uncertain ideas about the directions in which traffic can move, where cars can come from and go to, and so on (van Schagen and Rothengatter, 1986). If children are taught strategies in isolation from the reality to which they refer, and if at the same time they do not have a good conceptual grasp of how the traffic environment works, there is the real possibility that they may simply be going through a series of meaningless movements.

On the other hand, a child trained in making timing judgements is much more likely to look before crossing because *he can't make timing judgements without doing so.* He is no longer going through a series of head movements because someone told him to: he is picking up information and is making whatever movements are necessary to accomplish this. It is the *picking up of information* that is crucial, not the executing of movements. The difference between the two is fundamental.

Because this approach educates children in the information that they need to pick up when in traffic, their attention will also likely improve as they become more attuned to what is relevant and less to what is irrelevant. They might also be expected to be less distractible for the same reason. As Lee *et al.* (1984) point out, inexperienced children simply cannot be expected to know what to look for on the road, any more than the novice skier can be expected to know what terrain features are important in skiing down a mountainside. Giving children the opportunity to behave meaningfully in traffic, then, improves the chances of a number of capacities developing, not just the one specially singled out for treatment. Again, it is hard to see how this could happen in the classroom.

In spite of these advantages, behavioural approaches have received almost no attention, particularly in this country. Approaches change little, particularly in the heavy reliance placed on verbal methods. Of course, the introduction of behavioural techniques poses practical problems in that taking children to the roadside, whether individually or in groups, is clearly more time-consuming than gathering them together for a lecture in the classroom. Even with the relatively short training programmes discussed above, this still means quite a few trips out of the classroom. The question then arises: who is to undertake such training? And what are the financial implications of such proposals?

WHO SHOULD BE RESPONSIBLE FOR ROAD SAFETY EDUCATION?

It is certainly hard to see how the small number of safety and police officers who are currently responsible could possibly be expected to undertake such practical training on their own. For any large-scale introduction of such measures, a considerable change in resources and their management would be necessary. This leads to the commonest objection to such proposals, namely, 'it would be a good idea but is financially impracticable'. Such arguments are almost invariably a recipe for doing nothing or else for doing more of what we already know does not work. To a large extent, this reflects the whole attitude towards road safety education in this country as a marginal activity, kept ticking over, but without the commitment really to tackle the problem. As already said in this book, we seem almost to accept road accidents as an inevitable part of the modern world that we must learn to live with. It is an astonishing submission that would be hard to imagine in relation to any other threat to the health of children.

Before we accept the inevitable too lightly, however, let us consider the implications of the proposal a little more carefully. Is it, in fact, the case that behavioural training could not be implemented without massive injections of cash? Might not some more cost-effective way be found, providing there is the common will to do so?

Currently road safety education is undertaken in the main by road safety inspectors and police officers, who visit schools on an intermittent basis. These officers, in spite of sometimes valiant efforts, simply do not have the time or resources to cover current needs, let alone implement a detailed programme of behavioural training. Their role would seem to lie in *training the trainers* and in other ways providing back-up expertise, rather than in undertaking all the frontline child training themselves. This, of course, means that supplementary manpower needs to be found from somewhere else.

SHOULD THE SCHOOL BE INVOLVED?

Although the school is the agency responsible for most of the educational needs of children, road safety education is not currently one of them. As a result their role in this area is both haphazard and uncoordinated. Surveys show that attitudes towards road safety education vary widely amongst schools but most operate without any clear-cut policy on the issue (Singh, 1982). Where it appears at all, it tends to be infrequent and incidental. In fact, most schools' contribution extends no further than opening their doors to the occasional visits of police or road safety officers. The situation is not helped by the fact that teachers receive no training in road safety education whilst at college. No doubt this also partly explains why they tend to be unaware of the road safety materials that are available (Foot *et al.*, 1982).

Schools cannot really be blamed for this lack of involvement: they have no statutory requirement to teach road safety and have never come under particularly strong pressure to do so. In fact, surprisingly few people seem to see the schools as having a central role in road safety. Surveys show that most people see *parents* as the group with most responsibility for road safety (a view shared by parents themselves). And although almost everyone thinks that schools should make *some* input, most people (including teachers) have tended to take the view that the school's input should be occasional rather than regular. Only road safety officers apparently recognize the central role the school can play: in one survey, 80 per cent of them viewed road safety as a subject that should either be taught in its own right or should be integrated into other school subjects and taught at least once a week (Foot *et al.*, 1982).

The attitude of the road safety inspectors is, in fact, a very sensible one because it is doubtful if any other organization could possibly compare to schools in their access to children. Moreover, the educational system seems increasingly to regard itself as preparing children for life: how it manages to exclude itself from the task of *literally* preparing them for life is a strange anomaly that is hard to account for. If the school system took a more organized and active role in the road safety training of children, many of the resource problems discussed above would become less insurmountable.

Happily, education authorities have become increasingly aware of the important role that schools can play in this area and, indeed, the Local Authorities Association has recently issued a *Road Safety Code of Good Practice*, in which it is strongly recommended that road safety education be integrated into the school curriculum (LAA, 1989). It also recommends that the subject be taught in teacher training colleges. It remains to be seen how this integration into the curriculum is to be achieved and how it will figure amongst the curriculum's many other priorities. So far as I know, no detailed proposals have yet been forthcoming concerning who will teach the subject, how it will be taught, or how much time will be made available to it. Nevertheless, this development opens the door to real opportunities and must be welcomed as a potentially major initiative, provided local authorities choose to follow up on the recommendations with action.

It must be stressed that these opportunities are only potential ones because the benefits of school involvement depend not only on the amount of time that can be devoted to safety training but on the form that training takes. If it is approached in the usual way as another classroom activity to be taught by means of lectures, booklets and the like, then there is frankly little reason to expect dramatic changes. It cannot be emphasized too often that children's preparedness to face the road will not be improved simply by talking about it: they need *know-how* rather than mere *knowledge* and direct training seems the best way to get it. The formulation of programmes that can achieve this and the integration of these into the curriculum are problems requiring urgent attention.

WHAT CAN PARENTS DO?

Of all the groups who might have something to contribute, it is the parents who are most often seen as bearing primary responsibility for child pedestrian safety. This attitude prevails even amongst professional groups who clearly have something to offer themselves. For example, only 11 per cent of the headteachers interviewed by Colbourne and Sargent (1971) felt the school should play the major role in such education, a view endorsed by most teachers, police officers and, to a lesser extent, road safety inspectors (Foot *et al.*, 1982). The view is also strongly held by parents themselves (Sadler, 1972).

However, whilst parents certainly do have responsibility for their children's safety, substantial obligations also lie with the rest of society. It is too easy to call the problem the responsibility of parents and leave it at that. Those who plan the road environment (usually with little thought for the needs of pedestrians), the drivers who use it and the rest of us who benefit from it, all need to realize that its benefits are accompanied by risks which, for children, outweigh the risks they are likely to suffer from any other source. Yet these obligations are recognized only reluctantly, if at all. Little wonder that Singh (1982) declares that children's safety is 'everyone's concern but no-one's responsibility' (p. 73).

At the same time, we must recognize that parents have far greater opportunity to train children than anyone else, especially at an early age, and it seems foolish to ignore this 'resource' when considering children's road safety education. Particularly where practical roadside training is concerned, parents have a potentially crucial contribution to make. It is therefore worth exploring how this resource can be best utilized.

Unfortunately, there is no use just encouraging parents to teach road safety to their children and hoping for the best. Although they are naturally more concerned about their children's safety than anyone else, the fact is that most parents have little idea of what they should be teaching or how to set about it. Moreover, many parents seriously misjudge what their children are capable of doing, some tending to overestimate and others to underestimate their children's capabilities. For example, when Sadler (1972) interviewed a sample of over 2,000 mothers, she found that 25 per cent of them had introduced their children to only one or two specific roads by the time they were 8 years old. By contrast to this highly conservative approach, almost 20 per cent had introduced children as young as 3 years to 'very busy' roads and 13 per cent regarded their 2-year-old children as capable of crossing such a road unaided! The latter optimism (if that is what we should call it) seems to be depressingly common. We ourselves have quite frequently come across cases of parents allowing 3-year-olds to run errands to the local shops that entailed crossing several streets. It should be pointed out that such parents did not seem to be especially thoughtless, uncaring or stupid. They simply overestimated what their children were capable of doing and underestimated the danger of the road.

Finally, it has to be recognized that at the present time few parents take the teaching of road safety very seriously, as shown by most observational studies of parents accompanying children. The recent Scottish report discussed earlier, for example, found that only 10 per cent of parents made any attempt to give guidance to their children when crossing the road. Some 90 per cent simply crossed in the usual adult way, pulling their children after them by the hand. What is particularly disturbing is the effect this had on the children. Most became completely passive, paid no attention whatever to the road scene and deferred entirely to the adult's judgement. Clearly such children are learning nothing at all from the experience of being out with an 'expert' road user. This raises a rather pithy question: if children do not practise road-crossing skills when accompanied by an adult, when do they practise them? The answer seems to be when they are alone.

TRAFFIC CLUBS

If parents are not well equipped to train children, can this be changed? One approach that has been tried in several countries is the Traffic Club. In the UK the best known of these was the Tufty Club (discussed in Chapter 4), which until recently distributed stories and other material emphasizing good road behaviour to parents to read to their children. The material was originally intended for the under-5s but, in fact, proved popular with primary school children also. However, as we saw in Chapter 4, the approach was not very successful and the Tufty Club has in fact ceased operating.

A more elaborate attempt at the traffic club idea was developed in Norway where traffic materials were distributed to parents on a six-monthly basis. However, a marked feature of the Norwegian club was that it strongly encouraged parents to supplement the materials with practical training. Schioldberg (1974, 1976) evaluated the clubs by assessing the road safety knowledge, behaviour and accident rates of club members relative to non-members. The most superficially impressive result was that accident rates were found to be 20 per cent lower amongst club members, a difference that was even more marked in the only major conurbation in the country (Oslo). The children's road safety knowledge was also superior. These findings have led to the introduction of similar schemes elsewhere in Scandinavia as well as in Germany and Luxembourg. Currently, efforts are being made to establish a national Traffic Club in the UK (Downing, 1990).

A note of caution needs to be sounded with regard to the success of the Norwegian experiment, however, because the difference in accident rates was not matched by a similar difference in the road behaviour of members versus non-members. That is, there was no evidence that members were behaving more safely in traffic. Since membership was voluntary and only a third to a half of eligible children joined, it is very possible that the parents who enrolled their children were safety-conscious in the first place and that their children were less likely to have a road accident whether they joined the club or not. The only way in which this possibility could be ruled out would be to compare members before and after joining, to see what changes took place. This was never done. Once again, we come up against the problem of adequate evaluation in road safety research.

The fact that such clubs inevitably reach only a proportion of those for whom they are intended is a particularly important drawback of the traffic club concept. Indeed, it seems more than likely that the children whom the clubs fail to reach may be the ones most in need of help. For example, in a trial in the UK, Downing (1981) found not only that membership rates were low, but that the highest enrolment was achieved amongst the children of higher managerial and professional groups. Ideally, then, we need an approach that is less reliant on self-selective mechanisms and reaches a wider audience.

COLLABORATION BETWEEN PARENTS AND SCHOOLS

An intriguing approach that has been developed in the Netherlands is to set up a parent/child training programme through the schools rather than through autonomous clubs. In Holland, most children attend kindergarten between the ages of 4 and 6 and relations between the institutions and parents are generally good. The Dutch approach has been to use the institution as the focus for parent training, with the parents being taught and monitored by the teachers. This approach has several important advantages. Firstly, it ensures that a large proportion of parents will come in contact with the scheme. Secondly, it offers a systematic programme of training for the parents together with appropriate back-up, so they know what they are supposed to be doing and why. Thirdly, the child training is focused on a group of clearly defined problems that are known to be associated with risk. Finally, the training is primarily behavioural. An additional advantage is that it breaks the ice between parents and the school, which is almost certainly desirable in relation to the child's educational experience as a whole.

The approach has been evaluated in a number of studies (e.g. Rothengatter, 1981; van der Molen, 1983) and the results do show significant improvements in children's road behaviour. Moreover, these improvements have been found to persist six months after the end of the programme. Perhaps even more interesting, however, is the change that took place in the parents. Like the Scottish parents, untrained Dutch ones make little effort to teach road safety to their children. By contrast, unobtrusive observation of parents who had taken part in the programme showed that after training the likelihood of their giving guidance had risen substantially. An important benefit of the programme, then, is not just the immediate changes in child behaviour but also the heightened awareness shown by parents of their child's limitations. Furthermore, parents who have been trained to educate their children appear to develop a confidence in themselves as teachers which leads them to take a much fuller part in their children's road safety education.

This kind of integrated school/parent approach seems to have much to recommend it. It depends, however, on the nature of the relationship that exists between the school and the parents. In Luxembourg, for instance, road safety workers do not feel these are sufficiently flexible to permit adoption of the Dutch approach at the present time – a limitation which they greatly regret (Laroche-Reeff, 1988). It remains to be seen whether the approach could prove successful in this country. One or two attempts are currently being made, but the effectiveness of the schemes has not been evaluated.

Recently, our group at Strathclyde University and David Lee's group in Edinburgh have been jointly pursuing ways of involving parents and schools in such an integrated approach within the context of the Scottish school system, although the work is still at a very early stage. The aim is to teach timing skills and safe-place finding to 5-year-old children by means of a modifiable training programme that can be used both with individuals or groups. The success of the programme when taught by highly skilled researchers is currently being assessed, with very encouraging results. Later, our aim will be to see if similar improvements can be achieved by parents and teachers who have been trained for the job.

It seems likely that the changing relationship between schools and parents that is currently under way may lead to increased opportunities for such co-operative work to develop. An appealing aspect of the approach is that it does not simply pass on the responsibility for training to the school, thereby merely adding to an already heavy workload. Instead, it supposes the development of a working relationship between the school and the community and exploits that partnership in a mutually beneficial way. Whether the approach can be made to work remains to be seen. However, it seems to us to hold out considerably more hope than most others currently on offer.

CONCLUSIONS

At the beginning of this book, we stated that its aim was to put child pedestrian accidents in perspective. The facts can leave us in no doubt of the seriousness of this threat to our children. In spite of a welcome reduction over the past twenty years, accidents continue to outstrip almost any disease or disorder as a source of mortality or morbidity in the young. Happily, the seriousness of the problem seems finally to be making an impact, to the extent that government has declared its intention of reducing casualties by a third before the year 2000. Less happily, it is difficult to see how this target can be achieved in ten years, given the limitations of current approaches.

To improve on the situation, we believe that some freshness of approach is required, with respect to both the content of road safety programmes and the methods by which that content is taught. We have argued strongly for the introduction of practical methods, firmly aimed at developing the skills that pedestrians need in traffic and involving the child as an active participant from the start. Pep talks and simple drills are no substitute. Some indication of how these skills might be taught and by whom has also been offered, though the bare outline attempted in this chapter would require a considerable amount of development to turn it into a practicable programme. How this might be done is an important goal for road safety research in the immediate future. But unless education programmes are developed that do justice to the skills involved, it is difficult to see how present child casualty rates can be significantly reduced.

REFERENCES

American Automobile Association (1976) *Preschool Children in Traffic.* Falls Church, VA: Traffic Safety Department.

Ampofo-Boateng, K. (1987) *Children's Perception of Safety and Danger on the Road.* Unpublished doctoral dissertation, University of Strathclyde.

Ampofo-Boateng, K. and Thomson, J. A. (1990) Child pedestrian accidents: a case for preventive medicine. *Health Education Research: Theory and Practice*, **5**, 265–74.

Ampofo-Boateng, K. and Thomson, J. A. (1991) Children's perception of safety and danger on the road. *British Journal of Psychology* (in press).

Ampofo-Boateng, K., Thomson, J. A., Grieve, R., Pitcairn, T., Lee, D. N. and Demetre, J. (1991) Training children to devise safe routes to cross the road. *British Journal of Developmental Psychology* (in revision).

Antaki, C., Morris, P. E. and Flude, B. M. (1986) The effectiveness of the Tufty Club in road safety education. *British Journal of Educational Psychology*, **56**, 363–5.

Avery, G. C. (1974) *The Capacity of Young Children to Cope with the Traffic System: A Review.* Traffic Accident Research Unit. New South Wales, Australia: Department of Motor Transport.

Backett, E. M. and Johnston, A. M. (1959) Social patterns of road accidents to children: some characteristics of vulnerable families. *British Medical Journal*, **1**, 409–13.

Burton, L. (1968) *Vulnerable Children.* London: Routledge & Kegan Paul.

Chapman, A. J., Foot, H. C. and Wade, F. M. (1980) Children at play. In D. J. Oborne and J. A. Levis (eds), *Human Factors in Transport Research, 2. User Factors: Comfort, the Environment and Behaviour.* London: Academic Press.

Coates, G. and Bussard, E. (1974) Patterns of children's spatial behaviour in a moderate density housing development. In D.H. Carson (ed.), *Man-Environment Interaction: Evaluation and Application.* Pennsylvania: Dowden, Hutchinson & Ross.

Colbourne, H. V. (1971) Two experiments on methods of training children in road safety. Department of the Environment Report 404. Crowthorne: Transport and Road Research Laboratory (TRRL).

Colbourne, H. V. and Sargent, K. J. A. (1971) A survey of road safety in schools: education and other factors. Department of the Environment Report 388. Crowthorne: TRRL.

Colbourne, H. V. and Sheppard, D. (1966) Testing a poster for infants. *Safety Education*, **107**, 8–10.

Cyster, R. (1980) The use of video recording in traffic education in primary schools. *Traffic Education.* **5**, 5–6.

Demetre, J., Lee, D. N., Pitcairn, T., Grieve, R., Thomson, J. A. and Ampofo-Boateng, K. (1991) Errors in young children's decisions about traffic gaps: experiments with roadside simulations. *British Journal of Developmental Psychology* (in revision).

Deschamps, J. P. (1981) *Prevention of Traffic Accidents in Childhood.* Copenhagen: World Health Organization.

Downing, C. S. (1981) Improving parental road safety practice and education with respect to pre-school children. In H. C. Foot, A. J. Chapman and F. M. Wade (eds), *Road Safety: Research and Practice.* Eastbourne: Praeger.

Downing, C. S. (1990) Children's traffic clubs: the principles. Paper presented at PTRC Seminar on Child Pedestrian Safety, London, March.

Ekstrom. G., Gastrin, U. and Quist, O. (1966) Traffic accidents among children. *Proceedings of the Second Congress of the IAATM.* Stockholm: International Association for accident and Traffic Medicine.

Finlayson, H. M. (1972) Children's road behaviour and personality. *British Journal of Educational Psychology*, **42**, 225–31.

Firth, D. E. (1973) The road safety aspects of the Tufty Club. Department of the Environment Report LR 604. Crowthorne: TRRL.

Fisk, A. and Cliff, H. (1975) The effects of teaching the Green Cross

Code to young children. Department of the Environment Report 168UC. Crowthorne: TRRL.

Foot, H. C. (1985) Boys will be boys? *Safety Education.* **1**, 6–8.

Foot, H. C., Chapman, A. J. and Wade, F. M. (1982) Pedestrian accidents: issues and approaches. In A. J. Chapman, F. M. Wade and H. C. Foot (eds), *Pedestrian Accidents.* Chichester: John Wiley.

Gerber, D., Huber, O. and Limbourg, M. (1977) *Verkehrserziehung in Vorschulalter.* Cologne: Wolters Noordhoff.

Gibson, E. J. and Yonas, A. (1966) A developmental study of visual search behaviour. *Perception and Psychophysics,* **165**, 169–71.

Grayson, G. B. (1975a) The Hampshire child pedestrian accident study. Department of the Environment Report 668. Crowthorne: TRRL.

Grayson, G. B. (1975b) Observation of pedestrians at four sites. Department of the Environment Report 670. Crowthorne: TRRL.

Grayson, G. B. (1981) The identification of training objectives: what shall we tell the children? *Accident Analysis and Prevention,* **13**,169–73.

Grayson, G. B. and Hakkert, A. S. (1987) Accident analysis and conflict behaviour. In J. A. Rothengatter and R. A. de Bruin (eds), *Road Users and Traffic Safety.* Maastricht: van Gorum.

Grayson, G. B. and Howarth, C. I. (1982) Evaluating pedestrian safety programmes. In A. J. Chapman, F. M. Wade and H. C. Foot (eds), *Pedestrian Accidents.* Chichester: John Wiley.

Groos, M. (1977) Kennis van verkeersbegrippen bij kinderen van 4–7 jaar. Traffic Research Centre, Report WR 7702. Groningen: Rijksuniversitateit.

Gunther, R. and Limbourg, M. (1974) *Bedingungen fur das Erleben und Verhalten von Kindern im Strassenverkehr.* University of Tubingen, Germany.

Hakkert, S. and Hauer, E. (1987) The extent and implications of incomplete and inaccurate road accident reporting. In J. A. Rothengatter and R. A. de Bruin (eds), *Road User Behaviour: Theory and Practice.* Maastricht: van Gorum.

Heimstra, N. A., Nichols, J. and Martin, G. (1969) Analysis of road accidents involving young pedestrians. *Ergonomics*, **17**, 319–30.

Hobbs, L. A., Grattan, E. and Hobbs, J. A. (1979) Classification of injury severity by length of stay in hospital. Department of the Environment Report 871. Crowthorne: TRRL.

Hoffmann, E. R., Payne, A. and Prescott, S. (1980) Children's estimates of vehicle approach times. *Human Factors*, **22**, 235–40.

Howarth, C. I. and Repetto-Wright, R. (1978) Measurement of risk and the attribution of responsibility for child pedestrian accidents. *Safety Education*, **144**, 10–13.

Howarth, C. I. and Gunn, M. H. (1982) Pedestrian safety and the law. In A. J. Chapman, F. M. Wade and H. C. Foot (eds), *Pedestrian Accidents*. Chichester: John Wiley.

Howarth, C. I., Routledge, D. A. and Repetto-Wright, R. (1974) An analysis of road accidents involving young children. *Ergonomics*, **17**, 319–30.

Jackson, R. H. (1978) *Children, the Environment and Accidents*. London: Pitman Medical.

Johansson, L. E. (1967) Traffic instruction in a group of pupils seven years of age. Unpublished article referred to in Rothengatter, J. A. (1981).

Kenchington, M. H., Alderson, G. J. K. and Whiting, H. T. A. (1977) An assessment of the role of motion prediction in child pedestrian accidents. Department of the Environment Report 320. Crowthorne: TRRL.

Krall, V. (1964) Personality characteristics of accident repeating children. In W. Haddon, E. A. Suchman and D. Klein (eds), *Accident Research: Methods and Approaches*. New York: Harper & Row.

Kravitz, A. (1973) Accident prevention research. *Pediatric Annals*, **2**, 47–53.

Langley, J. (1984) Injury control – psychosocial considerations. *Journal of Child Psychology and Psychiatry*, **25**, 349–56.

Laroche-Reeff, M. (1988) La nouvelle brochure pour le préscholaire est en vente. *Circulation-Securité* (Bulletin périodique de la Securité Routière), **60**, 7.

Lee, D. N., Young, D. S. and McLaughlin, C. M. (1984) A roadside simulation of road crossing for children. *Ergonomics*, **27**, 1271–81.

Limbourg, M. and Gerber, D. (1978) Das Verhalten von 3 bis 7 jahrigen Kindern bei der Strassenüberquerung unter Ablenkungsbedingungen. *Zeitschrift fur Verkehrserziehung*, **2** (June).

Linden, H. R. van der and Goos, J. G. (1975) Gedrag en Verkeersonveiligheid bij Kinderen. *Verkeerskunde*, **12**, 624–5.

Local Authority Associations (1989) *Road Safety Code of Good Practice*. London: Local Authority Associations.

Maccoby, E. D. and Jacklin, C. N. (1974) *The Psychology of Sex Differences*. London: Oxford University Press.

McKelvey, R. K. (1978) A safe crossing interval discrimination training procedure for primary school children. Paper presented at joint ARRD/DOT Conference, Sydney, Australia.

Mackie, A. M. and Older, S. J. (1965) Study of pedestrian risk in crossing busy roads in London inner suburbs. *Traffic Engineering and Control*, **7**, 376–80.

Manheimer, D. I. and Mellinger, G. D. (1967) Personality characteristics of the child accident repeater. *Child Development*, **38**, 491–513.

Marcus, I. M., Wilson, K., Kraft, I., Swander, D., Southerland, F. and Schulhopfer, E. (1960) An interdisciplinary approach to accident patterns in children. *Monographs of the Society for Research in Child Development*, **25**, 17–19 and 39–54.

Marcusson, H. and Oehmisch, W. (1977) Accident mortality in childhood in selected countries of different continents 1950–1971. *World Health Statistics Report*, **30**, 57–92.

Matlin, M. W. (1987) *The Psychology of Women*. New York: Holt, Rinehart and Winston.

Meijer, C. J. W. and Vinje, M. P. (1978) Een onderzoek naar de kennis van verkeersbegrippen bij kinderen van 4–6 jaar. Traffic Research Centre, Report WR 7805. Groningen, NL: Rijksuniversitateit.

Michalik, C. (1978) Verhaltens Beobachtung 5–6 jahrigen Kindern im Strassenverkehr. Vienna: Kuratorium fur Verkehrssicherheit.

Molen, H. H. van der (1977) Observational studies of children's road crossing behaviour. In A. S. Hakkert (ed.), *Proceedings of the International Conference on Pedestrian Safety*. Haifa: Michlol Technion.

Molen, H. H. van der (1981) Child pedestrian's exposure, accidents and behaviour. *Accident Analysis and Prevention*, **13**, 193–224.

Molen, H. H. van der (1983) *Pedestrian Ethology*. Doctoral dissertation, University of Groningen, Netherlands.

Molen, H. H. van der (1989) World pedestrian training: experience and possibilities for worldwide application. *World Safety Journal*, **111**, 23–5.

Morris, J. P. (1972) *Road Safety Publicity: Quantifying the Effects of Public Service Advertising*. London: Chantrey House.

Newson. J. and Newson, E. (1976) *Seven-Year-Olds in the Home Environment*. London: Allen & Unwin.

Numenmaa, T. and Syvanen, M. (1970) A film as a medium of children's traffic teaching – an experiment. Report 49. Finland: University of Tampere.

Numenmaa, T. and Syvanen, M. (1974) Teaching road safety to children in the age range 5–7 years. *Paedagogica Europea*, **9**, 151–61.

O'Donaghue, J. (1988) Pedestrian accidents. In *Road Accidents Great Britain 1987: The Casualty Report*. London: HMSO.

Organisation for Economic Co-operation and Development (1981) *Methods for Evaluating Road Safety Measures*. Paris: OECD.

O'Shea, J. S., Collins, E. W. and Butler, C. B. (1982) Paediatric accident prevention. *Clinical Paediatrics*, **21**, 290–7.

Pease, K. and Preston, B. (1967) Road safety education for young children. *British Journal of Educational Psychology*, **33**, 305–12.

Preston, B. (1972) Statistical analysis of child pedestrian accidents in Manchester and Salford. *Accident Analysis and Prevention*, **4**, 323–32.

Preston, B. (1980) Teaching the Green Cross Code. *Traffic Education*, **5**, 3–4.

Rasmussen, J. (1985) Trends in human reliability analysis. *Ergonomics*, **28**, 1185–95.

Read, J. H., Bradley, E. J., Morison, J. D., Lewell, D. and Clarke, D. A. (1963) The epidemiology and prevention of traffic accidents involving young children. *Canadian Medical Association Journal*, **89**, 687–701.

Reason, J. (1985) Recurrent error forms in nuclear power plants and their implications for the design and deployment of intelligent decision aids. In *Proceedings NATO ASI Symposium on Intelligent Decision Aids in the Process Environment*. San Miniato: Pisa.

Road Accidents Great Britain 1987: *The Casualty Report* (1988). London: HMSO.

Rothengatter, J. A. (1981) *Traffic Safety Education for Young Children*. Lisse: Swets & Zeitlinger.

Rothengatter, J. A. (1987) Current issues in road user research. In J. A. Rothengatter and R. A. de Bruin (eds), *Road Users and Traffic Safety*. Maastricht, NL: van Gorum.

Rothengatter, T. (1984) A behavioural approach to improving traffic behaviour of young children. *Ergonomics*, **27**, 147–60.

Routledge, D. A., Repetto-Wright, R. and Howarth, C. I. (1974a) The exposure of young children to accident risk as pedestrians. *Ergonomics*, **17**, 457–80.

Routledge, D. A., Repetto-Wright, R. and Howarth, C. I. (1974b) A comparison of interviews and observations to obtain measures of children's exposure to risk as pedestrians. *Ergonomics*, **17**, 623–38.

Routledge, D. A., Repetto-Wright, R. and Howarth, C. I. (1976a) The development of road crossing skill by child pedestrians. In A. S. Hakkert (ed.), *Proceedings of the International Conference on Road Safety*, Vol. 1. Haifa: Michlol Technion.

Routledge, D. A., Repetto-Wright, R. and Howarth, C. I. (1976b) Four techniques for measuring the exposure of young children to accident risk as pedestrians. In A. S. Hakkert (ed.), *Proceedings of the International Conference on Road Safety*, Vol. 1. Haifa: Michlol Technion.

Ryhammer, L. and Berglund, G. W. (1980) Children and instruction in road safety. Uppsala Reports on Education, no. 8. Sweden: University of Uppsala.

Sadler, J. (1972) *Children and Safety: A Survey amongst Mothers.* London: HMSO.

Salvatore, S. (1974) The ability of elementary and secondary school children to sense oncoming car velocity. *Journal of Safety Research,* **6**, 118–23.

Sandels, S. (1974) Road accidents to children: what makes them happen? In *Proceedings of the Third Congress of the International Federation of Pedestrians,* Schevingen, Netherlands.

Sandels, S. (1975) *Children in Traffic.* London: Elek.

Sargent, K. J. and Sheppard, D. (1974) The development of the Green Cross Code. Department of the Environment Report LR 605. Crowthorne: TRRL.

Saska, S. (1971) Children's traffic parks as a place for action. Unpublished manuscript referred to in J. A. Rottengatter (1981) *Traffic Safety Education for Young Children.* Lisse: Swets & Zeitlinger.

Schagen, I. van (1985) Crossing at junctions: experimental application of a road safety education module for primary schools. In R. A. de Bruin (ed.), *Annual Progress Report of the Traffic Research Centre.* Groningen, NL: Rijkuniversitateit.

Schagen, I. van (1988) Training children to make safe crossing decisions. In J. A. Rothengatter and R. A. de Bruin (eds), *Road User Behaviour: Theory and Research.* Maastricht, NL: van Gorum.

Schagen, I. van and Rothengatter, J. A. (1986) Crossing at intersections. In *Proceedings of the 13th ARRB/5th REAAA Conference,* pp. 50–6. Sydney, Australia.

Schioldberg, P. (1974) Children, traffic and traffic training: an analysis of the children's traffic club. Unpublished report, Psychological Institute, University of Oslo, Norway.

Schioldborg, P. (1976) Children, traffic and traffic training. Paper presented at the *Fifth Congress of the International Federation of Pedestrians,* Geilo, Norway.

Scottish Development Department (1989) *Must Do Better: A Study of Child Pedestrian Accidents and Road Crossing Behaviour in Scotland.* Scottish Office, Central Research Unit Paper. Edinburgh: Scottish Development Dept.

Sheehy, N. P. and Chapman, A. J. (1982) Eliciting children's and adult's accounts of road accidents. *Current Psychological Reviews*, **2**, 341–8.

Sheehy, N. P. (1982) Accidents and the social environment. In A. J. Chapman, F. M. Wade and H. C. Foot (eds), *Pedestrian Accidents*. Chichester: John Wiley.

Sheehy, N. P. and Chapman, A. J. (1984) Accidents and safety. In A. Gale and A. J. Chapman (eds), *Psychology and Social Problems*. London: John Wiley.

Sheppard, D. A. (1975) Teaching pedestrian skills: a graded structure. *Safety Education*, **133**, 5–7.

Singh, A. (1982) Pedestrian education. In A. J. Chapman, F. M. Wade and H. C. Foot (eds), *Pedestrian Accidents*. Chichester: John Wiley.

Smith, H. T. and Howarth, C. I. (1981) Accidents: the consequences of human error? In C. I. Howarth and W. E. C. Gillham (eds), *The Structure of Psychology: An Introductory Text*. London: Allen & Unwin.

Svenson, O., Fischoff, B. and MacGregor, D. (1985) Perceived driving safety and seatbelt usage. *Accident Analysis and Prevention*, **17**, 119–34.

Thomson, J. A. (1989) Road safety education: How do we make our children streetwise? *Safety Education*, **3**, 13–16.

Todd, J. E. and Walker, A. (1980) *People as Pedestrians*. London: HMSO.

Transport and Road Research Laboratory (1972) Accidents to elderly pedestrians. Department of the Environment Leaflet 323. Crowthorne: TRRL.

Valavuo, T. (1976) *Verkehrsverhalten der Kinder und die Schulische Verkehrerziehung*. Doctoral dissertation, University of Innsbruck.

Vurpillot, E. (1968) The development of scanning strategies and their relation to visual differentiation. *Journal of Experimental Child Psychology*, **6**, 622–50.

Young, D. S. and Lee, D. N. (1987) Training children in road crossing skills using a roadside simulation. *Accident Prevention and Analysis*, **19**, 327–41.

Zwahlen, H. T. (1975) Distance judgment capabilities of children and adults in a pedestrian situation. *Zeitschrift fur Verkehrssicherheit*, **21**, 104–14.

FURTHER READING

Chapman, A. J., Wade, F. M. and Foot, H. C. (eds) *Pedestrian Accidents.* Chichester: John Wiley, 1982. Although based on the situation prevailing in the 1970s, this is still the best book available for readers seeking a detailed analysis of road accidents. The approach is multidisciplinary and includes chapters on driver behaviour and engineering measures.

Foot, H. C., Chapman, A. J. and Wade, F. M. (eds) *Road Safety: Research and Practice.* Eastbourne: Praeger, 1981. Based on reports from an international conference, the chapters are much shorter than in the above. Discusses both pedestrian and driver behaviour.

Rothengatter, J. A. and de Bruin, R. A. (eds) *Road Users and Traffic Safety.* Maastricht, Netherlands: van Gorum, 1987.
Rothengatter, J. A. and de Bruin, R. A. (eds) *Road User Behaviour: Theory and Research.* Maastricht, Netherlands: van Gorum, 1988.

These two volumes consist of short reports covering many aspects of road user behaviour. Like *Road Safety: Research and Practice* the contents were selected from papers presented at a major international conference. Extremely useful in bringing the situation reported in *Pedestrian Accidents* and *Road Safety: Research and Practice* up to date.

Plowden, S. and Hillman, M. *Danger on the Road: The Needless Scourge.* London: Policy Studies Institute, 1984. A detailed and cogently argued case in favour of a range of engineering measures. Also tackles the 'political' and institutional obstacles to progress in road safety.

The Royal Society for the Prevention of Accidents (ROSPA) publishes a journal, *Safety Education,* which often contains well-written review articles (and other information) on road safety. Several excellent examples can be found in the References.

INDEX